They Changed the World

OLD WORLDS TO NEW

The Age of Exploration and Discovery

They Changed the World

OLD WORLDS TO NEW

The Age of Exploration and Discovery

Janet Podell and Steven Anzovin

The H. W. Wilson Company
New York • 1993

Design by Elizabeth Rodger

Picture research by Margaret Glover and Ron Schick

Picture credits on page 276

Library of Congress Cataloging-in-Publication Data:

Old worlds to new : the age of exploration and discovery /
    editors, Janet Podell, Steven Anzovin.
        p.   cm. — (They changed the world series)
    Includes index.
    ISBN 0-8242-0838-2
    1. Biography—Dictionaries. 2. Explorers—Biography—
Dictionaries. 3. Scientists—Biography—Dictionaries.
I. Podell, Janet. II. Anzovin, Steven. III. Series.
CT103.043   1993
910'.92'2—dc20
[B]   92-19264
                                                    CIP

PRINTED IN THE UNITED STATES OF AMERICA

To our grandparents

and to the memory of
April Friedman
and
Robin Siegel

Contents

Science and Medicine

Picture Credits   276

Index   278

Preface

While this book was in preparation, the world was getting ready to observe the quincentenary of Columbus's arrival in the New World. This momentous event was being denounced by some people as the beginning of five centuries of racist oppression and hailed by others as the beginning of the process of change that led to the birth of a pluralistic United States.

The emotion invested by Americans, both celebrants and detractors, in assigning moral significance to the Columbus quincentenary is evidence that our sense of history remains strong, even though much of it may be based more on myth than on fact. We are often criticized as a people for whom the past is irrelevant, as a nation of consumers too occupied with the on-going business of our society—making money, spending money, and pleasuring ourselves with what money buys—to concern ourselves with finding out what happened in the world before our time. Our politicians and the people who run government agencies, including the State Department and the CIA, periodically demonstrate a disastrous lack of knowledge about the history of the regions they deal with. Our national holidays are mainly used as excuses for store sales. Our schoolchildren and teenagers are shown in study after study to be ignorant of both history and geography. Yet when fundamental historical issues do come to the fore, people respond vigorously. Their emotions can still be roused by events that happened decades and centuries before. The image of Columbus setting off through uncharted waters in search of Asia still has the power to evoke admiration, just as the image of Columbus ordering the mutilation of islanders because they could not bring him enough gold dust still has the power to evoke disgust and anger.

To bring forth an active response, to stimulate curiosity, the historian and the teacher of history must find ways of making the past come alive in the minds of students. The entertainment industry spends billions of dollars each year on movies and television shows to keep teenagers amused. Those same teenagers, if they could look into the past, would find real stories of danger, adventure, boldness, devotion, and terror that make the plots cooked up by screenwriters seem silly by comparison. Not only do these stories have all the elements necessary to hold a teenager's attention, but they have something that fiction rarely has: real consequences.

"They Changed the World," the series of which *Old Worlds to New* is the first volume, is intended to give history life by retelling the stories of certain people who lived in the past, in language that readers at the junior-high level can understand. Each volume of the series will contain about seventy-five biographical articles, organized around a time period or a theme. Biography is a natural genre for young teenagers, both because they are likely to have encountered plenty of biographical material about present-day celebrities (actors, musicians, and athletes, at least) and because they feel themselves to be the protagonists of their own life stories. A biographical account of an historical figure, if written with enought suspense and dramatic feeling, gives students a way of imagining the past, of putting themselves in the midst of long-ago action, of understanding what was at stake for the people who worried, reasoned, fought, and suffered in those days. By pairing, where possible, biographies of figures from different cultures who lived through the same events, the series also seeks to give students the opportunity to imagine these events from a variety of individual perspectives.

The people described in *Old Worlds to New* were all, in one way or another, part of the long process of change by which the world of the Middle Ages evolved into the modern world. Most of them were connected with the European campaigns of exploration and colonization. Others were people from non-European cultures who, like the Chinese admiral Zheng He and the Moroccan traveler Ibn Battutah, were explorers themselves, or who, like Queen Nzinga of Angola or the Aztec princess Malintzin, reacted in influential ways to the advent of the Europeans. The last section of the book contains articles about pioneers of Western science and medicine—explorers of a different but equally important kind.

Our background research for this volume uncovered scores of fascinating people whose lives deserve to be known by modern-day students. We could accommodate only a fraction of them. In making the selection, we bore several goals in mind. First, we wanted to concentrate on the colonization and resettlement of the lands that became part of the United States, since that story has importance for everyone who now lives here. Because that process was begun by Portugal and Spain, we wanted to describe in some depth their exploration activities and the growth of their empires, as well as the exploration activities of rival European nations. We hoped to include material on Asia and Africa, although for lack of space we were compelled to keep these sections brief. Above all, we wanted to be sure that, in addition to the major figures who could on no account be omitted, there was room for interesting people who were not so well known. And we tried to match people whose stories could provide alternative views of the same events (Cortés, Malintzin, and Moctezuma, for example, or Tisquantum and William Bradford).

The juxtaposition of so many historical figures from so many different regions and cultures presented us with the challenging problem of representing each of these cultures faithfully. We relied on recent scholarship to help us create accurate portraits, not just of the individuals themselves, but of their time and place, of the values, expectations, and principles that would likely have motivated them—information that should help readers make sense of these lives. On matters of controversy, such as the question of whether Columbus was hero or villain, we have tried to steer clear of making judgments about the events described in these accounts or about the national rivalries and theological assumptions that led to them. Our intent was to tell as much of each person's story as possible, in as comprehensible a way as possible, and in a manner that would foster understanding rather than resentment. We discovered that there was no need to sensationalize or fictionalize the lives of these figures to make them worth the attention of teenage readers. The things that happened to these people were inherently dramatic—Leeuwenhoek seeing for the first time the living organisms in a drop of water, Drake pausing in his game to assess the approach of the Armada, Estevanico running across the desert with his greyhounds in the guise of a god, Magellan with foolhardy confidence stepping ashore onto the beach at Mactan.

The authors wish to thank Diane Podell for assistance with research; David Podell for critiquing some of the articles; and Norris Smith, our editor at the H. W. Wilson Company, for helpful suggestions.

Janet Podell
Steven Anzovin
Amherst, October 1992

The Empires of Portugal and Spain

Henry the Navigator

Henry, known as The Navigator. In Portuguese, Henrique o Navegador. Born 1394 in Pôrto, Portugal. Died 1460 in Sagres, Portugal.

At the southwestern tip of Portugal is a rocky piece of land that juts out into the Atlantic Ocean, a lonely place that only mariners know. Atop its cliffs is an old fortress, with a lighthouse

Prince Henry the Navigator

built on top to guide approaching ships. It is called Sagres, the sacred place.

In 1420, when the fortress was new, it belonged to a prince named Henrique, or, as his English-born mother called him, Henry, the son of King João I. From the window of his room high on the cliffside, at the very edge of Europe, he could look out across the storm-ridden ocean and think about the unknown world that lay beyond it. Africa was out there, many miles to the south, and Prince Henry was consumed with curiosity about Africa. There were gold mines there, and Portugal needed gold to pay for its wars. There were people who knew nothing about Christianity, and he was eager to convert them. And somewhere in Africa, if old stories were true, was a lost realm of Christians under the kingship of a rich and powerful priest named Prester John. If Henry could find him, together they might be able to conquer the Muslims, who had ruled Portugal and Spain for hundreds of years and who were threatening to invade Europe again from their lands in North Africa.

But Henry was having a hard time finding sailors who were willing to sail down Africa's western coast. They refused to go past a certain place called Cape Bojador, on the coast of Morocco. All kinds of stories were told about the ocean beyond the cape, which was called the Green Sea of Darkness. It was said to be boiling hot, thick with slime, dangerously shallow, roiling with whirl-pools, and rife with sea monsters.

It was necessary to replace stories and rumors with facts. There had to be some central place where mariners could share their experience, exchange information. and develop their skills. Henry established this center at Sagres. He opened its doors to anyone who could contribute to his search for practical knowledge. To staff his observatory and to make nautical instruments, he hired Arab and Jewish scholars who specialized in mathematics and astronomy. To supervise his mapmakers, he brought in the master mapmaker Jehuda Cresques, trained at the Jewish cartography school on the island of Majorca. In his library he collected the reports of travelers, including those of his older brother Pedro, who had spent three years making his way across Europe. Pilots and captains from many countries came to visit Sagres and the nearby town of Lagos, where Henry had his shipbuilding factory.

Over the years, the members of Prince Henry's team found new and better ways of doing things. To replace the old-fashioned maps based on biblical legends, they drew maps based on information given to them by sailors, adding new details whenever they could. They designed and improved instruments like the compass, cross-staff, and quadrant, to help sailors find their location on the ocean. At Lagos they built a new kind of ship, the caravel, which was smaller and lighter than a cargo boat and easy to maneuver against the

Mariners of Prince Henry's era could find the latitude of a ship by using a cross-staff, like this one, to take sightings on the North Star.

wind. Much of the money that paid for these experiments came from a religious group called the Order of Christ, of which Prince Henry was the grand master. He also received from the pope in Rome the right to license all Portuguese expeditions bound for Africa and the right to collect one-fifth of the profits from these expeditions.

Visitors to Sagres can still see a vast compass made of earth and stones. Beyond it is a view of the Atlantic that Henry often saw.

Between the years 1420 and 1460, Henry sent out dozens of expeditions. Each time, he gave his sailors orders to push southward a little further along the African coast, or to bring back something new. In 1434, one of his squires, Gil Eannes, finally sailed around Cape Bojador and discovered that there was no Green Sea of Darkness lying beyond it. The following year, Eannes landed on the coast and saw that it was inhabited. Nine years and many trips later, he came back to Portugal with two hundred African people who were sold as slaves. (Though this was the beginning of the terrible European trade in African lives, it was not the beginning of slavery, which has existed all over the world for many centuries.)

By 1448, so many Portuguese ships were visiting the west coast of Africa that Prince Henry had a fort and a warehouse built on the island of Arguin, off the coast of Morocco. This was the first overseas trading post established by Europeans since the days of the Romans. The Portuguese sold wheat and woolen cloth to the Moorish merchants and Berber tribesmen, who paid for them with slaves and gold dust. One of Henry's captains, a man from Venice named Alvise da Cadamosto, went sixty miles inland up the Senegal and Gambia rivers and brought back to Sagres some of the first eyewitness reports by a European of life in Africa's interior. Among the things he described was the unusual way that salt was traded for gold. Berber caravans would bring chunks of rock salt from the Sahara Desert and send them out to customers along the Niger River, who needed the salt to survive in the hot weather. Each salt trader would put down a pile of salt at a particular spot and then hide. The African tribesfolk would find the salt, set down a pile of the gold they had dug out of their goldfields, and hide in their turn. If the trader thought the pile of gold was big enough, he would take it back to the caravan. If not, he would hide again, and the folk would come out of hiding to add more gold. In this way they did business without ever speaking to or even seeing each other.

Yet though Henry the Navigator masterminded many voyages of exploration, he never went on one himself. Three times he went to the coast of North Africa on military expeditions. The first time, when he was nineteen years old, he helped his father and his two older brothers capture the

The northwest coast of Africa

Muslim city of Ceuta, in Morocco, in the hope of gaining control of the riches brought there by Arab traders. But under Portuguese administration, the city no longer flourished. When Henry was forty-one he and his younger brother Fernando tried to expand their kingdom's territory by attacking nearby Tangier. It was a disastrous campaign, and Henry went home in defeat, leaving Fernando to die in prison. Finally, in 1458, he led a fleet against the Muslim city of Alcazar and succeeded in capturing it. He died two years later, so he never knew that Portugal's attempt to push the Muslims back from North Africa was destined to fail. But he did know that Portuguese mariners would continue to find out more and more about Africa as long as the royal family was willing to pay for their expeditions.

The Portuguese voyages down the African coast proved to the people of Europe that seagoing exploration was not only possible, but practical and profitable as well. Their success inspired other expeditions to yet more distant places. Without Prince Henry the Navigator, there would have been no Columbus to open a way to the New World from the Old. Nor would there have been a sea captain like Sir Francis Drake, who captured Henry's old fortress at Sagres for England in 1587. [See the articles on Columbus and Drake in this book.]

Pêro da Covilhã

Pêro da Covilhã (ku-veel-YAM). Born 1460 in Covilhã, Beira, Portugal. Died sometime after 1526 in Ethiopia.

King João II of Portugal had a secret mission in mind, and he needed an agent with unusual talents to carry it out. He was going to send the agent to India to spy on the Arab merchants who did business there. These merchants controlled India's busy coastal trade. They handled the sale of spices and other precious goods from various parts of Asia. Their ships were constantly criss-crossing the northern Indian Ocean, bringing goods to Arabia and East Africa.

The Portuguese, at the westernmost end of Europe, had to pay high prices for India's merchandise, and they were tired of it. They wanted to do business with India directly. But India was many thousands of miles to the east. Doing business with India would entail long journeys through hostile countries.

King João II of Portugal

The only alternative was to go by sea. But the Portuguese had been unable to find out whether the Atlantic Ocean and the Indian Ocean were connected. Portuguese explorers had been sailing south along the coast of Africa since the days of Prince Henry the Navigator, but they had still not reached its end. It seemed to go on forever. [See the article about Henry in this book.]

To settle the question, King João decided on a two-pronged plan. He would send a naval expedition down the coast of Africa as far as necessary to discover where it ended. [See the next article in this book, on Bartolomeu Dias.] He would also send a spy to India to discover the trade routes used by the Arab merchants. This spy would have to be trustworthy, alert, willing to risk everything for Portugal's future. He would also need to speak fluent Arabic in order to pass through Muslim countries without attracting attention.

The man chosen for the job was a knight named Pêro da Covilhã, who had been born in the same year that Prince Henry the Navigator had died. Though he was still in his twenties, Covilhã was battle-tested and cool-headed. He was gone on several secret diplomatic assignments to Spain and to North Africa, where he had learned Arabic. He knew a number of other languages as well.

Covilhã set out in May 1487. For the first part of his journey, he was accompanied by another agent, Afonso de Paiva, whose mission was to go to Abyssinia (the country now called Ethiopia) and make contact with a legendary Christian king named Prester John. Paiva and Covilhã traveled east across Europe, going from port to port along the Mediterranean Sea. Before they entered Egypt, they disguised themselves as Muslim merchants dealing in honey. They parted in the city of Aden, at the southern edge of the Arabian peninsula.

While Paiva headed across the Gulf of Aden to Ethiopia, Covilhã crossed the Arabian Sea by ship. He landed on the Malabar Coast in southwestern India and visited the cities of Cannanore,

Calicut, and Goa. What he saw astonished him. There were markets unlike anything to be seen in Portugal, where dealers sold cotton and silk, gemstones, porcelain, Arabian horses, medicines, and fragrant spices. He watched as these treasures were loaded on ships and taken away to be resold in distant places. Still posing as a merchant himself, he took passage on one of these ships. The route went westward across the Arabian Sea as far as the Persian Gulf, turned south to the Horn of Africa, and continued down the coast to the town of Sofala in Mozambique.

From Sofala, Covilhã sailed back to Aden and made his way by land to the Egyptian capital of Cairo, intending to sail for home as soon as possible. He had accomplished his mission. He could tell King João exactly what to expect in India and how his ships should set their course once they reached the Indian Ocean. Then he could go home to his wife and children, whom he had not seen for two years.

There were two messengers waiting for Covilhã in Cairo with a letter from King João. Afonso de Paiva had died without finding Prester John. The king commanded Covilhã to stay abroad until he had finished Paiva's mission as well as his own.

A Portuguese squire could not refuse an order from his king. Covilhã wrote a long report, describing everything he had learned about India and the Arabs who did business there. If the Portuguese could find a way to sail their ships around

Prester John, the legendary king of Ethiopia. This drawing appeared on a Portuguese map dated 1558, sixty-five years after Covilhã's journey.

the tip of Africa, they could get all the way to India by following his directions. One of the messengers returned to Portugal with the report, and Covilhã, after accompanying the other across Arabia to reconnoiter the city of Hormuz, turned his steps toward Ethiopia.

For centuries, the Portuguese had been hearing rumors about Prester John. He was said to be both prince and priest, ruling over a kingdom of Christians in a part of the world that was peopled by Muslims and pagans. He was said to live in a crystal palace and to have in his realm fabulous animals that breathed fire. King João hoped to make an alliance with him. With Prester John's help, the Christians could attack the Muslims from two sides and drive them from North Africa and eventually from Jerusalem.

After a harrowing climb over steep mountains, Covilhã found the royal court of Ethiopia. It was not what he expected. Instead of a crystal palace, he found a camp of red and white tents. Instead

Covilhã's route

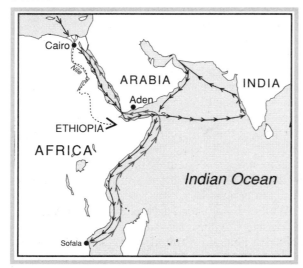

of Prester John, he found an emperor named Iskander who believed himself to be the descendant of Solomon, king of ancient Israel, and the Queen of Sheba. The emperor spoke from behind a veil, and his tent was guarded by four caged lions. He moved his camp every few months in an effort to suppress rebellions in his provinces and to prevent his Christian country from being overrun by one of the Muslim states that surrounded it.

Iskander's mother, the Empress Helena, was the only member of the court to recognize the importance of Covilhã's visit. Covilhã was the first European ever to reach Ethiopia. His presence was a sign that Portugal was an ambitious and energetic nation. Its rulers might be willing to help Ethiopia keep its independence.

But Iskander, thought he did not understand politics as well as his mother did, liked Covilhã's company. He refused to give him permission to return to Portugal. Other visitors from Europe who made their way to his court were likewise stranded by the emperor's decree. Covilhã never saw his wife and children again. Eventually he married an Ethiopian woman with whom he had several children.

As the years went by, Portugal succeeded in taking control of India's trade and building an empire in the Indian Ocean. [See the article on Afonso de Albuquerque.] In the year 1520, a group of Portuguese diplomats paid a visit to the royal court of Ethiopia. Covilhã served as their interpreter. He was then about sixty years old. When they left, they took his son Rodrigo to be educated in Portugal. But Covilhã himself died in the remote country to which King João had sent him.

Bartolomeu Dias

Bartolomeu Dias (DEE-osh). Born circa 1450, probably in Portugal. Died 1500 off the Cape of Good Hope.

In 1487, King João II of Portugal sent out two expeditions to India, one by sea and one by land. The land route was taken by a man named Pêro da Covilhã, who did reach India but never came back. [To find out why, see the article about Covilhã in this book.] The sea route was taken by a squire of the royal household, Bartolomeu Dias. His mission was to find out whether it was possible to sail around the continent of Africa, from the Atlantic Ocean on its western side to the Indian Ocean on its eastern side. If so, then Portugal would be able to send ships to India to buy the spices, medicines, and other precious commodities for sale in the markets there. The food of Europe was not much to taste without Asia's pepper, cinnamon, and ginger.

Portuguese mariners had been exploring Africa's west coast for many years without coming to the end of it. With each expedition they pushed further and further down the coast, but the shoreline ran on before them. Perhaps it had no end. That would explain why no ships had been known to come around Africa in the other direction, from east to west.

Dias was an experienced sailor. He planned his expedition with care and with the greatest secrecy, since the Portuguese did not want any other country to guess at their intentions. The main part of his fleet consisted of two caravels, the light, maneuverable ships developed by King João's kinsman, Prince Henry the Navigator. [See the article on Henry in this book.] The caravels were accompanied by a big, heavy cargo ship to carry food and supplies. This was the first time that an exploring expedition had needed a supply ship. Dias did not want the mission to fail if his food ran short or his sails were ripped by storms.

The best pilots in Portugal were assigned to Dias's expedition. His equipment included a number of the stone pillars called *padrões* with which Portuguese explorers marked their landings and established Portugal's claim to territory. The pil-

A carved stone pillar, or padrōe, *from the Cabral expedition on which Dias sailed. Portuguese explorers used padrões to mark land claims.*

lars were engraved with messages in three languages: Portuguese, Latin, and Arabic.

Dias's little fleet left Lisbon in August 1487 and headed along the North African coast toward the Gulf of Guinea. At various places along the African coast, he stopped to put ashore a number of women and men who had been kidnapped by earlier expeditions. Each one was given samples of gold, silver, and spices to show to the local inhabitants, so that they would understand what the Portuguese were looking for in the future.

The weeks and months went by. Dias and his crew passed the mouth of the Congo River, where a previous explorer, Diogo Cão, had set up a *padrōe* some years before. They passed another pillar more than a thousand miles further on, in what is now Namibia. That was the last. They had now gone farther than anyone else. But they could not turn back, for the coastline stretched ahead with no end in sight.

A violent storm seized the three ships as they sailed southward. Strong winds pushed them off their course and blew them out to sea. For two weeks, the two caravels ran before the wind, with no idea of where they were or of what had happened to the supply ship. When the storm died down, Dias tried to go back to his old course, to resume his patient progress down the coast. But the coast seemed to have disappeared. After a while he saw distant mountains to the north. It took him some time to realize that the caravels had been blown all the way around the southern tip of Africa.

The exhausted sailors dropped anchor in a place now called Mossel Bay, in South Africa, to repair their battered ships and to get fresh water. There were Africans herding cattle on the shore. They were startled by these strange-looking foreigners, and threw stones to drive them away. Dias shot one of the Africans with his crossbow.

The Portuguese continued eastward for another three hundred miles, as far as Algoa Bay. They had done the impossible. They had reached the other side of the African land mass. If they kept on going northeast, they would come at length to India. Dias was willing to try. But his

Dias's caravels were battered by a gale that blew for fourteen days and nights. In the cold weather, the sailors' hands froze to the ropes.

hungry, exhausted sailors refused to go any farther, and Dias turned the caravels back toward home. On the way, they set up a stone pillar at the cape that they had passed in the storm. Dias wished to call the place the Cape of Storms—in fact, it is one of the stormiest places in the world —but King João renamed it the Cape of Good Hope, the name it bears today.

The supply ship was waiting for them off the west African coast. It had been attacked by the local inhabitants, who had killed most of the crew. The survivors were taken aboard the caravels. The expedition arrived in Lisbon in December 1488, sixteen and a half months after its departure. Dias went immediately to King João's court to announce his success.

The news was received with jubilation in Lisbon, but it spelled disappointment for another explorer who had approached King João with a plan to find a sea route to India by sailing west rather than east. Dias's success put an end to the king's interest in this idea. Eventually the other explorer found support for his project from Queen Isabel of Spain. His name was Christopher Columbus. [See the article on Columbus in this book.] By a strange coincidence, when Columbus was forced to sail his battered ship into Lisbon

In this painting by Domingos Rebelo, emotion sweeps Dias's men as they realize where they are—500 miles east of Africa's southern tip.

Dias's route

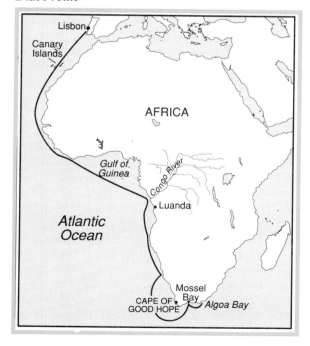

harbor after a storm on his return voyage, it was Bartolomeu Dias who approached him to check his documents.

Ten years went by before Portugal was ready to follow up on Dias's discovery. When Vasco da Gama's expedition was in preparation, Dias was put in charge of designing and building the ships. He went along as far as São Jorge da Mina, Portugal's fort and trading post on the West African coast, in what is now Ghana. Three years later, he was given the command of a caravel in the fleet of Pedro Álvares Cabral on his expedition to set up trading operations in India. [See the articles on da Gama and Cabral in this book.] When the fleet neared the Cape of Good Hope, it was struck by a hurricane. Dias's ship was lost, along with three others.

Seventy-five years later, Dias's grandson, Paulo Dias de Novais, founded São Paulo de Luanda, the first European city in southern Africa. [See the article in this book on Nzinga.]

Vasco da Gama

Vasco da Gama. Born circa 1460 in Sines, Setúbal, Portugal. Died December 24, 1524, in Cochin, India.

An unusual group of visitors was approaching the royal palace in the Indian city of Calicut. There were fourteen men, dressed in handsome clothes but walking with the gait of sailors long aboard ship. On their faces they wore an expression of combined weariness, determination, and amazement. Some of them carried the poles of a portable chair in which rode their commander, a

Vasco da Gama, from a Portuguese manuscript

stern man with a black beard and dark, piercing eyes. Curious people jostled the little group as it made its way slowly through the crowded streets.

Calicut was a busy port, despite the presence of crocodiles in its rivers. Gazing around him, the commander saw Muslim merchants bargaining over cargoes of merchandise from Ceylon, Malaysia, and China. Barrels of spices and bolts of silk were being carted into warehouses or loaded into the holds of the Arab boats called *dhows*.

Out in the harbor floated his own ships, with their huge square sails bearing the red cross of the Order of Christ and the snouts of cannons poking out from their sides. Those ships had brought him and his crew over the water for thousands of miles, from distant Portugal around the whole length of Africa.

Captain-Major Vasco da Gama had just taken the first step in Portugal's plan to reshape the world. He had made the first direct sea connection between Western Europe and Asia. The next step was to break the Arabs' monopoly on India's trade. Da Gama intended to fulfill that task, at whatever cost. The Hindu prince of Calicut, the Zamorin, was waiting for them in his palace, eating out of jeweled dishes, reclining on embroidered pillows. If he accepted Portugal's offer, so much the better. If he did not, then da Gama had no doubt that, one way or another, he would be persuaded.

The Portuguese had wanted to send a diplomatic mission to India ever since the explorer Bartolomeu Dias had proved that it was possible to get there by sailing from the Atlantic Ocean to the Indian Ocean around the southern tip of Africa. [See the article on Dias in this book.] Ten years had passed since Dias's return. There was a new king on the throne, King Manoel, who was eager to keep his country's ambitions alive. In 1496 he ordered work to begin on an expedition to open trade between Portugal and India. When that was accomplished, Portugal would no longer be forced to pay high prices to the Muslim and Venetian merchants who controlled everything that came from the East.

Vasco da Gama was a tough and reliable naval commander in his mid-thirties when he was chosen to lead this expedition. His boats were built under the supervision of the veteran explorer Bartolomeu Dias, who knew from experience what kind of ship would handle the voyage best. Instead of the highly maneuverable caravels that previous explorers had used, da Gama was given two *náos*, heavier ships that would stand up to the storms near the Cape of Good Hope. There were two supply ships, well stocked with food, supplies, and trade goods. Each ship was armed with twenty guns.

Much of the preparation for da Gama's voyage was done by the astronomer Abraham Zacuto, who provided the fleet with nautical instruments, maps, and mathematical tables, along with instructions on how to use them. Without his contribution, da Gama would not have succeeded in making the longest sea voyage yet attempted by Europeans. [See the article on Zacuto in this book. For the story of an even longer voyage that took place some eighty years earlier, see the article on the Chinese admiral Zheng He.]

Da Gama and his officers stayed awake the night before their departure, praying in a riverside church. There were 170 men in the crew when the fleet set sail on July 8, 1497. For three months they saw no land as the ships made a wide arc through the Atlantic. They stopped at the place they named St. Helena's Bay, in what is now South Africa, to take on fresh water. There was a skirmish with the Hottentot inhabitants, and da Gama was wounded in the leg by a spear.

A few days later, the ships rounded the Cape and began making their way north up the eastern side of the continent. They passed the farthest point reached by the Dias expedition and entered a part of the world that had been colonized by the Arabs and Persians. At each port city they stopped to search for a pilot who could steer them to India, but the Muslim sheikhs who ruled these cities were in no hurry to help them.

This part of the journey was full of trouble. The sailors became ill with scurvy because they had no fresh fruits or vegetables to eat. One of the ships ran aground on a shoal. Another was nearly captured by a crowd of people in the town of Mom-

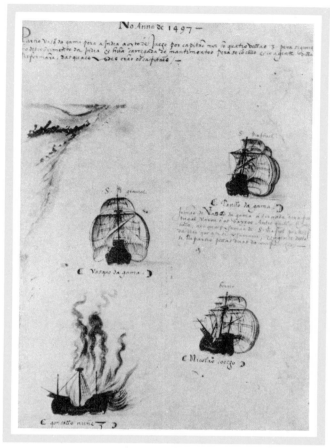

A drawing from 1497 shows da Gama's four ships, including a supply ship which was unloaded and burned during the voyage east.

basa, in what is now Kenya. Several pilots tried to lead them astray. Da Gama pushed forward. He kidnapped local people and tortured them to get information he needed. He captured merchant ships to take revenge for attacks on his own ships. He took hostages as a way of forcing the sheikhs to aid him. One of them finally provided an expert pilot from India who guided the fleet across the Indian Ocean, helped along by the monsoon winds that blow toward the east all summer long. The Portuguese reached the city of Calicut in May 1498, after a journey of ten months.

Calicut and the other cities along India's Malabar Coast were part of a great Hindu empire called Vijayanagar that covered all of southern India. The Portuguese knew nothing of Vijayanagar or of the Hindu religion, which they mistook for a version of Christianity. Their interest was in getting permission to trade. When da Gama, with his bodyguard of thirteen men, entered the Zamorin's palace in Calicut, he carried letters from King Manoel requesting this privilege.

But da Gama had underestimated the sophisticated tastes of India's monarchs. The Zamorin was insulted by the gifts of hats, coral beads, and sugar that da Gama offered. He refused to cooperate. At the same time, the city's Arab merchants realized that the Portuguese would be a threat to their business arrangements. They tried to bribe the Zamorin to have da Gama killed. Some Portuguese sailors were held for ransom, and da Gama retaliated by seizing Indian hostages. The expedition left Calicut in August, pursued by a Muslim navy. Still, da Gama had got a letter from the Zamorin promising to trade with Portugal in the future.

Da Gama dealt with Arab rulers in the port cities of East Africa. Such men were not impressed by the beads and hats he had brought to trade.

Da Gama had achieved a great feat of navigation and had accomplished his mission, but at a high cost to himself and his crew. On the way home they were attacked by pirates and ravaged by scurvy. So many sailors died that they had to abandon one of their ships for lack of a crew to sail it. Da Gama's brother Paulo was among the dead. Of the 170 men who had left Portugal three years before, only 44 returned. [A number of prisoners also survived the journey. Among them was a man named Gaspar, the Jewish admiral of the Indian city of Goa. For the story of his capture and his subsequent service to Portuguese exploration, see the article about him in this book.]

Da Gama accepted the title of Admiral of India from King Manoel. Over the next few years he married, had six children, and looked after his estates while other navigators took a turn at commanding Portugal's expeditions, using the sea route he had pioneered. They established trading posts at several other cities on the Malabar Coast and with some of the ports in East Africa.

By 1502 da Gama was ready to return to India, this time at the head of a fleet of twenty warships. His mission was now one of revenge. The Arab merchants of Calicut, with the Zamorin's approval, had attacked and killed a group of Portuguese traders. [See the article on Pedro Álvares Cabral in this book.] Da Gama intended to pay them back by diverting the entire Muslim trade in spices to Portugal.

When he reached the Malabar Coast, da Gama assigned a squadron of caravels to patrol the coastline. No trading ships would be allowed to pass unless the captain had a license from the agents of King Manuel. The Portuguese would also set the prices for all merchandise. Anyone who continued to do business with the Arabs would be punished by death.

Da Gama soon found an opportunity to demonstrate the seriousness of this threat. A ship owned by an Arab trader from Calicut arrived, carrying Muslim families on their way home from a pilgrimage to the city of Mecca. At da Gama's order, his sailors seized all the money and goods on board, locked the four hundred passengers inside the hold, and set the ship afire. Those who tried to escape by swimming were speared in the water. The only survivors were a few boys who were rescued and sent to Portugal to be baptized.

As da Gama's fleet approached Calicut, the Zamorin sent a messenger, offering to pay the Portuguese for the losses they had sustained in the massacre. Da Gama replied by bombarding Calicut with cannon fire. He ordered the messenger to be horribly mutilated and sent him back to Calicut in a boat filled with the cut-up bodies of Hindu fishermen caught trading with the Arabs. They had been hanged from the rigging and used for target practice.

The attack fleet that the outraged Zamorin sent against da Gama was defeated. Da Gama sailed for Lisbon with cargoes of pepper and cinnamon bought in the port cities of Cannanore and Cochin. He left agents in those cities to oversee the new Portuguese spice trade, protected by a squadron of warships.

For many years afterward, da Gama remained at home, serving as an advisor to King Manoel while the Portuguese built an empire in the Indi-an Ocean. Within a few years they had completely dislodged the Arabs. They set up forts and naval bases, extending their power westward to the Red Sea and eastward to the Malaysian Peninsula. Eventually they went as far east as China and Japan. They controlled all commerce in the Indies. [See the article on Afonso de Albuquerque, the Portuguese viceroy in India.]

But maintaining an empire is an exhausting business, especially for a small country. Many of the officials who were sent to administer its affairs turned out to be incompetent, greedy, or lazy. In 1524, the new king, João III, decided that it was time to reform them. He asked Vasco da Gama to undertake the job. Da Gama's combination of threats and punishments put an end to such activities as looting ships and selling the cannons from Portuguese forts. But da Gama was a sick man, and within four months he was dead.

Vasco da Gama's bones made almost as many

Portuguese sailors, determined to gain control over the Indian spice trade, fight their Arab rivals in a sea battle near the city of Surat.

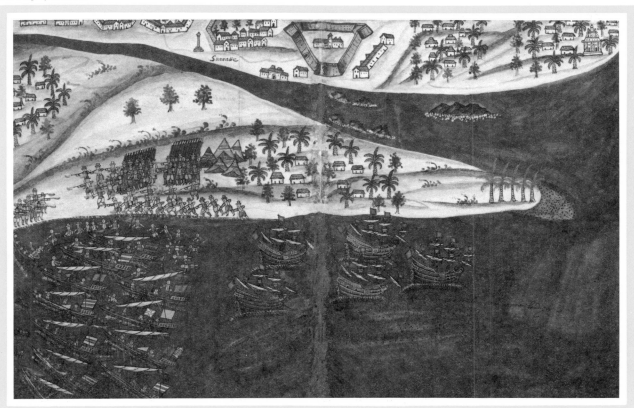

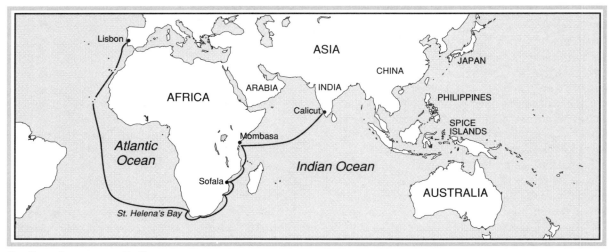

Da Gama's voyage to India

journeys in death as they had in life. First his body was buried in a church in India, in the Portuguese colony of Goa. Then, following the instructions he had left, it was dug up and sent back to Portugal, where it was buried in another church. Soon after, that church was rebuilt, and the bones were transferred to the new church. Finally, the government of Portugal had da Gama's skeleton moved to Lisbon, to the Church of the Jerónimos, which had been built in his honor on the site of the chapel where he had prayed all night before leaving for India on his first voyage. It turned out to be the wrong skeleton, so another one was dug up and buried in its place. To this day no one is quite sure if the bones in the tomb are really those of the great explorer.

Pedro Álvares Cabral

Pedro Álvares Cabral (ka-BRAHL). Born 1467 or 1468 in Belmonte, Portugal. Died 1520 in Santarém, Portugal.

When Vasco da Gama arrived in Lisbon in the fall of 1499, after going all the way to India and back again, he had good news for Portugal's King Manoel. The port cities of India were busy marketplaces for Asian products such as spices, gems, and medicinal herbs. The prince of the city of Calicut had reluctantly agreed to sell these products to the Portuguese, as well as to the Arab merchants with whom he usually did business.

Immediately King Manoel put together a trading expedition. The weary da Gama declined the

Pedro Alvares Cabral

honor of commanding it. In his place, the king chose a young nobleman, Pedro Álvares Cabral. On March 9, 1500, Cabral set sail from Lisbon with a fleet of thirteen ships manned by 1,500 sailors. One of his captains was Bartolomeu Dias, the veteran explorer who had been the first to go around the Cape of Good Hope. On board as special advisor was Gaspar of India, the master mariner whom da Gama had captured on his trip. [See the articles on Dias, da Gama, and Gaspar.]

Following the advice of da Gama and Dias, Cabral headed in a wide curve toward the west, intending to come back eastward toward Africa when he was closer to the Cape of Good Hope. This maneuver was intended to help the expedition take advantage of the strongest winds. At the widest point of the curve, the sailors sighted land, to which Cabral gave the name Island of the True Cross. In fact, it was no island, but the coast of South America, where Brazil is now.

The Portuguese set up a cross and said a Mass before an audience of uncomprehending but friendly tribespeople. When they set sail again, they left behind two convicts who were assigned to learn the local language and convert as many people as they could. They were probably eaten instead, for these tribes practiced cannibalism.

No one knows for sure whether Cabral came to Brazil by mistake or by intention. Previous sailors had sighted land in that area, and the Portuguese had an agreement with Spain that gave Portugal all the land east of an imaginary line drawn at 46 degrees 37 minutes of longitude. Cabral may have had secret orders from King Manoel to see what he could find.

Cabral sent a ship back to the king with news of the discovery, and he and his fleet went on toward the Cape of Good Hope. This was the place that Bartolomeu Dias had wanted to call "Cabo Tormentoso," the Stormy Cape. As they approached

On the left side of this 1502 map is the coast of Brazil, marked "Land of the King of Portugal." Also visible are Greenland, Europe, and Africa.

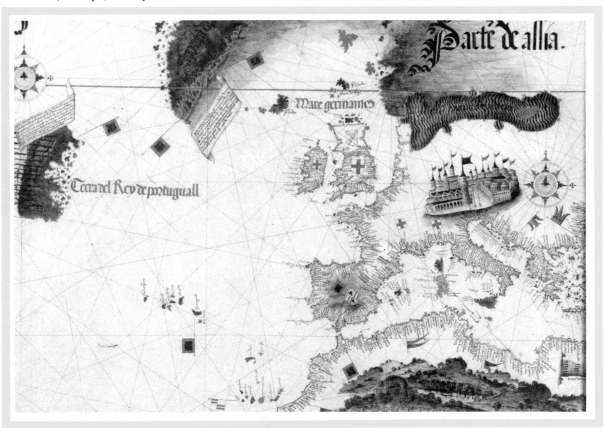

it, they were hit by a hurricane that capsized four of the ships. Bartholomeu Dias was among the dead. One of the surviving ships was blown far to the east and eventually landed on the island of Madagascar, off the east coast of Africa, where no Europeans had ever been seen before. The other ships found their way around the Cape of Good Hope and were reunited some months later in Mozambique. They continued northwards along the east coast of Africa, headed for the city of Malindi (in present-day Kenya), whose ruler had given Vasco da Gama a promise of help for the Portuguese.

King Manoel had instructed Cabral to capture Muslim ships and take their cargoes. Cabral now began to carry out this part of his mission. The first two ships he captured he had to give back; they were owned by one of the cousins of the king of Malindi. To the king himself Cabral sent expensive gifts, and in exchange the king gave the crew fresh food. By mid-September the expedition had crossed the Indian Ocean and arrived in Calicut.

Da Gama's old adversary, the Hindu prince of Calicut known as the Zamorin, seemed to be interested in Cabral's offer of trade. He gave the Portuguese a warehouse and a residence in the town. The group of merchants who had come with Cabral went ashore to live there, together with three Catholic missionaries. The Arab merchants who had been trading in Calicut for years were not pleased at the new competition. On the night of December 16, they came in a mob several thousand strong, attacked the Portuguese living ashore, and killed most of them.

The furious Cabral ordered his sailors to capture ten Muslim ships from the harbor, confiscate their cargoes, burn them, and kill the 500 men who were aboard them. On one vessel were three elephants, which the Portuguese slaughtered and ate. Then they bombarded Calicut

Portuguese vessels enter the harbor at Malindi. The East African ports had been ruled for some 300 years by families from Persia and Arabia.

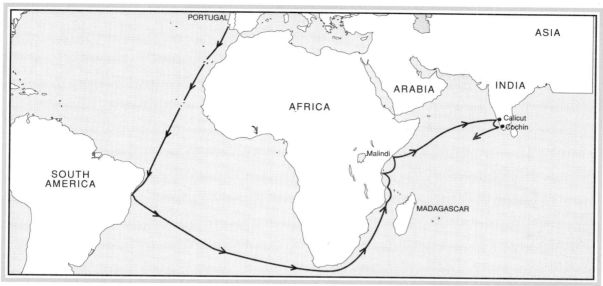

Cabral's route

with cannon fire. With Gaspar of India steering the flagship, they sailed to the city of Cochin, burning two more Muslim ships along the way.

The king of Cochin was an old enemy of the Zamorin. He was happy to help Cabral stuff his ships with valuable goods—cinnamon, ginger, pepper, cloves, camphor, amber, opium, and myrrh, as well as pearls, rubies, diamonds, perfume, and fine cloth. The Portuguese sailed for home just as a fleet of warships arrived from Calicut to take revenge.

Cabral's fleet, minus two ships that had foundered on the way back, entered Lisbon in July 1501 with more good news for King Manoel. In addition to Cochin, the cities of Carangolos and Cannanore were willing to do business with him. If Portugal invested enough money and manpower, it might become as prosperous as Venice, which for centuries had controlled most of the trade between Europe and India. Cabral himself went back to his estate in eastern Portugal and lived there until his death in 1520.

Afonso de Albuquerque

Afonso de Albuquerque (ol-bu-KER-kuh). Born 1453 in Alhandra, Portugal. Died December 15, 1515, off Goa, India.

For centuries, India had served as the central marketplace for the products of Asia. Its port cities were overflowing with necessary and desirable items—medicinal herbs that could cure illnesses, spices that could make food delicious and perfume the air, rubies and diamonds to delight the eye. A network of Arab dealers bought these goods and shipped them to other places. Some shipments went to the Egyptian port of Alexandria, where merchants from the Italian city of Venice collected them to sell throughout Europe.

This way of doing business was about to change. The people of the Western European nation of Portugal had developed their ability to move around by sea. Their explorers had succeeded in going all the way to India, even though it meant a

Afonso de Albuquerque

tremendously long journey around the continent of Africa. [See the preceding articles in this book]. By the beginning of the sixteenth century, Portuguese trading ships were going back and forth from Portugal to India by the dozen, competing for business that used to belong solely to the Arab and Venetian traders.

Portugal's King Manoel understood that his merchant fleet would need protection from these rivals. He summoned a knight named Francisco de Almeida, appointed him governor of India, and gave him the job of building forts along the coasts of India and East Africa. Almeida had been working at this job for three years when the sultans of Egypt and of several Muslim cities in India sent a navy to drive out the Portuguese. There was a battle off the Indian coast, and Almeida's son Lourenço was killed.

To avenge his son, Almeida in February 1509 led nineteen ships against a much larger Muslim fleet. The Battle of Diu lasted one afternoon. When it was over, the Muslims had been so thoroughly defeated that they could no longer challenge the Portuguese in India.

Almeida's successor was Afonso de Albuquerque, a member of a prominent family who had been an officer in the service of three Portuguese kings. He spent the Battle of Diu in a prison, where Almeida had put him to prevent him from taking over the governorship until the war of revenge was finished.

Albuquerque's conquests

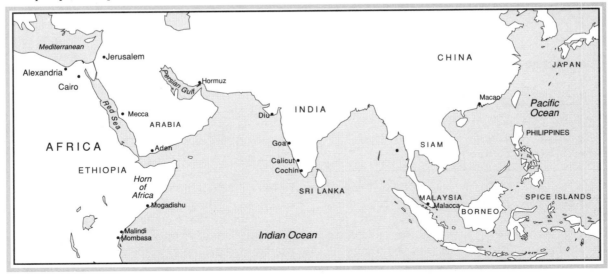

Under Albuquerque, the Portuguese succeeded in extending their control over a huge area. Albuquerque accomplished this feat in only six years through a combination of diplomacy and terror. He was already famous for the ruthlessness with which he had killed Muslim civilians and prisoners on his way to India. With the help of Hindu pirates, he captured the Indian city of Goa from the sultan of Bijapur [see the article on Gaspar of India, Goa's admiral] and killed some six thousand Muslim inhabitants. He repopulated the city by conducting forced marriages between its surviving women and his soldiers. Goa became the center of the Portuguese empire in India.

When he had finished subduing Goa and other important cities on the Malabar Coast, Albuquerque went east, to the Malay peninsula. He captured the port of Malacca in July 1511. That city became the eastern naval base for the Portuguese. From there they went on to Siam (now called Thailand), the Spice Islands (now called the Moluccas), and eventually all the way to China and Japan. The Portuguese navy patrolled the seas around the great Asian ports, so that no ship could come to the East to trade without Portuguese approval.

Then Albuquerque turned his attention to the west. In 1515 he led a fleet to take control of the Arab island of Hormuz, at the entrance to the Persian Gulf. His soldiers occupied part of Hormuz and built a fortress that allowed the Portuguese to control all the shipping that passed through the gulf. Albuquerque did not succeed in taking the city of Aden, at the entrance to the Red Sea, so Arab spice dealers were still able to ship their goods to the Venetian merchants in Alexandria. But even without complete control of the spice trade, the Portuguese now had an Asian empire, supported by a network of naval bases that stretched from East Africa across the Indian Ocean to Malaysia and beyond.

Albuquerque died aboard the ship that was taking him back from Aden to Goa. The empire that he built continued for more than one hundred years, yet it began to decline as soon as he died. The governors who replaced him were greedy and inept. The old admiral Vasco da Gama was sent out to India in 1524 to clean up the mess they had made of things, but within four months he too was dead.

An artist's rendering of Albuquerque on his ship, receiving armor, weapons, and tribute from the leaders of a surrendering Arab city.

It takes a great deal of money and effort to maintain a large, faraway empire. Eventually, despite the riches that flowed to them from the East, the Portuguese were exhausted. Their country became a Spanish dependency in 1580. In the seventeenth century, the Dutch and the English took away most of their Asian colonies, leaving them only the province of Macao, in southern China. The African colonies finally broke away on their own, as did Brazil, Portugal's most important possession in the New World. All that is left of the first modern European empire are a few islands in the Atlantic Ocean and the port of Macao in China.

Ferdinand Magellan

Ferdinand Magellan (ma-JEL-en). In Portuguese, Fernão Magalhães; in Spanish, Fernando de Magallanes. Born circa 1480 in Portugal, probably in Sabrosa, Pôrto. Died April 27, 1521, on Mactan Island (in the present-day Philippines).

Who was the first person to circumnavigate—that is, sail completely around—the world? Many people think it was the Portuguese captain Ferdinand Magellan, who sailed in the service of the king of Spain. They are partly right and partly wrong. Magellan never intended to go all the way around the globe; his purpose was to sail westward from Spain, find a waterway across the continent of South America, get to the Spice Islands (in what we now call Indonesia), and then come back home the same way. But Magellan was killed in the Philippine Islands, and his sailors, who had suffered terribly from hunger and illness on the trip across the Pacific, decided to keep sailing westward, even though it meant they had to cross the Indian Ocean and risk being captured by their enemies, the Portuguese. Two hundred and eighty men set out with Magellan in 1519, but only thirty-five came back; and these thirty-five were indeed the first to circumnavigate the globe.

Magellan came from a noble family in the north of Portugal and grew up at the royal court in Lisbon, where he was a page. As a young man he went east to serve under the viceroys Francisco d'Almeida and Afonso de Albuquerque as they fought to extend Portugal's control of the Indian Ocean. [See the article on Albuquerque in this book.] Then he went to Morocco to help subdue a Muslim city that had rebelled against Portuguese rule. He was wounded in the leg and left permanently lame. But his taste for adventure was not at all lessened, especially after he received a letter from a friend who had been shipwrecked off the Moluccas and who had decided to stay in those

beautiful islands for good. Magellan went to King Manoel with a plan for an expedition to the Moluccas to bring back the spices that grew there in plenty. But the king disliked Magellan and rejected his plan.

So Magellan, like Columbus before him, decided to try Portugal's neighbor and rival, Spain. [See the article on Columbus in this book.] And with the help of a crackpot scholar, Ruy Faleiro, he conceived an elaborate plan to prove that the Moluccas really belonged to Spain and not to Portugal. Both countries had agreed to abide by the Treaty of Tordesillas, which divided the earth in half along an imaginary line running north and south around the globe. All newly discovered lands on one side of the line were to belong to Portugal, and all newly discovered lands on the other side to Spain. It was reasonably clear where the dividing line lay in the Western Hemisphere, but no one could figure out exactly where it would fall in the Eastern Hemisphere.

Ruy Faleiro said that he knew where it was. He also said that the ocean on the other side of the American land mass—the ocean that the conquistador Vasco Núñez de Balboa had seen from Darién and had called the Southern Sea—was very narrow and could quickly be crossed by ship. [For more on Balboa, see the article about him in this book.] There was sure to be a passageway by water through the American continent. If the king of Spain would send ships to find the passageway and cross the ocean on the other side, Faleiro said, they would discover that the Moluccas were really on the Spanish side of the line of demarcation, and all the marvelous spices from those islands would belong to Spain.

The king of Spain, Carlos I, was interested in this idea. Even though his conquistadors were exploring huge new areas of the Americas, the Portuguese were making a great success out of their campaigns in Asia. It would be a fine thing if this captain Magellan could sail up from the other side of the world and claim the Moluccas for Spain. He made Magellan and Faleiro members of

Ferdinand Magellan as a young man

the prestigious Order of Santiago and promised them ships, crews, and money.

It was no easy task to prepare such an immense expedition. Magellan was planning to be at sea for at least two years. The money from the king's treasury was not enough to cover all his expenses. He had to go to private banking houses in several countries and ask for money in return for a share of the profits (for Magellan intended to come back with cargoes of spices to sell). The five ships given to him by the king turned out to be small and rickety, not at all in shape to go halfway around the world. In addition to supplies and food, Magellan had to purchase a large stock of items to give away and trade, including bells, beads, mirrors, mercury, copper and iron bars, velvet cloth, jewelry, and fishhooks. He also had to recruit sailors for the crew, and since few sailors were willing to go on so dangerous a voyage, he was forced to take on numerous criminals and gamblers trying to escape their debts.

The fact that Magellan was Portuguese made his job even more difficult. The king's officials were suspicious of him. They insisted that he hire Spanish seamen instead of Portuguese seamen with experience in Asian waters, and they gave him Spanish captains who did not like or trust him. The Portuguese, for their part, thought he was a traitor. King Manoel sent two secret agents to Spain to try to sabotage the expedition. Magellan, however, had an unusual amount of persistence and determination. On September 20, 1519,

his five ships set out from the port of Sanlúcar with himself in command as Captain-General. He left behind his wife and newborn son.

We know all the details of Magellan's voyage because one of the sailors who survived it wrote a long account of it. He was Antonio Pigafetta, a gentleman from Italy who joined the expedition in search of adventure and who later told his exciting story in all the courts of Europe.

The voyage got off to a slow start. For several weeks the ships were stuck in the doldrums at the equator, waiting for a breeze. In November they reached Brazil, and they spent the next three months going southward along the South American coast, looking for the channel, or strait, that Magellan was sure would be there. Every likely-looking place turned out to be a dead end, however, and by April many of the officers and men were tired and discouraged. Winter was coming on in the Southern Hemisphere, so Magellan ordered the fleet to dock at Port San Julian, a desolate spot on the coast of Patagonia, to wait out the bad weather.

Several of the Spanish officers decided that things had gone far enough. On the first day of April they launched a mutiny. Three of the five ships were soon under their control. But after a few quick fights, Magellan and the sailors loyal to him took the mutineers captive. One rebel leader was killed in the fighting, one was given the death sentence and beheaded, and two others were abandoned on the shore. The men who had joined them were sentenced to work all winter at hard labor, repairing the leaking ships.

Magellan sent the smallest ship to continue searching for the channel. It was wrecked on a sandbank many miles away from Port San Julian, and its crew waited there for months while two of their number walked all the way back to get help.

Meanwhile, Magellan had made a terrible discovery. The outfitters who had supplied the food for the expedition had cheated him. Instead of two years' worth of food, he only had enough for six months. The sailors caught fish and game to preserve, but Magellan knew they were likely to run out of food before the journey was over. Nonetheless, they added two more to the number of people they had to feed: two native tribesmen who were captured and put in chains. They were to be taken back to Spain and exhibited as specimens of the New World's inhabitants.

An antique woodcut of Magellan's ships threading the rocky strait under the gaze of several giant people and a curious mermaid.

When spring came, in October, the expedition began to move southward along the coastline once again, looking for the channel. In the end, they found it by accident, when two of the ships were blown into the channel by a violent storm. It was not the first time that bad weather had brought about a new discovery—Bartolomeu Dias had had the same experience when a storm blew his ship around the Cape of Good Hope.

All four ships now entered the strait and began to make their way across. It was a narrow waterway, zig-zagging between walls of rock, with dangerous currents and confusing inlets. Without Magellan's expert navigation, they might never have made it through. Finally, after a month's journey, they came out into the Southern Sea, which they renamed the Pacific ("peaceful"). But now there were only three ships remaining in the expedition. The fourth was on its way back to Spain, under the command of mutineers.

The officers of the other ships wanted to do the same. They informed Magellan that in their opinion the westward journey to the Moluccas was too risky to attempt. Magellan insisted that the expedition keep going in spite of the dangers. Perhaps he would have changed his mind if he had known what would happen next.

The three ships set out across the Pacific. It was now the end of November 1520. They did not reach land again until March of 1521. During that time they went more than nine thousand miles. The supply of food and fresh water soon ran out. In his account, Antonio Pigafetta tells of sailors eating dead rats, pieces of oxhide, sawdust, old biscuits swarming with worms. "Had not God and His Blessed Mother given us so good weather," he wrote, "we would all have died of hunger in that exceeding vast sea." Many did die of hunger and thirst, and many others died of scurvy or dropped dead from heatstroke or exhaustion. There were barely enough men left to sail the ships.

One thing was clear: Ruy Faleiro had been completely wrong about the size of the western ocean. It was much, much wider than the Atlantic. Spain would never be able to make this a trade route to the Moluccas. The whole voyage seemed to have been utterly in vain. But Magellan refused to accept this judgment. In fact, he swore to execute any sailor who spoke a word of discouragement.

At last the ships dropped anchor off the island of Guam. Out from the nearby village came tribespeople in canoes, bringing coconuts. The sailors, weak from illness and hunger, were happy to get the coconuts but fearful of the tribespeople, who boarded the ships and took away everything they could carry. On the following day a group of sailors went ashore to get water, fruit, and meat. There was a confrontation with the villagers, and before the expedition left, several tribespeople had been killed by crossbows and their village had been set afire. Magellan called these islands the Ladrones ("thieves"), but if he had not been in such a desperate plight, perhaps he would have been kinder to their inhabitants. One of the villagers was captured to serve as a guide.

The expedition continued on to the island chain now known as the Philippines and claimed it for Spain. Here they encountered friendly chieftains who had plenty of gold to trade for Spanish iron. They treated Magellan to a feast of roast pork and palm wine, and Magellan had his sailors help with the rice harvest. On the island of Cebu he and the expedition's priests began an aggressive campaign to convert all the tribespeople to Christianity, using both persuasion and terror (Pigafetta reports that one village was burned because its inhabitants refused to be baptized). The chieftain of Cebu asked Magellan to intervene in a dispute he was having with a rival on the island of Mactan, and Magellan, against the advice of his officers, consented.

On April 27, 1521, Magellan with a group of sailors attacked Mactan. The islanders fought back with poisoned arrows, lances, and *kali*, a traditional martial art. Magellan was wounded in the legs, and as he fell, the islanders rushed on him. He was killed by a man named Lapu Lapu, whom many Filipinos today regard as a national hero. Eight sailors and four islanders also died in the battle.

The chieftain of Cebu now threw off his new religion and decided to loot the expedition. To weaken the officers' resistance, he invited them to a banquet and gave them plenty of palm wine. When they were drunk, the islanders stabbed

twenty-five of them to death. Two escaped and rowed back to the ships to warn the others. As they sailed out of the harbor, the crew saw on the shore one of their officers, still alive and begging his friends to ransom him. But they were afraid to turn back, and they left him to die.

Little was left of the expedition that had set out from Spain with such grand ambitions. Most of the officers were dead. The sailors who still remained had survived hunger, thirst, storms, scurvy, shipwrecks, combat, and murder. They no longer had Magellan to lead them through their ordeals. One of their ships was a ruin and had to be burned, leaving them with only two. For the next few months they sailed around Indonesia, fighting among themselves and unable to decide what to do next. Should they go back across the Pacific and through the strait, the way they had come? That was unthinkable. Then should they go westward, across the Indian Ocean and around the Cape of Good Hope? If they did, the Portuguese might capture them. In the end they decided to try their luck with the Portuguese.

But their luck did not hold. In Brunei they narrowly escaped being taken prisoner by the sultan. After that, they lived more or less as pirates, bullying their way from island to island and doing whatever was necessary to stay alive. When they

After crossing the Pacific in a nightmarish journey of hunger and disease, Magellan was killed in a dispute among Filipino islanders.

got to the Moluccas—their original destination—they found the Portuguese firmly in control and had to hide on the island of Tidore. Here they loaded up two cargoes of cloves, enough to satisfy the investors who had financed the expedition. But before they could leave for Spain, one of the ships, the *Trinidad*, sprang a leak and had to be left behind for repairs, together with its crew. The other ship, the *Victoria*, set out alone for the last leg of the journey in February 1522, commanded by Juan Sebastian del Cano (also spelled d'Elcano and El Cano), a Basque seaman who had been one of the mutineers at Port San Julian. Its crew consisted of forty-four Europeans and thirteen Indonesians.

It was a long, hard voyage, almost as hard as the trip across the Pacific, except that now, instead of tropical heat, the sailors had to face bitter cold. There was nothing to eat but rice. Seven weeks of bad storms hit them as they tried to round the Cape of Good Hope, and once they had doubled it, they had to go two more months without fresh food and water. Hunger and scurvy were killing the crew, and those who were left alive could barely work the ship, which was leaking badly. At last they reached the Cape Verde Islands, controlled by the Portuguese, and sent a landing party of thirteen men ashore to take on supplies. But on their third trip the men were arrested, and the *Victoria* went on its way without them. There were twenty-two left alive

—eighteen Europeans and four Indonesians—when the ship arrived in Seville's harbor on September 8, 1522. Those eighteen were the first to go clear around the globe, at a terrible cost. The following day, dressed in their rags and barefoot, they carried candles to the church of Santa María de la Victoria to give thanks for their safe return. The thirteen sailors taken prisoner by the Portuguese came home some time later.

And what about the *Trinidad*, left behind in the Indies? It sailed for home in April 1522 with a crew of fifty-three, under the command of Gonzalo Gomez de Espinosa, who had been Magellan's constable. They planned to sail back across the Pacific to the Spanish colony of Darién, in Panama. In their first three months at sea they lost thirty-five men to sickness and malnutrition, and got only as far as the Mariana Islands. They gave up the attempt and went back to the Moluccas, where the Portuguese arrested them and put them all in prison. Three years later, in 1525, the crew of the *Trinidad* arrived back in Spain: there were only four of them left.

Yet after the whole ordeal was over, the one ship that came back—the *Victoria*—brought home enough spices to pay for the entire expedition and make a profit for the investors. No one gave Magellan much credit for this. The mutineers who had fled the expedition as it passed through the strait had had plenty of time to give King Carlos their own account of the voyage, and

The circumnavigation of the world by Magellan's expedition

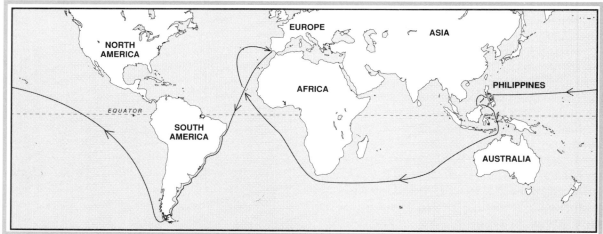

they had nothing good to say about Magellan. Antonio Pigafetta, after he recovered from the trip, spent his life touring Europe to tell *his* version of the story, which was much more favorable to Magellan.

A few years after the *Victoria* returned, Spain sent another expedition to attempt Magellan's route to the Moluccas. Del Cano went along as the pilot, and though he had survived the first trip, he died on the second. In 1529 King Carlos of Spain —now also Emperor Charles V of the Holy Roman Empire—renounced Spain's claim to the Moluccas in return for the sum of 350,000 ducats from Portugal. The Philippines, which Magellan had claimed for Spain, were colonized by the Spanish and remained under their control until 1898, when the United States acquired them in the Spanish-American War.

Gaspar of India and Abraham Zacuto

Gaspar of India, also known as Gaspar da Gama. Born circa 1458, possibly in Granada, Spain, or Poznan, Poland. Died sometime after 1526, probably in Cochin or Goa, India.

Abraham Zacuto (za-KU-toe or sa-SU-toe). Born 1452 in Castile, Spain. Died circa 1515, possibly in Damascus or Jerusalem.

Yusuf Adil Shah, the sultan of Bijapur on India's Malabar Coast, was not a man to take chances. His father had been the sultan of the Ottoman Empire. When his father died, his elder brother, next in line for the throne, had ordered all his male relatives strangled. Yusuf Adil had escaped to Persia and had come to India as a slave. Now that he had risen to become a king, he kept his armies and navies strong by welcoming into his service people from all over the region, including Arabs, Turks, Persians, and Jews.

The cities of the Malabar Coast were buzzing with talk about the strangers who had sailed into the harbor of Calicut a few months earlier. These strangers had come all the way from distant Portugal, around Africa and across the Indian Ocean, in order to trade. Their leader, Vasco da Gama, was a proud man with a fierce temper. [See the article on Vasco da Gama in this book.] His ships were now at Angediva Island, not far from the port of Goa in Bijapur, where they were being repaired before the trip home. Yusuf Adil Shah consulted with the admiral of his navy, a man named Gaspar. They made a plan that would allow Gaspar to spy on the Portuguese newcomers.

At dawn the next day, the Portuguese were hailed by a tall man who came ashore in a boat rowed by unarmed sailors. He was in his forties— not much older than da Gama—but his hair and beard were white. To the surprise of the Portuguese, the man spoke to them in perfect Spanish. He was taken aboard da Gama's flagship, where he told his story. He said he had been born to Jewish parents who had fled from the persecutions of Christian Europe and had gone to Egypt as refugees. Kidnapped as a teenager, he had been sold into slavery in Mecca, the Muslim holy city. After his escape, he had made his way to Bijapur, where he was employed by the sultan. He had come to the flagship with a message from the sultan, inviting the valiant Portuguese to settle in his country.

Da Gama was another man who did not like to take unnecessary chances. While Gaspar was talking, the Portuguese interrogated the sailors who had rowed him to the island. These sailors confessed that a fleet of warships was hidden nearby, with orders to attack on Gaspar's signal. Gaspar was seized and tortured. Eventually he admitted that he had come as a spy. He was taken prisoner along with his men. On the long voyage to Portugal, the men were set to work pumping water out of the leaking ships, while Gaspar served as pilot. He left behind not only Yusuf Adil

Shah, who now needed a new admiral, but also a wife and son.

It would have come as no surprise to the Portuguese to find a Jewish admiral in India. Jews had been living on the west coast of India since at least the twelfth century, and it was believed that the lost tribes of Israel might have found their way there much earlier. Columbus, when he set off to find the westward route to Asia, expected to find a Jewish community there, and brought along a Jewish interpreter, Luis de Torres, who was fluent in Hebrew. The interpreter on Vasco da Gama's first voyage, João Núñez, was also a Jew.

Since one of the goals of da Gama's expedition had been to seek converts to Christianity, his prisoners were baptized when they reached Lisbon. There was another reason to baptize Gaspar. In 1497, while the expedition was still under way, King Manoel had issued a decree that made it illegal for Jews to live in Portugal. Vasco da Gama served as godfather to his fellow admiral, who was given the name Gaspar da Gama, though he referred to himself as Gaspar da India. His expertise in navigation and geography caught the attention of the king, who frequently consulted him about Portugal's plans for exploration and trade. In exchange, the king gave him horses, clothes, and servants.

These conversations with Gaspar undoubtedly reminded King Manoel of discussions he had had with another Jewish expert in navigation,

Abraham Zacuto. Zacuto was not a mariner but an astronomer. For most of his life he had lived in Spain, where he had been a professor at the University of Salamanca. Among other things, he had designed a copper astrolabe (a device that determines the height of the sun) that was much more accurate than the old wooden models. He had also written an almanac containing astronomical tables. Both these things helped sailors to figure out their latitude and hence find the trade winds they needed to sail across the seas. Without Zacuto's research, the explorers of Spain and Portugal would not have been able to carry out the feats of seamanship that gave birth to empires.

Christopher Columbus was particularly indebted to Zacuto, whose almanac was one of the books that Columbus carried with him on his voyages. He consulted Zacuto when he was trying to convince King Fernando and Queen Isabel to fund his westward expedition to Asia, and Zacuto testified before the committee that was set up to evaluate the project. On Columbus's fourth voyage, when he was marooned on Jamaica, it was Zacuto's astronomical tables that enabled him to calculate the time of a lunar eclipse and hence to save himself from an attack by the islanders. [See the article on Columbus in this book.]

But just as Columbus's momentous first expedition was getting underway in the summer of 1492, Zacuto was forced to leave Spain along with all the rest of the country's Jewish population, some 300,000 people in all. Fernando and Isabel

The world of Zacuto and Gaspar

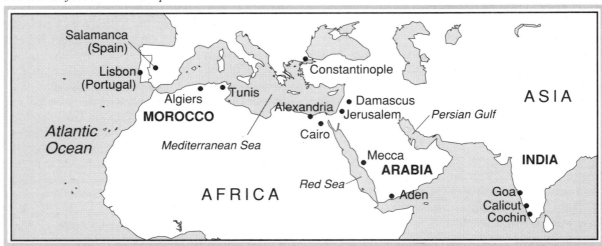

In this mural, Zacuto holds a copy of his famous almanac, with his name in Hebrew letters on the cover, as da Gama kneels before King Manoel.

had decided that the nation they were building out of four separate provinces must be entirely Christian.

Jews had come to Spain in antiquity, when it was still part of the Roman Empire. They had been there in the Middle Ages when it was conquered by the Vandals, the Visigoths, and finally the Moors (Muslims from North Africa). Under the Muslims, Spain became a center of learning where the classical works of Europe were studied when the Christian world had forgotten them. That is why most of the mapmakers, scientists, and physicians in Europe at the beginning of the era of exploration were Arabs and Jews. The civilization that they created is known as the Golden Age of Spain. It came to an end as Christian armies reconquered Spain piece by piece.

With the pope's consent, Fernando and Isabel established the Spanish Inquisition, a kind of religious police force whose job was to purify Spain and the Church of nonbelievers. Under their new rulers, the Jews of Spain were given a harsh choice: accept conversion to Christianity or undergo imprisonment, torture, and execution. "New

Christians," as Jewish converts were called, were burned alive if they were caught doing anything connected with the Jewish religion. To remove temptation from these "New Christians," and to fill up the royal treasury as well, Fernando and Isabel ordered all unconverted Jews to leave and confiscated their property. Some years later, they also expelled the Moors.

The Jewish refugees from Spain died by the thousands from drowning, exposure, sickness, starvation, and attacks by pirates and bandits. They sought shelter in whatever countries would take them in. In many places they were sold into slavery or forced to convert. In others, the officials demanded payment before they would give shelter to the refugees.

Zacuto was one of the luckier ones. When Portugal's King João heard about the expulsion, he invited the professor to come to Lisbon to serve as his court astronomer. King Manoel, who succeeded his cousin on the throne in 1495, asked Zacuto to help with the planning of Vasco da Gama's expedition to India. The fleet carried Zacuto's metal astrolabe and his astronomical tables, which he

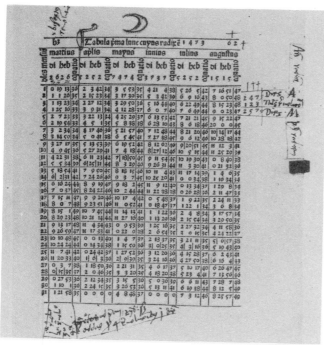

A page from the Latin edition of Zacuto's almanac, translated from the original Hebrew text. This book once saved Columbus's life.

A synagogue at Cochin, India. Jewish refugees from Spain and Portugal flocked to the many Jewish communities of the Malabar Coast.

taught the sailors how to use, as well as maps and sailing instructions that he provided. "I assure Your Highness," he told the king, "that this navigation between Portugal and India will become so easy that even small ships will be able to undertake it." He was correct.

But Zacuto never had the chance to learn the outcome of the expedition. In 1497, while da Gama was still in India, King Manoel gave in to the requests of his Spanish-born wife, the daughter of Fernando and Isabel, and ordered his Jewish subjects to leave the kingdom of Portugal. The decree covered only adults. Jewish children were ordered to stay behind to be baptized as Christians. Some families escaped this fate by committing suicide together. Others arranged to flee, but when the deadline for the exile arrived there were not enough ships to take all the refugees away. Those who were unable to leave— some 20,000 in all—were given a choice of baptism or slavery.

Zacuto and his son Samuel made their way to Tunis in North Africa, a dangerous journey on which they were twice taken prisoner. Zacuto stayed in Tunis for a number of years, writing a book on the history of Jewish law. Toward the end of his life he lived in Jerusalem.

King Manoel would have preferred Zacuto to accept conversion and stay in his job as court astronomer. The loss of scholars like Zacuto hurt Portugal's plans for building a maritime trading empire. So he was pleased indeed when da Gama brought him Gaspar, a top-notch mariner who had first-hand knowledge of India.

Gaspar proved to be a great help to the Portuguese. Six months after he arrived in Lisbon, he was back on board ship as interpreter and special advisor to Pedro Álvares Cabral, who was leading a fleet of thirteen ships to India to establish trading relations. [See the article on Cabral in this book.] The fleet reached India in September 1500 after a detour that brought them to Brazil. They set up a trading post in the city of Calicut. Within three months the Portuguese and the inhabitants were at war. Gaspar piloted the fleet to Cochin, where he negotiated a treaty that set the terms for future trade with the Portuguese.

On the way home, Cabral's fleet met another, bound westward from Lisbon to investigate King Manoel's new possessions in Brazil. One of the officers on this fleet was Amerigo Vespucci, the explorer whose name was given to the Americas. Before they parted, Vespucci sought out Gaspar to get his advice. He was, Vespucci wrote, "a trustworthy man who speaks many languages" and who had sailed the seas from Portugal (Brazil, in fact) to Sumatra.

Twice more Gaspar went to India in the service of King Manoel—in 1502, with Vasco da Gama's expedition to subdue Calicut, and in 1505, with Francisco de Almeida, the first viceroy of India. In 1510 he led an attack on the royal palace in Calicut. For many years he helped the viceroys in their dealings with local rulers, as advisor, interpreter, and diplomat. [See the article on Afonso de Albuquerque in this book.] He found his grown son living in the family's old house in Goa and his wife living in Cochin. But he could not persuade them to renounce Judaism and accept conversion. Gaspar's wife was a scholar and an expert in Jew-

ish law. It was through her that the Jews of Cochin purchased Torah scrolls (scrolls inscribed with the first five books of the Hebrew Bible) that had been looted from the synagogues of Lisbon.

After the expulsions from Spain and Portugal, Jews came to India in great numbers—so many, in fact, that the viceroy Albuquerque asked for permission to kill them, and the Catholic Church set up a branch of the Inquisition. Thousands more went to South America, but the Inquisition was established there too. So even in the New World and in Asia the Jews were not safe from the hatred that pursued them nearly everywhere in Europe. Until the founding of the modern state of Israel in the twentieth century, the most secure place for Jews was the United States, a nation that owed its existence to the first voyage of Columbus—ironically, a voyage that would never have been made without direct help from Spain's converted and unconverted Jews.

Christopher Columbus

Christopher Columbus, variant of name Cristóbal Colón. Born circa 1451, probably in Genoa, Italy; died May 19, 1506, in Valladolid, Spain.

The people of the Spanish port of Cádiz were used to the sight of prisoners aboard the ships that docked in their harbor. Many times they had watched as war captives, mutineers, and convicts were taken off ships under guard. But the prisoner who had just arrived from Hispaniola was different. White-haired, bent with arthritis, chained at the ankles so that he could barely shuffle, he wore his irons with a kind of furious pride. It was Cristóbal Colón, the Admiral of the Ocean Sea, the man who had been bold enough to cross the Atlantic in search of a sea route to Asia. Behind him came his brothers, Bartolomé and Diego, also prisoners. The whole family, so proud of its achievements, was coming home in humiliation!

But was it really such a surprise that this Colón

had fallen so far and so fast? After all, he had started out as a nobody, an obscure sailor and mapmaker. For years he had been obsessed by the idea that the Atlantic was a very small ocean and that he could cross it with hardly any trouble, despite what the most learned geographers said. Finally the queen of Spain had given him permission to test his theory. And what a moment of triumph it had been when he and his crew came back from that voyage alive, along with six brown-skinned people who spoke an unknown language —living proof that the expedition had reached land on the other side of the Atlantic.

Ever since that moment, things had been going badly for the Admiral. Twice more he had gone back over the ocean. He had found dozens of islands, but no evidence that they were really part of China or Japan. He had started a colony of Spanish gold-seekers, but it was now a chaotic place where disease and violence flourished. The famous mariner, the man whose feat had been the talk of all Europe, had become a pitiful failure. Even the queen and king were embarrassed when he knelt before them, still angry over the way he had been treated, and burst into tears.

Little did they know that five hundred years in the future, this Cristóbal Colón—or Christopher Columbus, as we call him—would be known the world over as "the man who discovered America." That label is not entirely accurate, of course. North, South, and Central America had been discovered thousands of years before by Asian immigrants who had come, by boat and by land, from Siberia. (These were the people to whose descendants Columbus mistakenly gave the name "Indians.") The Admiral himself did not realize that he had come to a place that was unknown to the rest of the world. To the end of his life, he believed that he had reached islands on the edge of the Asian mainland, and that Japan and China could not be far away.

Columbus was not even the first European to reach America. Leif Eriksson, a Viking sailor from Greenland, visited the coast of Canada in the year 1000, and his sister Freydis founded a short-lived colony there a few years later. But no one outside the Viking world knew anything about this adventure, and soon it was nothing more than an old story. [See the article on Leif Eriksson and Freydis Erikssdottir in this book.]

So what's all the fuss about Columbus? Just this: He changed the world, completely and permanently. He opened a pathway from the Old World

Christopher Columbus. This portrait is thought by some scholars to be a copy of one made from life.

to the New at the very time when the Old World was getting ready to move out of its old ways. Suddenly there was more to the world than the little kingdoms of Christian Europe, always fighting among themselves; the huge empire of the Muslims, stretching across three continents; and the faraway realms of Africa, China, and Japan. For the people of Western Europe who lived near the Atlantic and who could reach the other side by ship, Columbus's discoveries opened up great sources of wealth. For the peoples of the Americas, his arrival meant the loss of their land and the decline of their own cultures. For the peoples of Africa, the result was the horror of the transatlantic slave trade. Out of all this adventuring and suffering, the modern world was born.

Even if Columbus had stayed home, the Old World and the New World would have made contact sooner or later. The Western Europeans had the ability to sail long distances in their wind-driven ships. All they required was enough courage to take them into unknown waters very far from land, and a good reason to go there. It so happened that Columbus had both. He also had ambition. He was determined to make a great name for himself in the world, to be almost the equal of kings. And, being an intensely religious man, he felt that God was guiding his actions. "I am not the first admiral of my family," he once wrote. "Let them call me, then, by what name they will, for after all David, the wisest of kings, tended sheep and was later made king of Jerusalem, and I am the servant of Him who raised David to that high state."

What did Columbus mean when he said that he was not the first admiral of his family? No one is certain, for Columbus did his best to keep his origins a mystery. Although he is the most famous explorer who ever lived, the truth about his early life remains hidden. Most historians accept the idea that he was born in the city of Genoa, on the northwest coast of Italy, and that he was the son of a woolweaver and the grandson of a peasant. Genoa in the fifteenth century was a city of seagoing merchants who sailed far and wide in pursuit of trade. According to this version of events, Columbus first went to sea when he was a teenager, traveling along the Mediterranean coast and to the island of Chios on trading trips. In 1476 he accompanied a fleet of Genoese ships westward across the Mediterranean on their way to England. Near the Strait of Gibraltar the convoy was attacked by pirates, and almost everyone aboard was killed. Columbus, hanging onto an oar, swam six miles to the shore of Portugal and was pulled from the water by fishermen. When he recovered, he went to the city of Lisbon, where his brother Bartolomé was working as a mapmaker.

Some historians doubt that all of this is true. Columbus himself hardly ever referred to his past, and his son Fernando, who wrote a book about him, exaggerated some things and left out others. The only thing that is certain is that a man calling himself Cristóbal Colón arrived in Lisbon in 1476. Over the next eight years, in addition to helping his brother in the mapmaking business, he went on a number of sea voyages—north to Ireland and Iceland, south to the Portuguese gold mine at Elmina on the west coast of Africa. He married a young noblewoman and lived for some time on her family's estate in the Madeira Islands, Portugal's colony in the Atlantic. They had one child, a boy named Diego.

All this time, while Lisbon buzzed with news of the latest scientific research into navigation and the most recent attempt to sail southward along the African coast, Columbus was reading everything he could find on the subject of a westward route to Asia. The problem of how to get to Asia was a matter of concern to many Europeans in those days. Europeans wanted spices to make their bland food palatable. They needed gold to pay for wars. They needed medicines derived from Asian plants. To get these valuable items, they had to pay high prices to merchants from Genoa and Venice. The merchants obtained their goods from Arab dealers who did business in India and Indonesia.

The Arab monopoly on trade with Asia was one reason why the Christian kings of Europe were enemies of the Muslim empire to the east. Another reason was the danger that the Muslims might conquer Europe. Most of Spain had fallen to them long ago. Now they had conquered the Christians' Byzantine Empire and stood ready to attack Europe from the east. [Two hundred years later, the Muslims had come as far west as Hungary. See the article on John Smith in this book.] While the leaders of Christian Spain were fighting a long battle to push the Muslims out, Portugal's Prince Henry had set in motion a national effort to weaken the power of Islam by finding a

Columbus signed his letters to his family with this cryptogram. Scholars think that the symbols carry a hidden Catholic or Jewish meaning.

direct route between Western Europe and India. His explorers had been sailing further and further down the African coast, hoping to find a way eastward around Africa. [See the article in this book on Prince Henry the Navigator.]

But why an eastward route? Why not go west? The world was round—that was an accepted idea by now—so if a Portuguese caravel set out westward and sailed far enough, it would eventually come to Asia. That was the idea that consumed Cristóbal Colón night and day. No one knew if Africa really had a southern end. There might be no way to get around it. On the other hand, the first person who got to Asia by going westward would be rich, honored, famous throughout Europe. Even a lowly sailor might hope to make himself a prince if he could summon the courage to go on such a journey. For it would be a journey into the void, into a world of absolute mystery. There were no maps or charts for mariners to follow. There would be no landmarks, not a single familiar sign. When they reached the other side—*if* they reached the other side—they would be in China or Japan, countries where Europeans were complete strangers. Anyone who undertook the voyage would have to travel mainly on faith.

Faith was something Columbus had in abundance. He was certain that God had chosen him to carry out this mission, and that the Bible contained proofs that he would succeed. Again and again he read the works of the ancient Greek geographer Ptolemy and the Venetian merchant Marco Polo, who had visited China in the thirteenth century [see the article on Marco Polo in this book]. By his own calculations, all of which were mistaken, he convinced himself that the earth was smaller than it really is. He decided that the land mass of Asia was so wide that it must

A magnetic compass in an ivory box from the late 15th century. Sea captains often hid their compasses to avoid accusations of witchcraft.

stretch nearly all the way around the other side of the earth. A good seaman would require only a few weeks to cross the Atlantic and reach the Asian coast, Columbus thought. All he needed was a fleet of ships, men to sail them, and money to feed and pay them.

Most of the people who listened to Columbus decided that he was at best a dreamer, at worst a madman. That was the reaction of King João II of Portugal when Columbus presented his proposal in 1483. The best geographers in the country said that he was wrong. In the spring of 1485, therefore, Columbus went across the border to Spain. His wife had died, and he was accompanied by his little son, whom he left at a Spanish monastery to be raised by the monks.

Spain was a country undergoing enormous changes. Once broken up into four provinces, it was in the process of becoming united through the marriage of Queen Isabel of Castile and King Fernando of Aragon. The combined armies of the king and queen were making war against Granada, the last Muslim-held territory in Spain. Their ultimate goal was to produce a nation that was absolutely and entirely Christian. They would no longer tolerate the presence of Muslims, who had lived in Spain for 700 years, or of Jews, who had been there for at least 1,200 years, al-

though together the Muslims and the Jews had produced a culture of great learning while Christian Europe was locked in the Dark Ages.

In Columbus's proposal, Queen Isabel saw the possibility of extending Christianity yet further. There were millions of people in Asia who knew nothing about Christianity. Spanish priests could be sent over to convert them. And with the gold that Columbus expected to find in China—for had not Marco Polo said that the temples in China were roofed with gold?—she and the other Christian leaders of Europe might launch one more battle to take the city of Jerusalem away from the Muslims. Of course, a steady flow of treasure from Asia would help make Spain an ever more powerful nation. But in Isabel's mind, the search for gold would have a holy purpose too.

Nonetheless, for the time being, the monarchs were too busy with the war against Granada to give much thought to the grand ambitions of Señor Cristóbal Colón. Nor did they have any money to spare while they were running a military campaign. They referred his proposal to a committee of priests and professors, with instructions to examine it thoroughly and recommend a course of action. Some of the sharpest minds in Spain were on the committee, and they saw that Columbus's plan relied more on wishful thinking than on solid evidence. Again and again they asked him to explain his calculations. Columbus waited four years for their decision. Finally, they told Isabel and Fernando that Columbus's request should be denied.

Without support from a monarch, the "Enterprise of the Indies," as Columbus called his plan, was doomed. The kings of France and England, approached by Columbus's brother Bartolomé, were not interested. King João of Portugal said he was willing to look at it again, but at that very moment Bartolomeu Dias arrived in Lisbon with the news that he had sailed clear around Africa into the Indian Ocean. [For the story of Dias's journey, see the article on him in this book.] The eastward route to Asia was a success. Portugal had no need for a westward route any longer.

That was very nearly the end of Columbus's peculiar idea. Nothing more would ever have come of it if Luis de Santangel, the king's treasurer, had not changed the queen's mind. He and three other men donated money to help pay for the expedition. All four men were either Jewish or, like Santangel himself, from Jewish families that had been forced to convert to Christianity. In all likelihood, they paid for the trip in the hope that Columbus's voyage would make it possible for the Jews of Spain to settle in Asia. Many converted Jews were burned alive in Spain every year because they practiced Judaism in secret. And the unconverted Jews, too, desperately needed a place of refuge. In March of 1492, as soon as King Fernando and Queen Isabel had conquered Granada, they announced that the Jewish inhabitants of their kingdom had four months to sell their possessions and get out.

There was much delicate negotiating to be done before Santangel and other supporters of Columbus could persuade the king and queen to agree to the explorer's terms. Columbus insisted on receiving a noble title and a coat of arms, the right to be called the Admiral of the Ocean Sea (that is, the Atlantic), the right to govern whatever lands he found, and the right to collect taxes on all trade with those lands. In addition, he wanted these titles and rights to be passed down in his family throughout the generations. The contract by which the king and queen granted these conditions was dated April 17, 1492.

Over the next four months, Columbus rushed to get ready. He spent most of his time in the town of Palos, which had been ordered by the king and queen to provide two caravels for the expedition as a punishment for smuggling. (A caravel was a light, easily maneuverable ship, well suited for voyages of exploration. It had been developed by Prince Henry the Navigator's master shipwrights.) The third vessel, the *Santa María*, was a freighter that Columbus rented to be his flagship. With the help of an experienced sea captain from Palos named Martin Alonso Pinzon, he recruited ninety sailors.

The *Santa María* and the two caravels, the *Niña* and the *Pinta*, sailed at dawn on August 3.

Isabel and Fernando, the joint rulers of Spain. In backing Columbus's expedition, they extended their power to a new world.

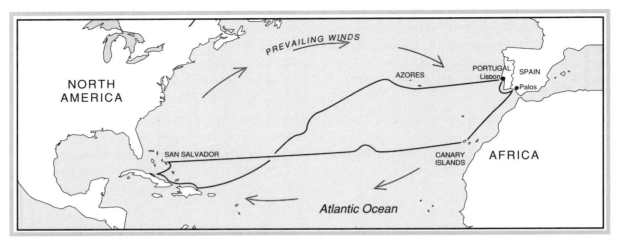

The route of Columbus's first voyage

As they left the harbor at Palos, they passed a number of little boats full of families with children. All the harbors of Spain were crowded with these boats, for the deadline for the departure of Spain's Jewish citizens had been midnight of the previous day.

Columbus's first destination was the Canary Islands, 800 miles southwest of Spain. His plan was to sail due west from the Canaries. From his reading of Marco Polo, he expected this course to take him straight to the islands of Cipango (or Japan, as we now call them). If by bad luck he missed Cipango, then he would arrive either at Cathay (that is, China) or the Golden Peninsula (Malaysia). To find his way, he relied on the method of navigation called "dead reckoning"—guessing the ship's speed from observing its path through in the water and then estimating how far the ship must have come. He also used astronomical tables prepared by a professor named Abraham Zacuto. [See the article on Zacuto in this book.]

In fact, though Columbus had nowhere near as much sailing experience as Pinzon, the captain of the *Pinta*, he seems to have had an inborn knack for navigating. He was lucky enough to find the westward-blowing trade winds, and for several weeks his ships coasted along under their power. The route he chose still remains the best route for sailing westward to the Americas.

Although Columbus's diary of the voyage no longer exists, a copy of it was made by Bishop Bartolomé de Las Casas, one of his first biographers. [For more information about Las Casas, who saw first-hand the aftermath of Columbus's expeditions—he went to Spanish America with the conquistadors and became their harshest critic—see the article on him in this book.] It tells how the enthusiasm of the sailors began to erode as they sailed farther and farther away into the unknown, and how close they came to rebelling against the admiral, especially when the ships lost the trade winds and fell into a dead calm. By the first week of October, everyone but Columbus wanted to turn back. But, says his diary, "The admiral added that it was useless to complain, since he had made up his mind to sail to the Indies and intended to continue the voyage until, God willing, he should reach them." A few days later the crewmen began to see shore birds, floating tree branches, and other signs of land. At two o'clock in the morning on October 12, they saw in the moonlight a thin white strip of beach, and at noon the next day they dropped anchor in a small bay on the coast of a small and rocky island.

Dressed in rich velvet, the Admiral of the Ocean Sea was rowed to shore. The captains and officers stood by as witnesses as he planted the banner of Fernando and Isabel and declared the island to be their property. Then they all knelt and kissed the earth. Nearby stood another group of witnesses, surprised and curious. They were members of the Taino people, inhabitants of the islands in the Caribbean Sea. They shared these islands with another and much more dangerous people, the Carib or Canib, from whose name the word "cannibal" is derived.

The island on which the Spanish ships had landed, called Guanahani in the Taino language, was renamed San Salvador by Columbus. It is part of the island chain that we now call the Bahamas. Columbus saw plainly that it could not be either Cipango or Cathay; those places were described by Marco Polo as rich civilizations abounding in gold, while Guanahani was the home of unclothed people who lived in simple huts. He decided that he must have landed somewhere northeast of Japan. By sailing southwest, he would reach his destination. So for the next few weeks the Spanish ships wandered through the Bahamas and along the coasts of two large islands, Cuba and Hispaniola, checking for gold at every Taino village they found.

By Christmas Eve, the flagship lay off the north coast of Hispaniola (the island now shared by the nations of Haiti and the Dominican Republic). Exhausted from the labor of sailing in rocky waters with nothing to guide them, Columbus and the crew of the *Santa María* fell into a dead sleep. And while they slept, the ship, with only a young boy at the tiller, ran aground on a hidden reef and was wrecked. The crew saved whatever they could, with the help of Tainos sent by the local chief, Guacanagari. Then, using wood salvaged from the *Santa María*, the sailors began building a tiny settlement that Columbus called La Navidad. Thirty-nine men volunteered to stay there and search for the gold mine that Guacanagari said was not far away. (One of these men was the brother of a young woman from Seville who had given birth to Columbus's second son, Fernando.) On January 16, 1493, the *Niña* and the *Pinta* sailed for Spain.

An artist's rendering of Columbus's three ships crossing the Atlantic in 1492. The route he took is still the best one for a westward voyage.

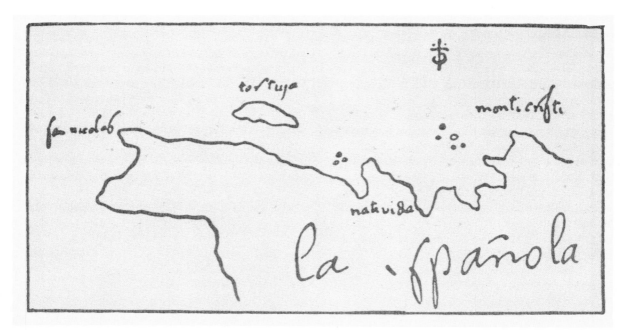

Columbus sketched this map of the north coast of Hispaniola. It shows La Navidad, the fort he built from the remains of the wrecked Santa María.

Thirty-two weeks after his expedition set out to find the westward route to Asia, Columbus arrived back in Palos on the *Niña*. He almost didn't get there. On the return trip, his ships had been caught in a violent storm. Columbus was so sure that the end had come that he wrote out an account of his journey and threw it overboard inside a barrel, in the hope that the knowledge of his discovery would not die with him. The *Niña* came to rest at one of the Azores Islands, where half the crew marched to the village church in their shirts to give thanks for their survival. But the Portuguese governor of the island had them thrown into jail on suspicion of using Portugal's sea route to Africa. Of course he did not believe them when they said they were returning across the Atlantic from the Indies.

Once the men were back on board, the *Niña* put out to sea again—and ran into a hurricane that lasted for six days and ripped the sails to shreds. Columbus was forced to land in Portugal, where he was summoned to appear before King João. The rivalry between Portugal and Spain had become so intense that some of the Portuguese courtiers tried to persuade the king to have Columbus executed.

Finally, on March 15, Columbus reached Palos. A few weeks later he was in Barcelona, at the Royal Palace, where he presented the full story of his adventure to the king and queen. He brought with him the evidence of his success: bars of gold from Guacanagari, colorful and aromatic plants, bright green parrots in wicker cages. There were also human beings—seven bewildered Taino islanders, the first New World inhabitants ever to see the Old.

Columbus was at the height of his triumph. Fernando and Isabel did not doubt that he had actually fulfilled his promise to go to Asia. They treated him with all the honor due a nobleman of the highest birth. (They had shown no honor at all to Martin Alonso Pinzon, captain of the *Pinta*, who had reached Spain before Columbus did and who felt that he deserved a share of the credit.) Columbus was even granted the right to wear royal emblems on his coat of arms. From this time on, he did not call himself Cristóbal Colón, but El Almirante, the Admiral.

The news of Columbus's voyage spread throughout Europe. While he was still on his way home, he wrote a letter to Luis de Santangel and another courtier, Gabriel Sanchez, describing his discoveries. Copies of this letter were printed up—an action made possible by the invention of the printing press a few decades before—and distributed in all the major cities. Thus, while Portugal kept its explorations a tight secret, Spain's new possessions were soon being discussed by interested people from England to Italy. Unable to decide for themselves how to share the enterprise of exploring the unknown parts of the world, Spain and Portugal appealed to Pope Alexander VI. He drew an imaginary line around the globe and gave Spain everything to the west of it and Portugal everything to the east. The location of this line was based on advice from Columbus.

By the time this agreement was reached, Columbus was on his way back to Hispaniola as the leader of a colony. He had embarked from the port of Cádiz in September of 1493 with a fleet of seventeen ships carrying some 1,500 men together with livestock, plants, and food. His instructions from the queen and king were to build a settlement dedicated to growing crops, mining gold, and converting the islanders to Christianity. This voyage was entirely paid for by the money and property that the royal treasury had seized from the exiled Jews. As the fleet neared its destination, Columbus sighted and charted dozens of new islands, including the ones we know today as Dominica, the Virgin Islands, and Puerto Rico.

But La Navidad was gone. It had been burned to the ground, and among the ashes lay the skeletons of the men who had lived there. They had

In this Spanish engraving, Columbus's men raise a cross, symbol of the Christian religion, while Taino Indians offer him golden treasures.

Columbus brought horses, cattle, chickens, and pigs to the New World. Large animals had to be hoisted aboard ship with pulleys and ropes.

brought the disaster on themselves. Throwing away all discipline and self-control, they had gone rampaging through the nearby villages, stealing the women. The villagers had attacked them and killed every one.

The expedition began building a second colony on Hispaniola, which Columbus called La Isabela. Within a very short time it became a place of disorder. It was built on marshy, mosquito-infested ground, and soon half the colonists were sick. Their food rotted in the humid atmosphere. A fort was constructed several miles away for storing gold, but no gold mines had yet been found, and the treasure-hungry settlers fought with one another and with the islanders.

Columbus's grand ambitions were quickly falling apart. If he did not find a good source of gold, Isabel and Fernando would lose faith in him, and

his dreams of honor and wealth would come to nothing. Leaving La Isabela to its squabbles, he took three caravels and headed westward, determined to find China and the Great Khan who was said to rule it. Sailing along the dangerous southern coast of Cuba, dipping down to Jamaica, constantly pressing the amazed inhabitants for some clue that would lead him to the right place, he finally convinced himself that Cuba was no island, but a peninsula—in fact, the Malay Peninsula in Asia. To support his belief, he assembled all his officers and sailors and demanded that they swear, under oath, that they agreed with him.

Some historians think that by this time the burden of his enormous undertaking had robbed Columbus of his reason. He was also suffering from gout, arthritis, rheumatism, and exhaustion. Though he was only in his mid-forties, all his hair had turned white, and his bones ached constantly. On the way back to the Isabela colony, he fell into a coma, and for weeks he was unable to get out of bed.

La Isabela was deteriorating day by day. The Spanish colonists had gone completely out of control, raiding villages without mercy, and the islanders launched a rebellion that Columbus put down with extreme violence. Since gold mines still had not been found, he forced every male islander to pay a tax of gold dust. Many islanders worked themselves to death trying to gather enough, and those who failed were punished by having their hands cut off. Instead of gold, Columbus sent back to Spain cargoes of Indians to be sold as slaves.

This went directly against the orders of Queen Isabel, who wanted her new subjects converted, not enslaved. The queen and king had heard, by now, plenty of complaints about Columbus's troubled leadership. Yet when he came to see them in the summer of 1496, having left Hispaniola in the care of his brother Bartolomé, they agreed to give him the money for a third voyage. His job this time was to check on reports from Portuguese explorers that there was a large land mass to the south of his islands, across the ocean from Africa.

After a hard journey, in which his three ships sat becalmed for days on end, baking in the tropical heat, Columbus arrived at an island he named Trinidad, off the coast of what is now Venezuela. The land was much different from the islands in the Caribbean: fields of corn grew there, and beds of pearl-bearing oysters flourished in mangrove swamps. To the southeast of Trinidad was something that appeared to be an even larger island, with a river flowing from it into the sea. An immense quantity of fresh water came pouring out of this river, more than any island could produce. (It was, in fact, the Orinoco, one of the biggest rivers in South America.) Columbus began to suspect the truth. He wrote in his notes, "I believe this land may be a great continent that has remained unknown to this day." He saw two possible solutions to the puzzle. Either the continent was an extension of Asia, or it was the biblical Garden of Eden.

During his absence, Columbus's brothers, Bartolomé and Diego, had abandoned La Isabela and built a new city named Santo Domingo, near the southern coast of Hispaniola. This was the first permanent European colony in the New World. It was a healthier and more beautiful place than La Isabela, and it was near a genuine gold mine, but it was plagued by the same intractable problems. Most of the Spanish colonists refused to submit to the authority of the Colón brothers, whom they ridiculed as incompetent fumblers. One group of rebels broke away and formed an alliance with the Indians. Columbus vacillated between hanging the rebels and giving in to their demands. He showed less mercy toward Indians who refused to be taxed and enslaved. They were hunted down and killed. Many others had already died from diseases that the colonists brought over from Europe.

Queen Isabel's trusted agent, Francisco de Bobadilla, was shocked to see the terrible conditions in Santo Domingo when he arrived there in the fall of 1500. He removed Columbus from his position as governor and sent all three brothers back to Spain in chains to face trial.

The king and queen had had enough of Cristóbal Colón. They forbade him ever to return to

The colony of Santo Domingo was so badly managed that Columbus and his brothers were sent back to Spain in disgrace by order of Queen Isabel.

Hispaniola, though he continued to receive his share of the colony's profits. They refused to read a book he had written containing biblical prophecies of Spain's role in capturing Jerusalem from the Muslims. Columbus wanted one last chance to push westward from Cuba and find the passage to the Indies that he felt sure must be there. To keep him from bothering them any further, they sent him on this final expedition. He sailed from Cádiz in May 1502 with a fleet of four caravels, accompanied by his brother Bartolomé and his son Fernando. In less than three weeks he was back in the Caribbean and had landed on a previously unknown island, Martinique.

It was impossible for Columbus to stay away from Santo Domingo, the city he and his brothers had founded and ruled. He set his course for Hispaniola. As he neared it, he recognized the signs of an oncoming hurricane. The new governor, Nicolas de Ovando, did not believe his warning and refused to allow his caravels to take shelter in the harbor. Columbus found another place to wait out the storm. But twenty ships just leaving Santo Domingo on their way to Spain were destroyed, with no survivors. Among the dead was Francisco de Bobadilla, the man who had sent Columbus home a prisoner.

Columbus took this as proof that God was still guiding him, in spite of all his disappointments. He headed westward, past Jamaica and Cuba. By early August he had come to a stretch of unfamiliar coastline. The fleet had reached Central America and the country that we now call Honduras, at the edge of the Mayan empire. Following along the shore, trying to avoid dangerous rocks and shallows, the caravels inched their way through a pounding rainstorm that lasted twenty-eight days and rotted all their food. Finally, more dead than alive, they reached the isthmus of Panama. It was a beautiful place where the inhabitants wore necklaces of solid gold.

This, Columbus was certain, must be China. The rainforest was thick and wild, the weather unbearably humid. Nevertheless, he ordered his sailors to begin building a mining colony at a riverside spot called Veragua. His dreams were about to be fulfilled. He would now have enough treasure to hire an army and lead it to Jerusalem.

The inhabitants of Veragua waited until the right moment, when the river was low and the foreigners were temporarily stranded. Then they launched their attack. When the battle was over, on Easter night, the Spanish were gone, leaving behind one of their caravels and the bodies of their dead comrades. The three remaining caravels were riddled with holes made by shipworms and were barely able to float. Soon the expedition was down to two ships, and Columbus, sick with disappointment and delirious from malaria, set his course for Santo Domingo. On the way they ran into a violent storm and came near to sinking. They were lucky to reach Jamaica, where they propped up the two useless ships on the beach at Santa Gloria Bay.

Columbus and his men were now marooned. They had no way of leaving the island. No one in Hispaniola had any reason to come looking for them. In all likelihood, they knew, they were destined to live out the rest of their lives in the makeshift huts they built on the decks of the caravels. Columbus wrote a a letter describing their ordeal, in the hope that it might someday reach Fernando and Isabel. "Today, may Heaven have mercy on me, may the earth cry for me, as I wait for death alone, sick and racked with pain," the letter read. "I am so far away from the Holy Sacraments that if my soul should here leave my body, not even God would remember it."

Yet Columbus, of all people, was not one to surrender to the inevitable. A miracle might still occur. His first problem was to keep all one hundred of his sailors alive and safe. As governor of Hispaniola, he had made terrible mistakes when it came to dealing with both colonists and natives. The same mistakes this time would cost them all their lives. To prevent his crewmen from interfering in any way with the islanders, he ordered them to stay on board the sandbound caravels. A handpicked team of sailors, headed by a particularly brave officer named Diego Mendez, was sent to negotiate with the chiefs of the nearby villages. In exchange for pairs of scissors, the chiefs agreed to supply the Spanish with bread and to let them hunt and fish.

Five hundred miles of choppy seas stretched between Jamaica and Santo Domingo. The only possibility of rescue lay in getting someone to cross those seas in a rowboat. Mendez and another officer volunteered. In two dugout canoes, with ten islanders in each one to work the oars, they set out across the channel, under the blazing July sun.

The marooned sailors at Santa Gloria had nothing to do but wait. Six months went by, and still there was no answer from Hispaniola. Half the men joined together in a mutiny and worked off their frustration by raiding Indian villages. The Indians themselves grew tired of supplying the Spanish with food. There were signs that they were preparing an attack on the caravels. It happened that Columbus had with him an almanac containing the dates of lunar eclipses. On the night of February 29, he invited the village chiefs to a meeting on the beach and warned them that the Christian God would punish them if any harm came to the sailors. As proof of this, he said, the moon would disappear. And so it did. Before it emerged from the shadow of the sun, Columbus had received promises of help from the chiefs.

In June 1504, one year after they were cast away on Jamaica, Columbus and his sailors saw the sails of two caravels on the horizon. Mendez and his group had not been drowned after all. After four days, half dead from thirst and fatigue, they had reached the westernmost point of Hispaniola. It had taken them until September to reach Santo Domingo, and when they did, Governor Ovando had been in no hurry to send a rescue mission. A friend of Columbus's had rented a ship and come in person to bring him home.

The Admiral of the Ocean Sea arrived back in Spain from his fourth voyage in November 1504. The ordeal of the past year had left him crippled, unable to move his legs. The success of the gold mines in Hispaniola had made him a rich man, but all his rights to ownership of the Indies had been stripped from him, and the king refused to reinstate them. The queen might have been more sympathetic, but she died a few weeks after his return. Columbus's appeal of this judgment was carried on for years after his death by his descendants. His claim was vigorously disputed by the heirs of Martin Alonso Pinzon, who said that without the help of the sea captain from Palos, Columbus would have discovered nothing.

It was becoming more and more evident—except to Columbus—that what he had discovered was not the eastern edge of Asia but a land mass that was unknown to the ancients and not mentioned in the Bible. Once Columbus had brought this mysterious new world into the consciousness of Europeans, they had proved eager enough to do what he could not—exploit it for their own various purposes. The colony on Hispaniola, soon to become the basis of an enormously wealthy Spanish empire, was only the beginning. Already, in 1497, the Venetian explorer John Cabot had gone to Canada in the service of the king of England, and in 1500 Pedro Álvares Cabral, on his way to India around the southern tip of Africa, had struck Brazil and claimed it for Portugal. [See the articles on Cabral and his navigator, Gaspar of India, in this book.] The history of Western Europe, from this point until well into the twentieth century, would be dominated by a long fight for control of the seas and the lands that lay beyond them.

Through most of that history, the man who had started it all was nearly forgotten. Columbus did not live long after he came back from his last expedition. In May 1506 he died and was buried in the city of Valladolid. Over the years, his bones were dug up repeatedly and reburied in Seville, then in Santo Domingo, then in Cuba, and finally in Seville again. No one is sure any longer if the remains in his casket are really his. The continents that he opened for exploration were not even called by his name, but by the name of the Italian navigator Amerigo Vespucci, who claimed the discovery of the New World for himself.

More than three hundred years passed before historians and geographers began to show much interest in Cristóbal Colón, and by that time, much of the information about his life had been lost forever. In the nineteenth century there was an unsuccessful movement in the Catholic Church to have him declared a saint. There was an explosion of interest in him in the twentieth century, and hundreds of books were written about him, but the result was that the real Columbus vanished behind a cloud of myths. By the 500th anniversary of his first voyage, in 1992, he was being hailed by some people as the greatest explorer of all time and damned by others as a fanatic who brought the curse of slavery to the Americas.

The fact is that the story of Columbus is like a mirror held up to history. You can point it in different directions, and it will always show something worth seeing. But it will never show the whole truth all at one time.

Vasco Núñez de Balboa

*Vasco Núñez de Balboa (bahl-BO-uh).
Born circa 1475, in Estremadura, Spain.
Died January 1519, in Acla, Castilla del
Oro (now Panama).*

Before the sweating, exhausted soldiers, the ocean stretched out, limitless and blue. Behind them were the dense green jungles of Panama, the narrow bridge of land between North and South America. The Spanish adventurers had hacked their way through the forest for nearly a month, in search of a rumored southern sea and an empire of gold. Four days earlier, their leader, Vasco Núñez de Balboa, had glimpsed the blue waters as he climbed a high hill. But now, standing on the beach, they were silent. This was no sea, but a vast ocean, just a few dozen miles from the familiar Atlantic. Now Balboa roused himself. As the first Spaniard to see the Pacific Ocean from the shores of America, he must mark the occasion with a show of greatness. Balboa drew his sword, held high the banner of Spain,

Balboa, with his company of soldiers and priests clustered behind him, salutes the Pacific in this romanticized engraving from the 19th century.

and marched into the surf. The sun glinted from his armor as he shouted, "By the grace of God, I claim all that sea and the countries bordering on it for the King and Castile!"

That was the high point of the career of Balboa, who was cut from the same cloth as the Spanish conquistadors Hernán Cortés and Francisco Pizarro. [Their adventures are described in the articles about them in this book.] Balboa even came from the same part of Spain as they did, the bleak province of Estremadura that bred many restless men in the sixteenth century. And he, like they, was the son of a family that had noble blood but little money or power.

In 1500, finding few prospects for advancement in Spain, Balboa decided to go to the New World, where Spain was just beginning a vast effort to conquer the inhabitants and set up its own colonies. He joined an expedition sent to explore the coast of present-day Colombia in South America. Later he set up a small farm on the Spanish-held island of Hispaniola (now the nations of Haiti and the Dominican Republic).

Balboa knew little about farming, and he soon fell into debt. In 1510 he heard that a ship was about to embark with supplies for the failing Spanish colony of San Sebastian on the Colombian coast. To escape his creditors, he hid in a wine barrel and was carried aboard the ship with the other cargo. Stopping at the town of Cartagena, Balboa's ship met up with the few surviving colonists from San Sebastian, led by Francisco Pizarro. The two adventurers banded together and established a new colony called Santa María de la Antigua, on the coast of Darién (as the eastern part of Panama was then called). This was the first permanent European settlement on the American mainland.

In 1511 King Fernando of Spain appointed Balboa governor and captain-general of Darién. His job was to secure the area for Spanish settlers and to send back any gold or other treasures he found. Balboa was quite successful at this work. He made key alliances with several Indian tribes, then began systematically to rob and enslave the rest, sometimes unleashing fierce war dogs into their villages to search out uncooperative inhabitants and tear them apart. Any chiefs who did not surrender their gold immediately were tortured. From one chief, who lectured the

Spanish on their greed for gold, Balboa learned of a sea to the south, beyond which was an entire empire of gold. [This was probably a reference to the empire of the Incas in Peru, which was later conquered by Pizarro. For more on the conquest of Peru, see the articles on Pizarro and Atahualpa in this book.]

In great excitement, Balboa wrote to Spain asking for weapons and men to help him carve a passage through the jungle to the sea and conquer the golden empire. The expedition was sent in 1514, but it was not placed under Balboa's command. The king, hearing of Balboa's misdeeds, put a hot-tempered old nobleman named Pedro Arias de Ávila (usually called Pedrarias) in charge of the expedition instead, and appointed him the new governor of Darién as well. With Pedrarias came several figures who afterward played important roles in the Spanish conquest of the Americas: Hernán de Soto, who discovered the Mississippi River; Francisco Coronado, who led an expedition into the interior of the American Southwest; and Bernal Díaz de Castillo, who wrote the most famous eyewitness account of the conquest of Mexico. [See the articles on Coronado, Estevanico, Cortés, Moctezuma, and Malintzin for more on these stories.]

But Balboa had already decided to make the trip on his own. On September 11, 1513, he set out through the Panamanian jungles with 106 Spanish soldiers, many Indian bearers, and a number of bloodhounds. Cutting their way south through the narrowest part of the isthmus, east of the present-day Panama Canal, the Spanish crossed the crocodile-infested Chagres River, then pushed through fever-ridden swamps, carrying their clothes on their heads to keep them from rotting in the foul water. The jungle was so dense that they did not see the sun for days at a time. After two weeks they began climbing the mountains that run the length of the country. It was from the height of one of those peaks that Balboa saw the Pacific Ocean for the first time. A few days later he and his men reached the water, and Balboa made his dramatic speech.

Over the next few years, Balboa spent his own money to build a number of ships on the Atlantic side of the isthmus and have them carried in pieces across to the Pacific side, where they were reassembled. He set sail to explore the Pacific in

At Balboa's command, a pack of dogs attacks a group of Indians from a village in Darién, including the brother of an uncooperative chief.

1517, but contrary winds blew him back to shore. So Balboa never saw the western coast of South America or made contact with the Incas, rulers of that rumored empire of gold.

Meanwhile, the king had to be informed. Balboa's messengers, bearing news of the great discovery and a gift of several hundred pearls Balboa had taken from the coastal Indians, caused a sensation at the Spanish court. Perhaps the sea beyond Panama lapped the shores of Asia, and offered an easy route to the spices and other riches of the East. (Indeed, the Pacific does link Panama to China, but no one knew then that many thousands of miles of ocean lie between.)

King Carlos, Fernando's successor, made Balboa governor of several provinces in Panama, but placed him under the authority of Pedrarias, the new governor of Darién. Pedrarias turned out to be even more ruthless than Balboa had been. Under his administration, tens of thousands of Indians were slaughtered, and many more were forced into slavery. Balboa did not trust Pedrarias, nor did Pedrarias trust Balboa. At length they came to an understanding and even agreed that Balboa would marry Pedrarias's daughter, who lived in Spain. But the two rivals could not stand each other for very long. Balboa publicly accused Pedrarias of incompetence and greed, and there was some talk that Pedrarias would be removed and put on trial. Pedrarias was sure that Balboa wanted the governorship for himself, which was probably true, and decided that the safest course was to dispose of this troublesome rival once and for all. In late 1518, he summoned Balboa to his headquarters on a pretext and ordered him arrested on charges of high treason and mistreatment of the Indians. The arresting officer was Pizarro, who thought nothing of sacrificing friends for his own gain. After a rigged trial, Balboa was taken to the town square, where Pizarro cut off his head.

Such was Balboa's bad luck that he is not even mentioned in the one great poem in English that mentions the discovery of the Pacific Ocean. The Romantic poet John Keats got it wrong and credited the feat to Hernán Cortés, the conqueror of Mexico:

> *. . . Then felt I like some watcher of the skies*
> *When a new planet swims into his ken,*
> *Or like stout Cortez when with eagle eyes*
> *He star'd at the Pacific—and all his men*
> *Look'd at each other with a wild surmise—*
> *Silent, upon a peak in Darién.*

Malintzin

Malintzin (mah-LINT-zin), also known as Malina, Malinal, Malinche, Doña Marina. Born circa 1501 in Paynala, Coatzacoalcos, Mexico. Died 1550 in Spain.

The march of the Spanish conquistador Hernán Cortés through Mexico into the heart of the Aztec empire in 1519 was a remarkable feat. With just a few hundred men, Cortés faced down the most feared people in Mexico and captured their king, the great Moctezuma. [See the articles on Cortés and Moctezuma in this book.] But Cortés could have done nothing without the help of an Aztec princess named Malintzin. She translated from the Aztec language into Spanish for Cortés. More important, she understood the situation better than Cortés did. She showed him the route he should take; she found out plots against him; and finally she used her skillful way of speaking to persuade the mighty Moctezuma to do Cortés's bidding.

Malintzin was the daughter of the Aztec chief and governor of the town of Paynala, on the eastern coast of Mexico. We are not sure about what year she was born, or even about her real name. It may have been Malinal or Malinche. (In fact, all the names we have for her may only be versions of Marina, the name later given to her by the Spanish.) Her father was a powerful man, but he died when she was still a child. Some time around the year 1510 she was sold into slavery, perhaps by kidnappers but possibly by her own mother, who had remarried after her father's death and did not want her to challenge the new marriage. Eventually Malintzin ended up as the servant of a chief on

Artists from the city-state of Tlaxcala drew this picture of Tlaxcalan envoys talking to Cortés. The largest figure in the scene is Malintzin.

the far southeastern border of the Aztec empire, where it met the empire of the Mayas.

When Cortés landed on the coast of Mexico in 1519, near where Tabasco is today, he was given twenty slaves as a gift by the local chief. Among them was Malintzin. She was "beautiful and intelligent and without embarrassment," wrote Bernal Diaz, one of Cortés's men, "truly a great chieftainess and the daughter of great chiefs and the mistress of lords, and this her appearance clearly showed." Cortés had the slaves (all of whom were women) baptized and made Christians; then he gave them to his captains. Malintzin, whom the Spaniards called Doña Marina (Lady Marina), he gave to the nobleman Alonzo Puertocarrero. When Puertocarrero was sent back to Spain with messages and gold for the king, Malintzin became Cortés's lover. They had a son named Martin.

To the Spanish invaders, Malintzin proved to be more valuable than any amount of gold. She could speak the Aztec language, Nahuatl, and the Tabascan language, which one of the Spaniards could understand, and she soon learned Spanish. When Moctezuma sent envoys to meet Cortés, it was Malintzin who explained to Cortés that the Aztec king thought the Spanish might be visitors from the gods, and showed him how to take advantage of this. As Cortés's small army marched through the town of Cholula toward the Aztec capital, it was Malintzin who uncovered a deadly ambush against them. Had it not been for her loyalty and her quick wits, the Spanish would have been destroyed before they reached the capital city.

When the Spanish reached Moctezuma's palace, Cortés decided to take the king hostage. Malintzin, Cortés, and a few armed men were admitted to his throne room. There Malintzin argued for hours with the king, urging him to come with them peacefully for his own good. Finally, he allowed himself to be persuaded. In fact, Moctezuma believed he was speaking with messengers from his gods. He believed that Cortés had come from the gods to reclaim the land of the Aztecs in fulfilment of an age-old legend. He also believed, as did all the Aztecs, that Malintzin and Cortés were two sides of the same being, so much so that they even called Cortés "Malintzin's Captain." In some of the pictures the Indians made of their first encounters with Cortés, Malintzin is drawn larger than any other figure, which shows how important they thought her to be. Whatever she said to Moctezuma (and her exact words were

The lake city of Tenochtitlán contained many teocalli, *or temples. The Aztecs had a separate group of priests for each god and goddess.*

never written down), it is clear that his decision to become a prisoner was due as much to the arguments of Malintzin as to Cortés's threats of force.

Despite their king's surrender, the Aztecs soon rose to kill the invaders. In the bloody battle that followed, Moctezuma was killed. Malintzin was one of only three women in the Spanish party to escape, protected by a group of Indian warriors allied with Cortés. Later she helped Cortés form an alliance with other Indian tribes that had been subject to the Aztecs. In the summer of 1521 the armies of Cortés laid siege to the Aztec capital. In three months of fierce fighting every Aztec warrior was killed, and despite Cortés's orders his Indian allies sacrificed many of the Aztec women and children.

Cortés and Malintzin never married. In 1524 he gave her in marriage to Juan de Jaramillo, one of his officers. Cortés himself married a Spanish noblewoman in 1528. Malintzin went with her husband to Spain, where she was well received at the royal court. The king had good reason to be grateful to Malintzin, for she had opened the way into Mexico for Cortés and enriched Spain with land and gold. To her own people, though, she seemed the embodiment of treachery. Even today in Central America, "malinche" is what people call a traitor, and Malinche is also the name given to one of the sleeping volcanoes in the heart of Mexico. Legend has it that shortly before his death the weary Moctezuma was heard to ask her and Cortés, "What more does Malinche want of me?" Malintzin left no record of her thoughts, so we do not know why she chose to help the Spanish against the Aztecs. But it is not hard to imagine reasons: her own people had made her a slave, and surely would have killed her and her child (or sacrificed them to the gods) if Cortés had been defeated. Cortés won her loyalty, and with it the land of Mexico.

Moctezuma

Moctezuma II (mawk-tay-ZU-mah), also called Montezuma. In Nahuatl, Motecuhzoma. Born 1466. Died circa June 30, 1520, in Tenochtitlán (now Mexico City), Mexico.

King Moctezuma was afraid and confused. For years there had been signs and portents that his priests could not explain. A pillar of fire had been seen in the east. Lightning and floods had struck the capital city. His people believed that some day a white-skinned, bearded god would return to rule their land. But a magic bird had shown him in a mirror that his people would be conquered by warriors riding on the backs of deer. Now a band of strangers was coming, people unlike any ever seen before. They were white-skinned and bearded, like the god. But they also rode on the backs of great animals, like the conquerors that the bird had shown him. Were they gods, to be welcomed and served? Or enemies coming to destroy his empire?

Moctezuma, whose name means "Angry Lord," was the last great king of the Aztecs, a people who built an empire in central Mexico in the fifteenth and sixteenth centuries. The lands that they controlled stretched from the Atlantic coast of Mexico to the Pacific. All the empire was ruled from the capital city called Tenochtitlán, located where Mexico City is today. The Aztecs themselves were also called the Mexica, from which we get the name of their country, Mexico.

The Aztecs loved things of beauty. Their houses were white and clean, and their city was well-planned, with wide streets and many gardens. Rich people wore beautiful cloaks of parrot feathers in all the colors of the rainbow. Their warriors even carried flowers into battle. And they were deeply religious, devoting much of their time to rituals intended to satisfy their gods. They believed that daily sacrifices of human beings were the only thing that kept the world from ending in

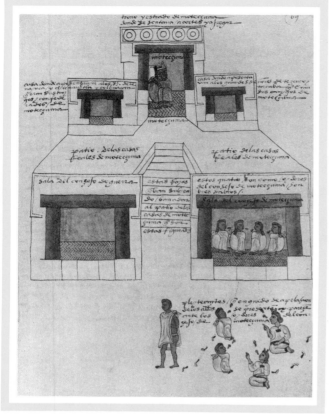

This picture of Moctezuma upon his throne was drawn by an Aztec artist. The descriptions were added later by a Spanish scribe.

fire, as it had, according to their legends, three times before. To the Aztecs, the most important reason for having an empire was that it enabled them to capture or take as tribute an endless supply of captives to sacrifice to their god, Huitzilopochtli. Most Indian civilizations of Central and South America practiced human sacrifice, but the Aztecs did more of it than anyone before or since. They needed thousands of people to sacrifice every year, and often went to war just to capture new victims. The peoples living under Aztec rule hated their masters, but few could outfight the Aztec warriors, who were skilled at catching their enemies alive. During Moctezuma's reign, this hatred would be the doom of the Aztecs.

Little is known of Moctezuma's early life. He was the son of Axayacatl, king of Tenochtitlán, who had died in 1481. In 1503 Moctezuma was elected to the throne upon the death of his uncle,

Ahuitzotl, a noted conqueror. For most of his reign, Moctezuma concerned himself with wars and conquests, gathering more and more sacrifices for Huitzilopochtli. He was also a cunning politician. In revenge for the execution of his sister, the queen of the neighboring Texcocan people, he tricked his allies the Texcocans and killed many of them. He then chose the next Texcocan king, even though the Texcocans never submitted to Aztec rule. However, all accounts of him agree that most of all he was a true believer in the gods, having been chief priest before becoming king, and that he was guided by what the powerful Aztec priests and astrologers told him.

In 1520 the Spanish conquistador Hernán Cortés landed on the Mexican coast near Vera Cruz. [See the article on Cortés in this book.] The world beyond Mexico was unknown to the Indians, and none had ever heard of Spain or seen a European. When descriptions of the Spaniards reached Moctezuma, the emperor thought that Cortés and his men might be messengers from the white, bearded god Quetzalcoatl, returning from the land of the sunrise (the east) to reclaim his realm. So the emperor sent ambassadors of peace to Cortés bearing rich gifts, including a great disk of gold and one of silver, and a helmet filled with grains of gold. But Moctezuma was cautious. He also sent a message warning the strangers not to come to the capital city.

Seeing these riches, Cortés was more determined than ever to press on into Mexico and meet with the great Aztec overlord. He and his small

The Aztec people prized beautiful things. This head-dress, made of brilliant quetzal feathers, was worn by a priest impersonating a god.

Aztec legend held that the god Quetzalcoatl, the Feathered Serpent, would arrive from the east. Many Aztecs thought Cortés was his messenger.

band of soldiers journeyed toward Tenochtitlán, at each stop sending messages of friendship to Moctezuma. Each time Moctezuma denied them permission to meet him. By the time Cortés reached the gates of the city, he had gained many allies among the peoples ruled by the Aztecs and had defeated a plot backed by Moctezuma to have him and his small army killed.

Acting on the advice of his astrologers, Moctezuma no longer tried to resist Cortés. The king, riding in a litter worked with gold and silver and crowned with green feathers, came to meet Cortés just inside the city. When Moctezuma stepped down, the people bowed their heads, and his followers laid fine cloaks upon the ground for him to walk upon. He wore a heavy necklace of gold and jewels, and sandals of solid gold. Cortés dismounted from his horse and made to embrace Moctezuma, in the Spanish way, but he was told that no one could touch the king. Once the priests had bathed Cortés in sweet-smelling incense, Moctezuma greeted the conquistador with friend-

ship and gifts. He then led the four hundred Spaniards and their followers to a huge palace where his father had once lived. Through his translators —a shipwrecked Spaniard who had learned an Indian language, and the Aztec princess Malintzin, Cortés's lover—Cortés tried to convince the emperor to accept Christianity. Moctezuma politely but firmly refused.

The Spaniards were impressed with the beauty of the lives of the Aztecs and the vast riches of their king. But they were horrified at the constant human sacrifices. Cortés became convinced that Moctezuma was waiting for the right moment to sacrifice the Spaniards as well. So he walked into Moctezuma's throne room with Malintzin and a few soldiers and quietly took Moctezuma prisoner. Malintzin persuaded Moctezuma to come with them to the Spanish palace along with his court, swear fealty to the Spanish king, and gather a great gift of gold to send back to Spain.

It is not clear, even today, why Moctezuma listened to the words of Cortés and Malintzin and agreed to become a prisoner. With just a gesture from the king, the four hundred Spaniards and their followers would have been crushed by thousands of fierce Aztec warriors, and the history of Latin America and of Europe would have been very different. Perhaps Moctezuma really did believe that these were people from heaven, and that he must obey them. Or perhaps he realized that the Spaniards came from a nation beyond the sea which the Aztecs could not hope to resist. In any case, his decision marked the beginning of the end of the Aztecs.

The Aztecs soon saw that their leader had surrendered his power to Cortés, and began to talk of killing the invaders. It did not help matters when Moctezuma betrayed several rebellious lords to Cortés, or when Cortés had the Aztec idols thrown down and crosses put in their place. Not long after, Cortés was called away to defend himself against a Spanish army that had been sent to take over his expedition. In Cortés's absence, Pedro de Alvarado, the officer in charge, stirred up more trouble in the capital by killing six hundred Aztec leaders celebrating a feast day. This so angered the Aztecs that they rose to attack the Spaniards, even though Moctezuma was still a hostage. Cortés returned and commanded Moctezuma to calm his people.

In the battle that followed, Moctezuma was fatally wounded. The Spaniards claimed that he was stoned or shot by the Aztecs, who had picked a new king who was less superstitious and more willing to fight. Mexican writers later said that he was strangled by the Spaniards themselves, but this is unlikely, for they had no reason to give up such a valuable hostage. A year later, the Aztec empire was no more, the beautiful city of Tenochtitlán was in ruins, and the mighty Aztec army had been slaughtered. [See the articles on Cortés and Malintzin in this book for more of this story.]

Hernán Cortés

Hernán Cortés (kor-TAYS). Born 1485 in Medellín, Badajoz, Spain. Died December 2, 1547, near Seville, Spain.

In the sixteenth century, Spain sent out *conquistadores*—the Spanish word for conquerors—to take possession of the vast new lands discovered in the Americas. The greatest of the conquistadors was Hernán Cortés. Part general,

Cortés, the conqueror of Mexico and founder of Spain's New World empire, is shown in this drawing holding a shield with his coat of arms.

part politician, part adventurer, and part missionary, Cortés led a small Spanish army into the heart of the powerful Aztec Indian empire of Mexico and, against great odds, conquered the entire country. This gave Spain a huge new territory in the New World and, in the process, wiped out a civilization that had been flourishing for a century.

Cortés was born in a small town on the harsh, windy plains of Estremadura in south-central Spain, an area that was also the birthplace of another great conquistador, Francisco Pizarro. [For the story of Pizarro's conquest of Peru, see the article on Pizarro in this book.] As the son of a family with much honor but little wealth, Cortés saw few prospects for advancement in Spain, but many in the New World. Tales of new lands and great riches lured him to the port of Cádiz, where Spanish soldiers and adventurers gathered to plan the conquest of the Americas.

In 1504, at the age of nineteen, Cortés sailed with a group of merchants to the island of Hispaniola (which is now shared between the nations of Haiti and the Dominican Republic) in the Caribbean Sea. Here Cortés bided his time, working a small farm and befriending the governor. When the governor sent a small army under Diego Velázquez to conquer Cuba in 1511, Cortés went along as treasurer, to tally any gold that was seized and make sure the king was given his royal fifth. By now Cortés had become a skilled politician and diplomat, learning to flatter those above him and outflank his enemies. He soon gained wealth and power as one of the new colony's chief officials, serving twice as mayor of Santiago, the Cuban capital.

Over the next few years Spanish explorers came to Hispaniola and Cuba with news of the vast wealth of the Indians of Central America. Cortés saw his chance to gain fame and honor. Mortgaging his lands and other holdings, he raised the money for an expedition to plant a Spanish colony on the Central American mainland. He was determined to succeed where other captains had failed, so he assembled a navy of six good ships and three hundred seasoned soldiers, provided his men with every necessity, and sought the support of Diego Velázquez, now governor of Cuba, who made Cortés captain-general of the expedition. But the more soldiers Cortés recruited, and the more people shared his enthusiasm for the expedition, the less the governor liked it. Velázquez began to see Cortés as a powerful rival, and he decided to revoke Cortés's appointment before the expedition could get underway.

But Cortés learned of the governor's plans, and, on the night of November 17, 1518, he secretly ordered his men to board the ships. The next morning, after taking all the meat from the town's butchers, he bid farewell to the furious Velázquez and set sail for the Cuban port of Trinidad, where he picked up additional ships and men, including such experienced captains as Pedro de Alvarado and Alonso Puertocarrero. They set off three months later for the mainland with eleven ships, more than six hundred men, plenty of weapons, and sixteen horses.

Cortés first landed on Cozumel, an island just off the Yucatán peninsula. Immediately he began shaping his men into an effective army, drilling them often until they became expert fighters. Cortés was careful to involve his men in all major decisions; he was such a good persuader that his men gave him their support willingly. He also set the pattern for all his future dealings with the Indians. He gave strict orders to his men that the Indians were to be treated fairly, and made every effort to make friends with the local chieftains. But he also threw down the idols of the Indian gods, set up crosses in their place, and put an end to human sacrifice, which was practiced by all the Indians in that part of the world. His strategy was simple but effective: to make alliances with the Indians while weakening them from within by attacking their beliefs with new ideas; and, if diplomacy did not work, to defeat them quickly.

An earlier Spanish expedition had met no trouble from the Indians when it landed at the mouth of the Tabasco River, so Cortés landed there also. Now, however, thousands of Tabascans attacked Cortés's small army. The Spanish soldiers fought back with sword, lance, musket, and cannon, but it was their horses that most terrified the Indians. They had never seen horses before, and to them the horse and its rider looked like a single, fearsome beast. The Tabascans surrendered, and Cortés, ever the diplomat, quickly got from them promises of peace and gifts of food. They could not

Cortés's expedition

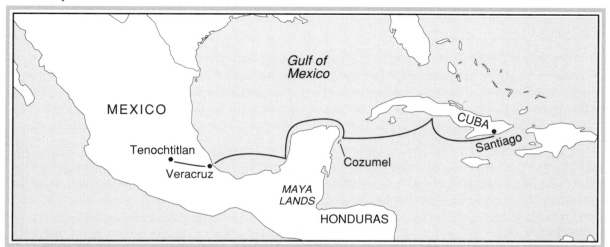

give him gold, they told him, because all of it was owned by their overlords to the west, the Aztecs, whom no European had ever seen. Instead, they gave him what turned out to be an even more valuable gift, a slave woman named Malintzin. She had been born an Aztec princess and could speak both Tabascan and Nahuatl, the language of the Aztecs. Malintzin became Cortés's interpreter, and later, his lover; her advice and quick wit saved the expedition several times in the months that followed. [See the article on Malintzin in this book.]

A few days later Cortés's ships landed on the coast farther west, near where the city of Veracruz is today. Almost as soon as they disembarked, the Spanish were met by two local chiefs, emissaries from the Aztec emperor, Moctezuma, who had heard of the fight with the Tabascans. [For more about the emperor and the Aztec way of life, see the article on Moctezuma in this book.] Cortés received their gifts of food and gold and let them watch as he and his men said Mass. To further impress the chiefs, who had every detail of the visit recorded in paintings on bolts of cotton cloth, he paraded his horses and men and fired his cannons. One of the chiefs asked to take a Spanish helmet back to Moctezuma. When the chiefs returned they gave Cortés the helmet, now filled with grains of gold, and more gifts of gold and silver, including a huge disk of pure gold shaped like the sun and a silver one shaped like the moon.

To Cortés's surprise, the chiefs bowed before him and called him a *teule*, which means a god. Cortés did not immediately grasp the importance of this, but Malintzin did. Among the Aztec gods, there was a bearded, white-skinned god named Quetzalcoatl. According to tradition, Quetzalcoatl had visited Mexico long before and would someday return to claim it as his realm. Moctezuma thought that Cortés and his men might be messengers from Quetzalcoatl. But he was not certain about this, so he refused to give Cortés permission to come to the Aztec capital, Tenochtitlán, located where Mexico City is today. Cortés was determined to go there anyway, even if he had to march hundreds of miles and fight tens of thousands of fierce Aztec warriors. He felt he was on a sacred mission to conquer Mexico for Spain and for the glory of God.

The first step was to silence any opposition among his own troops. Cortés had studied law as a young man, and he knew that he needed legal authority to carry out his plans. So he convinced his men to found a new town, Vera Cruz, and had himself elected its captain and chief justice. This act freed him from the authority of Diego Velázquez, the governor of Cuba, for by law the head of a Spanish town was responsible only to the king of Spain. Then Cortés quickly arrested those of his men who still supported Velázquez, letting them go as soon as they pledged their loyalty to him instead. Finally, he had all the expedition's ships burned, except for one that he sent back to Spain with the treasure he had acquired so far and a letter to the king. Now there could be no turning back.

The Spanish also needed allies among the Indians. Cortés discovered that many of the surrounding tribes hated the Aztecs, who had conquered them in order to have a steady supply of victims for their daily program of human sacrifices. The Aztecs believed that without human sacrifices, the sun would fail and the world would end. The conquered tribes were ready to rebel against Aztec rule, but needed someone to unite and lead them. Cortés skillfully made allies of the rebellious tribes, while at the same time assuring Moctezuma of his friendship.

On August 16, 1519, he struck out for Tenochtitlán with four hundred soldiers and an escort of Indian warriors. Their route took them over three mountain ranges and almost 250 miles of plains and deserts. Yet the hardships of travel were far less dangerous than the native peoples along the way. A major battle was fought with the fierce Tlaxcalans, sworn enemies of the Aztecs; in the end they too became Cortés's allies and sent many warriors along with him. The Tlaxcalans warned him that Moctezuma was planning an ambush at the town of Cholula, but Cortés marched for Cholula anyway, realizing that he had to face down each threat or lose the support of his allies. With the help of Malintzin he found out the details of the ambush and kidnapped the Cholulan chiefs before the attack began. Then the Spanish soldiers opened fire on the Cholulan warriors and slaughtered them.

Now Moctezuma was truly alarmed. He again sent messengers to Cortés promising his friendship and offering gifts, but still denying the Spanish

Cortés and Malintzin receive gifts of corn, birds, and a deer from Moctezuma. The Aztecs did not use chairs, however; the artist imagined them.

permission to enter Tenochtitlán. Cortés matched this double-talk with his own, assuring Moctezuma that he would learn things of importance when once he met Cortés.

On November 8, 1519, the Spanish forces entered Tenochtitlán, without opposition from the Aztecs. They beheld a gleaming white city in the middle of a lake, with wide avenues, blue canals, and beautiful gardens. Moctezuma came out to meet Cortés and offered the Spanish lodging in a great palace that had once belonged to the king's father. Near the palace was the main temple of

the Aztecs, and every day the Spanish could see people being sacrificed there to the Aztec gods. Weeks passed, and the Spanish began to worry that they were being kept for sacrifice as well. Cortés was not getting any closer to conquering Mexico by simply sitting in the palace. So he conceived a bold plan. With the help of Malintzin and a few soldiers, he placed Moctezuma under house arrest. Now Cortés was in a position to rule Mexico through the Aztec king without firing a shot.

But just as Cortés was consolidating his power, Spanish ships arrived off Vera Cruz. The fleet, captained by Panfilo Narvaez, had been sent to arrest Cortés and replace him with a man loyal to Diego Velázquez. Moctezuma was already secretly in contact with Narvaez through Aztec officials on the coast and hoped to use him to outmaneuver Cortés.

Cortés had to take decisive action. He marched back to Vera Cruz with 250 picked troops, leaving a garrison in Tenochtitlán under one of his chief lieutenants, Pedro de Alvarado. In a brief night battle Cortés surrounded and defeated Narvaez's army; Narvaez himself lost an eye in the fighting and was put in chains. His men went over to Cortés. But misfortune awaited Cortés back in Tenochtitlán. Alvarado, a reckless man who preferred fighting to talking, had massacred hundreds of Aztecs on a feast day. When Cortés returned, he found Alvarado besieged by thousands of warriors, and his hopes for a peaceful conquest were dashed.

Within a short time Moctezuma was deposed by his more warlike brother, Cuitlahuac, who moved to block the Spanish army's escape. Cortés's men had to fight their way out, street by street, bridge by bridge, burdened by tons of gold that they refused to leave behind, until in desperation they dumped it all in the lake (none of this gold has ever been found). Early in the fighting, Moctezuma was killed, probably by his own people, who were angry at how he had played into the hands of the Spanish. The Aztecs pursued Cortés and his men all the way to the borders of the Tlaxcalan republic, where they escaped to safety. They had lost hundreds of men and most of the horses.

But Cortés was not beaten. Over the next few months he rallied his forces, made new alliances with the Indians, and seized guns, ammunition, and horses from expeditions sent from Cuba and Jamaica. In December 1520 he marched back to the Aztec capital with nearly a thousand Spanish soldiers and perhaps as many as one hundred thousand Indians, mostly Tlaxcalans. The siege of Tenochtitlán and the surrounding towns was long and bloody. The Aztecs fought bravely, but they were driven back step by step. In the end, nearly every Aztec warrior was killed (many by their enemies, the Tlaxcalans). Those left alive were enslaved, including the new king, Cuauhtemoc, and the city was razed to the ground. The Aztec way of life was lost forever.

Cortés was now in complete control of Mexico, accepted as leader by Indians and Spanish alike. Had he wished, he could have carved out his own kingdom, independent of Spain. King Carlos

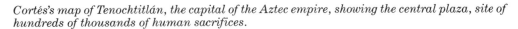

Cortés's map of Tenochtitlán, the capital of the Aztec empire, showing the central plaza, site of hundreds of thousands of human sacrifices.

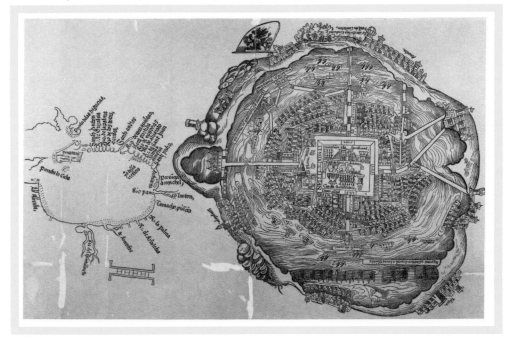

Aztec warriors defend Tenochtitlán against the combined armies of the Spanish, the Tlaxcalans, and other tribes tired of Aztec domination.

feared just that. But Cortés remained loyal to the Spanish crown. And he was eager for more conquests. In 1524 he undertook an expedition to the jungles of Honduras and Guatemala, where two of his lieutenants, Pedro de Alvarado and Cristóbal de Olid, were putting the torch to the Maya Indian civilization. Cortés wanted to capture Olid, who had rebelled against his authority. He also wanted to make sure that the bloodthirsty young Alvarado did not kill every Maya in the jungle.

The overland route from Mexico to Honduras was incredibly difficult; the Spanish had to hack their way through some of the densest rain forest in the world. Cortés took along Cuauhtemoc and the few surviving Aztec nobles. He did not trust the king out of his sight, even though there were no Aztec warriors left to lead in rebellion. During the campaign Cortés began to suspect Cuauhtemoc of plotting his murder, and left the last Aztec king hanging from a tree.

Meanwhile, back in Mexico (or New Spain, as the conquered territory was now called), there was another conspiracy against Cortés. When he returned from Honduras, having brought Olid to justice and curbed some of Alvarado's brutalities, he found that his political enemies had taken over the government. In 1528 Cortés was forced to return to Spain and defend himself to the king against the accusations of his enemies. Two years later, now married to a noblewoman and bearing the titles of marquis and captain-general (but not the higher title of viceroy, which the king refused to grant him), he came back to Mexico. But his further expeditions and business ventures in the New World were unsuccessful, and, in 1540, tired and disappointed, he left again for Spain, never to return. Cortés died in 1547, believing he had failed to achieve the lasting fame he thought he deserved for conquering an empire with his wits, his courage, and a few hundred men.

Francisco Pizarro

Francisco Pizarro (pi-THA-ro). Born circa 1475 in Trujillo, Cáceres, Spain. Died June 26, 1541, in Lima, Peru.

Few conquerors of any age showed more bravery, determination, and physical endurance than Francisco Pizarro, the sixteenth-century Spanish conquistador who in one swift stroke brought down the empire of the Incas in Peru. But it is also true that few conquerors were more treacherous, greedy, and cruel. Consumed by a passion for gold, Pizarro and a handful of Spanish soldiers looted and destroyed a great civilization, leaving little behind but poverty and war.

There are many legends about Pizarro's early

Francisco Pizarro

life, but few solid facts. We know that he was the son of Gonzalo Pizarro, a soldier who fathered many illegitimate children in the small town of Trujillo in southwestern Spain. His mother was Francisca Gonzalez, a village girl. Probably he was abandoned by both parents at birth. Growing up on his grandparents' small farm, Pizarro never attended school or learned to read and write; instead, he herded pigs. This was a point of embarrassment for him in later life, when he had to deal with the highest nobles of Spain. He did learn to ride and fight in the wars of the local barons; he may have fought alongside his father in Italy. Early on, like many young Spanish men of his time, he decided to seek his fortune in the New World. In 1502, at the age of twenty-seven, he sailed for the new Spanish colony on the island of Hispaniola (now shared between the countries of Haiti and the Dominican Republic).

Pizarro's first expedition was a complete disaster, but it showed his ruthlessness, and his luck. He went to Central America on an expedition authorized by Spain's King Fernando to establish two new colonies on the isthmus of Darién (the narrow bridge of land that we now call Panama). In 1509, the expedition founded a little town, not more than a few huts surrounded by a wooden palisade, called San Sebastian. Pizarro was left in charge while his commanders sailed back for reinforcements. They did not return, and the town, surrounded by hostile Indians and impassable jungles, began to run out of food. Pizarro, with only two small ships, could not evacuate all his men. His solution was to wait until enough men had died so that the survivors could fit into the ships. One ship sank immediately, but the other, captained by Pizarro, eventually met up with another ship carrying the explorer Vasco Núñez de Balboa. [See the article on Balboa in this book.] Pizarro now threw in his lot with Balboa and was with him in 1513 when Balboa first sighted the Pacific Ocean. But when the governor of Darién ordered Balboa arrested on charges of conspiracy, it was Pizarro who carried out the order. By some accounts it was also Pizarro, no great respecter of friendships, who beheaded Balboa in the town square of Old Panama City a short time later.

Filtering up from the south were rumors of a realm of gold, an empire richer than all the Aztec lands that had been conquered a few years earlier by Hernán Cortés. [See the article about Cortés in this book.] Pizarro had little enough to show for his two decades of hard work in the New World, and he wanted more. Together with Diego de Almagro, another hard-bitten adventurer, and Hernando de Luque, a well-to-do priest, he formed a partnership to explore the western coast of South America in search of this fabulous golden empire, which was called Peru.

Their first expedition, which departed on November 14, 1524, was hardly a success. The ships faced adverse winds and could make little headway down the coast. Running out of food and water, Pizarro and his men put to shore, but were attacked by Indians and finally fled back to some islands off Panama. But Pizarro did acquire some gold ornaments, and this made him eager to mount a bigger expedition. He and Almagro set out again in March 1526. By sailing well away from the coast, they were able to go as far south as the port of Atacames, in what is now Ecuador. This was the northern edge of the Incan empire, which stretched for hundreds of miles farther down the coast, and the adventurers could tell immediately by the stone buildings and well-planned fields that they were nearing their goal. But again the Indians were hostile, and Pizarro had to retreat to a safe island refuge. There he stayed with his men while Almagro returned to Panama to drum up new troops and supplies.

The new governor denied Almagro's request and instead sent an expedition to bring back Pizarro. When the ships arrived, Pizarro's men were starving and sick, with their clothes worn to rags, but Pizarro's will to go forward was unbreakable. According to one story, he drew a line in the sand with his sword. "There lies Peru with its riches," he said, pointing to the far side of the line, "and here, Panama and its poverty. Choose, each man, what becomes a brave soldier. For my part I go to the south." Thirteen men stepped over the line with him and stayed on the island. The rest sailed back to Panama.

Eventually a ship outfitted by Almagro returned for Pizarro. The Spanish set off for the south, making port in the Incan city of Tumbes, in present-day Peru. There they met an Incan nobleman and were shown temples sheathed in gold and broad stone roads leading up to the fantastic heights of the Andes mountains. Among the high peaks, Pizarro learned, was located the heart of the vast Incan empire. Further exploration down the coast convinced Pizarro that, after eight long years, he had finally found the empire of gold. But he had no money, no troops, and no official backing for a voyage of conquest. So Pizarro returned to Spain, where after a year he convinced the king to appoint him governor and captain-general of a colony to be founded in Peru—if he could conquer it. For his partner Almagro, Pizarro obtained only the governorship of Tumbes. Pizarro recruited his brothers Martín, Gonzalo, Juan, and Hernando to come back with him to Panama.

The route of Pizarro's expedition

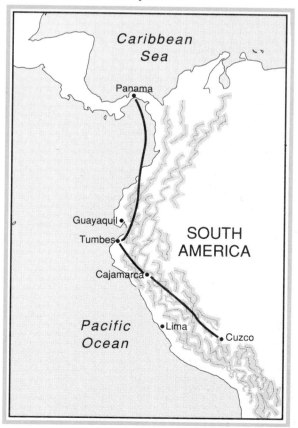

Almagro was bitterly disappointed over his small share of the future riches, but for the moment all disagreements were put aside in the larger adventure of conquest. It was agreed that Pizarro would again spearhead the expedition, and Almagro would follow later with reinforcements. Pizarro left Panama for Tumbes in January 1531 with three ships, 180 men, and 27 horses—a force even smaller than the one Cortés brought to conquer Mexico. It is hard to understand how Pizarro thought he could defeat a great empire with such a small army, yet he, like Cortés, was completely confident of success. And he had Cortés's example to inspire him.

But Pizarro was not the leader that Cortés was. His small navy was forced by bad weather to land on the coast some 350 miles north of Tumbes. Pizarro, overeager to begin the conquest, did not wait for more favorable winds but marched into the jungle to reach the city by land. Along the way he lost many men to heat and sickness. When the Spanish finally reached Tumbes, they stumbled right into a battle between the inhabitants of Tumbes and the Indians of a nearby island. Here Pizarro's luck came to his aid. He soon learned that the Incan empire was in the middle of a civil war between the forces of the emperor Atahualpa and those of his half-brother Huascar, who had a better claim to the throne. [See the article on Atahualpa in this book for more of this story.] Pizarro now saw the way to conquest. By playing the two sides against each other, he might be able to overcome both. (In fact, because of this civil war the Incan empire was at its very weakest just

The capture of Atahualpa took place in the plaza of Cajamarca, though this Spanish drawing from 1534 shows it happening outside the city walls.

as Pizarro appeared. Had he come a few months sooner or later, there would have been a secure leader on the throne, and then he probably could not have succeeded.)

Into the interior Pizarro marched with the pick of his men. For the first time, he tried to make allies of the Indians he met and recruit them for a possible war against Atahualpa. The small force crossed the heights of the Andes and marched to the northern hill town of Cajamarca, where Atahualpa was staying with his armies. Atahualpa knew of their coming, but seemed to be more curious than alarmed. Such a small force could hardly be a threat to an emperor who commanded tens of thousands of warriors. Atahualpa, who was camped outside of the deserted town, agreed to meet Pizarro. However, Pizarro did not plan a meeting but a massacre. He was determined to capture Atahualpa and rule the empire through him, just as Cortés had done with the Aztec emperor Moctezuma in Mexico. [See the articles on Moctezuma and Malintzin in this book.] Pizarro hid his men and horses throughout the town, and waited.

Atahualpa entered Cajamarca the next day, accompanied by six thousand unarmed escorts. A Catholic priest from Pizarro's party handed Atahualpa a Bible and tried to convert the emperor to Christianity. Atahualpa understood little of this and threw down the Bible in anger. At that, Pizarro gave the signal, and his men opened fire on the Indians in the square. The Incas fought back, but their bare hands were no match for Spanish swords, lances, and musket balls. Any who managed to escape the town were run down by Spanish cavalry. In less than an hour, all the Incas were dead save for Atahualpa, who had to be rescued from the blood-crazed Spanish by Pizarro himself.

By making Atahualpa his captive, Pizarro now had control of the empire. But Atahualpa had not played his last card. First he offered a great ransom in gold for his release. Then, hearing that Pizarro's men had met with his brother Husacar, he had Huascar assassinated so that Pizarro could not make Huascar emperor in his place. This angered Pizarro, and when the ransom treasure had finally been collected, he did not release the emperor as promised but had Atahualpa executed on charges of murder and heresy.

Meanwhile Pizarro had been joined by his partner Almagro, and the Spanish began stripping the empire of its wealth. In Cuzco, the Incan capital, they gathered thousands of pounds of gold and silver, including ten planks of solid silver twenty feet long, one foot wide, and several inches thick. (Much of this treasure never reached Spain. Some of it was captured by French pirates; some sank to the bottom of the sea in Spanish ships; and some was stolen by the conquistadors themselves.) In their lust for treasure, the Spanish gave little thought to caring for the people they now ruled. They emptied the Incan storehouses of food and did not bother to maintain the complex irrigation systems needed to raise new crops. Wherever the Spanish came, the Incas were soon starving, or dying from European diseases like measles or smallpox.

At this point Pizarro's luck began to run out. The new Incan emperor, Manco, a brother of Huascar, suddenly turned against Pizarro. He led an Incan army up into the mountains and started a guerrilla war against the Spanish that was to last for forty years. More trouble for Pizarro came from Almagro, who was still angry over the poor reward Pizarro had gotten for him in Spain. In

The immense silver mine at Potosí, known as "the hill that eats men," gave up its riches to Spain through the forced labor of Indians.

April 1537 Almagro seized the town of Cuzco for himself. Pizarro immediately marched on Cuzco with another army. Almagro and Pizarro arranged a truce, but Pizarro broke it as soon as he could round up reinforcements. In a bloody skirmish that cost more Spanish lives than any battle with the Incas, Almagro was defeated by Pizarro's brother Hernando. Then Hernando sentenced Almagro to death and had him strangled, just as had been done with Atahualpa.

Pizarro now turned his attention to building a new capital, Lima, on the Pacific coast west of Cuzco. But he did not have long to live. The son of Almagro plotted revenge, and on Sunday, June 26, 1541, assassins broke into the governor's palace. Pizarro held them off with a rapier and a cloak until he was so tired he could no longer lift his sword. Then the attackers stabbed him through the throat. As he died, Pizarro drew a cross on the floor in his own blood.

Atahualpa

Atahualpa (ah-tah-WAHL-pah; also spelled Atahuallpa and Atabalipa). Born 1502 in Cuzco (in present-day Peru). Died July 16 or August 29, 1533, in Cajamarca, Peru.

When the Spanish adventurer Francisco Pizarro first landed on the coast of Peru in 1527, he discovered an empire greater than that of the Aztecs in Mexico, richer in gold, and harder to conquer. [See the article on Pizarro in this book.] This empire was ruled by the Inca Indians, whose supreme king was Atahualpa.

Since the fourteenth century, the Incas had been masters of a vast empire stretching from the coast of western South America to the jungles of the Amazon basin, and from Peru to Chile (as we call these places now). Their land included some of the highest and most rugged mountains in the world, the Andes, and some of the driest deserts, like the Atacama, where rain never falls. The empire was tied together by an excellent network of roads, one of the finest in the world, guarded by many fortresses of stone. It was an orderly and well-organized realm, and all its subjects obeyed the Incan emperor, who was thought to be a god. But the Incas never were able to work out a peaceful and orderly way to choose new emperors. This helped Pizarro to defeat them.

Atahualpa's father was the emperor Huayna Capac, a great conqueror who died of smallpox in 1527, the same year Francisco Pizarro landed. Smallpox was one of several diseases brought to the New World by Europeans. The Indians, who had never been exposed to these diseases before, had no resistance to them; by some accounts, Huayna Capac died so quickly that he did not have time to appoint the next emperor. Another story has it that he had already decided to divide the empire into two parts, the northern part under the rule of his son Atahualpa, the southern part under another son, Huascar. Huascar was considered by most Incas to be the rightful heir, but Atahualpa had followed his father often into battle and was respected by all his father's generals. A Spaniard writing some years later noted that Huascar was "even-tempered and pious" but that his half-brother Atahualpa was "ruthless and vengeful, a man of greater determination."

Atahualpa was not satisfied with just half an empire. He wanted to be supreme ruler of all the Incas. In 1532 he came down from the north and attacked Huascar's armies. In a bloody battle near Cuzco, the Incan capital, his generals destroyed Huascar's army and took Huascar prisoner. Atahualpa himself made his headquarters in the town of Cajamarca, in the northern part of the empire. He was now supreme ruler, but Huascar still had some supporters.

While the Incas were fighting over the throne, Pizarro and his small army began a march through the mountains toward Cajamarca. Pizarro's strategy was simple: to capture the emperor, just as Cortés had done in Mexico with the Aztec leader

Two portraits of Atahualpa: on the left a European engraving and on the right a miniature painting discovered in Peru in the 1830s.

Moctezuma, and control the empire through him. [See the articles on Cortés, Moctezuma, and Malintzin in this book.] Atahualpa knew the Spanish were approaching, but he did nothing to stop them. Indeed, he seems to have been very curious to see these newcomers, with their horses and guns, and their strange religion that worshipped the son of a god, just as the Incas did. A meeting between Atahualpa and Pizarro was arranged.

When Pizarro arrived, Cajamarca was deserted. Atahualpa had moved his armies to a camp a few miles away. This was a mistake on Atahualpa's part, for it allowed Pizarro to hide soldiers throughout the city and lay plans for an ambush. And Atahualpa made a second mistake when he came for the meeting: he entered the

seemingly empty town with only an unarmed escort. Perhaps he was so confident of his power that he thought no one would attack him. If so, he was wrong. When Atahualpa and his followers entered the town square, a Spanish friar appeared, handed him a Bible, and urged him to accept Christianity. Atahualpa threw down the Bible in anger. With that, Pizarro gave the signal to attack. The Spanish musketeers opened fire, the cannon thundered, and Pizarro's cavalry charged into the square. Every Inca in Atahualpa's escort was killed; Atahualpa was spared only because Pizarro himself protected him at the cost of a sword wound in the hand.

Pizarro imprisoned Atahualpa in Cajamarca but allowed him to continue ruling the empire from

The Incas used llamas as beasts of burden, as well as for food, wool, hides, and fat. This silver Incan llama is wearing a pack-blanket.

prison. Through his agents, Atahualpa learned that Huascar had been talking with the Spaniards. Fearing that Huascar would strike a deal with the invaders to regain the throne, the emperor secretly had him murdered. Atahualpa did not yet realize that Pizarro was a more dangerous enemy than Huascar.

Seeing that the Spaniards were eager for gold, Atahualpa offered them a great treasure in exchange for his freedom. He said he would fill the hall that was his prison with gold to a point as high as he could reach. This was an immense amount of gold, for the room was 22 feet long and 17 feet wide, and the Inca could touch a point 7 feet above the floor. Pizarro agreed to the ransom, but when the gold was delivered he refused to keep his side of the bargain. Instead, the Spanish put Atahualpa on trial for crimes against the Christian religion—for having many wives, for worshipping idols, and so on—and for ordering the murder of Huascar. Atahualpa was found guilty by the judges, one of whom was Pizarro himself, and sentenced to death by burning at the stake. When the emperor saw he was to be burned, he asked to convert to Christianity so that he could be strangled instead. This was a less painful death, and one, he believed, that would spare his soul in the afterlife. The Spanish granted his request.

Atahualpa's murder was not the end of the Incan empire. Pizarro named Manco, the brother of Huascar, as the new emperor. But Manco led a revolt against the Spanish and later fled with an army into the remote mountains. It was not until 1572 that the last Incas were rooted out and killed by a Spanish army. By then Pizarro was long dead, murdered by his own men in a dispute over power and gold.

Bartolemé de las Casas

Bartolomé de las Casas (lahs KAH-sahs). Born August 1474 in Seville, Spain. Died July 17, 1566, in Madrid, Spain.

In the sixteenth and seventeenth centuries there was a great rivalry between Spain, France, Holland, and England, the seagoing nations of Europe. Part of this rivalry was religious, for Spain was a Roman Catholic country, while England and Holland were Protestant; France was torn between the two faiths. Part of the rivalry was economic, for Spain had established a mighty empire in the New World, and the other nations tried everything they could to loosen her hold on it. In this contest, one of the most potent weapons was propaganda, writings that aim to advance the ideas of a group or a country. Writers in France and the Protestant lands turned out numerous tracts painting the Spanish as villains who enslaved, tortured, and murdered their Indian subjects. This was known as *la leyenda negra*, "the Black Legend" of Spain's brutality in the

New World. The purpose of such writings was to loosen the hold Spain had on its colonies, and to show the rest of the world that the writer's own country was better fit, morally and legally, to rule the Americas. The most damning evidence against Spanish rule, however, was penned not by one of Spain's rivals but by a Spaniard, Bartolomé de Las Casas. Las Casas had seen the Spanish conquest for himself and was the first European to protest against the oppression of the Indians.

In 1502, Las Casas came to the New World as a soldier in the Spanish army occupying Hispaniola (the Caribbean island now shared between the countries of Haiti and the Dominican Republic). There he helped to subdue Hispaniola's Indian population. For his services the governor granted him an *encomienda*, an estate of land that included the Indians living on it. Under the encomienda system, these Indians were slaves of the owner in all but name. Some owners treated them well, and some treated them poorly, but in all cases the Indians had to work for nothing. Within a few years, most of the Indians in Hispaniola had been killed by endless work or by European diseases, mainly smallpox. So few native Indians were left alive that new Indian laborers had to be kidnapped from other islands. Soon the Spanish began importing slave laborers from Africa. (This was the beginning of the African-American slave trade, which lasted until the 1870s.)

The Spanish were of two minds about the Indians under their control. Most of them believed that it was their duty to turn the Indians into good Catholics. This could not be done if the Indians were being killed for their lands or worked to death as slaves. On the other hand, many Spanish also believed that they needed Indian labor to extract the riches of the New World. The rulers of Spain, under the influence of the Catholic Church, repeatedly made laws protecting the Indians. But Spanish colonists in the New World wanted to be sure of a free supply of Indian workers at any cost—even if it meant breaking the law.

At first Las Casas ran his encomienda in much the same way as the other Spanish landowners did. In 1513 he joined the Spanish expedition that conquered Cuba and was granted a second encomienda there. At about this time, Las Casas became a Catholic priest, probably the first to be ordained in the New World. He also underwent a change of heart about the Indians, whom he had seen slaughtered and enslaved by the thousands. Now he felt that it was wrong to hold the Indians in bondage. In a fiery sermon of 1514, he said that he would no longer be master of the Indians on his encomienda. He denounced the encomienda system, urged fair treatment for Indians under Spanish law, and argued that the Indians should be converted to Christianity by peaceful means only, not by bloody conquest. In 1515 he sailed to Spain to plead the Indians' case before King Fernando. A commission was formed to investigate, but when it reached the New World, it refused to carry out Las Casas's suggestions. His ideas seemed too extreme.

Las Casas decided to start a new colony of former encomienda Indians who would now be allowed to work their own lands. The new colony was located on the coast of present-day Venezuela, and it did not last long. It was attacked first by angry Spanish landowners, then by hostile Indians, and in 1522 it collapsed. So disappointed was Las Casas that he retreated into a monastery at Santo Domingo for ten years. During this time he grew more convinced than ever of the rightness of his cause. In 1537 he led a band of Dominican priests into an unconquered area of what is now northeastern Guatemala and peacefully converted several of the local Indian chiefs. His success gave him the confidence to return to Spain in

Bartolomé de Las Casas, from a painting by Felix Parra

1540 and once more petition the Spanish government on behalf of the Indians.

While Las Casas was in Spain he wrote his most famous book, *Brevísima relación de la destrucción de las Indias* ("A Brief Report on the Destruction of the Indies"). In the *Brevísima relación*, Las Casas warned that God's wrath would destroy the Spanish for the sins they were committing in the Americas. Such was the strength of Las Casas's arguments that Spain's King Carlos ordered new laws limiting the encomienda system. When the laws were put into effect, however, the colonists rebelled. To keep the peace, most of the new laws were modified or retracted. In the end, their main effect was to make the colonists hate Las Casas. The Spanish colonists of Chiapa, a town on the border between Mexico and Guatemala, threatened to kill him when he was sent to be their bishop in 1545.

Though he was now more than seventy years old, Las Casas did not abandon his cause. For the next twenty years he lived in Spain, writing books and debating the question of the treatment of the Indians. At the order of the king, Las

This engraving appeared in a French book published in Holland in 1620. The verse accuses the Spanish of delighting in cruelty.

L'Espagnol en prennant plaisir en meurtrerie,
Faisoit un meschant fact, & plain de vilainie,
Quand le peuple fort doux, & simple s'en fuyoit
Au temple de salut, & sa vie cherçoit
Il brusle les Seigneurs: O triste Tragedie
Faire mourir les gens, bien loing de maladie,
Mais il prend son plaisir au feu, comme meschant
NERO, mettant le feu au Rome fort plaisant.
E 2

Casas's works were published in full a few years after his death in 1566 at the age of ninety-two.

Las Casas was so eager to convince his readers of Spain's irresponsible conduct that he sometimes strayed from the facts. He would never admit, for example, that some of the conquistadors were less cruel than others. Hernán Cortés, the conqueror of Mexico, was, in Las Casas's view, among the worst of them. Las Casas wrote that Cortés had laughed and hummed a little tune while the Spanish slaughtered thousands of Aztecs at the town of Cholula. But Las Casas was not at the battle, and his account was based only on a single ballad, penned some years after the battle by someone who had not been there either. Most other contemporary accounts, even those of the Indians themselves, describe Cortés as a man concerned for the welfare of the Indians he conquered. But in many cases, Las Casas painted an accurate picture of events. His description of the cruelties committed by Francisco Pizarro during the conquest of Peru was right on the mark, for Pizarro and his men were little more than pirates. [For more on the conquest of Mexico and the battle at Cholula, see the articles on Cortés, Moctezuma, and Malintzin. The conquest of Peru is described in the articles on Pizarro and Atahualpa.]

Protestant propagandists used Las Casas's writings as proof of the Black Legend. Writing in 1583, the English translator of the *Brevísima relación* stated in his introduction that "posterity shall hardly think that ever so barbarous or cruel a nation had been in the world, if, as you would say, we had not with our eyes seen it, and with our hands felt it. . . . It is not hatred that maketh me write these things, as the author of the book is by nation a Spaniard, and besides writeth more bitterly than myself." Editions of Las Casas's book were often illustrated with horrific pictures of tortured Indians drawn by an artist named Theodore DeBry, who had never been to the New World. The irony is that the English, French, and Dutch, who later ruled their own empires in North America, were, if anything, more cruel to the Indians than were the Spanish. They did something the Spanish never did: they drove the Indians from the land and often tried to exterminate them completely. However, there was no fiery reformer like Las Casas to bring their cruelties to light.

Estevanico

Estevanico (es-tay-VAH-nee-ko), also called Estevanico the Black, Estevanico the Moor, Estevanico Dorantes, Estevan, and Stephen. Born circa 1500 in Asemmur, Morocco. Died May 1539 in Hawikuh (in present-day New Mexico).

For generations, life in the Zuñi Indian *pueblo* (town) of Hawikuh had changed little. Then one day a band of three hundred Mexican Indians marched into the village out of the southern deserts. At their head was a tall man with dark brown skin, unlike any man the Zuñis had seen before. Clothed in Spanish leggings and an Indian feather headdress, draped with turquoise jewelry, and flanked by two greyhounds, the man was an impressive sight. But what did he want, and what did his arrival mean? The Zuñi elders met that night to discuss his fate.

The man was Estevanico, a Muslim from North Africa who was now in the service of the Spanish governor of Mexico. Though most history books say little about him, Estevanico was one of the boldest explorers of the sixteenth century. Not only was he the first non-Indian to set foot in New Mexico, he also traveled entirely across North America from Florida to the Gulf of California.

Estevanico did not set out to be an explorer. He was born sometime around the year 1500 in the North African country of Morocco, across the Straits of Gibraltar from Spain. The Moors, as the Muslims from North Africa were called, had occupied Spain for centuries, but had been driven back to Morocco by Spanish forces in 1492. At that time it was a common practice for wealthy Spaniards to own Moorish slaves, and for wealthy Moors in North Africa to own Spanish slaves. We do not know anything about Estevanico's early life—whether he was born a slave or was captured by the Spanish and made a slave—but by about the year 1525 he was living in Spain as the slave of a Spanish nobleman named Andres Dorantes de Carranca.

In 1528, Estevanico went along with Dorantes on an expedition to Florida led by the conquistador Panfilo Narvaez. [For more about Narvaez, see the article on Hernán Cortés in this book.] Narvaez was a cruel and incompetent captain who

Estevanico's journeys

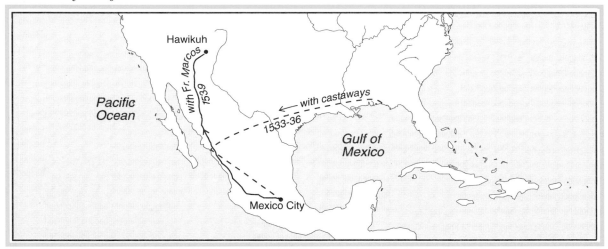

led his hundreds of men to disaster. In the jungles of Florida many of the soldiers died from fever; others were killed by Indian arrows. Finally the men tried to sail back to a Mexican port in five rickety, overcrowded boats built from hides and hand-cut planks. All the boats sank in the Gulf of Mexico. Only fifteen men reached the shore, somewhere on the coast of what is now the Florida panhandle.

Immediately, the castaways were captured and enslaved by the local Indians. Within a year eleven men had died, leaving four survivors: Estevanico, Dorantes, a captain named Castillo, and Alvar Núñez Cabeza de Vaca, the treasurer of the expedition. They endured four more years of hard labor and beatings before they found a way to escape. Slowly they made their way west, going from village to village. According to Cabeza de Vaca, who wrote a famous account of the trip, the three Spaniards by this time no longer treated Estevanico as a slave but as an equal. He learned the Indian languages more quickly than the others and was a better diplomat.

In exchange for food and shelter, the travelers offered to heal villagers who were suffering from illnesses. By the time they reached Texas, they had become famous as healers. As a medicine man Estevanico was treated with respect by the Indians and given the best of whatever they had. As he approached a village Estevanico always announced his coming by sending an Indian ahead with his dance rattle (a magical object carried by Indian medicine men).

Their route took them through what is now Texas and down into Mexico. Along the way the travelers heard tales of a great city or group of cities called Cibola somewhere to the north. Cabeza de Vaca saw some arrowheads said to be from Cibola that were made of a green stone that looked like emerald.

In March 1536, after crossing the entire breadth of North America, they met a company of Spanish horsemen on the Rio Sinaloa in northwestern Mexico. [Mexico had been conquered by Spain just fifteen years earlier; for that story, see the articles on Cortés, Moctezuma, and Malintzin in this book.] Escorted by the soldiers and hundreds of Indians, Estevanico and the others journeyed south to Mexico City. There Cabeza de Vaca, Castillo, and Dorantes were received with honors

A Zuñi dancer with a gourd rattle. As he roamed across the continent, Estevanico carried a rattle as a symbol of his power and authority.

by the viceroy, Antonio Mendoza. But the Spanish refused to recognize Estevanico's freedom, and he had no choice but to serve once more as the slave of Dorantes.

Hearing of the rumored riches of Cibola, Mendoza decided to send an expedition to find it. Francisco Coronado, governor of a northern province, was given command of the effort. [For more about Coronado's exploits, see the article on him in this book.] Mendoza and Coronado enlisted the help of a Spanish missionary priest, Friar Marcos de Niza, to go first and scout the way. With him went Estevanico, who was to act as guide, scout, and translator.

The Indians liked and respected Estevanico far more than they liked the friar. Estevanico freely took part in Indian ceremonies, practiced Indian medicine, and collected a hoard of Indian gifts, including several beautiful green plates on which his meals were always served. Friar Marcos thought all this did more harm than good to his mission, so he sent Estevanico on ahead to prepare the way to Cibola. According to the account of Friar Marcos, he told Estevanico to send back a small cross if he learned bad things about Cibola, and a large cross if he heard of great riches there. Within a few days, Estevanico sent back a cross as big as a man. Friar Marcos hurried forward, expecting to find a golden treasure waiting for him around every bend of the trail.

As Estevanico continued north, he gathered around him hundreds of Indians who believed that he was a holy man, perhaps even a god. He led Friar Marcos a merry chase through the deserts of Sonora and Arizona. Whenever the friar was about to catch up with him, Estevanico made sure to move on. Finally Friar Marcos was left far behind.

Sometime in May of 1539 Estevanico and his followers topped a rise near the Zuñi River in present-day New Mexico and saw the pueblo of Hawikuh. According to the Indians, this was one of the fabled cities of Cibola. As usual, Estevanico sent a messenger ahead with his dance rattle. The Zuñi did not greet Estevanico joyously, as he expected. Instead they led him and his followers to a house outside the village walls. While he waited, the Zuñi discussed what to do about him. Two days later, they came to a decision. Just after sunrise Zuñi warriors dragged Estevanico from the house and cut him to pieces. Then they sent the pieces to the chiefs of all the other pueblos, to show that Estevanico was no god but only a man, and not to be feared. None of his followers were harmed; some escaped to the south to bring the news to Friar Marcos.

Why did the Zuñi kill Estevanico? One account holds that they were angered by his dance rattle. Perhaps the Zuñi thought it came from an enemy. Or possibly they were suspicious of his claim that

A 19th-century view of the Zuñi pueblo at Acoma, New Mexico. It was built on a high mesa that kept the Spanish temporarily at bay.

he had magic powers and the friendship of the Spanish. Most likely, the Zuñi decided that the only way they would be left in peace was to kill any Spanish envoy who entered their lands.

Without Estevanico as his advance man, Friar Marcos could not go on. Although he claimed to have journeyed all the way to Hawikuh to see it for himself, it is clear from other evidence that he never came within one hundred miles of the place. Instead, Friar Marcos fled back to Coronado to boast of his own courage and of the riches to be found in Cibola. When Coronado arrived at Hawikuh a year later, he found no gold or silver, but plain adobe houses from which angry Zuñi shot arrows at him. Of Estevanico no sign remained, save for the green dishes and one of his greyhounds, now owned by a Zuñi chief.

Francisco Coronado

Francisco Vásquez de Coronado (ko-ro-NAH-do). Born circa 1510 in Salamanca, Spain. Died September 22, 1554, in Mexico City.

The weary column of Spanish horsemen suddenly pressed forward with new energy. Over the next rise, said their guide, was the city of gold they had been seeking for months. Their leader, Francisco Vásquez de Coronado, led the way, wanting the honor of being the first Spaniard to see the wealth that would soon be theirs. He rode to the top of the hill and looked down—and felt the taste of victory turn to bitter defeat. Instead of a golden city, he saw only a dusty Indian village.

Coronado was a wealthy grandee, or nobleman, who had made a good marriage and saw greater opportunities for advancement in the New World than in Spain. He sailed for New Spain (the early Spanish name for Mexico) with Antonio de Men-doza, the new viceroy, in 1535. By 1538 he had become governor of a province and was anxious for new conquests. Since the lands south of Mexico were already swarming with Spanish explorers and adventurers, Coronado looked to the north. A report by the Spanish explorer Alvar Núñez Cabeza de Vaca made vague references to a settled Indian people living in that direction; perhaps they were as rich in gold as the Aztecs and Incas the Spanish had so recently conquered in Mexico and Peru. [For an account of these conquests, see the articles on Cortés, Moctezuma, Malintzin, Pizarro, and Atahualpa in this book.] A Franciscan monk called Friar Marcos de Niza, who had been to Peru and seen the Incan gold, came to Coronado with rumors of yet another empire of gold somewhere to the north, the fabulous "Seven Golden Cities of Cibola." In 1539, with Mendoza's approval, Coronado appointed Friar Marcos to head a small expedition to find the Seven Cities. A Moorish slave named Estevanico, who had traveled with Cabeza de Vaca among the northern Indians, went along as guide and trans-

Coronado and his men pushing forward on their long march from Mexico to Kansas, as imagined by the American artist Frederic Remington.

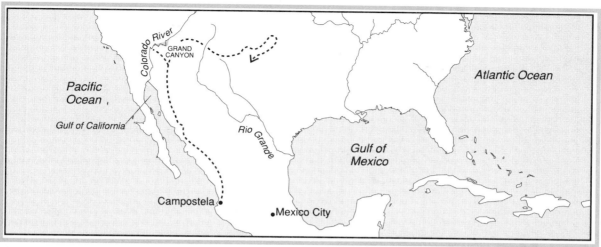

The route of Coronado's expedition

lator. [For more about Estevanico's adventures, see the article about him in this book.]

As they traveled, Friar Marcos sent Estevanico north ahead of the expedition to see if the Seven Cities were in that direction. Acompanied by some three hundred Mexican Indians, Estevanico eventually reached the Zuñi town of Hawikuh in the region we now call New Mexico. As the story goes, Friar Marcos had asked Estevanico to send back a cross as a message. If the country was poor, he was to make the cross small; if the country was rich, he was to make the cross large. Estevanico now sent back a cross as big as a man, though the only things of golden color he could have seen were the fields of Zuñi corn.

The Zuñi people, along with several other tribes of the American Southwest, lived in towns made of clay, called *pueblos*. (Hence their general name of Pueblo Indians.) Estevanico thought he knew the right way to approach the Zuñi. As he came into Hawikuh he displayed a dance rattle (a magical object carried by Indian medicine men). This may have angered the Zuñi. More probably, they did not like the news that there was a force of Spanish soldiers just to the south. Whatever the reason, they killed him. Estevanico's followers took this news south to Friar Marcos, who in turn fled back to Coronado with the idea that he had located the Seven Cities.

The next summer Coronado himself led a much larger expedition up the western coast of Mexico to the New Mexico area. He brought with him 300

horsemen, many Indians and camp followers, and livestock—pigs, cattle, and sheep. (A supporting expedition headed by Hernando de Alarcón sailed two ships on a parallel course up the Gulf of California and discovered the mouth of the Colorado River.) With a small party of cavalry Coronado left the main body of the expedition and struck out north toward the Zuñi. A second force under García Lopez de Cárdenas headed west until its way was blocked by a vast chasm, the Grand Canyon of the Colorado River, which they were the first Europeans to see.

Coronado's progress was broadcast by smoke signals from pueblo to pueblo, so his arrival at Hawikuh in July 1540 was no surprise to the Zuñi. The Zuñi warriors who had already gathered there had never submitted to an enemy before and they paid no attention to the Spanish demand for their peaceful surrender. Finally, despite a rain of Zuñi arrows, the Spanish attacked the town and took it in an hour. Coronado himself was knocked unconscious by a rock, but there were few other Spanish casualties.

The Spanish soldiers actually admired the Zuñi for their courage and their temperate, hardworking way of life, though that did not stop them from killing any Zuñi who resisted and taking others as slaves. There were blankets and corn to loot, but no gold or silver. In fact, the Zuñi had hardly anything that the Spaniards valued. The Zuñi pueblos were definitely not the Seven Golden Cities of Cibola.

A view of the Grand Canyon in northwestern Arizona. A band of Coronado's soldiers heading west had to turn back when they reached it.

Coronado's forces wintered not far from the present site of Santa Fe. In the spring Coronado met an Indian whom the Spanish had nicknamed "the Turk." The Turk claimed to know of a great and wealthy people living in a land called Quivira, far to the northeast. With the Turk as guide, Coronado and thirty horsemen set out for Quivira. The party followed the Pecos River north, encountering great herds of buffalo and the nomadic Plains Indians who hunted them. Finally they arrived at Quivira, which was located somewhere on the Arkansas River in Kansas. Coronado's hopes for glory were finally smashed as he realized that he had traveled many hundreds of miles to find nothing more than a small circle of Pawnee Indian lodges. To the Turk, the Pawnee were rich, as the Plains Indians reckoned wealth—in bravery, wisdom, and magical skills. But it seemed like an evil trick to Coronado. He beheaded the Turk on the spot and turned back to Mexico in disappointment. The Seven Cities were nothing more than an empty dream.

Coronado's expedition had opened a vast area for Spanish settlement, from Texas to the Gulf of

Zuñi warriors defending Hawikuh from attack by Coronado's soldiers. The Spanish admired the pueblo dwellers whose land they colonized.

California, and from the Arkansas River to the Rio Grande. After him came Spanish missionaries, traders, and ranchers. But Coronado himself was bitter that he had never found the Cities of Gold. On his return, the authorities were not pleased either and put him on trial for being an inept expedition leader and a corrupt governor. He was let off with a fine and resigned the governorship of his province in 1542. Little is known of Coronado's life afterwards.

Junipero Serra

Junipero Serra (SER-rah), birth name Miguel José Serra. Born November 24, 1713, in Petra, Majorca. Died August 28, 1784, in Carmel, California.

In the Spanish conquest of the Americas, missionary priests were as important as generals. Once the conquistadors (Spanish conquerors) had subdued a new territory, the padres (*padre* is the Spanish word for father or priest) secured it by converting the natives to Catholicism and spreading Spanish culture. One padre was worth a thousand soldiers, it was said. Indians who would fight or flee an army trusted the missionaries and accepted their faith. Missionaries made good explorers, too. Driven by religious zeal, willing to endure any hardship, they would go where no one else would. One of the most dedicated of the missionary explorers was the Franciscan padre Junípero Serra, who founded a string of missions that would later grow into the great cities of California.

Born on the Mediterranean island of Majorca in 1713, Serra became a Franciscan at the age of eighteen. The Franciscans are a missionary order of Catholic friars who take strict vows of poverty and humility, following the example of St. Francis of Assisi. When he was a student, Serra was too short to reach the lecture stand, and so sickly that he was excused from all heavy work. But he had a powerful intellect, and he soon became an honored scholar and preacher. His sermons moved one listener to say that his words could have been "written in gold." Serra's fellow Franciscans fully expected him to become bishop of the island.

Yet Serra always yearned for the hard life of a missionary. He saw even the modest comforts of his monastery as a temptation to worldliness. Nor did he desire to wield the power of a bishop. He felt that a life of comfort and influence was not the right choice for a Franciscan when there was so much work to do and so many souls to be saved in the New World. In 1749 Serra and his devoted student Francisco Palóu departed Majorca to do missionary work in Mexico. Serra and Palóu were

Junipero Serra

to be companions for many years; Palóu's biography of Serra is the source for most of what we know about him.

The two friars arrived in Mexico City on New Year's Day in 1750. Serra embarked on his first mission a few months later. He and Palóu walked for sixteen days to reach the remote village of Jalpan, in the Sierra Madre mountains northeast of Mexico City. The church in Jalpan was little more than an adobe hut, and few Indians came to worship there. Serra saw that the dramatic aspects of Catholic worship were most appealing to the Indians. He held colorful processions like the ones he had joined as a boy in Majorca, and put on religious plays with Indian children as actors. Villagers would come from miles away to take part in the processions and ceremonies of Lent and Holy Week (the week that ends with Easter). During his eight years at Jalpan Serra also built a stone church, taught European methods of agriculture, and helped the Indians build up trade with other villages.

In 1758 Serra's superiors summoned him back to San Fernando, the Franciscan convent in Mexico City. There Serra soon gained fame for his sermons. People from all over the city came to hear his words and to see him act out the punishments suffered by various saints. He welcomed a

The mission of San Antonio de Padua in Jolon, one of nine churches built in California by Junipero Serra in the late 18th century.

life of discomfort and self-discipline as a way of doing penance for his sins. He wore a woolen shirt made of bristles or a coarse coat with pieces of broken wire woven into it. Sometimes he would beat himself with a whip or a chain; other times he would strike his chest with a stone. He also ate little and allowed himself only four hours of sleep a night.

New developments far from Mexico City were to change Serra's life. In those days the area known as California was treated by the Spaniards as two territories: Baja, or Lower California (now part of the modern nation of Mexico), and Alta, or Higher California (now the state of California). The Spanish had planted several colonies in Baja California, but had left Alta California mostly untouched. But now they had a good reason to move quickly into Alta California. The Russians were pushing southward down the coast from Alaska. [Alaska was at that time a Russian territory; for more on the Russian expansion into North America, see the articles on Dezhnev and Bering in this book.] Without a solid claim to Alta California and settlements in the region to back it up, the Spanish might lose it and Baja California as well.

For many years the Jesuits, a powerful order of Roman Catholic teachers and missionaries, had built a network of missions throughout Spanish America, especially in the lower part of California. But now the Jesuits had to abandon their missions, their farms, everything but their prayer-books. The Spanish king, Carlos III, was jealous of the Jesuits' political influence and believed that their leaders had tried to kill him. In the summer of 1767 he ordered all the Jesuits to leave Mexico forever. Lacking food and water, with no time to rest, many of the older priests died along the way.

Once the Jesuits were expelled, King Carlos III appointed the Franciscans to expand missionary work in California. Serra's devotion and endurance made him the obvious candidate to lead the California mission. In 1769, with the expedition's military commander, Gaspar de Portolá, and a small group of priests and soldiers, he headed up the coast of Baja California to San Diego. This was farther north than the Jesuits had ever gone. There he founded the first of Alta California's missions, Mission San Diego, on July 16. Serra was in constant pain from a leg infection he had contracted when he first arrived in Mexico, but

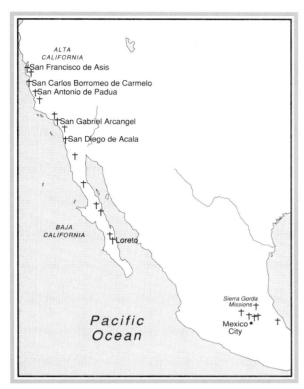

Spanish missions of Upper and Lower California

he refused to turn back. Over the next twelve years he founded eight more missions along the coast, including San Carlos in Carmel (near Monterey), which he used as his headquarters; San Antonio de Padua, in Jolon; San Gabriel, on the present site of Los Angeles; San Luis Obispo; San Francisco (also called Mission Dolores); San Juan Capistrano; Santa Clara; and San Buenaventura. (Many of these missions have been restored and can be visited today.)

Merely breaking ground for a church was not enough, as Serra knew from his days at Jalpan. He and the other padres worked hard to earn the trust of the Indian inhabitants. This was not always easy. He was in San Diego when for the first time an Indian family brought him a baby to be baptized. Serra believed that baptism would save the baby's soul from an eternity of pain. But just as he was about to pour water over the head of the child, a frightened uncle snatched the baby away and ran off.

The padres taught the Indians not only religion but also European agriculture and crafts. Within a few generations the traditional ways of life that had sustained the Indians for thousands of years had been destroyed. This was the secret of Spain's success in colonizing the New World. Yet Serra and the other padres did not see themselves as destroyers, but as the helpers and the friends of the people they had converted. Serra protected them from Spanish soldiers, traders, and settlers who tried to take advantage of them. This often brought him into conflict with the Spanish military authorities. But it also helped ensure the survival of the far-flung missions, which in the early years could have been overrun by hostile Indians.

By 1784 the elderly Serra, revered by Spanish and Indians alike, had visited each mission several times. His energy and support sustained the padres he left in charge of each mission and often made the difference between a mission's failure and its success. He died in August of that year at his mission in Carmel. Without him, the Spanish might never have colonized California—and the early history of the state might have been Russian rather than Spanish.

Mariners and Pirates

Giovanni da Verrazano

Giovanni da Verrazano (vay-raht-SAH-no; also spelled Verrazzano). Born circa 1485, in Italy, probably near Florence. Died circa 1529, in the Lesser Antilles, probably on Guadeloupe Island.

On early sixteenth-century European maps of the New World, the space between New-foundland and Florida was a mysterious blank. Mapmakers and mariners could only guess at what was there. Perhaps there was a great strait (a channel of water) that led right to exotic Cathay, as the Europeans called China in those days. Or there might be a narrow isthmus (a bridge of land like the isthmus of Panama) that linked the south and the north. Or maybe all these lands and waters were part of Asia, as Columbus had claimed. All these guesses and theories were disproven by the work of the Italian explorer Giovanni da Verrazano, who made a long cruise along the Atlantic coast in search of a route to China. But even he did not understand that the coastline he followed for so many miles was the edge of a solid continent.

Verrazano's patron was King François I of France, who loved all things Italian and decided to begin France's exploration of the New World with an Italian mariner. Not much is known for sure of Verrazano's earlier life, except that he was born of a noble family that lived in the Italian city of Florence, made voyages to Newfoundland and the eastern Mediterranean, and probably knew the explorer Ferdinand Magellan. [For Magellan's story, see the article on him in this book.]

Verrazano's reputation as a captain must have been good, for King François commissioned him to make the first French attempt to find a passage through the Americas to Asia.

In the spring of 1524, Verrazano set out for the New World in a single ship, heading on a northerly course to avoid the Spanish shipping routes to Mexico. He first sighted land at Cape Fear, off the coast of what is now North Carolina. Investigating along the coast, he found what he believed was a "an isthmus a mile wide and about 200 long, in which, from the ship, we could see the Orient Sea," as he wrote in his log, "the same which flows around the shores of India and Cathay." In fact he could not see the Pacific Ocean

Giovanni da Verrazano

at all, for it was 3,000 miles to the west. Verrazano was looking across the narrow Outer Banks, a line of islands, dunes, and shoals running along the coast of North Carolina, into what is now called Pamlico Sound. Nowhere did Verrazano find a channel through the Banks, or he would have quickly realized his error; instead, his report led mapmakers of the time to draw North America with a narrow waist at the Carolinas, and with the Pacific Ocean—which they called the Sea of Verrazano—covering about half the continent.

Verrazano continued north, still looking for a strait. He thought he had finally found it when he sailed through the narrow channel that bears his name—the Verrazano Narrows—into New York Harbor, as it is now known. He described this place as "a very pleasant spot situated between two hills where a very large river flowed into the sea." By "river" he probably meant the Narrows and the harbor itself. He did not venture much further in and so did not see the great river that was discovered by Henry Hudson in 1609 [see the article on Henry Hudson in this book]. If the French had followed up on Verrazano's discovery and planted a colony on the shore of this first-rate harbor, the main language spoken in New York City today might be French.

From New York Harbor Verrazano sailed all the way up the New England coast to Maine. It was his comparison of Block Island to the shape of the Isle of Rhodes in the Mediterranean that was later to give the state of Rhode Island its name. Eventually Verrazano reached Newfoundland, and from there sailed home to France. The king found his report interesting enough to send out another explorer, Jacques Cartier, some years later. [Cartier's explorations are described in the article about him in this book.]

Most of the Native Americans Verrazano met were friendly, eager to see the strange Europeans and to trade with them. A group of Carolina Indians even saved one of his sailors from drowning. Some Indians, however, perhaps having met Europeans before, were more suspicious. The Abnaki Indians of Maine would only trade with the sailors by lowering down a basket from a cliff. As the Frenchmen sailed away, wrote Verrazano, the Abnaki jeered at them and made "all signs of discourtesy and disdain . . . such as exhibiting their bare behinds and laughing wildly." Verrazano

On this copper globe from the year 1530, North America appears as a curved strip of land, with the Sea of Verrazano along its western shore.

named this coast "Land of Bad People." In 1528, Verrazano set out on another voyage, this time to pick up lumber on the east coast of South America. On his way, he stopped at an island in the Lesser Antilles, probably Guadeloupe, to take on water and trade with the Indians. The natives waved in a friendly way, and Verrazano waded ashore alone to meet them. What he did not know was that these were Carib Indians, who made a habit of eating strangers. They killed him quickly and devoured him there on the beach, while his crew watched helplessly offshore.

Through all his voyages of exploration, Verrazano never gave up hope that a passage to Asia would be found through the eastern coast of what is now the United States. Later explorers who studied the records of his voyage realized that no such strait exists. Searchers for a quick route to Cathay would now have to look in the far north. [See the articles on Barents, Cartier, Frobisher, and Hudson in this book.]

Jacques Cartier

Jacques Cartier (kar-TYAY). Born 1491 in Saint-Malo, Brittany, France. Died September 1, 1557, near Saint-Malo.

The riches that Spain and Portugal were reaping in the Americas and Asia during the sixteenth century inspired other European nations to mount their own voyages of discovery. France, like England, looked to the northern part of the New World, where no other nation had yet made a claim but where there might be lands to settle and direct passages to the trading ports of Asia. The first French-born captain of an expedition to the New World, Jacques Cartier, opened a water route into the interior of North America that France would later use to found Canada.

The fishing village of Saint-Malo, where Cartier was born, had for years been sending codfishing boats as far west as the Grand Banks off the coast of Newfoundland, clear across the North Atlantic. Cartier was already a respected mariner, with voyages to Newfoundland and Brazil to his credit, when King François I of France chose him to lead an expedition to "discover new lands in the New World."

Cartier's first voyage to Canada, begun in April 1534, was more a scouting and charting expedition than anything else. He carefully looked over the coasts of Labrador and Newfoundland Island, and sailed around the smaller islands and bays of what we now call the Gulf of St. Lawrence. He was impressed with the beauty of the country and the abundance of fish, game, and wild fruit. On this trip Cartier did not enter the St. Lawrence River, but he did meet the Huron Indian leader Donnaconna, who was on a fishing trip in the gulf with about 200 of his tribespeople. The two leaders got on so well that Donnaconna sent two of his sons back to France with Cartier as a token of friendship. Donnaconna hoped to make the French his allies against rival tribes.

In May 1535 Cartier set out again with orders from the king to find a possible passage to Asia and to scout out sites for a new colony. Secretly, he also hoped to find a place that had been mentioned to him by Donnaconna's sons, the rich Kingdom of Saguenay, where gold, silver, and diamonds could be had for the taking. When the expedition reached the Gulf of St. Lawrence, the two Huron boys directed Cartier to the mouth of the St. Lawrence River. The ships entered the river at the end of August and sailed up until they reached the Huron Indian village of Stadaconé, the home of Donnaconna and the site of present-day Québec City. The area around Stadaconé was called by the Indians "Canada," probably from

Jacques Cartier

As the Huron Indians watch with interest, Cartier and his men leave their ships and set out in boats to explore the St. Lawrence River.

the Huron word *cannata*, which means village. Soon this word was taken up by the French, who used it to mean the whole country.

Donnaconna welcomed Cartier warmly and pressed him to remain in Stadaconé, not to continue upstream, where the French might be tempted to become the allies of some rival chief. But Cartier was not moved by Donnaconna's offer of his niece and son as gifts, or even by three shamans, dressed as devils, who tried to scare the French into giving up their plan. In September 1535 Cartier and a picked crew continued up the river in one of the smaller boats. Soon enough it became clear that this was an ordinary river and not a route to China. A month later they reached the large Huron village of Hochelaga. (A hill there, which Cartier named *Mont Royal*, "King's Mountain," would later become the site of the city of Montréal.) Here Cartier heard more from the Indians about the Kingdom of Saguenay. But it

was getting late in the season, so Cartier returned to Stadaconé, where his men prepared to spend the winter.

Donnaconna was still hoping that the French would become his allies. When he realized that they were looking for a kingdom of gold, he began to tell them what they wanted to hear. He told Cartier that Saguenay lay westward along great rivers and that he himself had seen its strange creatures and untold riches. Though Donnaconna embellished his tale with all kinds of fantastic and ridiculous details, Cartier believed him, so much so that when summer arrived he kidnapped the unfortunate chief and took him back to France to tell his story to the king. Donnaconna convinced the king as well, but by the time a return trip was organized five years later, the chief was dead. No trace of Saguenay was ever found, but the mythical kingdom continued to be drawn on maps of North America for more than a century after.

Cartier's explorations

This third and final expedition was led not by Cartier himself but by a nobleman, Jean-François de la Rocque de Roberval, who had no exploring experience. While Roberval dallied at dockside in France, Cartier went ahead to Canada with five ships, taking along a number of convicts in the hope of starting a French colony. The Hurons of Stadaconé, seeing that the French planned to settle there and not just visit, were not as friendly as before, so Cartier and his men continued on to a site a few miles further west. There they build some huts and a fort to serve as a base for expeditions in search of Saguenay. The convicts planted gardens and began mining for gold and diamonds while Cartier made his way up the St. Lawrence. This time he reached the rapids above Montréal.

But again the Canadian winter closed in, and Cartier returned to the colony. Over the next few months the settlers were attacked by the Hurons,

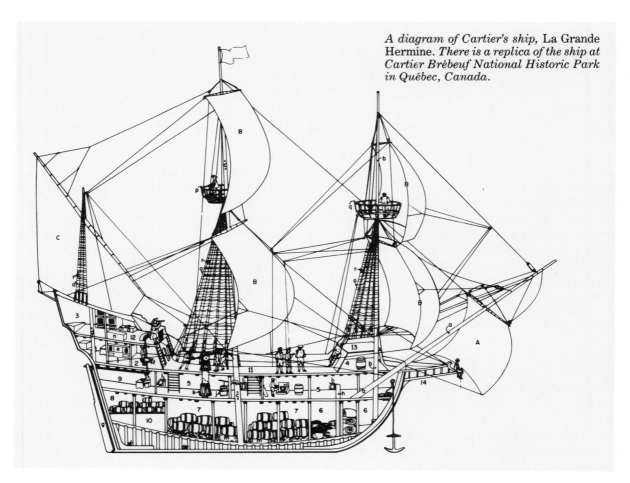

A diagram of Cartier's ship, La Grande Hermine. *There is a replica of the ship at Cartier Brébeuf National Historic Park in Québec, Canada.*

suffered from scurvy and other diseases, and shivered in the bitter Canadian winter, which was much colder than the winters in France. There seemed to be little worth staying for, so Cartier made up his mind to take his men home. Even when they ran into Roberval, arriving late off Newfoundland, Cartier refused to stay. Against Roberval's direct orders he upped anchor in the night and sailed back to France. The colony that Roberval then founded failed just as Cartier's had, and for the same reasons. The survivors returned to France after just one winter.

Faced with the failure of the trial settlements, the harshness of the Canadian winter, and the absence of diamonds and gold, the French put aside their plans to colonize the New World for a long while, and thus lost the chance to claim Canada entirely for their own. When they did return, however, it was Cartier's pioneering voyages that showed them the way into the heartland of Canada.

The "diamonds" and "gold ore" Cartier brought back for the king were just quartz and fool's gold, no more valuable than the rocks brought back from Baffin Island forty years later by the English mariner Martin Frobisher. [See the article on Frobisher in this book.] This doesn't seem to have hurt Cartier's reputation, though, for the king made him a present of two ships. Cartier rented out these ships and lived off his income on a small estate near Saint-Malo until his death at age sixty-six.

Francis Drake

Francis Drake. Born circa 1550–53 in Crowndale, Devonshire, England. Died January 18, 1596, off Portobelo, Panama.

The Spanish cargo ship *Nuestra Señora de la Concepción* was sailing northward along the west coast of South America, bound for the port at Darién—what we now call Panama. In the hold of the ship were thirteen hundred bars of silver from Spain's Peruvian mines, as well as fourteen chests full of coins. All this wealth was intended to enrich the treasury of King Philip II in Madrid, though some of it might never get there; pirates and privateers cruised the Atlantic Ocean, always on the lookout for Spanish treasure ships. But the captain of the *Nuestra Señora* was not worried. Here in the Pacific there were no privateers. A large, well-armed sailing ship had little to fear from native Indians in their canoes, and nothing at all to fear from rival European ships, which never came to these waters. This part of the world was Spain's alone.

A shout from the lookout called the captain's attention to a slow-moving merchant ship on the horizon, its Spanish flag flapping in the breeze. The *Nuestra Señora* changed course and headed toward the merchant ship to hear whatever news it might carry. Now the two ships were in shouting distance of one another. A cannon suddenly boomed on the merchant ship. There was a volley of arquebus shots and crossbow bolts, and the *Nuestra Señora*'s mizzenmast fell over with a crash. Up the side of the *Nuestra Señora* swarmed a gang of armed sailors shouting to each other in English. The amazed Spaniards were quickly captured and found themselves prisoners on a ship that, against all expectation, had come all the way from the English port of Plymouth, across the Atlantic, through the Strait of Magellan, and up the western coast of South America, right into the teeth of the Spanish empire. And while the English crew carried the silver bars and the money chests into the hold of their ship, the *Golden Hind*, the Spaniards were introduced to their captor, a short, vigorous man with a pleasant face and a look of determination. He was Francis Drake, the boldest and the best of Queen Elizabeth's master mariners, the captain with nerves of iron who attacked the Spanish and wrecked their plans time and time again. The

Sir Francis Drake at the age of forty-two, in a portrait by Nicholas Hilliard

Spanish called him *El Draco*, "the dragon," the fiery thief who never lost an opportunity to steal their gold.

There was a double rivalry between Spain and England in Drake's day: one was economic, and the other religious. England and the other maritime nations of Europe were jealous of Spain's vast holdings in the New World and angry that Spain refused to let them come there to trade. The English had also broken away from the Catholic Church and established their own Protestant state religion, and the Spanish were doing everything in their power to bring England back under the authority of the Catholic pope. English sailors captured by Spain were often tortured and killed as heretics or chained to oars in galley ships to work out their lives in slavery.

From his boyhood, Drake was an enemy of both Spain and Catholicism. He and his family—he was the youngest of twelve children born to Protestant tenant farmers—were chased from their home in Devonshire by English Catholics during the reign of Elizabeth's Catholic sister, Queen Mary. He learned his seamanship as a young teenager piloting a small merchant boat in the rough and rocky North Sea. By the time he was in his early twenties, he was on his way to the West Indies as second in command of a slave-trading

expedition led by his relatives, the Hawkins family of Plymouth. In 1568, on a second expedition to the West Indies, Drake survived a massacre at the Caribbean island of San Juan de Ulua when the Spanish killed several hundred English sailors after promising them safe-conduct out of the harbor. From that point on, Drake's life was dedicated to the quest for revenge against Spain.

Though Queen Elizabeth was not yet ready for a war with Spain, she was happy to allow her sea captains to plague Spain's colonial enterprises. She gave Drake a privateering commission—a document that allowed him to raid foreign ships and ports. Without this document, he would have been a mere pirate. [For more information on pirates and privateers, see the article on Henry Morgan in this book.] In 1572–73 he attacked three towns on the Spanish Main (present-day Colombia and Venezuela), crossed the Isthmus of Panama, and captured a mule train laden with treasure, making himself instantly famous and very rich.

Over the next few years, Drake organized a voyage that would strike at the Spanish where they least expected it—in the far western part of their New World empire, along the coast of the Pacific. Elizabeth had many first-rate captains in her kingdom, but only Drake had the nerve and the daring for something as dangerous as this. He set off from Plymouth at the end of 1577 with five small ships (soon reduced to three) and 164 men. The expedition was kept so secret that even the crew did not know where they were headed. They soon found themselves sailing south along the coast of Argentina, steered by a Portuguese pilot whom Drake had kidnapped from a captured ship, and bound for the strait that the great Portuguese navigator Ferdinand Magellan had found and crossed sixty-five years before. In his room, Drake kept a copy of Antonio Pigafetta's journal of that journey. So closely did he follow Magellan's tracks that when he put into the bay of Port San Julian to behead a disobedient officer, he found the remains of the gibbet on which Magellan had hanged two mutineers. [See the article on Magellan in this book.]

But Drake's expedition did not suffer the same fate as Magellan's, though it had its share of adventures. It passed through the strait in sixteen days, half the time that Magellan took, while the crew ate the meat of birds that the Welsh sailors named *penguins* (from the Welsh words for "white head"). As the ships entered the Pacific, they were hit by a terrible storm that sank the smallest ship and convinced the captain of another to turn back for England. Drake's flagship, the *Golden Hind*, was left to continue the mission on its own.

Up the coasts of Chile and Peru went the *Golden Hind*, making surprise attacks on the harbor settlements that Spain had established, looting warehouses and churches and taking valuable cargos from ships. Many times the Spanish authorities sent ships to chase them, but the only harm to Drake and his crew came from Indian tribesmen in Chile who killed and ate two sailors. Captured Spanish officers found Drake living a gentlemanly life on his flagship, dining on silver dishes to the sweet sounds of viols played by a company of musicians. His crew, they noted, treated him with awe. And though the outraged Spanish called him a barbarous pirate, eyewitness reports of his attacks say that his men, unlike real pirates, did not commit rape, murder, and torture. His prisoners were set free, sometimes with handsome gifts, as was the captain of the *Nuestra Señora*. The kidnapped Portuguese pilot, whom Drake freed in Mexico, later wrote that Drake read psalms, preached to the crew, and made sketches and paintings when he was not busy hounding the Spanish.

In April 1579, the *Golden Hind*, so packed with treasure that its sides were leaking, left Mexico and sailed up to Oregon, where the sailors encountered such bitter cold and "vile, thicke, and stinking fogges" that they retreated south again. Just north of what is now San Francisco they anchored in a little bay, where for five weeks they repaired the ship and made friends with the Miwok Indians. This area Drake named Nova Albion—that is, New England. So there was a New England in California before there was a New England in the East. [See the article in this book on John Smith, who gave the east-coast New England its name.]

It may have been Drake's intention all along to circumnavigate the world, or he may have decided that it was too risky to sail back the way he

Drake sailed around the entire globe in the Golden Hind, *harassing Spanish shipping and visiting the future site of San Francisco.*

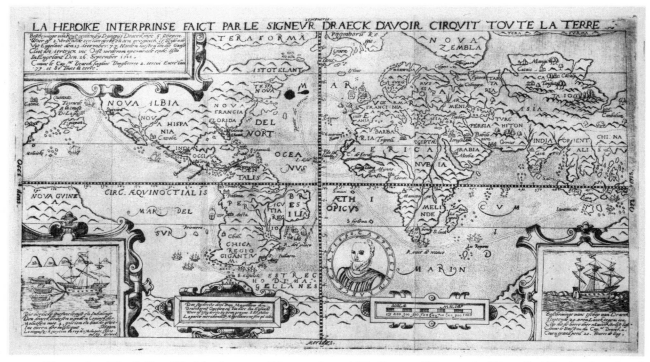

The route of the Golden Hind *is shown on this map from 1589. It was off the coast of Peru that Drake chased and captured the* Nuestra Señora.

had come, past the Spanish who would now be watching for him. He ordered the *Golden Hind* to take a course westward across the Pacific, a route completely unknown to English sailors. After two months, still generally following the trail of Magellan, the ship reached the Philippines and Indonesia, where it was nearly wrecked on a reef. Drake stopped at a number of islands to make trade agreements with their Muslim rulers before setting out across the Indian Ocean, avoiding the Portuguese shipping routes established long before. [See the article on Afonso de Albuquerque in this book for more about Portugal's Asian empire, which was just about to be swallowed up by Spain.] By the end of the journey the ship's company, now down to fifty-nine men, had run out of water and were drinking rain. They sailed into Plymouth harbor in September 1580.

Drake was now more than a famous captain; he was a national hero. He was the first captain ever to sail around the world (for Magellan had died halfway), and the first Englishman to sail three of the world's oceans (the South Atlantic, the Pacific, and the Indian). And he had brought back so

much treasure, especially the millions from the *Nuestra Señora*, that each person who had invested money in the expedition, including the queen, received back their investment ten times over—some say more than forty times over. It was a bigger haul than any ship from any nation had ever captured. Stories and songs about Drake's exploits rang throughout England. The Spanish ambassador demanded that Drake be arrested and the money returned to Spain, but Queen Elizabeth went down to the *Golden Hind* herself and knighted Drake before a cheering crowd.

For some time after this, Drake stayed home in Devon, managing his new country estate with his second wife, a local heiress, and serving as the mayor of Plymouth. He was called back to service in 1585 by Queen Elizabeth, who was now preparing for open war with Spain. With a fleet of twenty-nine ships, Drake sailed to the Caribbean and swooped down on three Spanish cities—Santo Domingo in the present Dominican Republic, Cartagena in Colombia, and St. Augustine in Florida—and did so much damage that Spain's finances were badly shaken and the Bank of Spain collapsed. King Philip needed constant loans to run his huge empire, and the banks of Europe refused to lend money to a king whose assets were threatened by pirates. [It was on this voyage that Drake took home the colonists from the first settlement at Roanoke established by Walter Raleigh. See the article on Raleigh in this book. See the article about Martin Frobisher to learn more about the captain who was Drake's second-in-command on this voyage.]

The furious Spanish had yet another reason to be angry with England: Queen Elizabeth was helping the people of Holland in their rebellion against Spain. For their part, the English had plenty of hatred for the Spanish, who had tried to start a Catholic revolution in England and had paid people to try to assassinate the queen. These two nations had gone beyond rivalry. The time for a showdown was approaching. King Philip drew up plans for an invasion of England that would end Elizabeth's reign and make it a Catholic country once again. His officials began building and outfitting a fleet of warships they called the Invincible Armada. This fleet would sail to Holland, collect the Spanish soldiers that had been fighting the rebellion there, and deliver them to the southern shore of England.

By the spring of 1587, the invasion force was nearly ready. Every part of Spain's empire, from Peru in the west to the Portuguese East Indies, had contributed ships, guns, and supplies. But the Armada did not sail that year, for on the night of April 29, four galleons under the Drake's command sailed straight into the Spanish port of Cádiz and opened fire with their heavy artillery on the eighty ships assembled there. Before the Spanish could get their land guns into position, Drake and his men had destroyed more than thirty ships, including the admiral's flagship. Then the English sped away up the coast, wrecking fishing villages as they went. Next they captured the fortress of Sagres, on the northwestern tip of Portugal, which had housed Prince Henry's navigation headquarters two hundred years before— the very place that had given birth to European sea power and exploration. [For more of that story, see the article on Henry the Navigator in this book.] For several weeks, Drake's 2,200-man fleet cruised along the coast of Portugal, destroying all the supplies that were being collected for

the Armada. Before heading home to Plymouth, they captured a huge Portuguese cargo ship loaded with treasure that would help Elizabeth pay for England's defense.

But Elizabeth had decided to try peace talks with Philip instead of war. A war would be expensive, and Elizabeth's money was stretched to the limit. Again and again her sea captains urged her to mobilize a navy without delay. "Prepare in England strongly and most by sea!" was Drake's advice. Eventually Elizabeth realized that Spain was moving ahead with its invasion plans, and a war council was formed. Among its leaders were Drake, his relative Sir John Hawkins, Martin Frobisher, and the other "seadogs" who had made England a maritime power. By the time the Armada was sighted in the Channel, on July 29, 1588, the English were ready to meet it.

Drake was never so cool and calm as when he heard that the moment of decision was at hand. He happened to be playing a game of bowls on the grass when the messenger arrived, and he made no move to go until the game was finished. "There is plenty of time to win this game," he supposedly said, "and thrash the Spaniards too." The Armada was a formidable fleet, the greatest threat England had faced in hundreds of years. But Drake had reason to be confident. Against Spain's massive floating fortresses, England was going to send a new kind of ship designed by Hawkins and Drake—quicker, lighter, more easily maneuvered, and armed with more powerful weapons. Instead of boarding enemy ships and capturing them in hand-to-hand combat—the kind of seafight Spain was used to—the English planned to blast them with cannon fire and sink them. Drake also knew that the Spanish sailors would be hungry and thirsty. For in his strike against Cádiz, he had burned the Armada's water barrels and ruined its food supply.

The battle in the Channel lasted more than a week. In skirmish after skirmish Drake and Hawkins harried the Armada and picked off its ships. Drake's tactics were so brilliant that the Spanish, who fought with great courage and tenacity, were convinced that he was using sorcery against them. His frequent displays of daring seamanship set an example for the English sailors. It was his idea to launch fireships, small boats covered with flaming pitch, against the Spanish

Although the Spanish attack fleet is closing in, the iron-nerved Drake calmly finishes his game of bowls before launching his defense plan.

English ships, fighting at close range under the command of Drake and his fellow seadogs, defeat the Invincible Armada in August 1588.

fleet in the hope of setting it on fire. The inexperienced Spanish sailors, many of whom were ordinary farmers and artisans forced against their will to serve in the Armada, panicked at the sight of the fireships and suffered a fatal loss of nerve. On the morning of August 8, the English fleet with Drake in the lead came sailing out of the fog, battered the Armada with a terrible rain of cannon fire, and chased what was left of it away from the English Channel and into the storm-racked North Sea. Many of the Spanish ships, filled with wounded and starving men, were wrecked on the long trip home. Of the immense host that had sailed with the Armada, some 30,000 men, only three or four thousand were left alive. The English had lost less than a hundred men.

The defeat of the Armada marked the beginning of the decline of the Spanish empire. It was the beginning of Drake's decline as well, for he would never again have such a moment of glory. In 1589 he set off with instructions from the queen to attack naval installations at the Spanish port of Corunna, but decided instead to plunder Lisbon.

The attack failed, and he lost more than half his crew. He went raiding in the West Indies in 1596, but the Spanish had learned something from his earlier raids and fought off his attacks on Puerto Rico and Panama. Drake never came home from this voyage. He died of dysentery aboard his ship off the Panamanian coast, dressed in his armor so that he could meet death like a soldier, and was buried at sea. His relative and colleague Sir John Hawkins, who had fought alongside Drake to save England's independence, also died on this final voyage. But the legend of the fearless Drake had already passed into English folklore. Like King Arthur, he was thought to be an undying hero, who would return in time of danger to defend his people. In a poem by the poet Alfred Noyes, he reappears as Lord Nelson at the Battle of Trafalgar:

> *Nelson was just . . . a ghost!*
> *You may laugh, but the Devonshire men*
> *Knew that he'd come when England called,*
> *And know that he'll come again.*

Martin Frobisher

Martin Frobisher (FRO-bi-sher). Born circa 1539 in Pontefract, Yorkshire, England; died November 22, 1594 in Plymouth, England.

Tiny Kodlunarn Island lies within a narrow bay on the coast of Baffin Island, a great island between Greenland and the mainland of Canada. In high summer—the only time when Kodlunarn is not covered by snow and ice—old trenches and a stone foundation can still be seen. These are not the marks of the Inuit (Eskimos), who have lived in this area for thousands of years without digging or building anything of stone, but of the English sea captain Martin Frobisher, who four hundred years ago was sent here on a fool's errand to search for gold.

Young Frobisher was raised by an uncle, Sir John York, a merchant who often sailed to Africa. By age fourteen, Frobisher was sailing to West Africa on voyages of trade and exploration. On one of these he was taken captive by the Portuguese, who dominated the area, and thrown in prison. After he regained his freedom he captained a privateer and looted French ships (legally, because France and England were then at war) and Spanish ships (illegally) for Queen Elizabeth of England. Sometimes he turned to out-and-out piracy, but even though he also spent time in an English prison, his reputation as a pirate did not do him much harm, for in the Elizabethan age a successful privateer was held in high regard.

Frobisher was a large, powerful man, a seasoned fighter given to outbursts of anger when crossed. The best portrait we have of him shows him gripping a pistol with one hand and resting his other hand on the hilt of his sword. But he was also known for his excellent seamanship, genuine concern for his sailors, and willingness to see a job through to the end, no matter how difficult or dangerous it might be. Thus he was just the man to seek the fabled northwest sea passage through North America to China (or Cathay, as Europeans then called it). England was eager to find a new trade route to the riches of the East, since all the known routes were controlled by the Spanish, Portuguese, or Turks. Many of England's best seamen, including Frobisher, believed that a

Martin Frobisher

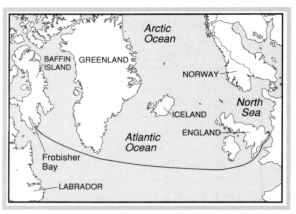

Frobisher's explorations

northwest route must exist, and, moreover, that it would be faster and easier than any of the established routes—if it could be found.

Frobisher proposed the idea of an expedition to find the northwest passage to several influential friends and eventually convinced a group of private investors put up the money for his first voyage. He set out on June 7, 1576, in the bark *Gabriel*, taking with him some of the best navigational instruments of the time. He was accompanied by two smaller ships, but one was not much more than a longboat with sails and was lost along the way. The rest of the expedition made a fast passage across the North Atlantic to Greenland, but then the second ship sneaked away amid the ice and fog and went back to England, leaving Frobisher and the crew of the *Gabriel* alone in the Arctic waste.

Sailing around the south end of Greenland and across what we now call the Davis Strait, Frobisher discovered what appeared to be the entrance to another strait. Could this be the hoped-for route to the East? In fact, it was only a narrow bay (now called Frobisher Bay) on the coast of Baffin Island, but Frobisher did not learn that on this first trip. He had missed by only a few miles a real strait, the Hudson Strait, which leads to the vast Hudson Bay in eastern Canada.

Frobisher did find a lump of black rock that seemed to have flecks of gold in it. But he lost five of his sailors, who were captured by the Inuit. Though Frobisher captured a Inuit in turn—according to the story, he leaned over the ship's side and hoisted the Eskimo, kayak and all, right out of the water and onto the deck—he could not persuade the tribe to exchange prisoners, so he sailed back to England without the five men.

All plans to locate a passage to China were dropped when one expert found a tiny bit of gold in Frobisher's lump of black rock. Now the English hoped to find in the north a source of the precious metal as rich as the mines the Spanish had tapped in Mexico and Peru. [For more on the Spanish conquests in the New World, see the articles on Cortés and Pizarro in this book]. Back went Frobisher to his bay in May 1577 with three more ships, the financial backing of a group of investors now calling themselves the Cathay Company, and the queen's personal blessing. His crew began to dig on Kodlunarn Island and elsewhere.

Almost immediately Frobisher had trouble with the Inuit, who attacked the boats and wounded him with an arrow. With some trickery his men managed to capture three Inuit to hold as hostages for the return of the five sailors kidnapped in the first voyage. Again, no trade of hostages was ever made, and nothing is known for certain about the fate of the five lost men. The Inuit—a man, a woman, and her baby (shown peeking out from his mother's hood in a drawing made at the time)—were taken back to England, where they caused a sensation. But within a month the effects of England's warmer, wetter climate had killed them, just as it had killed the Inuit man whom Frobisher had brought back from his first voyage.

While smelters in England worked to extract gold from the 200 tons of rocks he had carried home, Frobisher departed with fifteen ships on his third and last voyage to the New World. Off the coast of Greenland, losing his way in the ice

A drawing from a 1580 book about Frobisher shows an Inuit man hunting ducks from a kayak and an Inuit mother backpacking her baby.

and storms, Frobisher was blown into the large strait he had missed before. He was tempted to proceed all the way through to find the great body of water that had to be at the other end—this surely was the route to China!—but his orders were to mine ore, not to explore, so he turned back. Thus Frobisher barely missed being the European discoverer of Hudson Bay. [To find out more about the bay, see the article on Henry Hudson in this book.] He and his crew spent the rest of the summer mining rock on Kodlunarn and other islands at the mouth of Frobisher Bay.

The "gold ore" that Frobisher brought back was actually nothing more than rocks laced with iron pyrites—fool's gold, the same worthless mineral brought back by the French mariner Jacques Cartier years earlier on his last voyage to Canada. [See the article on Cartier in this book.] But it was years before the ore-smelters, who were charging the Cathay Company large sums of money for their services, would admit this. When the truth finally came out, many investors were ruined. They blamed Frobisher, and the angry queen

would no longer receive him. Frobisher could not even raise the small sum of money he needed to buy his old ship the *Gabriel* when it was sold at a great discount by the Cathay Company to help pay off its debts.

Nearly penniless, Frobisher took up his old profession of privateering. As usual, he was successful at this, and soon he was back in the queen's good graces. England now needed its bold master mariners more than ever, for its long rivalry with Spain was ripening into war. In 1585 Frobisher was appointed a vice-admiral on Sir Francis Drake's privateering voyage to the West Indies. [For more on that voyage, see the article on Drake in this book.] Later he and Drake became enemies over the division of some Spanish booty, but they fought together when the Spanish Armada attacked England in 1588. Frobisher distinguished himself as master of the warship *Triumph*, defeating a squadron of four Spanish warships not once but twice. For this he was knighted and given command of his own naval division. His last expedition for the queen was in

The explorer John White drew these pictures of the Inuit man, woman, and baby whom Frobisher took to England. All three died there.

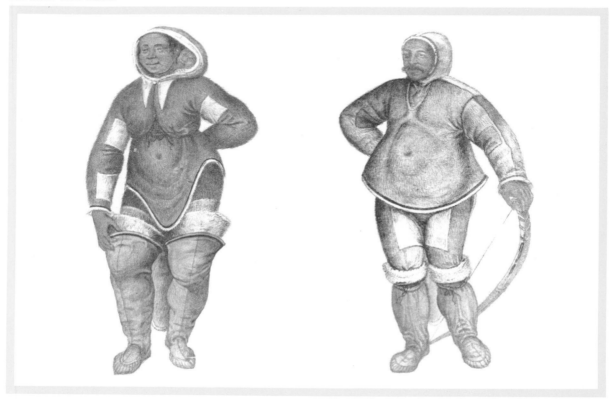

1594, when he led an attack against a fortified Spanish garrison in Brest, France. The garrison was taken, but in the battle Frobisher was shot in the leg. Carried back to the English port of Plymouth, he died of infection in the wound.

Frobisher's voyages yielded neither remarkable discoveries nor great wealth. Yet they laid the groundwork for England's colonization of Canada and were an important step in the development of a great seafaring nation.

Willem Barents

Willem Barents (BAR-ents), also known as Willem Barentzoon. Born circa 1550 in Holland. Died June 20, 1597, off Novaya Zemlya, eastern Barents Sea, Arctic Ocean.

Ice Haven is a small icebound bay on the north island of Novaya Zemlya, one of two large islands off the Arctic coast of Siberia. Only a few hundred miles from the North Pole, Ice Haven is often visited by polar bears and seals but rarely by people. In 1871, one of those rare visitors, a Norwegian walrus hunter named Elling Carlsen, stumbled upon an abandoned driftwood cabin built centuries before. Inside, Carlsen found everything just as it was when the builders left. Besides a few pieces of handmade furniture, there were broken tools, an oil lamp, a broken clock, a flute, a rusty musket, a old book on China, and a note on yellowing paper. The note told of the ill-fated last expedition of Willem Barents, the polar explorer who had sought a northeast passage through the Arctic Ocean from Holland to China.

The remains of Barents's final expedition were discovered in Novaya Zemlya three centuries after Barents and his crew starved to death.

In the sixteenth century, the seafaring countries of northern Europe, notably England and Holland, were anxious to find a northern sea route to China. The southern sea routes around the tips of South America and Africa were controlled by Spain and Portugal. Goods brought from the Orient were also traded at the eastern end of the Mediterranean, but Turkish pirates made that route dangerous too. And either way, middlemen forced the prices of silks and spices sky-high. So England and Holland mounted several expeditions to find a northern sea passage to the Orient—either a northwest passage over North America, or a northeast passage over Norway and Russia. A prize was offered by the Dutch government for the first ship to reach China by this last route, and a syndicate of Amsterdam merchants put up money for several attempts.

Among the great captains seeking northern sea routes were Henry Hudson and Martin Frobisher. [See the articles on Hudson and Frobisher in this book.] One of the ablest was Willem Barents, a Dutch seaman who was known for making accurate charts and keeping careful records of weather conditions on his voyages. Barents made three attempts to open a northeast passage. In 1594 he left from Amsterdam with two ships and made his way across the North Sea to a part of the Arctic Ocean now called the Barents Sea. But although he reached Novaya Zemlya at the far eastern end of the sea, he had to turn back owing to ice and bad weather. The next year Barents returned with seven ships. They sailed south of Novaya Zemlya through the narrow strait that separates it from the mainland and entered the ice-strewn Kara Sea. Beyond the Kara Sea, Barents sighted more ice-locked islands. Again, no northeast passage was found, but Barents reported confidently that it had to be just a bit farther than he had been able to go.

On May 10, 1596, Barents set off on what turned out to be his final expedition, this time with just two ships and a crew of twenty-seven men. Barents commanded the lead ship; the other was captained by another Dutchman, Jan Cornelizoon de Rijp. They sailed more to the north than before, believing that they could avoid the jumble of islands near the coast and sail clear round to China. A month into the trip they saw a sheer cliff of ice rising more than 1,000 feet from

the ocean. Barents's men killed a polar bear there and called it Bear Island. Further north, they discovered the island of Spitsbergen ("land of tall peaks"), now the northernmost part of Norway. Back at Bear Island, less than 15 degrees of latitude from the North Pole, the two captains had a disagreement about which way to go. Rijp wanted to head directly east, while Barents wanted to continue north. The ships separated; the captains never saw each other again.

At the extreme northeastern tip of Novaya Zemlya, Barents encountered thickening ice. It was fast becoming winter in the Arctic, and soon the ship could go no further. Worse, the ice quickly closed up behind the ship, making retreat impossible as well. What no one understood at the time was that pack ice closes the Arctic sea routes for nearly the entire year. Even if Barents had somehow managed to navigate around the ice, however, the expedition would still have been doomed to failure. Barents believed that the Kara Sea was the last barrier to a northeast passage, but he was wrong. The rugged north coast of Siberia actually extends eastward for thousands of miles to the Bering Strait; he would have had to navigate the strait and make a long voyage southward before reaching China.

Barents and his men left the trapped ship and walked to Ice Haven, where they built a hut from

Barents's route

Barents and his men, their ship frozen in the ice, shoot a polar bear for meat. Hungry bears often attacked them and stole the little food they had.

salvaged wood and stocked it with their few supplies. A large central fire heated the hut and water for bathing, and melted polar bear fat was used as fuel for the oil lamps. The site was marked by a frozen polar bear, which the men shot and set up on its hind legs. The ship's food was gone by late September, and the men were reduced to eating Arctic foxes and polar bear meat. There were no vegetables or fruit, and soon the men were all sick from scurvy, a disease caused by a lack of vitamin C. Barents himself suffered worst of all. Yet they kept up their spirits by playing a form of hockey on the ice. In the dark Arctic night they even staged their own plays. According to his journal, Barents was still sure they could reach China, if they could just survive the winter.

The long polar night began in November. The sun did not appear again until February, but the icepack did not break up until June. Even then

they could not sail away—the hull of their ship was still locked tight in ice. So Barents and the desparate survivors set out in two open boats with what little they could carry. A week later Barents and another crewman died and were buried at sea. Not until November did a few of the men, living on raw grass and seabird eggs, manage to reach the Russian port of Kola. There they met Jan Rijp's ship, which had wintered back in Holland and returned to search for them.

After Barents's tragic attempt, interest in a northeast passage waned for three centuries. It was not until 1878–1880, when Nils Nordenskjöld, a Swedish explorer, sailed completely around Asia and Europe, that the northeast passage was finally conquered. The relics of Barents's expedition, including a portion of his journal found in 1875, are now in the Naval Museum at The Hague in the Netherlands.

Henry Hudson

Henry Hudson. Date and place of birth unknown. Died 1611, Hudson Bay, Canada.

The greatest dangers to exploring mariners in the sixteenth and seventeenth centuries were not always storms at sea, hidden shoals, or hostile natives. Harsh conditions aboard ship and fear of the unknown would sometimes make a crew turn on its captain. An explorer who lacked the strength and nerve to control his crew could find himself marooned on a deserted coast or cast away in an open boat to die. This was the fate of Henry Hudson, the English explorer who was the first European to discover the river and bay that now bear his name.

Only guesses can be made about Hudson's early

Henry Hudson

life. He probably belonged to a family in England involved with overseas trade. He is not mentioned in any document until 1607, when he was chosen by the Muscovy Company, a group of English merchants and investors, to seek "a passage by the North Pole to Japan and China." His charter allowed him to try routes to the east or to the west. In 1607 Hudson sailed northwest to Greenland and then headed east along the edge of the polar icepack to the Arctic seas explored earlier by the Dutch captain Willem Barents. [See the article on Barents in this book.] He got as far as the island of Spitsbergen, but was not able to make much further progress because of the ice. The expedition had found nothing new—certainly no passage to Asia—but Hudson's description of abundant whales, walruses, and seals encouraged the English and Dutch to develop a whaling industry in these waters. Hudson's second voyage through the Barents Sea, in 1608, was also blocked by ice.

Perhaps because his English backers were reluctant to put up more money after the first two voyages, Hudson's next expedition to find a passage to Asia was underwritten by the Dutch East India Company. Flying the Dutch flag, Hudson took his ship the *Half Moon*, with a mixed Dutch and English crew, in a third attempt to find a passage to Asia by the northeastern route. But when the ship was blocked by ice off Novaya Zemlya, the icy islands that form the eastern border of the Barents Sea, the crew threatened a mutiny. Hudson convinced them that success was more likely on the western route, and they turned around to look for a passage along the east coast of North America. According to a report by the English explorer and soldier John Smith, who was a friend of Hudson's, there was a strait leading to Asia somewhere near what is now New York. [See the article on John Smith in this book.]

Cruising along the American coast, Hudson saw Chesapeake Bay and Delaware Bay. In September 1609 he entered New York Harbor. [He

Hudson's last two voyages

was the second European explorer to see the harbor. The first was Giovanni da Verrazano in 1524. See the article on Verrazano in this book]. At first Hudson imagined that this was the long-sought passage, but after heading up the great river that drains into New York Harbor—the river now called the Hudson—he realized that it was simply a large river and not a passage to the Pacific. But he sailed as far north as he could up the river, to the place where the city of Albany is today, before turning back. By coincidence, he came within less than a hundred miles of another European, the French explorer Samuel de Champlain, who was with a party of Indians on the lake in New England that is now named for him. [See the article on Champlain.] On the way back Hudson's expedition was threatened by Indians on Manhattan Island and killed several with cannon fire, an event the Indians would remember when the Dutch offered to purchase Manhattan in 1624. (In fact, it was the log from this voyage that spurred the Dutch to colonize the New York area.)

Hudson's explorations, building on those of Verrazano, showed conclusively that there was no strait to the Pacific Ocean between the Carolinas and Maine, and that there was no place in North America where only a narrow bridge of land separated the Atlantic from the Pacific. This was important information, but from Hudson's point of view, the voyage was a failure. To make matters worse, his crew began to threaten him again on the way home; they did not want to return to Holland. Finally he agreed to put in at the port of Dartmouth, in England, where he and his crew were quickly detained by the English authorities and told not to make any more voyages for other nations. The Muscovy Company, the British East India Company, and several private investors were now willing to back him for a fourth voyage, this time to explore a northern strait first seen by Martin Frobisher some years before. [See the article on Frobisher in this book.] Because of the furious rush of water that came through the strait at every ebb tide, it was thought to lead to a great sea, maybe the Pacific Ocean.

In 1610 Hudson and his crew set out in the ship *Discovery* to find this strait, which runs between Labrador and Baffin Island in Canada and which we now call Hudson Strait. Beyond the strait they discovered a vast bay, Hudson Bay, which is really part of the Arctic Ocean. Not sure which way to

In the Half Moon, *Hudson, searching for a route to Asia, entered New York Bay and sailed up the river that was afterwards called by his name.*

Set adrift by mutineers, Hudson, his young son, and seven sailors wait for death as their boat wanders among the icebergs in James Bay.

go, they wandered south along the eastern coast of the bay. As it turned out, this was a fatal mistake. When the *Discovery* reached the southernmost point of Hudson Bay, it was trapped by the growing winter ice and forced to spend the winter in a smaller bay now called James Bay.

Hudson was a master mariner and courageous explorer, but he did not know how to keep the loyalty and trust of his crews. During the long winter at James Bay he played favorites among the sailors and kept back food for himself. When the crew reported that food was missing, Hudson had the sailors' sea chests searched for hidden rations, as though they were the ones hoarding food. He demoted the mate, Robert Juet, for no good reason. And he offered a reward to a crewman named Henry Green, then took it back and gave it to another sailor.

All the crew's discontent was now focused on Hudson. Green and Juet plotted a mutiny and gained the crew's support. On June 22, 1611, once the *Discovery* was free of the ice, the mutineers seized the ship. Hudson, his son, and seven others (including several men who were sick) were forced into a rowboat and cast adrift in the icy bay, with no provisions. They were never seen again, and nothing for sure is known of their fate. The *Discovery* eventually made it back to England, where the mutineers were thrown in prison. But Green and Juet were not among them; Green was killed in a fight with Inuit (Eskimos), and Juet died on board ship during the trip home.

Semyon Dezhnev

Semyon Ivanov Dezhnev (DEZH-nyef; also spelled Dezhnyov and Deshnev). Born circa 1610 in Russia, probably in Pinega, Pomorye. Died 1672 in Moscow.

Two centuries before American explorers headed west into the prairies and mountains of the United States, Russian explorers headed east into the vast wilderness of Siberia, the northeastern part of Asia. Like the Americans, the Russians crossed endless plains, made great river journeys, and fought to subdue the inhabitants. Most of the early explorers of Siberia are unknown today, but the name of one, Semyon Dezhnev, has survived. In 1648 Dezhnev and a small group of Russian adventurers made one of the most difficult sea voyages of all time. In small boats they sailed several hundred miles through the Arctic Ocean along the northern coast of Siberia, rounded Siberia's forbidding northeastern tip, threaded down through the Bering Strait (the narrow channel between Siberia and North America), and finally entered the Pacific Ocean.

Most of the Russian pioneers in Siberia, including Dezhnev, were Cossacks, descended from warrior peasants who came from the heartland of Russia. Little is known of Dezhnev's early life. He was probably born in the northern part of European Russia called Pomorye, where most people made their living as fur trappers, fishermen, or boatbuilders. About the year 1630 he entered the service of the tsar, the emperor of Russia, as a collector of tribute—that is, payment extorted from one group of people by another, more powerful group. He was sent east to Tobolsk, the main city in western Siberia. Eight years later Dezhnev went further east to the frontier outpost of Yakutsk. Yakutsk was the base for Russians striking out for the frigid Siberian northeast, one of the coldest areas on earth.

In 1641 Dezhnev joined a party of Cossacks who had been ordered to build an outpost east of Yakutsk on the Indigirka River. Dezhnev's main job was to collect tribute from the local Siberian tribes, the Tunguses and the Yakuts. (These native Siberians, a few of whom survive today, are related to the Laplanders of Finland.) The usual Russian method of collecting tribute was to attack a village, capture hostages, and hold them until the tribute was paid and the Siberians promised to obey the tsar. This did not make for friendly relations between the Russians and the Siberians. An attack by the Tunguses drove Dezhnev's party north to where the Indigirka River drains into the Arctic Ocean. There they met a rival party of Russian pioneers. With Dezhnev acting as go-between, the two groups combined and made their way to the Kolyma River, farther east than any Russians had gone before. Heading up the Kolyma, they defeated the fierce Chukchi Siberians in a pitched battle and built an outpost.

The Kolyma basin proved to be a rich area for fur trappers. Furs, especially from the sable (an animal related to the mink), were the mainstay of the Siberian economy and the reason why most Russians went to Siberia in the first place. The Chukchi spoke of still richer areas farther east, on the Anadyr River. It was not clear, however, how far away that river was. In 1647, Dezhnev and a trader named Alekseyev, the agent of a wealthy Moscow merchant, tried to sail to the Anadyr, but thick ice prevented them from getting very far. The next year, Dezhnev, Alekseyev, and a former bandit named Ankudinov tried again. This time they led a party of about ninety Russians north along the Kolyma River to the Arctic Ocean. The plan was to sail east along the northern Siberian coast, looking for the entrance to the Anadyr.

The expedition used a kind of sailboat called a *koch*, a small wooden vessel with a flat bottom, gently rounded sides, and a double-thick hull. The koch was in all ways better suited to Arctic travel than the ships used by Western European explorers. It was smaller, more maneuverable, and

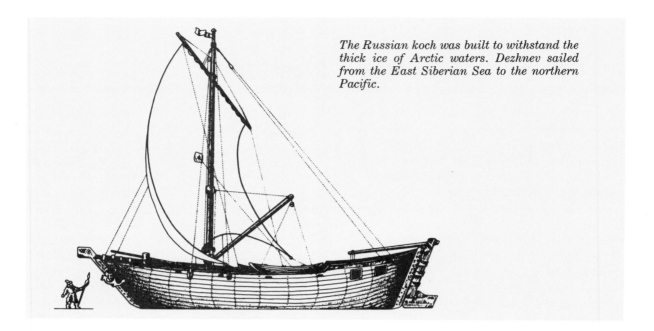

The Russian koch was built to withstand the thick ice of Arctic waters. Dezhnev sailed from the East Siberian Sea to the northern Pacific.

Members of the Tungus tribe, from central and eastern Siberia, set up a campsite. A baby rides in a basket atop a domesticated reindeer.

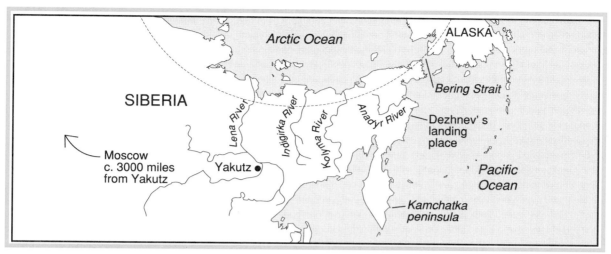

Northeast Siberia

less likely to break up when hit by ice. If the water froze over, the flat-bottomed koch could rest safely on top of the ice until it thawed.

By the time Dezhnev's expedition reached the sea, four of the expedition's seven koches had been shipwrecked. The survivors of the wrecks were caught and killed by Koryak Siberians, a people related to the Inuit (Eskimos) of North America. The other koches sailed slowly east, close to the shore. Since the men had no compass or maps, they did not venture into the open ocean. However, they could sail both day and night, for they were near the North Pole, and the summer sun shone for twenty-one hours of every day.

The details of this part of the journey are a matter of debate, because Dezhnev said little about them in his reports. But we do know that Dezhnev was excited to see a great walrus rookery not far north of the Bering Strait. Walrus skin, oil, and ivory were prized as highly as sable fur by Russians and Siberians alike. Rounding great rocky cliffs on the Chukotskiy Peninsula, the koches entered the Bering Strait. As far as we know, Dezhnev did not realize that he was passing just a few dozen miles from the continent of North America. [The polar explorer Vitus Bering, for whom the strait is named, passed through it one hundred years later and proved once again that Asia and North America are not connected. See the article on Bering in this book.]

South of the Bering Strait, a fierce storm blew up. The boats lost sight of one another in the icy fog and were wrecked on the eastern Siberian coast. Dezhnev and about twenty-five others made it to shore south of the Anadyr River. It was now late September and winter had arrived. Cold and hungry, naked and barefoot, the men walked northward for ten weeks to find the Anadyr. About half of them either died along the way or were lost in the wilderness just after they arrived. The crews of the other boats, including Alekseyev and Ankudinov, died of scurvy or were killed by Siberians.

Dezhnev and his men built new boats and sailed up the Anadyr. The explorers were greatly disappointed to find that the Anadyr basin was not nearly as rich in sables as the Chukchi had said. Nonetheless, Dezhnev successfully collected tribute from the local Siberians and explored further south as far as the Kamchatka Peninsula. The Russian empire now stretched more than 5,000 miles, from St. Petersburg on the Baltic Sea to Dezhnev's tiny outpost near the Pacific.

In 1664, after sixteen more years in Siberia, Dezhnev traveled to Moscow. Of the original ninety explorers, he was the only one to return to Russia, and probably the only one left alive. Though he was a fearless explorer, Dezhnev certainly never became rich in the tsar's service. In his letters to the tsar he complained often that he was never reimbursed for basic supplies like fishing tackle, nets, powder, and shot.

For almost a century afterwards, Dezhnev's adventures were forgotten. Later explorers of Siberia, such as Vitus Bering, knew nothing of his voyage. In 1728 Bering did hear rumors from Chukchis living on the Kamchatka Peninsula that a Russian boat had come that way some seventy or eighty years before. This story sparked the interest of an historian named G. F. Müller, who talked with Bering and who in 1736 discovered some of Dezhnev's reports in the tsar's archives at Yakutsk. Almost all we know about Dezhnev comes from these reports, written some years after the voyage. When Müller published them few years later, there was intense excitement all over the world, because people realized that Dezhnev must have found the long-sought Northeast Passage from Europe to the Pacific. [See the article on Bering in this book. For more on the search for the Northeast Passage, see the articles on Willem Barents and Henry Hudson.] But the sea route around Siberia was too icebound for the larger sailing ships of the eighteenth century. Some historians doubt that Dezhnev actually sailed it himself. They say he must have traveled overland instead. (The sea route was not navigated again until Nils Nordenskjöld's expedition in 1878.) Yet Dezhnev's reports show clearly that he and his party were the first people, and for 230 years the only people, to sail entirely around the northernmost point of Asia.

Vitus Bering

Vitus Jonassen Bering (BAY-ring). Born 1681 in Horsens, Denmark. Died December 19, 1741, on Bering Island, Siberia.

The place was called the "Big Land" by the Siberians. Gazing from the deck of his ship, the *St. Peter*, the Danish-Russian explorer Vitus Bering agreed—there seemed to be no end to it. In the distance he could see ranks of snow-covered mountains disappearing into the interior, beyond sight. Whales and porpoises spouted from the ocean on either side of the ship. The coast was lined by scores of small islands on which lived millions of seals, walruses, and plump seabirds. This land of Alaska was a great prize. He would claim it for his employer, the tsarina (the empress of Russia). But the man for whom the Bering Sea, the Bering Strait, and Bering Island are named did not live to bring her news of it.

By the early eighteenth century, the Russians had been pushing for two hundred years into Siberia, the vast northern part of Asia. Earlier Russian explorers such as Semyon Dezhnev had extended the Russian empire all the way from the Baltic Sea to the Pacific Ocean. [For more on the little-known exploits of Dezhnev, see the article on him in this book.] Now the Russian were poised to cross the Pacific and explore the west coast of North America. However, little of Siberia had been explored in a systematic way, and there were few dependable maps. Without a detailed understanding of Siberia, the Russians would be unable to open new trade routes to China, south of Siberia, or cross the sea to Alaska.

During his long reign (1682–1725), Tsar Peter the Great tried to put current knowledge about Siberia on a more scientific footing. In 1724 Peter hired the Danish-born captain Vitus Bering to see if Siberia and America were joined in the extreme north. (At that time no one realized that Semyon Dezhnev had already proved the existence of a sea passage between the two continents.) His orders to Bering were short and direct. Bering was "to sail along the shore which runs to the north and which seems to be a part of the American Coast. To determine where it joins with America. To learn the name of the coast and take it down in writing, make a landing, obtain detailed information, draw a chart and bring it here."

Bering had been sailing for the Russians for some twenty years. He was an experienced and courageous captain, but a very cautious one. He rarely took risks unless he was sure they were worth it. With the help of two junior officers, Martin Spandberg and Alexei Chirikov, both notable explorers in their own right, he set out on the long overland journey—a distance of some 4,500 miles—from Moscow to eastern Siberia. Not until the spring of 1728 did Bering's party reach the east coast of Kamchatka. There they built a boat, the *St. Gabriel.*

In July of that year they set out. Sailing northeast through what is now called the Bering Sea, Bering made contact with a band of native Siberians called the Chukchi who lived near the mouth of the Anadyr River. The Chukchi told him that if he kept on following the coast north and west he would eventually reach an "ice-filled sea"—the Arctic Ocean—and there he would find the mouth of the Kolyma River. Bering continued north through the Bering Strait that bears his name. Beyond that passage, where the land masses of Asia and America nearly meet, Bering could see the waters widening again, so he assumed (correctly) that there was no land connection between the two continents. Chirikov argued that they should make absolutely sure by pressing on around the tip of Siberia to the Kolyma, but Bering ordered the ship to turn around, feeling he had fulfilled his commission.

On his return in 1730, the Russian authorities did not see things that way. Bering had not gone far enough to be absolutely sure there was no land bridge across the strait, they said, so he had not carried out his instructions. By this time Peter the Great was dead; his successor, the tsarina Anna, refused to pay Bering. But Bering's friends at court took his part and he was soon back in favor. In fact, he was enlisted by the Russian Admiralty and the Academy of Sciences to head an even bigger expedition: to map the entire north and east coasts of Siberia from the port of Arkhangelsk near Finland to the mouth of the Anadyr River on the Pacific.

This was an ambitious undertaking indeed—perhaps more ambitious than anyone understood at the time. Siberia has perhaps 10,000 miles of coastline, including numerous bays, islets, and river mouths. The water and land along the Arctic Ocean are frozen solid from September to June. In summer the tundra, or plain, along the Siberian coast turns into a sodden bog, impossible to walk or ride on. No one foresaw that the Great Northern Expedition, as it was called, would take ten years (roughly 1733 to 1743) and the efforts of hundreds of explorers, many of whom would die in the attempt. Some of these explorers left their

On board Bering's expedition for the Russian Academy of Sciences were naturalists who made notes on marine animals like these walruses.

names on the map of Siberia and the Arctic. The Laptev Sea is named for Kharitov Laptev, who was shipwrecked in its waters. A navigator named Chelyuskin gave his name to icy Cape Chelyuskin, the northernmost point of Asia.

Bering spent most of the years from 1733 to 1740 overseeing the vast effort and once more making the long trek from Moscow to the Pacific coast. In 1741 he set sail from Kamchatka for the coast of Alaska. He was in charge of two ships: the *St. Peter*, which he commanded himself, and the *St. Paul*, commanded by Chirikov. The ships were separated in a storm, and Bering continued in a northeastly direction until he made landfall on Kayak Island off the Alaskan coast. There he saw great numbers of seals, walruses, and sea otters. He also found a deserted village belonging to the native inhabitants of Alaska, people known as Inuit or Eskimos, whose ancestors had come from Siberia tens of thousands of years earlier, when a bridge of land still linked Asia with North America.

Bering was not the first European or Asian to discover Alaska. The Chukchi Siberians, who are related to the Inuit, had known of it for thousands of years. He was not even the first Russian to set foot in the "Big Land." Alaska had been visited by a Russian, the geographer Mikhail Gvosdev, just a few years before. In 1732 Gvosdev had gone to the eastern Siberian port of Okhotsk, where he took command of Bering's old ship, the *St. Gabriel*. Sailing east into the Bering Sea, he came upon what he took to be a large island. In fact, Gvosdev had reached the coast of Alaska. The results of Gvosdev's voyage were not made public until some years after Bering's, so it is Bering who is usually said to have discovered Alaska.

With no clear idea of where to go from Kayak Island, Bering wandered down into the Aleutian Islands. Frequent storms and heavy fogs slowed the ship's progress until the crew was running low on food. Most of the men, including Bering, were sick with scurvy when they reached the island now called Bering Island, in the Bering Sea. Here the crew spent the winter, huddling in pits dug in the frozen ground. Bering, exhausted and discouraged, died within a month. The others survived on seal and otter meat and what scraps they

A native man travels by dogsled through the Arctic winter on Siberia's Kamchatka peninsula, from which Bering launched his expedition.

Siberia and Alaska

could salvage from the *St. Peter*, which ran aground in a gale. Their most vexing problem was the packs of blue foxes that stole their food and even nibbled on the men who were too sick to fight them off.

In the spring the survivors built another boat out of the wreckage of the *St. Peter* and made it safely back to Kamchatka. Chirikov, who was only a few days behind Bering for much of the voyage,

also returned that summer, in such poor health that he died not long after. Their fate did not discourage the Russians, however. Bering's discoveries spurred the Russians to expand into North America, an expansion that continued for a century and extended as far south as California. They did not give up their claim to land on the North American continent until 1867, when they sold Alaska to the United States.

Henry Morgan

Henry Morgan. Born 1635 in Wales, probably in Llanrhymney, Glamorgan. Died August 25, 1688, in Jamaica, probably in Lawrencefield.

In the 1600s, almost the whole of the Caribbean Sea was under the control of Spain. The Spanish colonies along the coast of Central America produced great quantities of gold, which was sent across the Atlantic to Spain in well-guarded galleons. Other maritime countries of Western Europe were determined to force their way into the West Indies, set up their own colonies, and get a

share of the treasure. In 1655, the English navy seized the island of Jamaica, which then became a British colony. One of the sailors who helped to take Jamaica was a young Welsh ensign named Henry Morgan. He was to become the most famous of the buccaneers who terrorized Spain's Caribbean settlements for decades.

Morgan is often called a pirate, but that is not precisely the right term for him. Pirates were gangs of rogue sailors who raided towns and ships and stole whatever they could. They were outside the law, and if they were caught and brought to trial, they could be executed. Morgan was not a pirate but a privateer. He and his crew behaved exactly like pirates, but they were protected by

Sir Henry Morgan

Morgan and his privateers torture the people of a town on the Spanish Main to make them reveal the places where they hid their gold.

English law because they were robbing England's enemies. All Morgan's attacks on Spanish property were authorized by Thomas Modyford, the colonial governor of Jamaica. Spain complained bitterly to the king of England about the ravages of the privateers, and the English government instructed Modyford to restrain them. But Modyford insisted that the privateers were a necessary evil. If they were stopped, the Spanish would certainly attack Jamaica and take it back, and England would lose its foothold in the Caribbean—as well as its share of the privateer's winnings. Modyford kept on giving the privateers help and encouragement, and the Jamaican town of Port Royal was soon a haven for privateers and for pirates as well (the term "buccaneers" covers them both). The Dutch and the French also had settlements in the Caribbean, and the buccaneers of all these nations were more than happy to attack one another's settlements whenever their home countries went to war.

Between 1655 and 1667, Morgan served in various privateer expeditions against the Spanish and the Dutch. He was elected leader of the English privateers in 1668, and with Modyford's permission he organized a raid on the Spanish city of Puerto Príncipe (now called Camagüey), on the island of Cuba. This was a city of rich tobacco plantations. The privateers had to march fifty miles through woody areas to reach it. When they got there, they found that the city had been warned; the people had hidden their money, and a citizens' militia marched out to meet them. The battle lasted four hours. Then the victorious buccaneers locked the townspeople into the churches while they tore the town apart in search of the hidden money. They tortured their prisoners until every one had given up every bit of gold. Then they took as a ransom a thousand head of cattle, which they butchered on the spot. Most of the women and children of the town died of hunger in the cathedral where they had been imprisoned.

The treasure gained from the plunder of Puerto Príncipe was not enough to satisfy the privateers, so Morgan decided on a particularly daring plan. He sailed his fleet across the Caribbean to Darién (what we now call Panama and Costa Rica) and prepared to raid the very rich town of Portobelo, the loading place for ships on their way back to Spain. This was a town so well defended that no one thought any buccaneer would ever dare attack it. There were two strong forts at the entrance to the harbor, and another fort on an island in the middle. Morgan's men crept up from behind, along the landward side, captured one fort and blew it up, together with all its defenders. They captured the island fort by forcing priests and nuns from the town to carry ladders, under fire, along the causeway that connected the island to the mainland. The third fort surrendered. For a month the privateers plundered the town in their usual way—torturing and raping the townspeople, feasting and drinking in their homes, stuffing the ships with their slaves, money, and valuables. Even the best guns from the forts were stolen.

The triumphant Morgan sailed back to Jamaica and started recruiting ships and sailors for his next exploit. He had his eye on a large French ship that had stolen supplies from an English vessel. He tricked its officers into coming on board his frigate, arrested them, took possession of their ship, and then had a handsome dinner served to his own captains to celebrate. The drunken buccaneers began firing guns for fun. One bullet hit a powder keg and the frigate blew up, killing almost everyone on board, including the French officers. Morgan was one of the few to escape.

Despite this setback, Morgan now had a reputation in the Caribbean as the best admiral among the buccaneers, and he had no trouble assembling a fleet of ships to attack Spanish settlements on the shores of Lake Maracaibo, in Venezuela. Their first target was the city of Maracaibo, which they found to be easy pickings: the townspeople had fled into the mountains, and the houses and churches were undefended. There was another haul of treasure from the town of Gibraltar, across the lake. But when the privateer fleet made ready to go home, they found their exit from the lake blocked by three Spanish warships. Morgan's usual resourcefulness did not fail him now. At his orders, the crew took a small vessel, outfitted it with explosives, set it afire, and sailed it toward the warships. At the last minute they jumped and swam for their lives. One of the warships caught fire and sank, the second fled, and the third was captured.

But the privateers were still trapped under the guns of the Maracaibo castle. While his sailors

Trapped inside Lake Maracaibo by Spanish warships, Morgan launches a floating bomb—the same tactic Drake used against the Armada.

brought up a fortune in coins and jewels from the wreck of the sunken warship, Morgan considered his situation. He decided on an elaborate trick. The Spanish gunners in the castle watched with alarm as the rowboats of the privateers went back and forth between the ships and the shore, apparently dropping off dozens of men armed with muskets and cutlasses. Thinking they were going to be attacked from the land, the Spanish shifted their cannons to the other side of the castle. They did not know that the rowboats were not really dropping anyone off—they ferried the same group of men back and forth each time, sitting up on the way to shore and lying down on the way back. When darkness came, the privateers, now safe from the guns of the castle, sailed away back to Port Royal.

Morgan's last and most notorious raid took place in August 1670, at Panama, the biggest and richest city on the Spanish Main. While he was making his preparations, word reached Modyford that England had signed a peace treaty with Spain; but either Morgan never heard the news, or he simply ignored it. He left Jamaica with a fleet consisting of thirty-six ships and nearly nineteen thousand men, including some French.

This expedition ran into many more difficulties than the raid on Maracaibo. In order to get to Panama the ships had to sail up the Chagres River, and to do that they had to pass the fortress of San Lorenzo, high on a cliff and surrounded by earthworks and wooden palisades. The storming of San Lorenzo cost Morgan more than a hundred men. Then six of the buccaneer ships were

The Caribbean

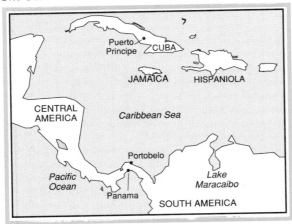

damaged on a reef at the entrance to the river. Leaving a detachment of men behind to guard the castle and the fleet, Morgan led the main part of his forces up the river in rowboats. They found the river so clogged with sandbars that they had to go on foot through the jungle. They had brought no food and as the days went by they began to starve. Soon they were reduced to eating tree bark and leather bags. If the residents of Panama had attacked them at this point, they could easily have overcome the buccaneers, put an end to the Morgan's career, and saved themselves from an ordeal. But the governor had decided to stay home and wait for the attack, and the buccaneers had time to refresh themselves by eating dried corn they had found in a barn and all the cats and dogs they could grab on the way.

The defenders of the city came out to meet Morgan and his men with an army of horsemen and infantrymen and a herd of charging bulls. Morgan drew up his forces with the best sharpshooters in front. Their volleys cut down the Spanish horsemen and sent the bulls off in a panic. The fighting lasted only two hours before the city fell. But the inhabitants had their revenge, after a fashion, for in the course of the night the whole town burned to the ground. Some say Morgan ordered it burned, but the more likely explanation is that the defenders fired it themselves. The buccaneers had to sift through the ashes and search the countryside to find what was left, and they took six hundred prisoners to hold for ransom. It was a disappointing outcome for such an ambitious campaign, and many of Morgan's crew suspected that he had kept most of the plunder for himself.

The Spanish were furious, and complained to King Charles in London over the broken peace treaty. This time it seemed Morgan had gone too far. The king replaced Modyford as governor of Jamaica, had him arrested and sent back to England, and imprisoned him for a while in the Tower of London. Morgan too was called back to England, but powerful friends intervened for him, and instead of being punished, he was knighted and appointed the lieutenant governor of Jamaica. He undertook no more privateer adventures. He spent his time on his Jamaican plantation, playing at island politics and polishing his reputation. When two London publishers brought out a biography of him, written by a former crew member, that painted him as a merciless cutthroat, he sued them for libel and forced them to apologize. In fact, the more respectable Morgan became, the more he became an enemy to his fellow buccaneers. As governor, he even executed a number of them for piracy. Now that the Caribbean was open for trade, the buccaneers were no longer useful, and the nations that had supported them before made them outlaws.

Alcoholism now caught up with Morgan, and before he had much time to enjoy his retirement, he died and was buried in the Port Royal cemetery. A few years later Port Royal was hit by an earthquake and a tidal wave, and most of the town, including the cemetery, collapsed into the sea. It was said among Jamaicans that Morgan had reached back from the grave to commit a last act of terror.

Abel Tasman

Abel Janszoon Tasman (TAHS-mahn). Born circa 1603 in Lutjegast, Groningen, Holland. Died October 1659, probably in Batavia (now Djakarta), Java.

During the fifteenth and sixteenth centuries, Portuguese and Spanish explorers pushed their trading empires eastward from India into Southeast Asia. In the archipelagoes (chains of islands) of Malaysia, Indonesia, and the Philippines could be found the spices and other goods that Europeans had long sought to obtain from the East. [For more of this story, see the articles on Afonso de Albuquerque and the other Portuguese explorers in this book.] As economic troubles at home weakened first Portugal and then Spain, other countries were eager to establish their own trading empires in this region. Chief among these new contenders was Holland. In 1602 the Dutch government created a merchant enterprise called the United Dutch East India Company (usually called the VOC, after the initials of its name in Dutch), which was granted the right to regulate all Dutch trade and sea traffic in that part of the world. It could also appoint the governors of Dutch colonies (such as the ones on the islands of Java and Sumatra), maintain a navy, and build fortified posts. Within a very short time, the VOC had set up headquarters in the town of Batavia (the present-day city of Djakarta) in Malaysia and had extended its au-

thority over Dutch shipping from the tip of Africa to the coast of China.

The job of the VOC was to enrich those who had invested in the company: merchants, bankers, and the government of Holland. To this end, the company was willing to sponsor voyages of exploration if there seemed to be a good chance that profitable new trade might result. Without the permission of the company, however, no Dutch trader could do any legal business in the East Indies or even sail there by the two known routes (westward through the Strait of Magellan near the southern end of South America, or eastward around the southern end of Africa). Traders who were caught breaking the VOC rules had their goods and ships confiscated and often ended up in prison.

Even captains who sailed to the East Indies by other routes were likely to fall afoul of the company. In 1616, two Dutch explorers named Jacob Le Maire and Willem Schouten became the first mariners to reach the East Indies by sailing around Cape Horn, at the southern tip of South America. They had discovered a new route to the Pacific, one that hadn't been claimed by the VOC because no one knew it existed, but the VOC officials did not believe them and their ship was taken from them anyway. We now know that Le Maire and Schouten lost not only their ship, but also the chance to become the European discoverers of the island continent of Australia. While sailing through the Pacific some 1,600 miles west of Peru, Schouten, the navigator, decided to turn the ship northward to get a better gauge of their position. Had he borne straight on, his ship would have hit the east coast of Australia.

The fact is, it is not known for sure just who was the first European to see Australia. Scattered rumors of lands in that area had been brought back by Portuguese and Spanish mariners who sighted a strange coastline or anchored briefly in a deserted bay. Even Ferdinand Magellan's crew may have made a brief landfall on Australia during their epic 1519 circumnavigation of the world. [See the article on Magellan in this book for more on this voyage.] None of these sailors realized that they were setting foot on an undiscovered continent. But of all the strange stories about Australia, the strangest was that of a Dutch captain named Abel Tasman, who was actually sent to explore the island continent and sailed clear around it without even seeing it.

Tasman, a seasoned mariner with eight years' experience in the confusing waters of Southeast Asia and the western Pacific, had shown himself willing to take on the hard and sometimes dangerous work assigned him by the VOC. Between 1634 and 1642, Tasman had led several trading voyages to Japan, Cambodia, Formosa (modern Taiwan), and Sumatra; joined an expedition searching for "islands of gold and silver" somewhere east of Japan; and captured a Chinese pirate who was preying on Dutch shipping.

At that time, maps of the world showed a large blank area in the southern Pacific. This part of the globe was well south of the usual trading routes, and the geography there was still a mystery. In the early seventeenth century, shipping between Africa and Java increased, and Dutch captains blown off their course now began to encounter Australia's western coast with some regularity. The Dutch gave the name "New Holland" to this vast and unsuspected land. Many geographers began to wonder if a great continent might exist in the unexplored waters of the South Pacific. New Holland might be its western edge, and it might include as yet undiscovered lands extending almost all the way to South America. This huge rumored continent was given a name: Terra Australis, or the Great South Land.

In 1642, Anthony Van Diemen, the governor-general of the Dutch East Indies, chose Abel Tasman to lead an expedition to find the Great South

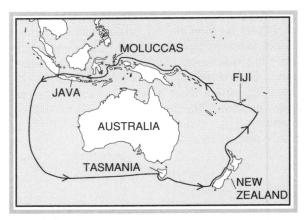

Tasman's route

Land. Van Diemen wanted to know where this land was, how large it was, and whether sailors could follow its coast along a new trade route across the Pacific to South America. Van Diemen assured Tasman that his efforts would be repaid "with certain fruits of gain, and undying fame."

Tasman set sail from Batavia in August 1642 with two ships. He dropped well to the south; then, finding no land, headed to the east. On November 24, he finally sighted a barren coast which he named Van Diemen's Land in honor of the governor-general. The surf was so rough that Tasman decided not to try landing a boat; instead, his ships skirted along south of the coast until they reached a bay where the water was calmer and Tasman's pilot could lead a party ashore. They found thick, hollowed-out trees and heaps of mussel-shells. Smoke could be seen rising from the woods, and suddenly the sailors heard a shrill sound like a trumpet. Fearing an attack, the sailors hurried back to their ship. The next day the men returned to put up a marker, but no contact was made with the inhabitants. On December 5, Tasman and his officers decided that Van Diemen's Land did not merit further exploration, so the expedition sailed further east. The route Tasman took made it impossible for him to see that Van Diemen's Land is really a large island separated by a strait from the mainland of Australia.

About a week later, the expedition again sighted land. It was the western coast of the South Island of New Zealand, never before seen by Europeans. When the Dutch dropped anchor in a peaceful bay and rowed ashore, they were chased back to their ships by fierce warriors paddling after them in sleek outrigger canoes. The next day the warriors attacked again, killing four Dutch sailors, then paddling away so quickly that they were out of range before the Dutch could fire their cannon. Tasman saw little point in staying at this dangerous spot; he named the harbor "Murderer's Bay," weighed anchor, and headed north. After sailing up the coast of the two main islands of New Zealand, without realizing that they were islands, he suddenly found himself in the wide ocean again.

Tasman concluded that New Zealand, which he called "Staten Land," was the western part of the Great South Land, and that the rest of it must stretch away to the east, perhaps as far as the tip of South America. The swell of the ocean north of New Zealand convinced Tasman that at that latitude there was clear water all the way to South America, so the Great South Land had to be entirely south of that latitude. Continuing northeast, Tasman came to the Tonga Islands, then turned west along the north coast of New Guinea, and finally made port in Batavia in June 1643.

Van Diemen was disappointed with Tasman's report. The exact size and shape of New Holland and the Great South Land were still unknown, nor had Tasman ventured all the way to the coast of South America, as he had been instructed to do. Worst of all, no riches had been found. But there was no one with the experience to finish the job but Tasman himself, so the next year he was sent out again, this time to find out whether New Guinea was attached in some way to the Great South Land.

Convinced by his previous voyage that the rumored continent had to be much farther south and east, Tasman sailed through the strait between New Guinea and Australia, dipped into the Gulf of Carpentaria on Australia's north coast, rounded Cape York (the tip of the peninsula that juts northward from Australia like a knife pointing toward New Guinea), and headed partway down Australia's east coast. Tasman saw a few people on shore, whom he described as "naked, beach-roving wretches, miserably poor and in many places of a very bad disposition." (Such ideas were uttered often by Europeans who had

Four of Tasman's sailors were killed by New Zealanders at Murderer's Bay. Tasman drew this picture of the attack in the journal he kept.

Terra Australis, the Great South Land, stretches across the Southern Hemisphere in this old map. Tasman searched for it, but it does not exist.

no understanding of the life and culture of the aboriginal Australians. One of the few who held a different view of them was Captain James Cook; see the article on him in this book.) On this voyage, Tasman proved that New Guinea is an island not connected to any land to the south, but the true geography of Australia, New Zealand, and the supposed Great South Land was as much a mystery as before. Upon his return Tasman retired from exploring, but continued working for the VOC until his death in 1659.

On neither voyage did Tasman find anything that interested the Dutch. Plainly there were no profits to be made in trading with the shy inhabitants of New Holland or Van Diemen's Land, and neither place seemed to be rich in natural resources. New Zealand, on the other hand, offered stands of tall timber and green fields for farming, but these were well defended by the ferocious

Maoris, as the warriors Tasman had encountered called themselves. So the Dutch East India Company turned its attention to developing its Asian colonies, and Australia remained unexplored for another century. Then, beginning with the 1769 voyage of Captain Cook, the British began the exploration and settlement of both New Zealand and Australia. The eastern coast of Australia was made into a famous penal colony, where British subjects convicted of crimes were sent as a punishment. Another penal colony, famous as a hellhole where prisoners were brutally treated, was located on Van Diemen's Land, whose name was changed to Tasmania in 1853. The result of these activities was the extinction of the native inhabitants of the island, who had all been killed by 1876. New Zealand was not settled by the British until the mid-nineteenth century, when colonists signed a peace treaty with the Maoris.

James Cook

James Cook. Born October 27, 1728, in Marton, Yorkshire, England. Died February 14, 1779, in Kealakekua, Hawaii.

What balances the earth as it turns in space? That was the mystery that baffled the geographers of the eighteenth century. In those days many scientists believed that the land masses of the planet had to be balanced between north and south, or the earth would wobble as it spins. Almost all the land they knew of was in the northern hemisphere. So it was thought that there had to be a huge undiscovered continent somewhere to the south to balance the weight of all the land in the north. This unknown continent was even given a name—*Terra Australis*, the Great South Land—but no one knew where it lay. A young English navigator with a passion for science, James Cook, solved the mystery of Terra Australis and forever changed the picture we have of our earth.

Cook was the most skilled captain of his time. He had learned seamanship by sailing coal ships in the North Sea, along the most dangerous coasts in Britain. Then he gave up a promising career as a merchant captain to join the Royal Navy, where his expert seamanship, dedication, and quiet air of command made a strong impression. Cook was also interested in science, which was rare for a sea captain, and rarer still for a man who had had little or no formal schooling. In his spare time he studied mathematics and navigation. When he observed an eclipse of the sun off Newfoundland, where he spent each summer charting the coast, he sent a paper about it to the astronomers of the Royal Society of London.

So in 1769, when the admirals of the Royal Navy was looking for a commander to lead a scientific expedition to the island of Tahiti in the Pacific Ocean, Cook seemed to be the perfect choice for the job. In the ideal conditions afforded by the clear Pacific air, a team of astronomers were to observe the transit of the planet Venus across the face of the sun. From their observations, they hoped to determine the exact distance from Earth to Venus and from Venus to the Sun. A young botanist named Joseph Banks and a naturalist named David Solander were to go along to gather specimens of plants, animals, and minerals from the South Seas. For his ship, the practical Cook chose the *Endeavour*, a coal freighter like the ones he had sailed in the North Sea. These Whitby colliers, as they were called, were sturdy, roomy, and sat high in the water, advantages Cook knew were not shared by any other kind of English ship.

The Royal Navy also gave Cook a second, secret assignment: to discover the Great South

James Cook

Land, or prove once and for all that it did not exist by sailing as far west as the island of New Zealand, discovered by the Dutch explorer Abel Tasman more than a century before. [For Tasman's story, see the article on him in this book.] Britain was worried that French mariners, who had already visited Madagascar (the large island off the east coast of Africa) and sighted the ice of Antarctica, were near to discovering Terra Australis and claiming it for France.

When the job in Tahiti was completed, Cook, following his instructions from the Navy, sailed the *Endeavour* south and southwest, a route that had never been tried by any explorer. The crew sighted New Zealand on October 6, 1769. Cook charted every feature of the dangerous New Zealand coast, a task that took six months. He sought as little contact as possible with New Zealand's inhabitants, the proud and warlike Maoris, who threw stones and warclubs at his sailors whenever they approached.

Cook then faced the choice of returning east by way of stormy Cape Horn, at the tip of South America, or continuing west, following Tasman's course in reverse to Australia. West seemed the safer course for the battered ship. Several days later, the *Endeavour* reached the flat east coast of Australia, which Banks likened to the rump of a scraggly red cow. After sailing up the coast Cook harbored his ship in a bay he named Botany Bay, after the many new types of plants Banks and Solander found there. (Botany Bay later became the site of a famous penal colony, a place where British subjects convicted of crimes were sent as a punishment. Sydney, the capital of modern Australia, is located there today.) Cook, Banks, and Solander tried to make contact with the inhabitants of Australia, but with little success. "All they seemed to want is for us to be gone," Cook wrote. But he did not share the low opinion of them held by most on board. "They may appear to some to be the most wretched people on earth, but in reality they are far happier than we Europeans. . . . They live in Tranquility which is not disturbed by the Inequality of Condition."

After leaving Botany Bay, Cook made his way through the Great Barrier Reef off the north coast of Australia, some of the most hazardous waters in the world. The passage demanded all his navigational skills. One night the *Endeavour*

struck a fang of coral and nearly sank, but luckily the fang broke off and partially plugged the hole. Even so, the ship would have sunk if one of the midshipmen hadn't suggested an old sailor's trick of using a sail to blanket the hole and slow the leak. The sail was lowered over the side on ropes until it covered the hole, then the ropes were tied all round the ship. This formed a kind of bandage for the hole. Now the leakage had slowed enough so that Cook could beach the ship to repair the damage. This took seven weeks, during which time the crew first saw kangaroos, a flying fox, and other animals unique to Australia. Cook described the kangaroo in his journal. "It was of a mouse colour, very slender and swift of foot. I should have taken it for a wild dog, but for its walking or running in which it jumped like a Hare or a dear. Excepting the head and ears which was something like a Hare's, it bears no sort of resemblance to any European Animal I ever saw. [One night] we din'd of the animal & thought it excellent." On August 20, 1771, Cook, Banks, and Solander raised the British flag on a small island off present-day Cape York and claimed all of eastern Australia for the British Empire. They called the territory "New South Wales."

Sailing through the East Indies and the Indian Ocean, Cook rounded Africa and made port in England nearly three years after setting out. He had circumnavigated the world. One of the most remarkable things about this voyage was the good health of the crew. Some of the men had died from a fever they caught when Cook docked at a Dutch port on the island of Java, but none of the crew had suffered from scurvy, the disease that killed hundreds of men on the voyages of Ferdinand Magellan, Vasco da Gama, and other early explorers. [See the articles on Magellan and da Gama in this book.] We now know that scurvy is caused by a lack of fresh fruits and vegetables containing vitamin C. Sailors on long sea voyages used to get the disease because they had nothing to eat but salted meat and dry biscuits. It was Cook's interest in science that saved his men. He had heard that some foods could prevent scurvy, so he had his men eat malt, sauerkraut and various kinds of sea grasses. In combination, these provided enough vitamin C to keep the crew healthy. He even experimented with a kind of instant broth he called "portable soup." (At about this time it was discovered that citrus fruits were the best cure for scurvy. Eventually the Royal Navy made sure that each crewman ate a lemon or lime every day. That is how British sailors got the nickname "limeys.") Cook also enforced strict rules of cleanliness aboard ship and provided fresh meat and vegetables for his crew whenever possible.

Cook hadn't found Terra Australis on this voyage, but he hadn't proved for sure that it didn't exist, either. So in 1772, only a few months after his return, the Navy sent him on a second voyage, this time to circumnavigate the globe in the far southern Antarctic latitudes—the last place left to look for the missing continent. If Terra Australis wasn't there, it could not be anywhere.

This was Cook's greatest and most dangerous exploration. It covered 70,000 miles and took more than three years. Cook's two ships, the *Resolution* and the *Adventure*, sailed down the west coast of Africa to Cape Town in South Africa. Two weeks later, still sailing south, they entered a sea filled with floating mountains of ice. Cook wrote in his log that this scene was wondrously beautiful, but he knew that it was deadly as well. All around were huge blue-white islands of ice in fantastic shapes like castles or cathedrals, each capable of crushing a wooden ship in a moment. The ships' sails and rigging became stiff with ice, and the sailors' hands were burned by the cold. Menaced by storms, heavy seas, and thick mist, the ships could not sail further south. Cook turned northeastward without reaching or seeing Antarctica itself. The two ships were separated in a dense fog but met again to pass the winter in New Zealand.

Over the next two years, Cook continued to circumnavigate Antarctica, exploring the southern Pacific and Atlantic during the winter months

Sailors from Cook's ship Resolution *chop ice to melt into drinking water. Fortunately for them, icebergs are made of fresh water, not salt water.*

An artist aboard Cook's ship drew this portrait of a Hawaiian man. Hawaiians prized garments made from the feathers of native birds.

home in 1775, Cook reported confidently that he had finally put an end to the notion of Terra Australis. In the process, he had sailed entirely around Antarctica, charted much of the South Atlantic and Pacific, and lost only four members of his 112-man crew—none of them to scurvy.

The Royal Navy had one more mystery for Cook to solve. In those days, the voyage from Europe to the Pacific was long and dangerous. Ships had to sail east around Africa and across the Indian Ocean, or west across the Atlantic, braving the treacherous Straits of Magellan at the southern end of South America. A shorter passage from the Atlantic to the Pacific had been sought for years. Most attempts were made by starting in the Atlantic and sailing northeast or northwest through the Arctic ice pack, but each try met with failure. [For more on the attempts to find a Northeast or Northwest Passage, see the articles on Barents, Frobisher, and Hudson in this book.] The Navy had offered Cook a safe job on land as a reward for his services, but instead of taking it, Cook volunteered to see if the Northwest Passage could be made from the other direction, from the Pacific to the Atlantic.

Cook proved that such a passage did not exist. (We now know that there is no passage at all through the Arctic that can be dependably traversed by sailing ships. Only modern icebreaking ships or nuclear submarines can navigate the Arctic ice pack.) Cook and his two ships, the *Resolution* and the *Discovery*, entered the Pacific in 1777 and reached the Hawaiian Islands. From there, they headed north to the Oregon coast, and up to the Bering Strait, the narrow channel of land between Siberia and Alaska. The strait is almost always hidden by a thick mist. But as Cook watched, the mist lifted for a few hours and he saw the continents of Asia and North America at the same moment.

But this voyage was to be Cook's last. The ships had been poorly fitted out at the Royal Navy dockyards and now they were falling apart. Cook was forced to anchor at Hawaii to make repairs. While the work was going on, a group of Hawaiian villagers stole some metal tools and one of Cook's rowboats. Cook went ashore to retrieve the goods. The villagers, angered by his strict insistence on getting back a pair of tongs, and hearing that another British search party had killed

and dipping down toward Antarctica during the summers. He discovered New Caledonia and charted Easter Island and the islands of Tonga in the Pacific, then saw other islands in the South Atlantic. Approaching the Antarctic coast in 1774, he made it further south than anyone had before, but was again stopped by the pack ice from reaching Antarctica itself. He was not entirely disappointed. "I who had Ambition not only to go Farther than any one had done before, but as far as it was possible for man to go, was not sorry at meeting this interruption, as it . . . shortened the dangers and hardships inseparable with the navigation of the Southern Polar Regions." Nowhere did he find the Great South Land. There *was* no mysterious continent in the southern hemisphere, except for Australia and New Zealand, and whatever land lay hidden beyond the barrier of ice and fog. Even taken together with South America and southern Africa, these lands were not enough to balance the land masses of the northern hemisphere. Returning

Bent on revenge after an argument over stolen goods, Hawaiian islanders killed Cook at Kealakekua Bay and ate parts of his body.

one of their chiefs, began to attack with spears and stones. Their woven war shields protected them against the sailors' guns, and Cook's men had to retreat to the beach. As Cook turned his back to help launch the boats, he was struck on the head by the villagers and then stabbed to death as he fell on his face in the surf. The Hawaiians dragged his body away. Later they returned his remains, and Cook was buried at sea with a ten-minute salute of guns.

As an explorer, navigator, and discoverer, Cook has few equals. Among English mariners, he is nearly as famous as Francis Drake [see the article on him in this book]. Cook's charts of the Pacific, the South Atlantic, and Antarctica clarified vast areas of the globe that had been the subject of rumors and legends for centuries. But he is best remembered for what he did not discover—the mythical Great South Land, and the Northwest Passage.

The Settlement of North America

Erik the Red, Leif Eriksson, and Freydis Eriksdottir

Erik the Red. Born Erik Thorvaldson circa 950 in Norway. Died circa 1010 in Brattalid, Eriksfiord (now Julianehåb), Greenland.

Leif Eriksson. Born circa 971 near Vatnshorn, Iceland. Died after 1010 in Greenland.

Freydis Eriksdottir. Born after 971 near Vatnshorn, Iceland. Died after 1010 in Greenland.

The land was the most beautiful the Vikings had ever seen. Their leader, Leif Eriksson, reached down to the grass and brought the dew to his mouth to taste its sweetness. There was plenty of rich pastureland for their cattle, and the rivers teemed with huge salmon. There were forests of hardwood trees, which were scarce and valuable in the cold Viking lands. Most amazing of all, there were wild grapes, which did not grow in any land that the Vikings had ever lived in. "Hereafter, we will have two tasks," Leif told his men. "Every day we will either gather grapes and cut vines, or cut timber to make a cargo for the ship. And I will give this land a name in keeping with its products—I will call it Vinland."

Vinland ("Wine Land"), which Leif Eriksson visited in about the year 1000, was probably located somewhere on the eastern coast of Canada. Four hundred and ninety-two years before the first voyage of Christopher Columbus, Leif and his crew became the first known Europeans to set foot in the New World. He was a member of an adventurous family that included his father, Erik the Red, who founded a Viking colony on the island of Greenland, and his sister Freydis, who was a leader of the first European settlement in America. Their exploits, as well as the adventures of an Icelandic trader named Thorfinn Karlsefni, are told in a series of *sagas*, or stories, written down by the Vikings a few generations later. Almost all we know of the Viking adventures in the New World comes from these sagas, which still make exciting reading today.

From about the ninth to the eleventh centuries, the waters of the North Atlantic were controlled by the Vikings, a fierce people who lived in Norway, Denmark, and neighboring lands. The Vikings (who are also called Norsemen) practiced farming and fishing and made long trading voyages, for they were skilled mariners; during the summers the more bold among them went out raiding for plunder and glory. There was hardly a settlement on the coasts of England, Ireland, Scotland, or France that had not been raided by the Vikings. They would suddenly appear in their swift longships, raze a village to the ground, steal its goods and animals, kill most of the inhabitants, and make slaves of the rest. Then they would sail away in search of another target. (The word *viking* means a pirate raid, and may come from an earlier word that meant "creek" or "bay," which is where the Vikings would hide before launching their attacks.)

Until the late tenth century, the Vikings were believers in an ancient pagan religion. (The names of four Viking gods and goddesses—Tew, Woden, Thor, and Frigga—survive in the names of weekdays Tuesday, Wednesday, Thursday, and Friday.) The Vikings despised Christians and liked to attack isolated monasteries and Christian religious communities because they were easy prey. Many Christians, especially those from Ireland, fled west to Iceland, hoping to stay one step ahead of their enemies. But in the year 870, the Vikings caught up with them. They killed, enslaved, or drove off all the Christians in Iceland, then settled the island themselves. Some of the surviving Christians headed further west to Greenland.

About the year 963, a Viking boy named Erik Thorvaldson came to Iceland along with his father Thorvald, who had been exiled from Norway for killing several men. Erik, who was nicknamed Erik the Red for his flaming red hair, grew up to be a forceful, ambitious, and ruthless man. Like many Icelanders of the time, he soon became involved in a blood feud, a series of revenge killings between two families. Iceland is a small island, and by the middle of the tenth century it was so thickly settled that there was not enough land to go around. Settlers were always coming into conflict over land rights and other legal matters, and then drawing their relatives and friends into the quarrels. The Viking code of honor demanded blood vengeance for any insult or injury. Sometimes a complaint could be settled peacefully by arbitration or fines, but more often it was settled by killing. There was so much killing that it was rare indeed for a man to die in his bed of old age.

Erik himself killed several men and in the year 980 was exiled from Iceland for three years. During his exile, Erik decided to raid the Irish Christians in Greenland. He did not even have to sail blind, for another Viking had already been out to Greenland some years before and returned with detailed instructions on how to get there.

The voyage was brief, for Greenland is only 175 miles from Iceland. (On a clear day it is even possible to see Greenland from the high peaks of western Iceland.) Erik sighted the barren east coast and then turned southward, looking for Christian settlements. These he never found, for there were no longer any Christians left in Greenland—they had all died or sailed away. But Erik did spot good grazing land on the southwestern tip of Greenland, better land than any he could hope to get in Iceland. He formed a new ambition: to start his own colony in Greenland.

When his three years of exile were up, Erik returned to Iceland and organized a colonizing expedition. It was at this time that he gave Greenland its name, hoping to lure colonists with images of a green and fertile country. (Weather in the North Atlantic was warmer in the tenth and eleventh centuries than it is today, and southern Greenland enjoyed a much milder climate then.) Twenty-five ships and some seven hundred Viking colonists set out from Iceland in the year 985. Only half of them finally made it to Greenland, the rest being wrecked or forced to turn back. Those who completed the voyage settled along the fiords (glacial inlets) near present-day Julianehåb.

A few months later, an Icelandic trader named Bjarni Herjolfsson arrived at the Greenland settlements. He told a tale that greatly interested Erik's son Leif, who was then about thirteen or fourteen years old. On the way to Greenland, Bjarni said, a storm had blown his ship far south of his course. He found himself in sight of forested lands. Historians generally agree that what he saw was the coast of Canada, or perhaps even northern New England. (Thus, Bjarni, not Christopher Columbus, is the first known European to have seen America.) But according to the sagas, Bjarni and his men did not land. Instead, they headed back north along the coast in hopes of finding Greenland. Only Bjarni's skill as a navigator got them through.

Bjarni's tale of a new land to the south inspired Leif Eriksson to mount an exploring voyage of his own a decade later. Probably Leif was looking to build his own reputation as a daring leader, perhaps in preparation for taking control of the Greenland colony after his father died or stepped down. Erik, on the other hand, seems to have had no intention of handing power over to his son or anybody else any time soon, and may have welcomed the chance to get Leif out of Greenland for a while. He helped Leif buy Bjarni's excellent ship. Sometime between the years 997 and 1000, Leif and his crew, sailing in Bjarni's ship, set off for the southern lands.

Although he could easily have sailed eastward across the Davis Strait to the southern tip of Baffin Island, and from there south along the coast of Labrador and Newfoundland without losing sight of land for more than a day or so, Leif decided instead to sail directly across the open sea, a much riskier course. He landed somewhere on the North American coast, perhaps as far south as New England, at the place he named Vinland. The exact site of the landing has never been determined and is a matter of heated debate among historians.

One point of argument is whether Leif really found grapes in Vinland. Nowadays, grapes do not grow as far north as Newfoundland, which is why some historians believe that he must have landed in Maine or Massachusetts, where they grow in abundance. But Leif may have meant berries instead of grapes, or it may be that in the warmer climate of the tenth century grapes did indeed grow in more northern regions.

In any case, the Vikings built a house and wintered in Vinland. In the spring, Leif and his men sailed back to Greenland with a cargo of timber, as well as valuable trade goods he picked up from a Norwegian ship wrecked off the Greenland coast. The journey brought him considerable prestige and earned him the nickname "Leif the Lucky." His father Erik attempted a voyage to Vinland two years later but was blown off course and barely made it back to Greenland.

In the year 1003, two Icelandic merchant ships arrived in Greenland, full of trade goods from Norway and carrying many new colonists. Heading this venture was a Viking named Thorfinn Karlsefni. He and Erik began to discuss where the newcomers should settle, since all of the best land in Greenland had already been claimed. They decided to start a new colony in Vinland. There was much enthusiasm for the trip, and most of the Icelanders decided to go along. Some of the Greenlanders decided to go along too, including

In this romantic painting by a 19th-century artist, Leif Eriksson and his Greenland followers come ashore on the rocky coast of Vinland.

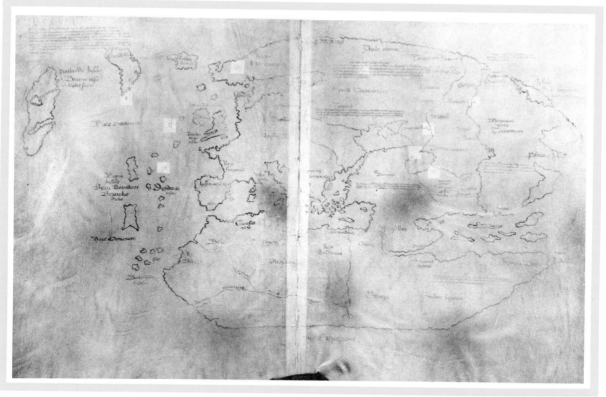

The Vinland Map is thought to have been drawn circa 1440 from lost Viking charts. If authentic, it is the earliest known map of the New World.

Leif's brother and sister Thorvald Eriksson and Freydis Eriksdottir.

Why didn't Leif, the boldest explorer among the Greenlanders, lead this expedition? As it happened, Leif himself was no longer interested in going back in Vinland—in fact, he refused to give the colonists precise directions on how to get there. He had a new conquest in mind. Leif had become a Christian a short time before, and was now the leader of a growing band of converts. Leif hoped to turn all the Greenlanders into Christians, but one person stood in his way: his father Erik, who held fast to the worship of Thor. The Greenlanders now split into two groups: Christians led by Leif, and pagans led by Erik. In spite of their quarrelsome habits, though, father and son managed to avoid a big battle over religion. After Erik's death about the year 1010, Greenland became a Christian country, as Leif wished.

Meanwhile, the colonists took four ships laden with goods and livestock and set out for Vinland in the spring of 1004. They spent some weeks sailing along the coasts of Labrador and Newfoundland without finding a place that looked like Leif's Vinland. Finally, some of the Greenlanders disembarked and set up a winter camp near the strait that separates Newfoundland from Labrador. Thorfinn, Thorvald, Freydis, and most of the Icelanders continued south to seek better land. They landed somewhere on the southwest coast of Newfoundland, where the Vikings built shelters and put their livestock out to graze.

A few days later the Vikings sighted a number of small skin boats coming into the bay. In the boats were people wearing furs and twirling long poles. The Vikings had trouble deciding whether the people were men or women. They had the bodies of men, but they were short in height, wore their hair long, and dressed in robes. The Vikings called them *skraelings*, or dwarves.

The people in the boats were most likely a hunting party of Dorsets, a people related to the

Eskimos. The tall Vikings, with their beards, helmets, and metal shields, must have looked as strange to them as they did to the Vikings. After staring for a while, the Dorsets paddled off. The Vikings did not see them again until the next spring, when a larger number of Dorset boats paddled up to the shore. This time the Dorsets had come to trade. At first the Dorsets wanted to exchange their furs for Viking weapons, but Thorfinn was no fool, and he convinced the Dorsets to accept cheese and yogurt instead.

Suddenly a bad-tempered bull that belonged to the Vikings came crashing in among the huts. The Dorsets panicked and tried to escape. Thorfinn, thinking the Dorsets had decided to attack, killed one of them who tried to take refuge in his hut. There were probably other killings too, and finally the Dorsets raced back to their boats and paddled away.

It was customary among the Vikings to avenge any defeat in battle, and they expected the Dorsets to do the same. The colonists built a stockade around the huts and set up an ambush for any

The remains of a Viking settlement were found at L'Anse aux Meadows, in Newfoundland, where archaeologists have reconstructed a sod house.

attackers. Three weeks later a great number of Dorset boats approached the shore. Thorfinn assumed that these were the same Dorsets seeking revenge, but they may well have been an entirely different group, interested only in trade. In any case, as soon as the boats landed, the Vikings launched their ambush. The Dorsets knew how to defend themselves, however, and their harpoons and bows and arrows proved better weapons than the Viking swords and axes. The sagas make mention of one especially frightening weapon the Dorsets used, a black, ball-shaped object that whizzed overhead and made a loud bang when it hit the ground. (Today we know that these were nothing more than inflated seal bladders attached to the Dorsets' harpoons.) Gradually the Dorsets drove the Vikings back against a cliff, leaving them no escape.

According to the sagas, as the Vikings retreated, Freydis, who was pregnant, came out of her hut and accused them of being cowards. "Why are you running?" she shouted. "I should have thought such brave men as you would slaughter them like cattle. If I had a weapon I could fight better than any of you!" Seeing a dead Viking man near her, she snatched up his sword, turned on the Dorsets, let fall her dress, and slapped her chest with the naked blade. Now it was the Dorsets' turn to be terrified. They ran back to their boats and put out to sea.

The Vikings were badly shaken by the attack. Vinland was plainly unsafe for Viking settlement. Thorfinn decided that it was time to pack up and leave, and after some further adventures, including one with a strange one-legged creature that shot arrows at them (it was probably a Beothuk Indian, a member of the other group of people who inhabited Newfoundland at the time), he and his followers returned to Greenland.

A group of Greenlanders stayed behind in Vinland for one more year, under the leadership of Freydis. One of the sagas tells how Freydis returned to Greenland and then organized a final voyage to Vinland, perhaps around the year 1007. This time the Vikings found the house built years ago by Leif Eriksson. Freydis claimed that Leif had given it to her. Two brothers named Helgi and Finnboggi arrived just before Freydis, and wanted to share the house and land with her. But the harsh-natured Freydis would have none of

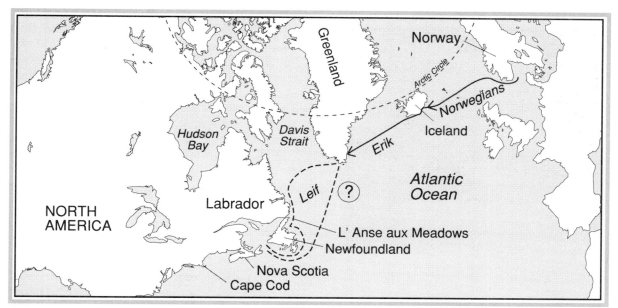

Viking lands

that. She tricked her husband into killing the brothers, and then she herself killed their wives with an axe.

This colony, like the others, did not last long. After a few years, Freydis sailed back to Greenland for the last time, and by the year 1015 there were no more Vikings in Vinland. When the weather turned colder in the thirteenth century, the colony in Greenland also began to fail. By the end of the 1400s, the Viking settlements in North America had been forgotten, except in the sagas. Later explorers of the New World, including Christopher Columbus, knew nothing of them, and they had no permanent impact on the history of the Americas. Not until the twentieth century, when archeologists discovered Viking remains in Newfoundland, were the Vinland sagas found to be more than tall tales.

Walter Raleigh

Walter Raleigh (RAW-lee or RAH-lee; also spelled Ralegh). Born 1554 in Hayes Barton, Devon, England. Died October 29, 1618, in London.

The Tower of London, the fortress on the edge of the Thames River, is not a particularly comfortable place in which to write a book. But behind its damp stone walls, Sir Walter Raleigh was hard at work on his *History of the World.* He had a been a prisoner in the Tower for thirteen years, since the year 1603, when he had been convicted on charges of conspiring against King James. Under James's predecessor, Queen Elizabeth, Raleigh had been a high-placed courtier, the sponsor of England's first colony in the New World, the explorer who had gone to South America in search of El Dorado, the soldier who had led attacks against Spanish cities. Now he could go roaming only in the world of his imagination.

Sir Walter Raleigh

Raleigh came from a prominent family in the seagirt West Country region of England. By the age of fifteen he was already a soldier, fighting with the Huguenots (French Protestants) against the Catholic army of France. Ten years later, after studying law and skippering a ship in the privateer fleet of his older half-brother, Sir Humfry Gilbert, he went to Ireland as captain of a company of foot soldiers to help put down, with great ruthlessness, an uprising in the province of Munster. On his return he was bold enough to recommend to the queen a change of policy with regard to Ireland: Instead of trying to conquer all the Irish chieftains, which would mean a long and costly campaign, England should support the lesser chieftains against the higher ones, whom they much resented.

The queen, who always appreciated intellect, wit, and charm, was impressed by this young captain. She installed Raleigh as a regular member of her court, in the role of her confidant and advisor, and helped him make his fortune by awarding him huge grants of land, as well as control of income-producing items such as wine licenses, broadcloth exports, and Cornish tin. With the profit from these lands and offices, Raleigh set out to do something that many Elizabethans had dreamed of but none had yet accomplished—to start an English colony in North America. He began by taking over a charter that the queen had granted to Sir Humfry Gilbert to search out new lands and establish settlements of English people there under his governorship. The queen promised that these settlers and their descendants would have the same rights as any subject of the English crown. Sir Humfry had died in 1583 in an attempt to plant a colony along the Penobscot River in what is now Maine. Raleigh renewed the charter in his own name and made plans to put a colony on the North American coast much further south.

First, Raleigh sent out a small scouting expedition, which cruised up the coast from Florida and landed in what is now North Carolina. The Algonkian Indians who befriended the expedition called the place Windgancon. It was, the scouts reported to Raleigh, a beautiful place, with abundant wild game, a temperate climate, and a long growing season that produced good crops; the soil, they added, was "the most plentifull, sweete, fruitfull and wholesome of all the world." Raleigh called the area Virginia, in honor of Elizabeth, who was known as the Virgin Queen, and made plans to send over a group of settlers. That would cost a lot of money, so he sent out a crew of privateers, which captured French and Dutch ships and took their cargoes.

Since Elizabeth refused to let Raleigh lead the expedition himself, it sailed in April 1585 with his kinsman Sir Richard Grenville in command. There were 108 colonists, all of them men. Among them were a scientist, Thomas Hariot, whose job was to describe the inhabitants and the natural resources of the area, and an artist, John White, who was to provide illustrations for Hariot's reports. Thus Raleigh started a tradition among English exploring and colonizing expeditions of helping to increase scientific knowledge. (Hariot later drew the first known map of the moon.)

Set ashore by Grenville on Roanoke Island, the colonists built a fort and began to explore the area. But their tiny settlement lasted for only one year. Though they depended on the Algonkians for most of their food, they managed to provoke the Indians' resentment, in part by failing to keep their cows and pigs out of the tribe's cornfields. There was a battle, and the tribe's chief was killed. When the great privateer Sir Francis Drake stopped off at the colony on his way back from raiding Spanish towns in the West Indies, the starving Englishmen jumped at the chance to go home with him. [For more about Drake's exploits, see the article on him in this book.] A few weeks later, Sir Richard Grenville arrived. Finding the colonists gone, he sailed back to England, leaving eighteen of his men behind to maintain the English claim.

Raleigh lost no time in organizing a second expedition. This time his group of settlers included fourteen farm families, among whom were two pregnant women. They sailed for North America in April 1587, intending to start a new colony in a better location, on the islands in Chesapeake Bay. But the expedition's captain, eager to go privateering, insisted on putting them ashore on Roanoke. In the ruins of the fort, they found the bones of Grenville's men, who had been ambushed and killed.

Without help from the Indians, the colony could not thrive. Its supplies quickly began to run low. The governor, John White, sailed home to get what they needed. (White had been the artist with the first Roanoke group. He had also been part of Martin Frobisher's expedition in 1577, and he painted the Eskimo mother and child whom Frobisher brought back from Canada. See the article on Frobisher in this book.) The first relief expedition that Raleigh tried to send was ordered to stay home and help defend England against the Spanish Armada. The second relief expedition failed because its captain picked a fight with two French warships and lost. Finally White was able to make the journey aboard a privateer. He arrived at Roanoke in August 1590

But the settlement was deserted. White could find no sign of the settlers except for the word CROATOAN carved on a post. This signified to White that the colonists had gone to Croatoan Island under the protection of its chieftain, Manteo, who had twice visited England with Raleigh's earlier expeditions and who had been the colonists' guide and interpreter. But the privateer captain refused to stay and look for them. White had no choice but to leave his own daughter and

In this drawing by expedition artist John White, ships carrying Raleigh's colonists approach the Hatteras sandbar and Roanoke Island behind it.

granddaughter and one hundred other colonists somewhere in the wilderness. Possibly they were killed by the Powhatan tribe, but they may have joined Manteo's tribe and moved with them to the interior of what is now North Carolina. There is a tribe there whose language is said to include words of Elizabethan English and whose children sometimes have fair hair.

That was Raleigh's last attempt to found a North American colony, though over the years he sent out several ships to look for the lost settlers. He had spent the enormous sum of £40,000 and had little to show for it except for some potato plants that Hariot had brought back, along with other botanical specimens. These plants are thought to have ended up on Raleigh's estates in Ireland, and to have spread from there to the rest of the country, where they quickly became the main source of food. (Raleigh was thus indirectly responsible for the mass emigration of the Irish to the United States in the 1840s, when the potato crop failed.) Raleigh also popularized another plant from the New World, tobacco, which he

Another drawing by White shows the Indian village of Secotan, with its cornfields, gardens, hunting grounds, and ceremonial dance circle.

smoked in a silver pipe. Within a few years nearly all the men at court were imitating him and had become addicted to tobacco.

By now, Raleigh had been knighted and held the important posts of master of horse and captain of the queen's guard. He had been instrumental in preparing England's defense against the Armada and had contributed much of his own fortune to do it. He was a man of accomplishments: a poet, a shipbuilder, a musician, a businessman. He never hesitated to display his scorn for old-fashioned ways of thinking and behaving. His rivals at court were jealous of his elegant clothes and of the attention the queen paid him. But his days of enjoying Elizabeth's favor had reached their end. She was furious to learn that Raleigh had secretly married one of her ladies-in-waiting, Elizabeth Throckmorton, and punished them both with a month's imprisonment after their first child was born.

Exiled from court, and hoping to impress the queen once more, Raleigh decided to venture far away "to seek new worlds, for gold, for praise, for glory," as he wrote in one of his poems. In 1595 he set off from Plymouth, England, at the head of an expedition of one hundred men. Their goal was to find El Dorado, the fabled city of gold, which was rumored to be in the mountains of Guyana, in South America. [The tale of El Dorado had gotten its start during the conquest of Peru by Francisco Pizarro. See the article on Pizarro in this book.] Raleigh was sailing directly into enemy territory, for the whole region was held by Spain. On his way, he had the good fortune to capture Hernando de Berrio, a conquistador who had spent years looking for the same city. The expedition sailed up the Orinoco River until it was stopped by impassable cataracts. [See the article on Alexander von Humboldt in this book for the story of how the dangerous Orinoco was finally explored.]

The following year, Raleigh took part in a naval and military attack on the Spanish city of Cádiz. Its purpose was to weaken the Spanish in their ongoing rivalry with England for control of the seas, and particularly to punish Spain for an incident in 1591 in which Sir Richard Grenville, in the ship *Revenge*, had singlehandedly held off a fleet of Spanish galleons while five English ships made their escape, at the cost of the *Revenge*, its crew, and his own life. More than a hundred ships took part in the surprise attack. Raleigh himself, in command of one of the fleet's five squadrons, set the strategy and led the assault that broke through the city's naval defenses. The people of Cádiz set fire to thirty-six of their own merchant vessels, together with all their cargoes, to keep them out of English hands.

The sack of Cádiz succeeded in undermining Spain's reputation and devastating its finances, and Raleigh was partly restored to Elizabeth's good graces. He was permitted to serve in the summer of 1597 as a squadron commander under the Earl of Essex, his replacement as the queen's favorite, in an expedition to destroy the Spanish warships that King Philip was planning to send against England. Instead, Essex led them to the Azores islands, in the Atlantic, in a vain attempt to intercept the Spanish treasure fleet as it sailed home from the West Indies laden with gold. Ra-

leigh distinguished himself by capturing a fort and by walking across a battlefield unarmed, in a display of courage that won him much renown. The queen rewarded him by appointing him governor of the island of Jersey, in the English Channel, in 1600.

Three years later, Elizabeth was dead, leaving no heir, and James Stuart became king. James and Raleigh had never had much fondness for each other. They differed over the issue of Spain: James was ready to make peace with England's old enemy, but Raleigh was not. Besides, Raleigh had been the beneficiary of the estates taken from a Catholic gentleman who had conspired to assassinate Elizabeth and replace her with James's mother, Mary, Queen of Scots. Raleigh was now accused of conspiring against James, and despite his spirited defense, he was convicted and sentenced to be beheaded. Just before the axe fell,

Chipping away at Spain's naval might, Raleigh leads a fleet of English warships (foreground) in a raid on the Spanish harbor of Cádiz in 1596.

the king commuted the sentence to imprisonment in the Tower. Raleigh's lands and his manor were given away to others. And in the Tower he stayed as the years went by, writing his history of the world from Adam and Eve forward, working on his poetry, and receiving visits from princes and ambassadors. He did scientific experiments in a little laboratory that had once been a henhouse. "Only my father would keep such a bird in a cage," the king's son said in scorn.

There was still one opportunity left for Raleigh to gain his freedom. In 1616 he was allowed to gather an expedition to return to Guyana in search of gold, with the hope of enriching King James and winning his pardon. But by the time they reached Trinidad, Raleigh and most of his men were ill with fever. A landing party went up the Orinoco, but instead of gold, it met disaster. Berrio, the Spanish conquistador whom Raleigh had captured and freed on his first visit, had built a fort on the Orinoco that blocked the group's way. There was a fight in which Raleigh's son Walter was killed. The Spanish ambassador, angry at this incursion into Spanish territory, demanded Raleigh's execution, and James agreed.

Raleigh was described by an Elizabethan writer as "fortune's tennis-ball," raised up to great heights and thrown down again. None of his attempts at New World colonization succeeded. El Dorado was never found and the Roanoke colony disappeared into thin air. But his fascination with the New World was contagious, and by trying and failing he opened the way for others who would, in time, build a world-shaping empire.

Pocahontas

Pocahontas (po-ka-HON-tas). Tribal name Matowaka; married name Rebecca Rolfe. Born circa 1595 in present-day Virginia. Died March 21, 1617, in Gravesend, Kent, England.

At the village of Werowocómoco, in the long-house of the great Algonkian chieftain Powhatan, a debate was under way. Two hundred people had crowded inside to hear their leaders decide the fate of the stranger who stood before them. He was one of the group of light-skinned men who had come in a ship a few months before and built a fort on an island in the river, right on a prime piece of hunting ground. These men wore bizarre clothing and spoke an unknown language. They would frequently come to nearby settlements and ask to buy corn, using gestures and a few words of Algonkian. It was obvious that they knew hardly anything about growing and catching their own food. But they were not entirely laughable, for they had dangerous weapons, black sticks that spat fire a long distance.

Powhatan presiding over a council in his longhouse (detail from John Smith's Map of Virginia)

Now this man had been caught in the woods. He was probably spying. And yet he was clearly a person of importance. What should be done with him?

Powhatan, dressed in a robe of raccoon fur, strands of pearls around his neck, sat on a raised seat in front of a hearthfire, listening to the arguments of one speaker after another. Many agreed with his brother Opechancanough, the head of the Pamunkey tribe, who said that they should kill the spy and then wipe out the tiny colony. This Englishman, who called himself John Smith, was clearly lying when he said that his group was simply taking refuge for a little while to recover from a sea fight with a Spanish ship. Powhatan suggested that caution might be the wisest course for the time being. If these Englishmen wanted to keep their little fort, perhaps it would be best to let them have it. There was still plenty of land for Powhatan's people, hundreds of miles of land, especially since he and his father had conquered the local tribes and made them part of the vast union called the Powhatan Confederacy. But Opechancanough was still wary. Why had the English come here, if not to take this land away from the people, as the Spanish had done in Florida? Why not get rid of them now, when they were still few and weak?

Powhatan made his decision. At his signal, a group of warriors dragged the prisoner over to a pair of huge stones and forced him to kneel. They raised their rock-studded wooden clubs over his head. It was clear from the look in his eyes that he expected to be killed, but he did not flinch or cry out. He plainly had courage; he was in command of himself even in the face of death. That was as it should be. That was just the manner in which Algonkian warriors hoped to meet their own deaths.

Out of the crowd, from somewhere near Powhatan's seat, a girl ran forward and threw herself down on top of the prisoner. The executioners stopped themselves from clubbing her just in the nick of time. They recognized Powhatan's daughter Matowaka. She was young in years, but old enough to be counted among the women rather than the children. Women among the Algonkians had the right to adopt captured prisoners if they wished. Of course, it was unusual for them to adopt pale-skinned foreigners. But Powhatan

At a festival held in Jamestown, the survivors of Virginia's Pamunkey tribe reenacted the rescue of John Smith by the young Pocahontas.

gave another signal, and the executioners put down their clubs. Before they sent Smith back to his fort, Powhatan and his warriors held a ceremony in which they made him part of the tribe and gave him an Algonkian name.

The tale of John Smith's rescue by Matowaka— who became known to the English colonists as Pocahontas—is a famous one, and hundreds of poems, plays, and stories have been written about it. Yet no one can say for sure exactly what happened to the captain at Werowocómoco. In his book *A Generall Historie of Virginia*, published in sixteen years later, in 1624, he wrote that he was captured, brought before Powhatan, condemned to death, and saved from execution at the last moment by Pocahontas, who protected him with her own body. [For Smith's version of these events, and for more information about the English colony at Jamestown, Virginia, see the article about him in this book.] Some historians suspect that Smith invented the whole incident. Anthropologists who have studied the customs of the Algonkian tribes say that Smith may very well have been telling the truth, but that he probably did not understand the meaning of what had happened. They suggest various possibilities. Perhaps Powhatan really did intend to execute Smith, and Pocahontas saved him by exercising her right to adopt him as a war captive. Or perhaps Powhatan arranged for Smith to undergo a traditional death-and-rebirth ceremony so that he could be tested for courage before being adopted into the tribe with Pocahontas as his sponsor. It is certain that from that time on, Pocahontas watched over the captain's welfare. She came often to visit him, gave him and his fellow colonists gifts of food when they were starving, and warned him of danger.

Pocahontas was about thirteen years old in January of 1608, when Captain Smith met Powhatan. (Powhatan was the name of the federation of thirty tribes ruled over by Pocahontas's father. The chief's own name was actually Wahunsonacock, but he was known to the English by the name of his people.) She was the favorite of the many children who had been born to Powhatan by several wives, and she had spent most of her childhood at Werowocómoco, her father's village on the banks of the Pamunkey River. She did not have to work as hard as other girls in her tribe, and wherever she went, she was attended by servants. Both of her names, Matowaka and Pocahontas, come from words meaning "playful" and "frisky." When visiting Jamestown, she used to round up the younger boys and turn cartwheels with them all over the fort. But when she was not playing, she carried herself with the majesty and pride that was proper for the daughter of a king, and she took very seriously her responsibility toward the man she had sponsored for adoption.

The winter of 1608 was full of suffering for the Jamestown colonists. Sickness had already killed half of them. Then a fire burned down their shelters and their storehouses of food. All the colonists would have died if Pocahontas and her servants had not brought frequent supplies of deer meat, turkey meat, cornmeal, and bread to feed them. "She next under God," wrote Smith later, "was still the instrument to preserve this colony from death, famine and utter confusion." On several occasions she served as her father's ambassador. When seven of Powhatan's warriors were captured at Jamestown and accused of plotting to kill the colonists, he sent Pocahontas to negotiate with Smith for their release. In October, when

Smith and a group of his men came to Werowocómoco only to find Powhatan away, they were given a warm welcome by Pocahontas, and were present when she led a dance ceremony in celebration of the autumn harvest.

But Powhatan's patience was on the wane. The arrival of more settlers at Jamestown convinced the chief and his counselors that Opechancanough was right—the English had come not merely to trade with them, but to take possession of their lands. His son Namontack, half-brother of Pocahontas, had gone to visit England as a passenger in one of the colony's supply ships and had come back with the news that the settlers' home country was wealthy and well-populated. These colonists at Jamestown were only the beginning; many more would be coming.

One day in the winter of 1609, Smith and a party of men arrived at Werowocómoco for a meeting with Powhatan. They found the village empty. Without telling them, Powhatan had moved his headquarters to another village thirty miles farther up the river. It was too late for the Englishmen to go home, so they settled down to sleep in Powhatan's deserted longhouse. They were awakened in the dead of night by the arrival of Pocahontas, who had run thirty miles through the forest in the darkness to tell them that they were in danger. Powhatan had ordered a group of warriors to take them by surprise in the morning and kill them. She brought this warning at great risk to herself, for if her father discovered that she had betrayed him, she would have been executed. Not long after this, she prevented her father's warriors from killing another colonist who was traveling through the woods with a message for Smith.

Yet Smith sailed back to England in September 1609 without telling Pocahontas that he was going. The new leaders of Jamestown allowed her to think that he was dead. This was a mistake, for the close relationship between the captain and the chief's daughter was the only thing that had enabled the colony to survive. Pocahontas never came to Jamestown again, and without her gifts of food, the colonists, still unable to provide for themselves, starved to death by the hundreds. The few who were left abandoned the colony in June, and only the sudden arrival of new colonists from England saved Jamestown from disappearing forever. Powhatan ordered his people to stop trading with the English. The English retaliated by raiding the Indians' villages. The two sides were soon in a state of war.

For some years the colonists heard little about the young woman who had been their benefactor. She was rumored to have married a warrior named Kocoum. According to another rumor, she had been sent by her father on trading missions to distant tribes. Some people thought that she must be hiding from the anger of her father because she had been disloyal, others that she had gone away so that she did not have to witness the constant killing.

In March 1613, a Jamestown captain sailed up the Potomac River to buy corn from the Patawamake tribe. The Patawamake lived deep in the interior, so far from Powhatan's headquarters that they could disobey the great chief's order against trade. The Englishman was excited to discover that Pocahontas was living secretly among the Patawamake. Bribing the chief, he tricked Pocahontas into visiting his ship, seized her, and took her as a captive to Jamestown. A ransom message was sent to Powhatan, demanding a large quantity of corn as the price for the release of his daughter, along with the return of English prisoners and of tools and weapons stolen from the colony.

For a long time there was no word from Powhatan. Pocahontas stayed at the colony, not in prison but in the house of a minister. Her conversion to Christianity became the special project of Jamestown's governor. Within a few months she had become the colony's first convert and had been given the biblical name Rebecca. When at last she accompanied the governor up the river to collect the ransom from Powhatan, she refused to speak to the Algonkians, and Powhatan, after agreeing to the ransom terms, instructed the English to keep his daughter. The two leaders then made a peace agreement, called the Peace of Pocahontas. It lasted five years.

A little more than a year after her capture, Pocahontas married an English widower, John Rolfe, and went to live at his plantation on the James River. In 1615 she gave birth to a boy. John Rolfe was the man who finally made the Virginia colony an economic success, after nearly a decade of starvation and misery. He did it by growing tobacco, a New World plant that had been introduced to Europe by the Spanish colonizers of America and that had been popularized in England by Sir Walter Raleigh. [See the article about Raleigh in this book.]

Smoking tobacco had long been a part of Native American religious ceremonies, as a way of offering thanks to the gods. In Europe, tobacco was smoked for pleasure, and people quickly became addicted to it, since it is a powerful drug. King James of England, for whom Jamestown was named, hated tobacco and was reluctant to permit the Virginians to grow it. But there appeared to be no other way for the colony to pay for itself. Although native North American tobacco was harsh and bitter, John Rolfe had found a way to grow the same fragrant species of tobacco that the Spanish were growing in the West Indies. Eventually the English government gave the Virginians a monopoly on tobacco—that is, it refused to allow the Spanish to sell their tobacco in England, so that Virginia's tobacco would have no competition—and the Jamestown colony flourished at last.

But in 1616, it looked as though the Virginia Company—the group of stockholders that had provided the money to establish the colony—was going to collapse. The company desperately needed some good publicity that would encourage more English people to invest their money in the colony. The marriage of an Indian princess to an English gentleman was a fascinating piece of news in England. The company decided to bring Mistress Rebecca Rolfe and her family across the sea. A number of Algonkian servants went with them, as did Pocahontas's sister Matachanna, who took care of little Thomas Rolfe, and her uncle Uttamatamakin, who went as an ambassador from Chief Powhatan. They arrived in London in June 1616.

Copper-skinned people from America had been seen before in England. [See the article in this book on Tisquantum, the Patuxet Indian who was kidnapped from the coast of Maine in 1605 and afterwards saved the Pilgrims from starvation.] But Pocahontas's royal bearing commanded everyone's attention. She was soon one of the most celebrated people in London. She had her portrait painted, was invited to plays and dances, and was sought out by courtiers and noblemen. The king and queen received her many times at Whitehall

An unknown artist painted this portrait of Pocahontas in 1616 during her visit to England, when she was about twenty-one years old.

Pocahontas is known to have had a pair of shell-and-silver earrings like those in this portrait, but her son was a baby when she died.

Palace, and when the royal court gathered on Twelfth Night, 1617, to see a masque written by the famous playwright Ben Jonson, Pocahontas sat at the king's right hand.

But London was not a healthy place to be, especially for people who were used to breathing clean air. Garbage and waste from the city's thousands of human and animal inhabitants sent up foul-smelling fumes and helped spread disease. By the winter of 1617, most of the Algonkian visitors were sick, including Pocahontas, her sister, and her son, who were taken to a house in the countryside to get well. There Pocahontas received an unexpected visit from Captain John Smith, who was still very much alive and very busy trying to arrange another trip to America. For the space of two or three hours she would say nothing to him, and when she did speak, she said: "They did tell us always you were dead, and I knew no other till I came to Plymouth; yet Powhatan did command Uttamatamakin to seek you, and know the truth, because your countrymen will lie much."

In the early spring, the Rolfe family boarded ship to return to Virginia. Part way down the Thames River, at the town of Gravesend, the captain stopped to have Pocahontas carried ashore. She was too ill, probably with tuberculosis, to go any farther. Neither the leeching and purging treatments of the physicians nor the healing ceremonies performed by Uttamatamakin had any effect. Pocahontas died at Gravesend and was buried in the local church. She was then about twenty-two years old.

When the ship reached Plymouth, in the west of England, it stopped once more. Pocahontas's two-year-old son Thomas was too weak from illness to make the journey across the Atlantic. He was given into the care of relatives, who raised him in England. When he was in his early twenties, he came to Jamestown and became a lieutenant in the colony's militia.

John Rolfe went back to Virginia and married a third time. He and his new family barely escaped the massacre of March 1622, in which the tribes of the Powhatan Confederacy made an attack on the English settlers, killing more than three hundred. Opechancanough's views had finally prevailed over those of his brother Powhatan. But despite these losses, and the loss of five hundred more colonists from hunger and disease in the course of the following year, the English did not give up their hold on Virginia. After the massacre, which ended the Peace of Pocahontas, the English launched a war of extermination against the Powhatan Confederacy. By 1646 the few remaining members of the tribes of coastal Virginia had been confined to a region in the north, the first Indian "reservation." By the end of the century, the tribes were extinct. Yet today there are thousands of Virginians who, through her son, are descended from Pocahontas.

John Smith

John Smith. Born January 1580, in Willoughby, Lincolnshire, England. Died June 1631 in London.

The winter of 1607–1608 was the coldest winter in memory—the Great Frost, people called it. The English settlers in the fort at Jamestown, in the country they called Virginia, were living miserably in ramshackle wooden huts that barely kept out the cold. They had nothing to eat but the dried corn they bought from the Algonkian Indian tribes who lived in the area. Half the colonists had already died from disease since the group's arrival in the spring of 1607. Every day there was talk of giving up the whole venture and going home.

Captain John Smith was determined they should stay. He made trip after trip up the nearby rivers to explore the area and to bargain for food, using the few words of the Algonkian language he had learned. A veteran of two wars, during which he had been captured and enslaved, he knew how to survive. His motto was, "To overcome is to live."

In the middle of December, 1607, Smith sailed up the Chickahominy River and went ashore in the company of an Algonkian guide, leaving his men to guard the boat. The two had not gone far when they heard from behind the cries of men under attack, and found themselves dodging arrows. Smith, holding his guide before him as a shield, fired back with his pistol as a crowd of warriors surrounded him. He began to inch backwards towards the shore. The next thing he knew,

he and his hostage had fallen into a frozen creek. The Algonkians pulled them out.

Over the next few weeks, the prisoner—the only one of the exploring party left alive—was led from one village to another. Sometimes Algonkian shamans came in and performed ceremonies in his presence. He was allowed to send a written message to Jamestown, the first example of writing that his captors had ever seen. Finally he was taken to the village of Werowocómoco on the James River, to be questioned by Powhatan, the chief of the Powhatan tribe and the supreme chief

John Smith (detail from his map of New England)

of an alliance of thirty Algonkian tribes that he and his people had conquered.

In Powhatan's longhouse, two hundred warriors and numerous chiefs, male and female, had assembled to discuss what they should do about the prisoner and his fellow colonists. In reply to Powhatan's questions, Smith said truthfully that the English had come in search of a water route to the Pacific Ocean. He also said, untruthfully, that the colonists planned to leave as soon as their ship came back for them. In fact, the Virginia Company of London, which had financed the colony, had received permission from the King of England to make permanent settlements in America. Once the English were well established, they planned to expand throughout most of the continent, just as the Spanish had done further south.

A decision was made. The prisoner was hauled over to a pair of huge stones, and his head was forced down on them. Powhatan's warriors raised their clubs and prepared to kill him. At the last moment, the king's daughter, Pocahontas, ran forward and laid her own head on the prisoner's.

There are some historians who think that Smith told many lies about his life and that the story of his near-execution was one of them. Other historians think that it did happen, and that Pocahontas was following Algonkian tradition by adopting a war prisoner into the tribe. [To read more about that idea, and about the lives of Pocahontas and her father, see the article about her in this book.] If it is true, it was only the most famous of Captain Smith's many narrow escapes.

Smith was the son of a prosperous farmer from Lincolnshire. He was born eight years before the Battle of the Armada, and as a child he heard all about the deeds of such adventurers as Francis Drake and Walter Raleigh. [See the articles about them in this book.] At the age of fifteen he left school to be apprenticed to a merchant, but after the death of his father he struck out on his own. He may have gone to Holland, like many young Englishmen of the time, to serve as a soldier in the Dutch rebellion against Spain. It is known that he accompanied the sons of a local nobleman on a journey through Europe and survived a shipwreck on his way home. He spent the next year reading books about the art of war and learning the art of horsemanship from an Italian riding master.

The place for an aspiring soldier to go in 1600 was Hungary, which was being torn apart by a three-way conflict between the Holy Roman Empire, the Turkish Empire, and the native Magyars, Wallachians, and Transylvanians. Smith set off, but on the way he was robbed of all his money. He took ship for Italy with a crowd of Catholic pilgrims headed for Rome, but a storm came up and the superstitious pilgrims threw him overboard. The ship that rescued him turned out to belong to a privateer (a captain who captures and raids other ships). Smith joined his crew long enough to qualify for a share of their booty, and then he made his way at long last to the city of Graz, in Austria, where he joined the Hungarian army. [Among the refugees who had to leave Graz because of the war was the astronomer Johannes Kepler. See the article about Kepler in this book.]

Smith fought in many battles and quickly earned a name for himself as an expert in fireworks and explosives. He showed his officers how to use flares as signals, how to frighten horses with fire, and how to catapult small bombs filled with gunpowder and musket balls over high stone walls. With his help, the army captured a town that had been held by the Turks for fifty years. A little later, the army attacked a city that was held by a gang of bandits. Their leader issued a challenge to single combat—a battle to the death between two champions from the opposing armies. Smith, who liked to think of himself as a medieval knight, accepted the challenge. In short order, he killed the bandit chief and two of his men and cut off their heads. Prince Sigismund Bathory, the prince of Transylvania, rewarded him with a gift of money and a coat of arms showing three Turks' heads on a shield.

Smith's last battle in this war took place at the fortress of Rotenthurn, where eleven thousand Christian Hungarians met thirty thousand Muslim Tatars in a general slaughter. The victorious Tatars found Smith lying wounded among the dead bodies, took him prisoner, and sold him to a Turkish nobleman as a slave. He was lucky, for many wounded prisoners were simply killed on the spot. Passing through several masters on a long journey eastward, he eventually arrived in a castle in Tartary (a region north of the Caucasus Mountains that later became part of Russia). An iron ring was riveted around his neck, and he was set to work threshing grain alongside many other slaves, both Christian and Muslim. One day, after his owner beat him, he killed the man and escaped on a stolen horse. He made his way home through Europe, across some two thousand miles of foreign territory. He was twenty-four when he reached England towards the end of 1604.

The Virginia Company, at this time, was making arrangements to send a group of colonists to the part of the New World claimed by England. The Spanish had been actively colonizing South America for several decades, to their great profit, and the French had fur-trapping outposts in a large area of eastern Canada. The English wanted their own share of New World's rich natural resources. They also wanted to find a water route that would allow them to reach the East Indies by going west. And, like the Spanish and the French, they were eager to convert the inhabitants of America to Christianity, which they all believed was the one true religion (though the Spanish and French were Catholics and the English were Protestants).

The first attempts to plant an English colony in America had been made by Walter Raleigh, who had spent an enormous amount of his own money without success. The Virginia Company was now ready to try. It was led by powerful noblemen who persuaded King James to give his permission for the attempt. To raise the money that was needed for ships and supplies, they formed a joint stock company to collect money from investors. Anyone who contributed money would receive a share of the profits from the colony. The colonists would have a council of leaders who would make the day-to-day decisions. There would also be a Royal Council, back in London, which would issue general instructions.

Three ships left England in February 1607 with the first group of settlers, numbering about one hundred. Their leaders included one captain who had sailed with Drake, another who had discovered Cape Cod five years earlier on an expedition financed by Raleigh, and Captain John Smith. For the first six weeks of the journey, they did nothing but ride at anchor off the coast of England, waiting for the wind to change, while the crew and passengers got sicker and hungrier every day. Finally, on May 14, they arrived at their destination in Chesapeake Bay, Virginia. They chose for the site of their fort an island in a river. Both the fort and the river they named after King James.

As it turned out, the settlers of Jamestown were not at all prepared for the harshness of life in their new home. Many of them were well-born gentlemen who refused to do any hard work. Many others were men of bad character who were not wanted in England. The leaders constantly quarreled among themselves. There was no sense of community, and since everything the settlers did was for the benefit of the company, not for their own benefit, they could see no reason to do their best.

By the time autumn arrived, the settlers who had survived the epidemic of typhoid and malaria were living in rotting tents, with nothing to eat but a little fish and a handful of boiled grain every day. It was not long before the resourceful Captain Smith began to take charge. His expeditions up the rivers to buy food from the Algonkians kept the colonists alive.

It was on one of these trips that he was caught and brought before Powhatan for judgment. On his return to Jamestown, where only thirty-eight settlers were still left alive, he was put on trial for losing his men in the Algonkian attack, and came close to being hanged. A few days later, the fort caught fire and burned to the ground. In the freezing weather, many of the settlers died of exposure. Every one of them would probably have died if Smith had not come under the protection of Powhatan's daughter Pocahontas. Over the next two years, she kept the colonists from starvation by bringing gifts of food, and helped prevent acts of violence between her people and the foreigners. Smith himself nearly died after being stung by a stingray while he was fishing.

From June to September of 1608, Smith was away from Jamestown on a series of long explorations up all the rivers connected with Chesapeake Bay, noting the natural resources and making contact with the inhabitants. The result was a map of Virginia that was published in England some time later. The map was so well drawn and so full of detail that it continued in use for many years. It was used to fix the boundaries of the neighboring colony of Maryland, and in the eighteenth century it was the basis for the surveying of the Mason-Dixon line, which divided Pennsylvania from Maryland and the free states of the

The famous map Smith drew for his Generall History of Virginia *was based on his explorations up the rivers of Chesapeake Bay.*

North from the slaveholding states of the South.

By the summer of 1608, most of the colony's original leaders had either died of illness, been shot for mutiny, or gone back to England. The only one left was Smith, who became the president in September. He put all his effort into forming the settlers into a disciplined community, like the regiment of an army. He enlarged the fort and drilled the men in the use of their guns. Every man had to do his share of the labor. "He that will not work shall not eat," Smith ordered. Anyone who used foul language got a can of cold water poured down his sleeve. Smith also made demands on the Algonkians, driving hard bargains for corn even though they had little to spare and needed to feed their own families. By this time, he had learned to speak the Algonkian language and no longer needed an interpreter.

Life in Jamestown was usually miserable. But Smith liked the New World much better than the Old. In Virginia, where energy and determination meant more than wealth or family connections, a farmer's son like John Smith could be a man of importance. He would gladly have stayed there forever, but in September 1609 he hurt his leg when a bag of gunpowder exploded, and a few weeks later he sailed back to England. Deprived of his leadership, the colony foundered and nearly collapsed. [See the article on Pocahontas for more about this.] Yet when he reached London, the Virginia Company accused him of mismanaging their affairs, and refused to pay him.

It took Smith several years before he could find investors willing to give him enough money for another trip to America. This time, his destination was further north, along the coast of Maine. The expedition left England in March of 1614. Its passengers included a Patuxet Indian named Tisquantum who had been captured by English mariners some years before. [See the article on Tisquantum in this book.] For several months, Smith traveled along the coast, making another of his finely detailed maps. He was particularly impressed with Massachusetts, where there was plenty of wood, fish, fur-bearing animals, fruit trees, and everything a settlement might need. He called the whole area New England, as a counterpart to the place on the west coast of America that Francis Drake had named New Albion (Albion is another name for England).

When he returned to England, Smith set about organizing a New England colony that would support itself by fishing and shipbuilding. The expedition left Plymouth Harbor in March 1615 and was making its way westward when a storm struck and forced it to turn back. By June, Smith was ready to try again. This time, his ship was chased by French pirates, who took him prisoner

The English place names on Smith's detailed map of the New England shoreline were chosen by Prince Charles (the future King Charles I).

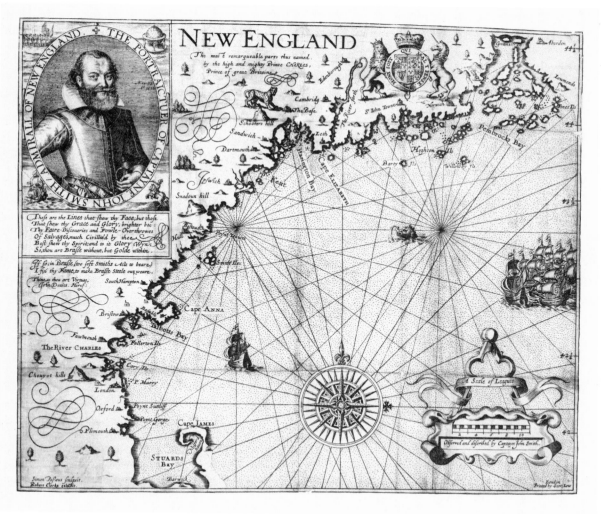

aboard their vessel. Abandoned by the captain of his own ship, who sailed back to England, Smith had no choice but to stay aboard the pirate ship for several months, writing his book *A Description of New England* and sometimes taking part in the pirates' attacks on Spanish ships. One night he escaped and made his way in a small boat to the shore of France. Shortly afterward, the pirate ship sank and everyone aboard drowned.

Smith spent the rest of his life trying to find some way to get back to America and encouraging other people's interest in it. When the Separatists (or Pilgrims, as we now call them) were getting ready to start a permanent colony in Massachusetts in 1619, he offered to go with them as a guide and protector. But though they had picked Massachusetts because of the glowing account of it in his book, they declined to take him along. Their refusal, he later wrote, "caused them, for more than a year, to endure a wonderful deal of misery, with an infinite patience; saying my books and maps were much better cheap to teach them, than myself." [For the Separatists' story, see the article in this book on William Bradford.] When the Powhatan Confederacy massacred the settlers at Jamestown in 1622, Smith volunteered to go back to Virginia to organize their militia, but this offer too was refused.

So most of bold John Smith's later years were spent writing books. The most famous of these were his *Generall Historie of Virginia* (published in 1624) and his *True Travels* (published in 1630), which were largely autobiographical. During the nineteenth-century conflict in the United States over slavery, some historians from the North, seeking to discredit Smith and thus to bring shame on Virginia and the South, declared that he was a liar who made up most of what he wrote. Later historians have found him to be mainly trustworthy.

After having escaped war, slavery, starvation, sickness, execution, piracy, and many another danger, Smith died in his bed at the age of fifty-one. Although he did not know it, he was the founder of Britain's empire. Jamestown, the first permanent English settlement in America, was England's first overseas colony. Plymouth and Boston, the first permanent English settlements in New England, were founded as a direct result of his explorations. Even the city of New York owes its existence to him, for he was the one who suggested to his friend Henry Hudson that he should look for the Northwest Passage in that area. [See the article on Hudson in this book.] In short, if John Smith had not had such a taste for adventure, there would have been no English colonies ready to seize their independence 150 years later and no Virginian statesmen to lead them toward democracy. Smith is thus the earliest "founding father" of the United States.

Tisquantum

Tisquantum (tuh-SKWANT-um), also known as Squanto. Born circa 1580 in present-day Massachusetts or Maine. Died 1622 at Manomoyick Bay (present-day Chatham Harbor), Massachusetts.

The chieftain Massasoit, leader of the Wampanoag Indian tribes in the area called Pokanoket (now part of eastern Massachusetts and Rhode Island), was getting ready for a journey. He and a group of warriors would be traveling forty miles across their territory to visit the people from over the sea who had made themselves a settlement on the shores of the great bay. Ever since their arrival in the autumn of the year, Massasoit had been hearing reports of these people. They had built mud huts on a hillside. Some of them lived in the huts, and some in the great ship that had brought them and that was still floating in the bay. They spoke the same language as some of the fisherman who came across the sea to catch cod. These fishermen had been coming every year for a long time now, but they had always gone back home; none of them had ever stayed all winter before, and none of them had brought their families with them. But this group had women and children as well as men. What were their intentions? Did they plan to come and live in Massasoit's territory?

An Abnaki Indian man named Samoset, who was visiting Massasoit over the winter and who knew some English, had gone to talk to the newcomers in the early spring. There seemed to be about fifty of them. They had a supply of food and tools for growing crops. They called their town Plymouth. Plainly they meant to stay and grow corn in the old fields that had been cleared by the Indians long ago.

At the end of March, Massasoit reached the English settlement in the company of sixty of his warriors. He and the leader of the English talked together through an Indian interpreter who spoke very good English, even better than Samoset spoke. The two men shared a meal and agreed that the wisest course would be one of peace. They promised that their people would do no harm to each other, would not take each other's property, and would help each other if either one was attacked. [This promise was kept on both sides for forty years, until Massasoit died. To find out what happened after that, read the article on Massasoit's son Metacom, also known as King Philip, in this book.]

When the ceremony was over, Massasoit went home with most of his escort, but he left behind the man who had served as the interpreter. This man had been living with the Wampanoag for several years, although he was not a member of the tribe. His name was Tisquantum, which means "door" or "entrance," and he knew much more about the place the settlers called Plymouth than any of the settlers did, because it was his home. He had lived there when it was a village called Patuxet, inhabited by a community of Patuxet Indians. Every one of them, including all his family, had died of a terrible illness that they had caught from the fishermen from Europe. Tisquantum was the only one left alive.

And how had he escaped the sickness himself? the English settlers wanted to know. It had happened this way. When Tisquantum was a young man, he had been kidnapped by a band of English

A statue of Massasoit.

explorers and taken back to England. Certain noblemen who were interested in starting colonies on the continent across the Atlantic had asked these explorers to capture a few of the people who lived there so that they could be questioned about things like its weather, its animals, its geography, and its inhabitants. Ten years went by before Tisquantum found a way to come home again, as part of the expedition of 1614 led by Captain John Smith—the same expedition in which Smith, mapping the coastline, gave the Patuxet village the English name of Plymouth. [See the article on

Smith in this book.] Smith put him ashore on Cape Cod. He had not been there long when another English sea captain, thinking that it would be more profitable to trade in slaves than fish, captured him and nineteen other Patuxet Indians and sold them into slavery in Spain. Tisquantum escaped and made his way to London, and after making a round trip to Newfoundland and back to England, in 1619 he came westward across the Atlantic for the last time, as a ship's pilot.

But when he reached his village on the shore of Cape Cod Bay, it was deserted. His family was gone, all the people he had known were gone, and the fields where they had grown corn were strewn with their bones. The sickness brought by the fishermen—it may have been smallpox, yellow fever, or measles—had killed thousands of people along the New England coast, decimating the tribes of the Patuxets, the Wampanoags, and the Massachusetts. Massasoit's people had given Tisquantum a new home. Now he would stay in his old home with the English settlers.

Tisquantum explains to several Pilgrim farmers the Algonkian Indian method of using fish to make the soil of their cornfields more fertile.

It was fortunate for the Pilgrims of Plymouth that Tisquantum (or Squanto, as they called him) chose to stay, for his help saved their lives. They had already been weakened by illness during their first winter in North America, and had lost half their group. [For more of their story, see the article on their governor, William Bradford, in this book.] They had brought seed for peas and wheat with them from England, but these crops failed to grow. They would have starved if Tisquantum had not shared with them the secrets of finding and growing food that his people had been studying for thousands of years. He showed them how to plant the multicolored corn called maize, a crop native to America that the English did not know; how to catch the small fish called alewives and bury them in the cornhills to fertilize the soil; how to keep watch over the fields so that animals would not dig up the alewives; and how to harvest the corn and cook it. He also showed them how to catch lobsters, crabs, and clams, and how to find wild pumpkins, squash, and berries, but it took the Pilgrims a long time to become accustomed to new kinds of foods.

The colonists also benefited from Tisquantum's help in their struggle to get Plymouth on a good economic footing and to keep it safe and secure. For their income, the Pilgrims depended on trade with the Indians. They bought the skins of beavers trapped by the Indians and sent them back to England to be made into beaver hats. Tisquantum, as their interpreter, helped them in their negotiations. So did a Wampanoag Indian warrior named Hobomok, who also came to live with the colonists and who was something of a rival to Tisquantum.

There was disagreement among the tribes of New England about how to deal with the English and the French who were arriving in increasing numbers. The Narragansett tribe wanted to attack the English and drive them out. They sent a war challenge to Plymouth in the form of a rattlesnake skin tied around a bundle of arrows. Tisquantum explained what it meant and went back to the Narragansetts with Governor Bradford's answer—the same snakeskin stuffed with bullets. There was no attack, but the Pilgrims built a stockade around their village. On another occasion, Tisquantum was captured by a Wampanoag chief who was planning to overthrow

Massasoit because of the peace treaty he had made with Plymouth. By killing their interpreter, this chief hoped to make things difficult for the colonists. But the Plymouth militia made a night attack to free Tisquantum, and the plot against Massasoit failed.

Despite this, Massasoit was none too pleased with Tisquantum, who had tried to use his position among the English to give himself authority among the Indians. (For one thing, he claimed that the deadly sickness that had killed so many Indians was kept locked up in the settlers' storehouse, and that he could unleash it on his enemies if he chose.) In March of 1622, a group of Wampanoag warriors came to Plymouth to demand that Tisquantum be handed over to them to be killed, as punishment for spreading a rumor that Massasoit was planning to attack the English. The terms of their peace treaty required Governor Bradford to do what they asked. But while he was stalling for time, the discussion was interrupted by the arrival of an English ship with a new contingent of colonists. Eventually Massasoit relented.

The following November, Tisquantum accompanied a party of Plymouth men on a boat trip around Cape Cod to buy corn and beans, for with the arrival of more colonists, the Pilgrims were running out of food. With his help, they bought enough to last for some months. But at a place called Manomoyick Bay (now called Chatham Harbor), Tisquantum fell ill with fever, and though Bradford tended him, within a few days he was dead. His friend the governor, who viewed all earthly events as acts of heaven, wrote in his history of Plymouth and the Pilgrims that "Squanto . . . was a special instrument sent of God for their good beyond their expectation."

William Bradford

William Bradford. Born March 1590 in Austerfield, Yorkshire, England. Died May 9, 1657, in Plymouth, Massachusetts.

The tiny English settlement in the North American wilderness had had a rough first year. First there had been the crossing of the Atlantic, sixty-five days at sea, with 102 miserable passengers crowded into their foul-smelling, storm-shaken ship, the *Mayflower*. When they reached land, there were six more weeks of waiting below decks in the dark and cold while some of the men scouted out a site for the colony they had come to build. Then there was the terrible sickness that had lasted all winter and killed nearly half their number. They had buried the dead at night to prevent the Indians who lived nearby from finding out how few were still alive.

The survivors had built little wooden houses roofed with thatch. Now that winter was coming on again, they were collecting firewood, stuffing the chinks of their houses with mud to keep out the cold, and gathering in the harvest from their twenty acres of corn.

William Bradford, the young governor of the settlement, thought it was time for a fresh start. In the Dutch city of Leyden, where he and his friends had lived in exile from England for eleven years, there was an annual day of thanksgiving to celebrate the end of the Spanish siege of 1574, in which thousands of Leydeners had died. The Bible, too, contained examples of thanksgiving days. And it was traditional in England to celebrate the ingathering of the harvest with a holiday called Harvest Home. Bradford proclaimed a holiday on which the colonists would hold a general feast and thank God for having brought them this far.

The meal was eaten communally, all the colonists together. They ate mostly what they found in the woods and streams: wild turkey, shellfish, eels, and greens, as well as hasty pudding made from corn. All this food was cooked and served by the handful of women and older girls who had survived the year (of the fourteen married women on the *Mayflower*, only four were still living). Massasoit, the chief of the Wampanoag Indians, came to the meal along with ninety members of his tribe, bringing five deer to be cooked and shared. For entertainment, there was musket practice, led by the colony's hired soldier, Captain Miles Standish; dancing and singing by the Wampanoags; and outdoor games in which both the English men and the Indian men took part.

It was Bradford who described the settlers as "pilgrims," but in their own day they did not call themselves by that name. The core group of colonists who settled at New Plymouth on the shore

This statue of Governor Bradford stands in the modern town of Plymouth. A few miles away is a reconstruction of colonial Plimoth Plantation.

of Cape Cod Bay were members of a larger group that refused to obey the rules of the Anglican Church, the official Church of England. They felt that the Anglican Church, though it had cast off the authority of the pope (the worldwide leader of the Roman Catholic Church), had not gone far enough in its reforms. To them, the proper form for a church was a voluntary community of believers, modeled on the earliest Christian communities and dedicated to biblical ideals of moral behavior under a "covenant" with God.

Since these reformers wanted to withdraw from the Anglican Church, they were called Separatists. But in England, the king or queen was (and still is) the head of the official Church. Any threat to the Church's authority was a threat to the idea of government by kings. Most people of the time thought of the Separatists as dangerous revolutionaries. Those who approved of their ideas were often imprisoned, beaten, or hanged.

William Bradford joined the Separatists when he was a teenager. He had been born in a little town in the north of England to a family of farmers. His father and mother died when he was young, and he was brought up by two uncles, who were none too pleased when he began to visit a group of Separatists that met in the nearby town of Scrooby. When the Church of England decided to crack down even harder on the Separatists, some of the group's members, Bradford among them, decided to leave England secretly and go to Holland, a country famous for its tolerant attitude toward the Jews and other people who needed a refuge from religious persecution. Their first escape attempt ended in disaster when the captain of the ship they had hired betrayed them to government officials, who took their belongings and marched them through a jeering crowd in the marketplace of the English city of Boston. The second attempt proved even worse: while the Separatists were boarding the ship, someone gave the alarm. The captain immediately sailed for Holland, taking with him the men who had already come aboard and leaving the women and children still on shore. But little by little, most of the group made their way to Amsterdam. Bradford was eighteen years old when he arrived in the spring of 1609.

Holland was enjoying a brief period of peace, after fighting for forty years for its independence from Spain. The Separatists from Scrooby settled in the university town of Leyden, where they were free to live in accordance with their understanding of God's will. But these English farmers found it hard to fit into the economy of Holland, which was built on manufacturing and trade. They learned how to work as cloth makers, tailors, and printers, but though they worked long hours, they stayed poor. Bradford became a weaver, and with the money he had inherited from his parents, he bought a house and married a girl named Dorothy May, with whom he had a son.

The Separatists began to realize that they would never prosper in Holland. They thought about going to some isolated place where they could acquire land and go back to farming. After reading several books about the New World, they decided to go to the territory of Virginia, where an English colony had been in existence since 1607. [For more information about the efforts of the English to colonize America, see the articles on Walter Raleigh and John Smith in this book.]

In addition to growing their own food, the Separatists intended to engage in trade, sending fish and furs bought from the Indians back to England. A group of London merchants whom they called the "merchant adventurers" agreed to provide money and supplies to help get the settlement started, but their terms were hard. When the *Mayflower* sailed from the English port of Plymouth in September 1620, bound for the northern part of Virginia (which in those days extended clear up to Manhattan), only a third of the passengers were members of the Leyden Separatist church. The rest were farmers and artisans who wanted to go to America in search of a better living. Most of the Separatists had to stay behind in Leyden. Bradford was on board, along with his wife, but their little son did not come with them.

Two months later, the ship reached the New World and rested at anchor—not at Manhattan, but farther north in Cape Cod Bay, where it had been driven by bad weather. The Separatists decided to stay and build their settlement nearby, at

Surrounded by ice and snow, the Mayflower *rides at anchor in Plymouth Harbor in December 1620 after a three-month journey.*

The first houses built by the Plymouth colonists were crude wooden huts roofed with thatch. The hilltop fort, made of logs, served as a church.

a place that John Smith had called Plymouth when he mapped the coast in 1614. To establish a political organization for the colony, and to assert the authority of its leaders over those settlers who did not belong to the church, the Separatists asked every male adult to sign an agreement. This document, called the Mayflower Compact, which Bradford helped to draft, committed the colonists to "combine ourselves together into a civil body politic . . . and by virtue hereof to enact, constitute, and frame such just and equal laws, ordinances, acts, constitutions, and offices, from time to time, as shall be thought most meet and convenient for the general good of the colony." The idea of a government whose authority rested on the consent of the governed—an idea that was modeled on the Separatists' religious covenant—was the basis of all future political arrangements at Plymouth.

The place the Pilgrims chose for their colony was a deserted Patuxet Indian village. All the people who lived there had died of a sickness they had caught from visiting European fishermen. Bradford was one of the scouts who went out in a snowstorm to find the site. When he returned to the ship, he was told that his wife had drowned. She had fallen or thrown herself overboard.

The colonists began to build crude shelters of wattle and daub (branches covered with mud). They had barely gotten started when they too were stricken with a terrible sickness, and many of them died. In the spring, after the death of the man they had chosen to be their governor, the surviving colonists elected Bradford in his place. He was thirty-one years old.

For the rest of his life, Bradford was the leader of the Pilgrims and the one person on whom the success of the Plymouth colony most depended.

His power was enormous. He carried out the laws that he helped to write, and served as the colony's principal judge. He also managed Plymouth's business affairs, kept its accounts, assigned jobs, made arrangements to import food and supplies and export trade goods, conducted its negotiations with the Indians and with other colonies, supervised its defenses, and made all its major decisions. Anyone who wanted to stay in Plymouth, even overnight, had to get his approval.

The first few years were hard ones. The Pilgrims knew nothing about fishing or raising grain suited to New England's soil and climate, and they were so weakened by disease that they barely had enough strength to do the work. A Wampanoag Indian named Hobomok, one of Massasoit's warriors, came to live with them and teach them how to survive in the wilderness. A Patuxet Indian named Tisquantum, who had lived in England and spoke English, saved their lives by showing them how to plant hills of corn and fertilize them with dead fish. [For Tisquantum's story, see the article about him in this book.] Their plan to operate as a trading colony fell through for lack of equipment, and the merchant adventurers, instead of sending them what they needed, sent visitors with whom the colonists had to share their houses and food. Under the terms of their agreement with the merchants, the colonists were not allowed to work for themselves as individuals but had to live communally, and Bradford was responsible for rationing food, cloth, and other goods out of the common stock. In 1627, Bradford and eleven others freed the colony from the agreement by volunteering to pay its debts themselves, in exchange for control of all its trade. Little by little, and amid many setbacks, Plymouth began to prosper.

The founding of the Puritan colony at Massachusetts Bay in 1630 proved the biggest challenge of all. The Puritans held certain ideals in common with the Separatists, but instead of withdrawing from the Church of England, they wanted to take it over and "purify" it from within. They did not share the Separatist insistence on keeping the church free from government interference; instead, they wanted to make the government a theocracy, in which the laws made by the state would be based on Protestant religious teachings. The arrival of the Puritans in the New World brought wealth to the people of Plymouth, who made money by selling the newcomers animals, seeds, and tools. But the new colony was much bigger, and soon it was competing with Plymouth and trying to expand into territory that the Plymouth settlers claimed for their own. Bradford had to be very careful in his dealings with Massachusetts Bay and its governor, the lawyer John Winthrop, but he could not prevent Plymouth from becoming embroiled in such messes as the Puritans' massacre of the Pequot Indians in 1639. [For more information about the Massachusetts Bay Colony and about colonial attitudes toward the Indians, see the articles in this book on Metacom, Anne Hutchinson, Roger Williams, and William Penn.]

A 1634 map of New England shows Plymouth outnumbered by the Puritan settlements near Boston. The word "sagamore" means "chief."

For all his work, Bradford was paid no salary until 1639, and most of his expenses came out of his own pocket. He was reelected almost every year from 1622 to 1656, and even in those few years when he was not the official governor, he served as one of the governor's assistants. One of his chief projects was to bring many of the remaining Separatists from Leyden to Plymouth (although the Separatists were always a minority in the colony). In this group was Alice Southworth, who became his second wife. They had three children and also reared three children from their previous marriages, a nephew of Alice's, and four boys whose parents had died.

Virtually nothing would be known about the history of the colony if not for Bradford. In his spare time, he wrote down the events that took place, year by year. The manuscript, called *Of Plimoth Plantation*, disappeared after the Revolutionary War and was not found again until 1855. Its publication helped bring about a revival of interest in the Pilgrims. (An annual thanksgiving day had been observed in New England towns since 1630, but it did not become a national holiday until President Lincoln declared it so in 1863.) Bradford's history showed plainly that not only Thanksgiving but also New England's traditions of local self-government and the town meeting,

together with the civil marriage ceremony, had their origins at Plymouth.

The first pages of the manuscript contain exercises in Hebrew, in Bradford's hand. Bradford, like most of the Pilgrims, had had hardly any formal education. (His foster father William Brewster, the deeply respected elder of the Plymouth church, was the only Pilgrim who had studied at a university, while the Puritan colony at Boston had many university-trained lawyers and theologians.) Yet Bradford had picked up some learning in Leyden, acquired many books, and tried to start a college at Plymouth to rival Boston's Harvard. In his later years he taught himself Hebrew so that he could understand "that most ancient language, and holy tongue, in which the Law and Oracles of God were written." This project helped to keep him from dwelling on what he considered Plymouth's failure, for as the colony prospered, its members began to move farther and farther away in search of more land, and the close-knit community of believers drifted apart and was a community no longer. The church that had held together in the face of persecution in England and poverty in Holland lost its purpose in the New World. In 1691, thirty-four years after the death of Governor Bradford, Plymouth Colony was absorbed by the Massachusetts Bay Colony.

Samuel de Champlain

Samuel de Champlain (shahm-PLANH). Born circa 1567 in Brouage, France. Died December 25, 1635, in Québec.

Since the voyages of Jacques Cartier in the 1530s, French fishermen and fur traders had returned often to the Gulf of St. Lawrence in the wilderness of Canada. [See the article on Cartier in this book for more information on his discoveries.] These trips were so profitable that the governor of the French port of Dieppe, Aymar de Chastes, asked King Henri IV for exclusive con-

trol of the fur trade, offering to finance and oversee the trade in return for a profit on every beaver, lynx, and bear pelt sold. In 1603, an expedition backed by de Chastes was sent to the St. Lawrence area to report on how best to set up a permanent trading colony there. As Geographer Royal, de Chastes chose French mariner and explorer Samuel de Champlain, who had made a name for himself with an account of his voyages to the West Indies and Mexico. This choice was a fateful one, for Champlain was to devote the rest of his life to founding a new nation for France on the shores of the New World.

The expedition surveyed the islands of the Gulf

of St. Lawrence and traveled west along the St. Lawrence River to the present site of Montréal, where Cartier had visited the Indian village of Hochelaga sixty-eight years before. There was no trace left of the village, but the location seemed a good one. On the expedition's return to France, Champlain told Henri IV that there was excellent potential for a permanent French colony in North America, and the king authorized a second voyage in 1604 under the patronage of Pierre de Montes, who had taken over de Chastes's fur monopoly. Two ships set out under the command of an experienced fur merchant named du Pont Gravé, who had been Champlain's captain on the first voyage; Champlain again acted as geographer and surveyor. One of the ships carried eighty colonists.

Over the next three years, Champlain surveyed the coasts of the areas we now call New England, Nova Scotia, and Newfoundland, looking for the best sites for colonies. He was the first European to map Massachusetts Bay, and he visited Plymouth Harbor sixteen years before the Pilgrims landed there. [See the article on William Bradford in this book.] The first year, the expedition set up a settlement in Acadia, on the St. Croix River along the boundary between Maine and Nova Scotia, but about half the men died of scurvy during the winter. The next year the survivors moved to Annapolis Basin on the Bay of Fundy, where they fared somewhat better. But when de Montes lost his monopoly in 1607, the colony was disbanded and the entire expedition returned to France.

The English were trying to establish their own competing colony in Acadia, so the French now focussed on the area around present-day Québec. Champlain led an expedition there in 1608. No longer just a surveyor and reporter, he was now in command of a ship and thirty-two colonists. Again, his goal was to establish a permanent French colony. The colonists set about building houses and a small fort, plowing land and sowing seeds on the present site of Québec City, only a short distance from the place where Cartier had spent the winter some seventy years before.

All did not go smoothly the first year. Almost immediately a group of colonists plotted to murder Champlain and deliver the little fort into the hands of the Spanish or the Basques, who were

Samuel de Champlain

also exploring the region. Luckily for Champlain, a French supply ship arrived on the very day the mutineers intended to carry out their plan. One of the conspirators confessed to the ship's captain, and the captain told Champlain. The ringleader was hanged, and three accomplices were sent back to France. During the winter, cold and scurvy again killed most of the colonists; only nine were still alive when a new shipment of settlers arrived in the spring. But the colony hung on, and by 1635 it extended all along the banks of the St. Lawrence from Québec to the Gulf.

Champlain understood that the settlement's existence depended on the good will of the surrounding Indian peoples, mainly Algonkians and Hurons. He learned much about their languages and customs while trying to develop trade with them and convert them to Christianity. But he found that the best way to ensure their support was to help them against the Mohawk Iroquois, whom they had been fighting for years over control of land in the Adirondack Mountains. In the summer of 1609 Champlain and two other Frenchmen agreed to accompany a Huron and Algonkian raiding party in an attack on an Mohawk town. The party traveled in canoes along the St. Lawrence River and the River Richelieu until they reached Lake Champlain, nestled in the mountains between what are now the states of Vermont and New York. Champlain was the first European to see it.

As their canoes drifted along the great lake, the three Frenchmen were amazed at the beauty of the countryside. There were fish, birds, and game in great numbers; many kinds of tall trees that they had never seen before; groves of fruit trees and fields of grain stretching beyond sight. One night, Champlain dreamed that the Mohawks were all drowning in the lake. The Algonkians believed that his dream predicted victory.

Near the falls of Ticonderoga, the Algonkian canoes surrounded a Mohawk town. All night the two sides shouted taunts and insults at each other, and at dawn the battle was joined. The Algonkians won it with the help of Champlain. He loaded his arquebus (an early form of shotgun) with four balls and with one shot killed two Mohawk chiefs and wounded a third. A few more shots from his two companions scared off the rest of the Mohawks. (After the battle Champlain used his arquebus once more, this time out of mercy, to kill a Mohawk warrior who was being tortured to death by the Algonkians.) For this and other acts, the Algonkians and Hurons pledged their friendship to the French. But the Mohawks and their allies in the Iroquois confederacy hated the French, and eighty years later they sided with the English against the French in the French and Indian Wars.

Champlain returned to France in 1610 to give his report to the king. While he was there he married Helen Boullé, daughter of the secretary of the king's chamber. This marriage assured Champlain's financial security—his wife's dowry was 6,000 *livres* —but since she was only twelve years old, the couple had to wait several years before they could live together. By then Champlain had been made commandant of New France (as Canada had come to be called), with complete authority over all settlements. He moved quickly to restore the failing fur trade and formed a company of merchants to finance more colonies and voyages of exploration.

In 1615, Champlain made his last and longest expedition, canoeing west to Lake Huron, one of the Great Lakes, to aid the Hurons and the Algonkians in another attack on the Mohawks. With him for part of the trip was his protégé, Étienne Brulé, a young explorer who had taken part in an "exchange program" devised by Champlain. Brulé had spent several years living in a Huron

Champlain's map of New France, from the Atlantic to the Great Lakes, showing the location of French settlements and Indian villages.

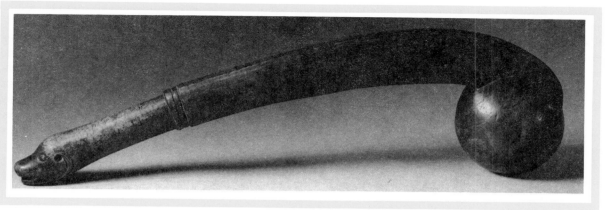

Firearms were unknown to the Iroquois until Champlain used his arquebus. Their own weapons included clubs like this one, hatchets, and knives.

village, while a Huron youth went with Champlain to live in France. Champlain and Brulé were separated before the battle with the Mohawks, which did not go as well for the Algonkians as the earlier one. Champlain was wounded, but made it back safely to Québec. Brulé was captured by the Mohawks and tortured, but he too survived. Later, with Champlain's encouragement, Brulé traveled west, perhaps as far as the future site of Duluth, on Lake Superior. But though he spent most of his life among the Huron Indians, Brulé

was never truly accepted by them, and in 1633 they killed him.

Champlain himself devoted the rest of his life to building up the colony at Québec, even convincing England to restore the colony to France after English privateers captured it in 1628. He died in Québec in 1635, at the age of sixty-eight. It was mainly due to Champlain's hard work and determination that the French colony in Canada flourished and grew. That is why Canadians often call him the father of their country.

René-Robert Cavelier de La Salle

René-Robert Cavelier de La Salle (lah-SAHL). Born November 22, 1643, in Rouen, Normandy, France. Died March 19, 1687, near the Brazos River, present-day Texas.

The Jesuit fathers at the Collège Henri IV at La Flèche, France, were concerned about one of their students, René-Robert Cavelier. They noted that he had excellent ability and a talent for mathematics, but also that he showed poor judgment and little prudence. Cavelier, who

is known today as the French explorer La Salle, was haunted throughout his adventurous career by the very traits noticed by his teachers when he was a boy. Seeking to carve out a grand empire for France in the midst of North America, he navigated the length of Mississippi River from the Great Lakes to the Gulf of Mexico in 1682, and established France's claim to the vast territory of Louisiana, which included most of the land between the Mississippi River and the Rocky Mountains. But every one of La Salle's grand schemes came to nothing because of his pride, impatience, and plain bad luck.

La Salle, the son of a wealthy merchant family,

was born in the French port town of Rouen. For nine years he studied for the priesthood at schools run by the Jesuits, a missionary order of Catholic priests. But the scholarly and priestly life was not for him, and his teachers knew it. When in 1666 the General of the Society flatly refused La Salle's third request to be sent to the Jesuit mission in China, he left the order and set sail for New France, the French colony in Canada. For the rest of his life, La Salle believed the Jesuits were plotting against him, though historians have found no evidence of this.

On his arrival in Montréal in 1667, La Salle was granted an estate of land in the southern part of the colony. He began at this point to style himself a noble, taking the title "Sieur de La Salle" from the name of a small estate owned by his family in France. La Salle was not cut out for the life of a farmer any more than that of a missionary. He dreamed of building a rich empire for France in Canada, as the Spanish conquistadors had done for Spain in Mexico and Peru. At the same time he hoped to gain glory and wealth for himself.

Tales La Salle heard from Indians made him think that there was a route to the Pacific Ocean by way of the Ohio River, which he confused with the Colorado River. (At this date no European knew just how wide North America was. The Ohio River is more than a thousand miles from the Colorado River, and some two thousand miles from the Pacific Ocean.) In 1669, with the backing of the governor of Canada, he sold his land to raise money for an official expedition to the Ohio Valley. However, his grasp of the geography of the area was at best vague, and he may never seriously have planned to look for a waterway to the Pacific. More likely, he intended to use his commission and the money he raised to establish himself as a fur trader in the region. This was the quickest way to make a fortune, because furs were the most profitable export from Canada.

Over the next few years, La Salle traveled parts of the Ohio River, crossed Lake Erie, Lake Huron, and Lake Michigan, and probably canoed down the Illinois River. He did not find a water route to the west, but he did make a name for himself as one of the chief fur traders in Canada. In 1672 he came to the attention of the new governor of Canada, Louis de Buade, Comte de Frontenac. Frontenac was also interested in extending

French power farther into the continent. La Salle became his right-hand man.

Their most important venture together was to build Fort Frontenac, a stronghold on Lake Ontario. One reason for building Fort Frontenac was to hold back the Iroquois Indians, who had been enemies of the French since the days of Samuel de Champlain [see the article on Champlain in this book]. But the chief purpose of the fort was to control the valuable Great Lakes fur trade. For years fur merchants from the Dutch colony of New Amsterdam (later taken by the English and renamed New York) had been encouraging the Indians to trade with them instead of with French traders from Montréal. This endangered the entire economy of New France. Fort Frontenac, which overlooked the main trading route from the upper Great Lakes to New Amsterdam, was an ideal place to divert the New Amsterdam fur trade back into French hands. La Salle convinced many Indians to sell their furs to him instead of to English or Dutch traders farther south. The schemes of La Salle and Frontenac did not stop there, however. French merchants were incensed to discover that the governor and his assistant were also getting hold of furs bound for Montréal. The profit from each fur was split between La Salle and Frontenac, who had many debts to repay back in France.

Territory explored by La Salle

The first European view of Niagara Falls was drawn by Louis Hennepin, a Franciscan friar who served as chaplain to La Salle's expedition.

La Salle was soon in the grip of creditors himself. In 1677 he won from King Louis XIV a patent (a royal license) to explore the western parts of New France, especially the Mississippi River valley. To finance the expedition La Salle borrowed large sums of money from French bankers and merchants, promising to repay them in furs he hoped to collect on his travels.

Over the next five years La Salle devoted more effort to holding his creditors at bay and establishing his own trading empire than to satisfying the terms of the king's patent. He was beset by one disaster after another. La Salle built a sailing ship, the *Griffon*, to travel on the Great Lakes. It was the first rigged vessel ever seen in those waters and caused great excitement among the Indians. In 1679 the *Griffon*, carrying a large store of

furs and other goods, disappeared somewhere on Lake Michigan. To get new supplies La Salle was forced to make a grueling 65-day journey overland in the spring rains to Fort Frontenac. There he found that all the furs he had stored for himself had been stolen by his agents. More money had to be borrowed to resupply the expedition. Meanwhile, an outpost that he had built near the Illinois River was looted and burned by mutineers. La Salle spent most of the next two years searching the wilderness for the remnants of his expedition and returning again to Montréal to borrow even more money. Not until February of 1682 did he start down the upper waters of the Mississippi.

La Salle and his men drifted downstream in a flotilla of some twenty elm-bark canoes, using their paddles to push away the winter ice floes.

By the middle of March they had reached the land of the Arkansas Indians. Farther down the river they made contact with the Taensas and other Indian peoples. At each meeting La Salle attempted to set up a trade agreement. By spring they were in the lower reaches of the river; the weather was warm and now the French had to push away alligators instead of icebergs.

On April 6 La Salle's party finally reached the mouth of the Mississippi, where it empties into the Gulf of Mexico. Shouting and firing their muskets into the air, they claimed all the land along the Mississippi for France. The new territory, which La Salle called Louisiana after the king of France, contained much of the most fertile land in North America. (The present state of Louisiana occupies only a small part of the Louisiana Territory.) Then they made the slow journey back up the river to Canada, arriving at the trading town of Michilimackinac (in present-day Michigan) in September 1682.

Though La Salle had finally fulfilled the king's commission, he found himself in worse difficulties than ever. His creditors refused to lend him any more money, and he could no longer count on the protection of Governor Frontenac, who had been relieved of his position. The new governor, Antoine Levebre, Sieur de La Barre, had his own favorites and was hostile to La Salle. La Barre seized La Salle's remaining property at Fort Frontenac and refused to support a new settlement La Salle built on the Illinois River near the present site of Ottawa, Illinois. La Salle knew he was ruined unless he could found an entirely new trade empire, separate from New France. In 1683 he went to France one last time and convinced the king to let him develop a new colony and a warm-water port at the mouth of the Mississippi. At the same time La Salle was to survey Spanish forts in the area and if possible capture them.

This expedition was La Salle's last chance at greatness, or so he believed. It may be that he was so anxious that he could no longer tell good choices from bad. The ships he chose were too small to carry the supplies and men needed for such an ambitious expedition. He quarreled with everyone involved. Hoping to use this expedition to pay off his debts, he spent money on trade goods that should have been spent on food and ammunition. He took along civilian colonists in place of hardened soldiers and explorers. Worst of all, he had no idea how to find the mouth of the

Standing at the mouth of the Mississippi River, La Salle lays claim to the Louisiana Territory in this modern and highly romanticized painting.

La Salle and two others lie dead near the Brazos River, mourned by Hennepin and a companion. The assassins are lurking in the bushes nearby.

Mississippi from the Gulf of Mexico, though he claimed otherwise to the king.

On July 24, 1684, La Salle set sail from France with four ships and 400 men and women. After five months the expedition entered the Gulf of Mexico, but missed the Mississippi and landed some 500 miles to the west, near what is now Matagorda Island in Texas. By then one ship had been captured by the Spanish, who patrolled the entire Gulf and considered it part of their empire in the Americas. Two more were shipwrecked, with the loss of needed supplies. The remaining ship left the expedition and returned to France, but La Salle decided to stay. He build a fort near the landing place and used it as a base to search northwards for the Mississippi.

La Salle was a proud and arrogant man. He expected instant obedience from his followers but did little to earn their trust and respect. Even one of his few admirers wrote that "all his fine qualities [were] offset by a haughtiness of manner which often made him insufferable, and by a harshness towards those under his command which drew upon him an undying hatred." After two unsuccessful attempts to find the Mississippi, the colonists had had enough of La Salle. On March 19, 1687, he was lured into an ambush by mutineers, shot to death, and left unburied.

With the failure of La Salle's expedition, King Louis XIV lost interest in the New World and turned his attention to making war with his European neighbors. That ended any possibility of a great French empire in the midst of North America. The vast territory of Louisiana was sold to the United States by Napoleon Bonaparte in 1803 to finance his conquests in Europe.

Anne Hutchinson

Anne Hutchinson. Born June or July 1591 in Alford, Lincolnshire, England. Died August or September 1643 in present-day Pelham Bay, New York.

The little church in the village of Newtown was packed from wall to wall with people, all of them bundled up in hats, capes, and overcoats. It was a raw day in November, and the unheated church was icy cold. Along the benches sat the important officials of the Massachusetts Bay Colony—thirty-one town deputies, nine magistrates, eight ministers—with the governor, John Winthrop, at their head, seated behind a table in a padded chair. Every bit of space left over was taken by spectators who had come to watch the trial of the woman who for two years had kept the colony rocking with her bold criticisms of its churches and ministers. The colony's leaders had made up their minds to silence Anne Hutchinson, and if she refused to be silent, to rid themselves of a troublemaker.

The defendant stood alone before them. Forty-six years old, she was the mother of fifteen children, a midwife and nurse of many years' experience, a devout Protestant who had come all the way from England to be near her favorite preacher and who held lectures in her home to teach other women. She stood before them for hours, on this day and the next, answering the ministers and magistrates and countering their arguments with a deftness that enraged them.

Anne Hutchinson was not the first of her family to stand trial for refusing to obey religious authorities. Her father, Francis Marbury, a preacher in the Lincolnshire village of Alford, was jailed three times and barred from preaching because he had denounced the bishops of the Church of England, the official state church, for appointing ignorant and incompetent ministers to lead congregations. After many years he promised to obey the bishops and was given a parish in London. Anne was the third of his thirteen children, and she grew up in a home where learning was respected and religious matters were always being discussed. In 1612, when she was twenty-one, she married William Hutchinson, a cloth merchant, and went back with him to Alford. Her husband's business prospered, and Anne spent her days taking care of her family, studying the Bible, teaching groups of women who gathered in her house, and helping her neighbors in times of sickness or childbirth. She gave birth to fourteen children in twenty-two years.

England in that era was seething with religious controversies. The official Church of England, headed by the king, was being challenged by reformers known as Puritans who wanted England to adhere to the moral standards of the Bible, which they felt had been corrupted. In their view, the Church of England, like the Roman Catholic Church which it had replaced, put obstacles between the individual and God. As followers of the Swiss reformer John Calvin, they believed that God would save only a chosen few for the rewards of heaven. Anne and William Hutchinson were among many English people who took these matters very seriously. Whenever they could, they rode the twenty-four miles to the city of Boston in Lincolnshire to hear the preaching of the famous Puritan minister John Cotton. At one point, Anne came close to joining the Separatists, a Protestant group that insisted on complete withdrawal from the Church of England. [For more information about the Separatists, now called the Pilgrims, who founded Plymouth Colony in 1620, see the article about William Bradford in this book.]

In 1625 King Charles I was crowned, and began his long power struggle with the Puritan-controlled Parliament, England's national legislature. His bishops cracked down on the Puritans, jailing some and exiling others. Some Puritan leaders made plans to start a colony in North America where their people could live without constant harassment from the king and the Church. The first members of the Massachusetts Bay Colony crossed the Atlantic in 1630 and began to build a network of villages on the coast and further inland.

As the trouble in England grew worse, Puritan sympathizers began to come across in large numbers. The main port of the colony was named Boston, in honor of the Lincolnshire town where John Cotton was preacher. By 1633 Cotton himself had escaped from England in disguise and had settled in the new Boston, where he did his preaching from the pulpit of a white clapboard meetinghouse instead of an ancient stone edifice. The same ship that brought him across the sea also brought Anne and William Hutchinson's eldest son and William Hutchinson's brother. Merchants like the Hutchinsons were finding it hard to keep their businesses going in England because of the high taxes and other restrictions imposed by the king, and they looked to the New World for a chance to do better. In September 1634, Anne and William arrived in Boston with a few belongings and their eleven surviving children, the youngest of whom was not yet a year old. They built their new home near the meetinghouse, across the street from the house of John Winthrop, one of the magistrates (executives) and the colony's chief founder.

Life in the Bay Colony was made up of three things: hard work, religion, and politics. There was no relief from the extremes of New England weather or the problems of trading, farming, and raising families except for attendance at long church services and constant discussions about matters of religious doctrine or the running of the colony. The Hutchinsons quickly became prominent members of the community. William did a good trade in imported cloth and headed an organization of local businessmen. The freemen of Boston chose him to serve on the town council and elected him to be one of their representatives on the General Court, the colony's legislature. Anne ran the household, helped mothers give birth, and tended sick neighbors, using remedies made from plants. The colonists of Boston learned to rely on her skills as a nurse and midwife, and called on her at all hours to come and help them. She gave birth to another child, her fifteenth, in the spring of 1636.

This statue of Anne Hutchinson stands on the lawn of the State House in Boston, the city from which she was banished in colonial days.

Within a few months of her arrival, Anne resumed her practice of holding meetings for women. She would summarize sermons that had been preached in church, answer questions, and add her own commentary. The women of Boston, who trusted her in times of distress, came by the score to hear her, and her reputation began to grow. Often eighty women at a time crowded into her living room. Though the Puritan ministers did not allow women to speak in church or to teach in public, Anne Hutchinson's listeners found that she knew her Bible as thoroughly as any preacher and had her own ideas about its lessons. Even more astonishing, she declared that the "covenant of works" preached by the Puritan ministers should be replaced by a "covenant of grace," and that their stolid reliance on the letter of biblical law should be replaced by a more open and flexible understanding of Scripture. The most important thing, she taught, was a close, loving, direct connection between the individual and God. She criticized all the colony's ministers except John Cotton, and on one occasion, she and a group of women walked out of the Boston meetinghouse to protest the views of the preacher who was giving the sermon. The insulted ministers were outraged, and denounced her as an antinomian—a heretic who did not obey the laws set forth in the Bible.

Anne's teachings were welcomed by many of Boston's men as well as its women. Prosperous merchants and traders began to attend her lectures, intrigued by her emphasis on individual responsibility and liberty of conscience. A visitor to New England in the summer of 1636 was told: "I'll bring you to a woman that preaches better than any of your black-coats that have been at the ninneversity, a woman of another kind of spirit." A body of followers, something like a political party, took shape, with Anne at its head. They challenged the colony's leaders over unfair practices in land distribution (bigger plots of land were given to wealthier colonists) and taxes (the businessmen of Boston paid much higher taxes than

The Puritan leader John Winthrop, governor of the Massachusetts Bay Colony, presided over the banishment of Hutchinson and Roger Williams.

the farmers of the outlying villages). In 1636 they succeeded in getting a Hutchinsonian, Sir Henry Vane, elected governor and sent other Hutchinsonians to represent Boston in the General Court. When Massachusetts Bay and three other English colonies went to war against the Pequot Indians, the Boston church congregation, under Anne's direction, refused to send either money or men, in protest against the appointment as military chaplain of a preacher whom they despised.

The Massachusetts Bay Colony now began to split into two factions. In no way did it resemble John Winthrop's original idea of a peaceful, harmonious, orderly place, a model for the rest of the world, whose inhabitants would practice perfect obedience to the laws of the combined church and state. The founders of the colony were afraid that Hutchinson and her allies would wreck their entire venture. More than once, King Charles had tried to put the colony under royal control. The same ship that brought Anne and William Hutchinson to North America had also brought a letter from England ordering the colony to give up its charter and submit to the king's rule, which Winthrop refused to do. The Hutchinson dispute threatened to weaken the colony just when it had to be strongest. Already the leaders had banished several troublemakers, including the young minister Roger Williams, who had had the nerve to declare that the charter was null and void because it had not been negotiated with the Indians. [For the rest of Roger Williams's story, see the article about him in this book.] Now here was Mistress Hutchinson making Massachusetts boil with her criticisms of the Puritan ideas that were the very foundation of the colony.

The orthodox Puritan leaders decided to counterattack. A law was passed allowing the colony to deny entrance to anyone thought to be a danger, and it was used to keep out some relatives of the Hutchinsons who had just come over from England. Hutchinson's brother-in-law, a preacher, was thrown out of Massachusetts for giving a sermon defending the Covenant of Grace. Seventy-five colonists, including several members of the Hutchinson family, signed a petition protesting his conviction; they were fined and forced to give up their firearms, and some were jailed. In the summer of 1637, John Winthrop was elected governor, defeating Hutchinson's friend Sir Henry

Vane. One of Winthrop's first acts was to call a conference of ministers to deal with the problem of Anne Hutchinson. The conference ruled that Anne's meetings were "disorderly" and that she had no authority to resolve questions of doctrine. She was ordered to appear before the General Court the following November. That gave Winthrop enough time to make sure that two of the deputies elected to the Court by Boston's freemen, both of them supporters of Hutchinson, would not be allowed to take their seats.

The trial was held not in Boston but in Newtown, a village on the other side of the Charles River, where Hutchinson had few friends. It was held in the village church, at a session of the legislature. Governor Winthrop and the colony's ministers and magistrates acted as both prosecutors and judges. Most of them had been educated at universities in England, and the governor himself had been trained as a lawyer. The defendant, who had had no such education, was not allowed even a lawyer's advice. Yet hour after hour—without a single break for food or rest—she stood before them, matching argument for argument, quoting the Bible to refute their quotes, and insisting that whatever she had done was a matter of conscience and not against any law. Several of her judges had themselves stood trial in England because of their Puritan beliefs, and many of them had seen their families helped by her in times of sickness or childbirth, but none of them showed her any compassion; in fact, they silenced the few witnesses who spoke in her defense. Still they could not make her bend to their authority.

It was Hutchinson's claim to prophetic revelation that finally gave her judges the grounds they needed to convict her. She declared that God's word was not confined to the Bible, but could come directly to individuals, and that she herself had received many such revelations. That was too much for the orthodox Puritans; it meant that the authority of the Bible, the basis for their government and all their behavior, was not final, and that anybody, no matter how poor or unlearned, could make rules of their own. Could there be an orderly society under such conditions?

Governor Winthrop read out the sentence: "Mrs. Hutchinson, the sentence of the court you hear is that you are banished from out of our jurisdiction as being a woman not fit for our society,

A defiant Hutchinson stands trial before the ministers and magistrates of the Massachusetts Bay Colony whose authority she questioned.

and are to be imprisoned till the court shall send you away."

"I desire to know wherefore I am banished," the defendant insisted.

"Say no more," answered the governor. "The court knows whereof and is satisfied."

Over the winter, Hutchinson was kept under house arrest in the village of Roxbury, where her family came to visit her. In March, she was taken to the meetinghouse in Boston and formally excommunicated from the church after another two-day trial. (As she left the room, she was accompanied by a young woman named Mary Dyer, the only person left among all her friends and followers who was brave enough to stand by her. Some twenty years later, when the leaders of Massachusetts were persecuting Quakers for preaching the authority of the "inner light," Mary Dyer was among those they executed.)

Roger Williams, the exiled minister, had made arrangements with the chiefs of the Narragansett Indian tribe to allow the Hutchinson family and a number of their friends to take refuge on the island of Aquidneck, sixty-five miles from Boston. In this new settlement they began to experiment with ways of putting into practice Anne's religious and political ideas. Women and men alike were allowed to preach. Some became pacifists and would not bear arms, even to defend the settlement. A few families, including the Hutchinsons, became anarchists: they decided to recognize no authority but that of individual conscience, and refused to have any kind of government.

The Puritans in Boston were shocked but not surprised to hear about these developments. They had always maintained that the devil was using Anne Hutchinson to undermine the stability of their society, and that the ultimate end of her teachings would be a complete breakdown of moral standards. Several Massachusetts colonists, most of them women, were excommunicated or banished for continuing to believe in the things she taught. Winthrop and his colleagues made it clear that if they possibly could, they would annex the Williams and Hutchinson settlements and root out everyone who did not agree with them. They even accused Hutchinson of being a witch. This was the most dangerous charge that a New Englander could face, for witchcraft was a capital crime punishable by hanging, and it could never be disproved.

Perhaps it was the fear of Puritan retaliation that made Anne Hutchinson leave Aquidneck in 1642, after the death of her husband. By now she was a grandmother. Some of her older children were in their twenties, married and with children of their own. Together with her six youngest children, she moved southward, to a site on what is now called Pelham Bay, on the shore of Long Island Sound. The territory was being colonized by Dutch settlers, but relations between the Dutch and the resident Indians had been badly mismanaged, and by now the area was in a state of constant warfare. One day at the end of the summer of 1643, a group of warriors came to the Hutchinson house and killed Anne Hutchinson, her son-in-law, and five of her children. The only member of her household to survive the massacre was her ten-year-old daughter, who was held captive by the Indians for four years until she was ransomed.

John Winthrop and many of his fellow Bostonians were certain that God had punished Anne Hutchinson as she deserved. Later generations have held her in much higher regard for daring to challenge the state and to raise issues of responsibility and equality. Statues of Anne Hutchinson and of Mary Dyer now stand on the lawn of the Massachusetts State House in Boston.

Metacom

Metacom (MEH-ta-com), also known as Metacomet and Pometacom, and as King Philip. Born circa 1640 in Pokanoket (in present-day Rhode Island). Died 1676 in Mount Hope (now Bristol, Rhode Island).

For the second time in two years, the Wampanoag Indians were mourning the death of their leader. The old chief Massasoit had died in 1661, after more than fifty years as sachem. His eldest son Wamsutta, one of his five children, had taken his place. And now he too was dead, killed by a fever on his way home from the English town of Plymouth, where he had been taken by force to answer questions about whether he was plotting a war. Some people said the English had poisoned him. Others said he had died of humiliation and anger, because the colonists treated him with such fear and contempt.

The new sachem was Metacom, Wamsutta's brother—or Philip, as the English called him. He was in his early twenties, too young to remember what the world had been like before the enormous changes that had happened during his father's lifetime. Back then, this land—the land that the colonists called New England—had been inhabited by dozens of tribes, all speaking dialects of the Algonkian language. There had been more than three hundred villages along the seashore and the rivers, with many thousands of people living in them. Out of the thick forests they had cleared large cornfields and beanfields. They had fished, they had hunted, they had gathered, and they had tilled, for many generations.

Then fishermen from across the sea had begun to visit, in their large wooden sailing ships. They looked different from the Algonkians, and they suffered from diseases that no one had ever seen. In the year 1617, one of these diseases began to spread through the seacoast villages. The epidemic raged for three years. Whole families disappeared, and then whole tribes. The Wampanoags alone lost two-thirds of their people.

From his headquarters at Mount Hope at the northern edge of Narragansett Bay, Metacom's father Massasoit had considered the situation. The huge Narragansett tribe to the west had been lucky. They had many healthy warriors, and they were now in a good position to overwhelm the Wampanoags and take over their territory. And what about the strange doings to the east, on the shore of Cape Cod Bay? The empty village of Patuxet, a place of ghosts, was said to be inhabited again by a group of foreigners from across the ocean. They had arrived at the wrong time of year, at the beginning of winter, and now in the spring they were looking very weak. They did not seem to know much about planting corn and fishing, although they did have powerful weapons.

Metacom knew well what had happened next. Massasoit had gone to visit the English newcomers and had spoken with them, using as his interpreter Tisquantum, who had been kidnapped to England many years before. [For the rest of Tisquantum's story, see the article on him in this book.] Massasoit and the English made a peace treaty, promising that they would not harm each other and that they would lend military aid in time of need. For the time being, the Wampanoags were safe from the Narragansetts.

The English at Patuxet—which they called Plymouth—needed plenty of help from Massasoit

Metacom, according to one 19th-century artist's idea

during those early years. One of his warriors, Hobomok, stayed at Plymouth and taught the colonists how to get food for themselves from the fields, the woods, and the water. And the English helped Massasoit in their turn. Once, when the sachem was so sick that he expected to die, a Plymouth man saved his life with broth and medicine. [See the article about William Bradford in this book for more about Plymouth Colony.]

But the world was changing rapidly. In a few years more English began to come, thousands more. They crowded into the villages they had built on the shore of Massachusetts Bay. And they began to spread out, up and down the coast, up the rivers. They were eager to buy beaver skins from the Algonkians. Back in England, the fur would be made into hats. The English traders paid the Indians in goods—blankets, metal pots,

This tobacco pipe, carved from soapstone, was found at an Indian burial ground near Mount Hope. Scholars think it belonged to Metacom.

fishhooks, rifles, bullets. Neither group trusted the other very much. But each had something the other wanted, and for a time it seemed that they would be able to live together peaceably.

Suddenly the trade in furs came to an end. People in England were bored with beaver hats, and so many beaver had been killed that there were hardly any left to trap. The traders began shipping farm products back to England instead. Land was the only thing they still wanted to buy from the Indians, and the more land the tribes sold, the fewer fields and hunting grounds they had left, and the harder it was for them to keep up their independence. Many times they would agree to sell a piece of land as long as they could continue to hunt or gather food there. But when they did, the colonists would accuse them of trespassing and bring them to their judges for punishment. Rarely, however, did the colonists punish English people who let their cows and sheep trample Algonkian cornfields.

That was one of the things that angered Metacom the most. Many English colonists had no respect for the Indians. Their laws, their religion, their family life, their leadership—none of it was worth anything to these English who were so proud of their own accomplishments. Now that the older generation was passing, there was hardly anyone left who remembered the early days when the English had looked to the Indians to save them from starvation, and the Indians had given generous help.

The younger people among the Wampanoags were saying that the time had come to save themselves. Plymouth Colony was rapidly eating up their territory. They would soon be squeezed into one small peninsula in Narragansett Bay. They had to fight now or lose everything. Of course they could not do it alone. They would have to make alliances with other, bigger tribes, especially their old enemies to the west, the Narragansetts, who were losing their own land to the colony of Rhode Island.

It was not long before the English colonists, always wary of the Indians, heard rumors about war plans. In April of 1671 the leaders of Plymouth Colony ordered Metacom to appear before them and took away all the weapons he and his warriors carried with them. A few months later they forced him to declare publicly that he was subject to the authority of the colony. To pay the fine they imposed, he had to sell yet more land.

One day, in the winter of 1674–75, an Indian named John Sassomon, a Christian convert who had once served Metacom as a translator and ambassador, told Plymouth's governor that Metacom was planning an attack on the colony's village of Swansea. Soon after, Sassomon's body was found in a lake. He had been executed as a traitor. But the English refused to recognize any system of justice beside their own, and they hanged three Wampanoag men for his murder.

This was more than the Wampanoags could tolerate. Although their preparations for war were not finished, they decided to act. The women and children were sent away to live under the protection of the Narragansetts. On June 24, 1675, a band of Metacom's warriors struck Swansea, burned its buildings, and killed six colonists on their way home from church. An army of colonists (including some pardoned pirates) marched out to the Indians' headquarters at Mount Hope, but they found it deserted. Metacom and his sister-in-law Weetamoo, chief of one of the Wampanoag groups, had left in canoes, together with their warriors, and were hidden in Pocasset Swamp, where the English could never find them.

That was the beginning of King Philip's War, the costliest war New England ever fought. For many months, the Wampanoags and their allies from the nearby tribes roamed across the land, raiding one English village after another. Up and down the Connecticut River, along the colonies' western frontier, homes and barns went up in smoke. The Indians could move speedily through the woods without being seen or heard, along a network of trails they knew well. The colonists found it impossible to defend themselves. If they went out to their fields to work, they risked being ambushed and killed. They never knew where their enemies would strike next.

A few weeks after the war broke out, the leaders of the Bay Colony sent a mission to the Nipmuck tribe, to ask them not to join the rebellion. (The mission's doomed leader was Edward Hutchinson, the son of Anne Hutchinson, who had been exiled from Massachusetts in 1637 for rejecting the authority of the Puritan church. To read her story, see the article about her in this book.) The men, riding on horseback, were ambushed in a narrow place between a swamp and a steep hill, and had to charge straight into musket fire to escape. Those who survived raced back with the wounded to the tiny farm village of Brookfield, where they holed up, along with the village families, in one of the houses. For more than two days they were besieged by Nipmuck warriors, who kept up a constant stream of gunfire and played football with the head of a captured man. Three times the warriors tried to set the house afire but were stopped by rain. The siege ended when a troop of English soldiers arrived, alerted by a colonist who had escaped from the house in the darkness. Several pregnant women in the house gave birth during the siege.

Seeing the success of the uprising, more local tribes decided to join in. The English began to abandon their frontier settlements. Their attempts to launch a counterattack were mainly failures. The deeply religious Puritan leaders of Massachusetts Bay Colony believed that this was God's way of punishing them for being disobedient. They declared days of fasting and penance, and they enacted strict laws against any kind of behavior that differed from the standards of the Puritan church. Quakers, because they refused to fight or to recognize the authority of the ministers, were singled out for harsh treatment.

It took the colonists a long time to realize that they would never succeed unless they received help from Indians who were not part of the rebellion. Many Indians who had converted to Christianity had been rounded up and imprisoned on an island in the Bay. Some of them were now released so that they could serve as scouts and guides for the English. The Mohegan and Niantic tribes were willing to help in order to demonstrate their loyalty to the colonists.

As the cold weather came on, some Wampanoags took refuge for the winter at a fortress that the Narragansett were building on an island in the Great Swamp, near present-day South Kingston, Rhode Island. Inside the fortress, protected by a stone wall topped with wooden spikes and a moat bridged by a single tree trunk, was a camp occupied by warriors and their families, more than a thousand people in all. The English learned the secret route to the island from a captured Narragansett. In the middle of December, the colonial army and a group of Mohegans attacked the fort and set it afire. Some six hundred of the people inside were burned or shot to death, and three hundred more taken were prisoner.

The furious Narragansetts, the strongest and most independent tribe in the area, now joined the uprising with a will. Throughout the spring of 1676 the Indian alliance pushed eastward, nearly all the way to Boston. Even the town of Providence was burned, though its founder, Roger Williams, had been good friends with the Nar-

Indians crossing a tree-trunk bridge to escape their burning camp are attacked by the waiting English colonists during the Great Swamp Fight.

ragansetts for thirty years and had tried to negotiate an end to the hostilities on several occasions. [See the article on Williams in this book.]

To the colonists, all this was the doing of the terrible King Philip. But in fact, once the war was under way, Metacom had little to do with running it. The real military leaders of the Algonkians were Muttawmp, sachem of the Nipmucks; Canonchet, sachem of the Narragansetts; and a few others.

From the Pocasset Swamp, where he had hidden after the first attack at Swansea, Metacom and his warriors had escaped to the Nipmucks' country, pursued by English troopers as they went. After that, he spent most of his time journeying from one tribe to another, convincing them to join the alliance. An English woman named Mary Rowlandson, who was captured by the Narragansett and held hostage for several

weeks, met Metacom on the trail. According to her written account, he comforted her when she despaired and gave her pancakes to eat, and she in turn made a shirt and a cap for his nine-year-old son. During the Great Swamp Fight, he was in the northern part of present-day New York State seeking help from the Mohawks, formidable fighters of the Iroquois tribal group who often raided the Algonkians. They chased him off, and Metacom continued his wanderings.

By May of 1676 the rebellion was running out of steam. Despite the complete destruction of thirteen English villages and the deaths of nearly seven hundred colonists, the English had not yet been conquered. The Algonkians could not afford to keep the war going indefinitely. They also had lost many hundreds of their people. The colonists outnumbered them; nor would the colonists ever run short of ammunition, because they could get more supplies from England. And if the Indians did not stop fighting soon and start planting corn, there would be no harvest, and they would all starve.

The alliance began to fall apart. Its collapse was hurried along by the execution of Canonchet, who was captured by Mohegans helping the English, and by a costly Algonkian defeat at Peskeompskut (now Turner's Falls, Massachusetts). By summertime, the Algonkian forces had dwindled to a few groups of fugitives hiding in the woods. When Metacom's wife Nanuskooke and their child were captured at the beginning of August, Metacom lost what was left of his fighting spirit. He went back to his old camp at Mount Hope. One of his own men betrayed him to the English and helped them set up an ambush in which Metacom was killed. The English cut off his head and took it back to Plymouth, where it was stuck on a pike and displayed to the public for twenty years. Metacom's wife and son were sold into slavery in the Spanish colony of Bermuda, along with many other Indians who had surrendered or been taken prisoner.

The defeat of the Indians was complete. Even the mighty Narragansetts were broken. The people who had lived in America for thousands of years would become servants and laborers for the people from across the sea. The colonists could now do what they liked with New England.

Roger Williams

Roger Williams. Born circa 1603 in London. Died 1683 in Providence, Rhode Island.

In the main village of the Narragansett Indians, a council of war was under way. The tribe had gathered to listen to messengers sent by the Pequots, their neighbors to the west. The angry Pequots were planning to attack the four English colonies—Massachusetts Bay, Connecticut, Plymouth, and Providence—that had sprung up over the past several years.

The Pequot ambassadors spoke plainly. The English settlers would soon destroy everything that had been there before. Every year they took more tribal land for their own use. They declared that the land belonged to a king who lived somewhere across the ocean. They insisted that the inhabitants submit to the colony's judges, even though the judges were unfair to them. It was time to forget old quarrels and join together to get rid of these arrogant intruders, the ambassadors said. If not, first the Pequots would be destroyed, then the Narragansetts, and eventually all the Algonkian tribes that inhabited what the settlers called New England.

The Narragansett warriors were inclined to agree, and so were their leaders, the chiefs Canonicus and Miantonomo. It was indeed high time to show the English that the Algonkians were their own masters.

A lone Englishman came to the door, his clothes soaked through with rain and spray. Canonicus welcomed him in. It was the preacher and trader Roger Williams, the only Englishman who could speak to the Algonkians in their own language, and the only one who understood their way of life. Canonicus liked Williams so much that he had given him a piece of land when he was banished by the leaders of Massachusetts Bay for challenging their authority. More than once he had stepped in to mend a conflict between one tribe and another. Today he had come through a storm, alone in a canoe, to ask the Narragansetts not to make an alliance with the Pequots. Williams and the Pequot messengers argued the matter back and forth for three days, until the Narragansetts decided to stay out of the war.

It was only one of many times that Williams served as a mediator between the Algonkian tribes and the English settlers. But though the settlers were glad of his help in matters like these, they considered him to be mainly a troublemaker, forever threatening them with foolish and

Statue of Roger Williams in Providence, Rhode Island

Williams was born in London, probably in 1603, the same year that Queen Elizabeth died. He grew up in the bustling riverside neighborhood of Smithfield, where his father, a well-to-do merchant, kept a shop. Close by his house were the execution fields where several generations of England's religious martyrs were burned alive. In the same neighborhood was the house of John Smith, the founder of the English colony in Virginia and the would-be colonizer of New England. [See the article on Smith in this book.] Though his own family was content to be part of the Church of England, the national Protestant church led by the king, Williams when he was still a boy joined the reformers known as the Puritans, who wanted to remove from the Church all traces of Roman Catholicism and to restore a "pure" form of Christian worship based on the Bible.

From an early age, Williams spent long hours at school, studying Latin and English. He learned Dutch from refugee children who lived in Smithfield. One day, while he was taking shorthand notes on a sermon in church, he came to the attention of Sir Edward Coke, England's Chief Justice. (He was the man who prosecuted for treason Sir Walter Raleigh, the man who founded the first English colony in the New World. See the article on Raleigh in this book.) Coke hired Williams to take notes in the special court called the Star Chamber, where people were tried for illegal religious and political activities. With Coke's help, Williams was admitted to a high school—a rare privilege for a merchant's son in those days—and went on to Cambridge University, where he studied for the ministry. Then he took a job as chaplain in the house of a rich family.

The changes in English society after the death of Queen Elizabeth were bringing England closer and closer to a civil war. Parliament, the nation's legislature, was fighting to limit the powers and privileges of King Charles, while the leaders of the Church of England were dealing out harsh punishments to their Puritan critics. Some of the leading Puritan ministers left England to start a colony in the New World, on the shores of Massachusetts Bay. Williams decided to join them. In February 1631, after a two-month journey, he and his wife Mary arrived at the town of Boston.

The leaders of the Bay Colony were friends of Williams's, and they quickly offered him the job of

dangerous ideas. The Puritans of Massachusetts Bay were trying their hardest to build a place of perfect holiness where everyone accepted the same church, the same morality, and the same God. Williams said that in order to come at the truth, people must be allowed to search wherever their consciences led them. His little colony of Rhode Island was a haven for religious groups—Quakers, Anabaptists, Jews—who had been hounded out of the other English colonies. One day, the Puritans hoped, they would take Rhode Island away from Roger Williams and get rid of everyone who had found a home there.

junior minister at Boston's church. It took them by surprise when he turned them down, saying that their brand of Puritanism was not pure enough for him. Williams had become a Separatist, someone who believed that the Church of England was beyond reforming and that no true Christian could have anything to do with it. Like all Puritans, he thought that the true church of God consisted of a very small number of believers in whom the grace of God was active. But he went further: he thought that those who felt themselves chosen by God were not permitted to pray alongside the "unregenerate."

Williams surprised his friends further by insisting that the colony's judges, known as magistrates, had no right to punish people for religious offenses such as breaking the Sabbath. Ancient Israel had had a single civil and religious law, said Williams, but the New Testament made a separation between the things that are Caesar's (that is, matters for the civil government) and the things that are God's (religious matters).

To the Puritans, Williams was an extremist, and a threat to everything they were trying to achieve. They were happy when he went off to be a preacher at the Separatist colony of Plymouth. [For the story of the Plymouth Separatists, see the article in this book about their governor, William Bradford.] But within a short time, he shocked the Plymouth settlers too by declaring that the Christian kings of Europe, including England's king, had no right to claim for themselves the lands of the New World, which belonged entirely to their non-Christian inhabitants. If Williams was correct, then the royal charters for the English colonies in America were not valid, and the colonies were illegal.

By August 1634, Williams was back in Massachusetts Bay colony as the minister of the church in the town of Salem. Hardly a month went by when he did not do something to anger the colony's leaders. He denounced his fellow ministers for conspiring to force a single kind of worship on everyone, saying that it was no different from what the Church of England had done back home. He refused to swear an oath of loyalty to the colony on the ground that any kind of oath or vow was strictly a religious matter, and hence could not be required by a government. He refused to give up his views on Indian ownership of the land. This really upset the Bay colony's magistrates, for King Charles was trying to put them under the control of a royal governor, and Williams's claim might have given the king the excuse he needed.

It was clear to Williams's former friends that there was no place for a man like him in Massachusetts Bay. In October 1635 they put him on trial for his "new and dangerous opinions against the authority of magistrates." He was found guilty and ordered to leave the colony by springtime. But because he continued to voice his dangerous opinions to others, the magistrates sent soldiers to seize him and put him on a ship bound for England. When the soldiers knocked on his door, they found that he had gone into the wilderness three days before, leaving his family behind.

It was the middle of January when Williams set out to the southwest, through one of the coldest and stormiest winters on record. He hoped to find shelter with some of the Indians, whose language he had already begun to learn. People from the Wampanoag tribe found him in the woods and brought him to their village of Sowams, where their chief, Massasoit, had his court. [In addition to saving Roger Williams's life, Massasoit had already saved the lives of the Pilgrims at Plymouth. For more about that story, see the article on Tisquantum in this book.] During his three months at Sowams, he helped resolve a dispute between the Wampanoags and their neighbors and rivals, the Narragansetts.

In the spring, Williams, accompanied by five men who had joined him from Salem, made his way to a piece of land on the eastern shore of the Seekonk River that he had bought from Massasoit. They built shelters there and planted crops. Then a message came from Plymouth, informing them that they were inside the colony's boundaries and asking them to move farther away. Crowding into a canoe, the men crossed to the other side of the river, where they were greeted in English by a group of Narragansett Indians. With the permission of Canonicus, they picked out a site for a village which Williams called Providence, "in a sense of God's merciful providence unto me in my distress." They were soon joined by their families and other refugees from Massachusetts Bay.

From the beginning, Williams intended that this new colony, which afterwards received the name of Rhode Island, would be a different kind of place from the other English colonies, and from England as well. The land that he had bought from Canonicus was shared among the settlers. Every new settler would also be given a share of the land. The town government was set up on clear democratic principles. Decisions would be reached in townwide meetings at which all heads of households could speak their minds. Most important to Williams, the government would confine itself to civil matters only. It would have nothing to do with the practice of religion. Providence would be a refuge "for such as were destitute for conscience' sake." Anyone who had been persecuted for a religious belief could come there.

These principles were put to the test the following year, when the lay preacher Anne Hutchinson was exiled from Massachusetts Bay for teaching that God's revelation could come to individuals directly, rather than through Scripture. [See the article on Anne Hutchinson.] She and a group of her followers came to live on Aquidneck Island in Narragansett Bay, a few miles from Providence. Williams had bought the island from Canonicus for them. Within a short time, the Hutchinsonians began quarreling among themselves over religious and political ideas. One ambitious man nearly succeeded in taking over Aquidneck and making himself governor for life. Some Rhode Islanders tried to undermine Williams's plans for fair distribution of land by secretly changing documents and trying to defraud the Narragansetts of territory that they had never agreed to sell. Others refused to obey the colony's laws.

That was one point on which Williams was adamant. Freedom of conscience was guaranteed to all members of the colony. But that did not give them the right to defy the colony's government. He compared a community of people to a ship on the ocean. The passengers are all welcome to pray in different ways, but for the good of everyone aboard, they must obey the orders of the captain.

Wampanoag Indians offer shelter to Williams after his banishment from the Massachusetts Bay Colony in the dead of winter in 1636.

Williams had no patience with colonists who said that they were pacifists and refused to serve in the militia. He did his best to keep the peace and he often succeeded, but when he failed, he saw it as his duty to work for a responsible victory.

The Pequot War was one example. After Williams persuaded the Narragansetts to stay out of a military alliance with the Pequots, things happened very much as the Pequot ambassadors had predicted. War broke out between the Pequots and the English colonies, who had made their own alliance with the Mohegan tribe. In letters to Governor John Winthrop of Massachusetts Bay, Williams kept Boston informed about developments in the war. He also passed along a battle plan that had been recommended to him by the Narrangasetts, in which the English army would pretend to retreat, then make a surprise attack on the main Pequot fort. The English followed this advice, but to Williams's disgust, they not only attacked the fort but burned it to the ground with the hundreds of people inside it, including women and children. The surviving Pequots were hunted down and slaughtered or enslaved. Afterwards, Williams negotiated a settlement between the colonies and the various Algonkian tribes that was intended to avert further bloodshed.

When he was not helping out with the colony's affairs, Williams spent his time farming his land, preaching, and selling goods to his Algonkian neighbors at a small trading post that he reached by canoe. But it began to look as if his tiny colony would soon be swallowed up by Massachusetts Bay. The Bay leaders were afraid that the unorthodox ideas brewing in Rhode Island would infect their own people. They sent agents to London to get permission for a takeover of Rhode Island. In 1643 Williams went to London himself to get a charter that would protect Rhode Island from this threat. (On his way to the Dutch colony of New Netherlands to take ship—for he was still banned from the port at Boston—he saw the beginning of the Indian uprising that resulted in the death of Anne Hutchinson.)

When he arrived, he found London in a ferment. The Civil War had broken out at last. Parliament, led by Puritans, controlled the government, and the leaders of the Church of England had been imprisoned. During the fifteen months that Williams waited for his charter, he wrote a

Settlements in Rhode Island

short book entitled *The Bloudy Tenent of Persecution for Cause of Conscience*, in which he set forth his belief that God gives to a nation's people the right to form whatever kind of government they choose—a shocking idea at the time. He also wrote that there was no basis in the teachings of Jesus for a national church and scolded the Puritans of New England for their refusal to allow freedom of religion after they themselves had experienced religious persecution. He published more works of the same kind when he came again to London in 1651 to get a revised charter. Both charters upheld liberty of conscience as a guaranteed right in Rhode Island, which made that colony the only place in the English-speaking world where people could pray as they wished.

In insisting on religious freedom, Williams was not simply being generous and open-minded. He thought that the true church described in the New Testament had disappeared during the centuries when Christian teachings were controlled by the Roman Catholic Church. Until the Second Coming of Jesus, no one could know exactly what form worship should take; hence, the civil authorities could not discriminate among different religions, including non-Christian religions. But Williams himself was a stickler for Puritan principles, and ridiculed other beliefs as "error." Eventually he gave up preaching and joined the

Seekers, who rejected all church worship and religious sacraments, gathering instead for prayer in private homes. Late in his life, he had a public argument with the Quakers, who had made many converts in Rhode Island after being hounded out of Massachusetts Bay. As one who relied entirely on the authority of the written Scripture, Williams regarded with contempt the Quakers' notion that the Holy Spirit was present in their own bodies. [See the article in this book on William Penn, the founder of the Quaker colony of Pennsylvania and another early champion of religious freedom.]

From 1654 to 1657 Williams was president of Rhode Island. Even in his old age he was kept busy as an interpreter in discussions between the English settlers and their Algonkian neighbors. The Pequot War had subdued the Pequots, but the conflict between the colonists and the other tribes had continued to simmer for years. Miantonomo, Canonicus's nephew and fellow chief, had been assassinated by the Mohegans with the approval of Massachusetts Bay. Canonicus and Massasoit were dead, and the new chiefs of the Wampanoags and the Narragansetts found it hard to suppress their resentment over their treatment by the colonists. Finally, in 1676, they rebelled. [For more of this story, see the article on Metacom, also known as King Philip, in this book.]

Williams met with his old friends among the Narragansetts to try to prevent the outbreak of war, but it was too late. Over the next year, the tribes made guerrilla attacks on English settlements and destroyed town after town. Most of Providence, including Williams's house, was burned to the ground, though he went personally to ask that the town be spared. In the end, the tribal alliance was defeated, and the Narragansetts, who in former days had been able to put three thousand warriors in the field, were exterminated. The few who survived were enslaved.

This was a sad sight for the man who once wrote, "It was not price nor money that could have purchased Rhode Island. Rhode Island was purchased by love." Williams continued to serve on the town council until a year before his death, early in 1683. By that time, the democratic principles on which he had founded Providence were being abandoned by the next generation, which had found a source of great wealth in the slave trade. Three hundred years after Williams was banished from Massachusetts, his sentence was revoked by the state. But ironically enough, by that time both Massachusetts and Rhode Island, in the grip of anticommunist hysteria, were insisting that schoolteachers sign oaths of loyalty to the government—one of the very issues that had brought about Williams's exile in the first place.

William Penn

William Penn. Born October 14, 1644, in London. Died July 30, 1718, in Ruscombe, England.

In a small town in Ireland in the year 1666, a group of Quakers quietly began to gather for their prayer meeting. A famous Quaker preacher, Thomas Loe, would be speaking that night, and there was much anticipation among the Friends, as the Quakers call themselves.

One person at the meeting stood out from the others. He was a handsome young man of twenty-two, dressed in the lace-trimmed costume of a cavalier and wearing an elegant black wig. The gleaming sword hanging from his belt made him seem out of place among the peace-loving Quakers. He had the air of a soldier, but he talked with the cleverness of a legal scholar.

It was rare to see a cavalier attending a Quaker meeting. The cavaliers were well-to-do English people who were militant supporters of the English king, Charles II. The Quakers were radical

Protestants who refused to fight for the king or even doff their hats to him. They lived in obedience to the promptings of an "inner light" that they felt came directly from God. For this heretical idea, and for their defiance of authority, they were persecuted and harassed throughout the kingdom.

The young cavalier, whose name was William Penn, was the eldest son of a rich family that belonged to the official Church of England and detested the Quakers. If Penn's father, an admiral and the king's good friend, had known his son was at this meeting, he might well have disowned him. But Penn was interested in what the Quakers had to say. As a boy, he had heard Thomas Loe preach, and through his years as a student, soldier, sailor, and manager of his father's lands, he had not forgotten Loe's moving words. Now, when Loe rose and preached, "There is a faith that overcometh the world, and a faith that is overcome by the world," Penn began to weep. From that night forward, he was a dedicated Quaker.

Despite his new convictions, Penn was still more a man of action than a man of peace. A few weeks later, he was at a Quaker meeting when a soldier burst in and began to make trouble. Penn picked the man up and was about to throw him down the stairs when he was stopped by the other Quakers, who insisted that violence was not their way. The soldier scurried off to the authorities, and soon the whole group was under arrest for "riotous assembly." When the judge saw Penn in his expensive clothes, he ordered the soldiers to release him, saying that there must have been a mistake—no man of Penn's class could be a Quaker. But Penn refused to accept his release. The mistake was all on the judge's part. In a letter of protest to the judge, Penn wrote, "Diversities of faith and worship contribute not to the disturbance of any place." Religious tolerance, he continued, was necessary for true freedom. Though this was not a new idea in England, the government considered it a dangerous notion and few people of the time were prepared to act on it. Penn was one of the first to put the principle of religious tolerance into practice—not in England, but in the New World.

When Penn became a Quaker, England was in political and religious turmoil. The country had just been through a civil war that started out as a

William Penn as a young man

struggle between the king and Parliament, the English legislature, but soon became a religious battle and a social revolution as well. The Puritans, led by Oliver Cromwell, seized control of the government, and in 1649 they shocked the world by executing the king as a traitor. In 1660, after Cromwell's death, the dead king's son, Charles II, returned from exile in France, defeated his enemies, and regained the throne. But religious tensions still ran high. The king and his supporters feared a new rebellion by radical Protestants. The Protestants feared that the king planned to make Catholicism the state religion again, as it had been up until a century before.

Small sects like the Quakers (who, though Protestants, were neither Puritans or Anglicans), suffered the worst in this confusion. Because Quakers refused to do such things as swear an oath of loyalty to the king (Quakers do not swear oaths of any kind), they were thought to be untrustworthy. Malicious informers would sneak into Quaker meetings and report to the authorities that they were plotting rebellion. Then the Quakers would be arrested and imprisoned.

Penn himself was imprisoned a number of times for his Quaker beliefs. In one of the most famous cases in English law, Penn and another Quaker, William Meade, were seized in London for preaching before a Quaker gathering. Penn insisted on a jury trial and pleaded eloquently for the right to see a copy of the charges against them and the text of the laws they were accused of breaking. These rights were guaranteed by English law, but the judge, the Lord Mayor of London, refused Penn's request. The Lord Mayor made it clear that he intended to convict Penn and Meade one way or another. When Penn accused the mayor of having "sinister and arbitrary designs" against them, the mayor had Penn and Meade shut into an iron cage in a corner of the courtroom.

Eventually, the jury returned a verdict of not guilty. The Lord Mayor angrily declared it no verdict at all. "If 'not guilty' be no verdict," returned Penn, "then you make of the jury and Magna Charta [the ancient English bill of rights] a mere nose of wax." But the Lord Mayor had the last word. He sent Penn to Newgate Prison for contempt of court, and threw the whole jury into jail as well for insisting on their right to reach an independent verdict. The jurymen pressed their case from prison and finally won the right for all English juries to be free from the control of judges.

Persecution of the Quakers became worse over the years, especially after Penn and a few other important Quakers began supporting the Whigs. The Whigs were a new political party, made up mainly of Protestants, that opposed the king and believed that Parliament should be free of royal control. After the elections of 1679, in which the Whigs won brief control of Parliament, King Charles postponed Parliament sessions for a year and hanged quite a few Whigs.

Penn began to think there might be little future for the Quakers in England. For years he had dreamed of starting a Quaker settlement in England's North American colonies. Several Quakers had already been to the colonies, but they had not met with a warm reception there, especially not from the Puritans of New England. [For more on religious controversies in New England, see the articles on William Bradford and Anne Hutchinson in this book.] In 1655 the first two Quakers in the Puritan colony of Boston, Mary Fisher and Ann Austin, had been imprisoned, accused of witchcraft, and exiled to the island of Barbados in the Caribbean.

In 1677 lands in the colonial province of West New Jersey (an area that is now part of the state of New Jersey) came into the hands of a few prominent Quakers, including Penn. Here was a place where Quakers and other dissenters could live in peace, free from the persecutions they suffered in both England and New England. That year, two hundred settlers arrived at a spot near the Delaware River and founded the town of Burlington. Penn, who was already famous for his pamphlets defending Quaker beliefs, drafted for the settlement a charter of liberties that later became one of the models for the American Constitution. In it he guaranteed to the settlers many new freedoms: free and fair trial by jury, freedom of religion, freedom from unjust imprisonment, and free elections. The guiding idea of his charter, he explained, was "to put the power in the people."

The West New Jersey settlement prospered, and some years later Penn saw an opportunity to expand it. In 1680 King Charles II granted him title to a vast tract of land south and west of New Jersey as repayment for loans made to the king by Penn's father. It was the king's idea to name the land Pennsylvania ("Penn's Woods"). At one stroke Penn became one of the greatest landowners in history, since Pennsylvania is about the same size as England itself. King Charles made it clear that Quakers, Whigs, and other troublesome dissenters would be welcome to leave England and settle in the new territory. Without spending a penny, wrote Penn, the king was able "to be rid of us at so cheap a rate as a little parchment."

As proprietor of Pennsylvania, Penn was given complete authority over the colony; he had to answer only to the king. But Penn had no desire to rule a kingdom of his own. He framed a government for the new colony in which representatives elected to a general assembly would make the laws, and a governor and council would enforce them. Each branch of government would keep the other from gaining too much power, so that no leader would be able to assume complete control and "hinder the good of the whole country." Free elections and fair trials were guaranteed. Anyone of any religion could live in the colony, and no one could be "molested or prejudiced for their religious persuasion."

The political freedom and rich soil of Pennsylvania attracted not only English but also Scotch, Dutch, and German colonists. But Penn himself continued to live in England. He made two brief trips to America, the first from 1682 to 1684 and the second from 1699 to 1701. During the first trip he spent most of his time turning his political ideas into a working government, exploring the interior of the province, and attending Quaker meetings. Penn also worked hard to make friends with the Indian inhabitants of the province. He saw to it that the Indians were paid for their lands and that they were treated with respect. In a famous letter addressed to the Indians, Penn wrote: "I am very sensible of the unkindness and injustice that hath been too much exercised toward you by the people of these parts of the world [meaning Europeans]. . . . But I am not such a man, I have great love and regard towards you." If any of the settlers wronged an Indian, Penn continued, there would be a fair trial, with "an equal number of just men on both sides." Never before in any European colony had the Indians been offered political and legal equality of this kind. The result was that the colonists and the Indians lived in peace for much longer in Pennsylvania than in the other English colonies. [See the articles in this book on Pocahantas, Tisquantum, and Metacom.]

A well-known story has it that Penn signed a treaty of peace with the Indians at a place called Shackamaxon. There, standing under a giant elm tree, he pledged to Chief Tamament (also known as Tammany) of the Lenni Lenape tribe that the Quakers and the Indians would always be friends. The story goes on to say that Penn then bested the Indians at a variety of outdoor sports, but

Penn pledges mutual friendship with the Lenni Lenape Indians at Shackamaxon. This episode has become part of American historical folklore.

given that Penn would have been nearly forty years old, was rather stout, and did not approve of games, this part of the story is unlikely to be true.

In 1685 Charles's brother James became king. Penn, who was now back in England, had long been James's friend and was able to convince the king to release more than a thousand Quakers from prison. But when James was deposed in 1688 for his pro-Catholic policies, Penn himself was accused of disloyalty to England and even of being a secret Catholic. For two years he had to stay out of politics. Then Penn was saddened by the deaths of his first wife, Guli, and his favorite son, Springett. On top of that, there was growing political strife in Pennsylvania, where the governor (who was chosen by Penn) and the General Assembly quarreled constantly. Penn found that the rough-and-tumble democracy he had created had none of the courtesy and harmony of a Quaker meeting.

"For the love of God, me, and the poor country," he wrote to one argumentative group of colonists, "be not so governmentish, so noisy, and open in your dissatisfactions!"

Penn's troubles prevented his return to Pennsylvania until 1699. During his second stay, he put forward the first plan to unite all of England's American colonies in a federation. According to some stories, Penn also tried to reduce or eliminate slavery in Pennsylvania, but this is not likely, for he owned and traded in slaves himself. He did believe in good treatment for slaves, however, and other Quakers in Pennsylvania were early founders of the antislavery movement.

Penn had hoped to settle permanently in the city of Philadelphia, which he had planned and laid out himself, but political events in England forced him to return in 1701. There he discovered that his trusted financial advisor, Philip Ford, had

The original design of Philadelphia, drawn in 1682 from Penn's plans, shows an orderly city with a public square and four wooded parks.

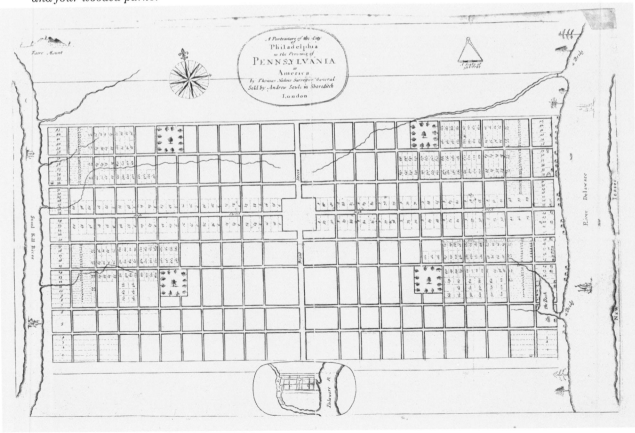

cheated him out of thousands of pounds. Through legal trickery, Ford almost won possession of Pennsylvania. Lawsuits between Penn and the Ford family dragged on for years. At one point the Fords had Penn thrown into debtor's prison.

Tired of running his colony's affairs from across the ocean, Penn decided to sell Pennsylvania back to England. The deal was still being discussed when Penn suffered a stroke in 1712. Unable to speak or to care for himself, he was nursed by his second wife, Hannah, until his death six years later at the age of seventy-four.

The colony of Pennsylvania remained in the hands of the Penn family until the American Revolution. Though Penn himself did not spend many years in America, he had a profound effect on the development of the United States. In fact, every country that is governed by a constitution owes a debt to Penn's very modern ideas of fair government and freedom of religion.

Daniel Boone

Daniel Boone. Born November 2, 1734, in Berks County, Pennsylvania. Died circa September 26, 1820, in St. Charles, Missouri.

He was called the American Adam, the American Moses, and the Achilles of the West. Poets hailed him as "The Mountain Muse" and the man "happiest among mortals." Famous artists painted his portrait, though only one artist ever drew him from life. He was Daniel Boone, the eighteenth-century American frontiersman, and there are probably more legends, tall tales, and outright lies about him than about any other American. While much of what is commonly told about him is not true, there is no doubt that Boone's real life was filled with enough adventure for any legend.

Boone was born to a family of Quakers who had moved from England to the British colony of Pennsylvania in 1717. [For information about the founding of Pennsylvania as a Quaker refuge, see the article about William Penn in this book.] At the age of twelve he was given his first gun—a long-barreled rifle that was taller than he was—and began learning how to live off the land using his rifle, his woodcraft, and his wits. He never went to school but worked the family farm in the spring and summer, hunted deer in the fall, and trapped beaver, otter, and bear in the winter. His father taught him blacksmithing, so he could make his own traps and repair his own gun.

In 1751 he and his family moved to North Carolina, settling on the banks of the north fork of the Yadkin River. To the west, on the other side of the Appalachian Mountains, lay the hidden land of Kentucky, the shared hunting ground of the Cherokee, the Shawnee, and other Indian tribes. The only way into Kentucky was by the Warrior's Path, an old Indian trail that vanished west through a notch in the mountains called the Cumberland Gap, at the meeting of the present-day states of Virginia, Tennessee, and Kentucky. Rumors of the beauty and natural wealth of Kentucky spread through North Carolina, but few settlers were willing to go find out for themselves. The Indians who owned that land protected it fiercely.

After a stretch in the British colonial army, Boone settled down and in 1756 married a neighbor's daughter, Rebecca Bryan. She had to manage their home on her own most of the time, for her husband was usually gone hunting, trapping, or exploring the lands leading to the Cumberland Gap. We can follow his travels today because he would often stop and carve a message into a handy beech tree, like this: "D. Boon killed a bar [bear] on tree in the year 1760," or "Come on boys here's good water." It was an old woodsman's trick, part of blazing a trail. Some of these carvings were photographed in the nineteenth century; traces of others can still be seen today.

Richard Henderson, a local judge, had a grand scheme to make Kentucky the fourteenth British colony, and Boone was the logical choice to lead a party of exploration. Boone, his brother Squire Boone, and a few companions entered Kentucky in 1767, and again in 1769. On both trips they had trouble with the Indians. Boone was captured twice by a Shawnee hunting party and both times was let go with a warning never to return. Several times all his gear was stolen, along with the furs of the animals he had caught—major setbacks for a man who had little money and was often in debt. Once he had to leap from a cliff into the top of a tree to escape the Shawnee, who, he suspected, would not be so kind if they caught him a third time.

Although Boone had not been the first white man to explore Kentucky, as is often claimed, he now knew it better than anyone else. In 1773 he set out with forty settlers to found a colony there. They had traveled only a few miles when they were attacked by Cherokee warriors and driven

Daniel Boone, portrait by an unknown American artist

back. Boone's young son James was captured, tortured, and killed. A short time later the Cherokee agreed to sell Kentucky to a group of whites, including Judge Henderson. As employees of Henderson's Transylvania Company, Boone and twenty-eight other frontiersmen cut a road along the Warrior's Path through the Cumberland Gap. This road, called the Wilderness Trail, was used by all the early Kentucky settlers. Boone himself founded a new settlement called Boonesborough. He moved there with his wife and family in August 1775.

Boone was out hunting one day in 1778 when he was captured by a group of Shawnee warriors. Their leader, a chief named Blackfish, proudly adopted the well-known hunter as his own son. Shortly after, Boone learned that the Shawnee were planning a surprise attack on Boonesborough. One night he slipped out of the village on horseback. With the Shawnee close behind him, he rode the horse until it dropped, then ran the rest of the 160 miles to Boonesborough. Boone's warning gave the town enough time to repair the stockade and lay in supplies. A few weeks later the town was besieged by a war party of four hundred Indians (including Blackfish) and forty British and Canadian soldiers. (This was during the Revolutionary War, when the British often used Indian allies to attack American settlements.) The Indians tried to burn down the town with fire arrows, but rain came and put out the flames. Indian and British snipers began to pick off the defenders one by one, while Boone and the other frontiersmen fought back desperately with their long rifles. They were saved by a relief force of eighty backwoodsmen who arrived from another settlement.

Henderson's grand scheme to create a fourteenth colony failed because he could not obtain legal title to the land. When Kentucky was made a county of the new state of Virginia at the end of the Revolutionary War, Boone also lost his title to the lands he had claimed. (Kentucky did not become a state in its own right until 1792.) Despite this setback Boone stayed in Kentucky, earning money to buy new claims to his holdings and collecting money from the other settlers who wanted to buy legal titles to their lands as well. In 1780, on the way to Richmond, the capital of Virginia, to purchase the titles, he was robbed of $40,000—

A group of settlers bound for Kentucky in the mid-1770s make their way through the Cumberland Gap with Boone as their guide.

all he had collected from the settlers, plus his own life savings. It took Boone thirty years of hard work to pay back the settlers' money. When he finally did, in 1810, he was left with just a half-dollar to his name.

Over the next few years Boone served as a delegate to the Virginia legislature (while Kentucky was still a part of that state) and held many local offices such as sheriff and county surveyor. So familiar was he with the land that he was often asked to draw up land-claim maps from memory. But Boone, who was completely at home in the wilderness, was not so familiar with the workings of civilization. Again he lost all his holdings, as, one by one, all the land-claims he had drawn up for himself and others over the years were declared invalid. That made him some lifelong enemies. In 1788, bitter and nearly penniless, he left Kentucky for good. Moving first to Kanawha County in what is now West Virginia, Boone in 1799 went

with his son Daniel Morgan Boone to Missouri, in what was then the French-owned Louisiana Territory. After Rebecca died in 1813 Boone lived with another son, Nathan, until his own death in 1820 at the age of eighty-six.

Boone's reputation as trailblazer and Indian fighter was unsurpassed even in his own lifetime. His friend James Filson made him famous by writing about him in a history of Kentucky published in 1784. Filson's book was full of tall tales about Boone made up by Filson himself, but it fired the imaginations of other writers. The English romantic poet Lord Byron put Boone into his satiric poem *Don Juan*, contrasting the frontiersman with Europeans of the time. The character of Natty Bumppo in the American novelist James Fenimore Cooper's *Leatherstocking Tales* was based on Boone. To these writers, Boone was a man completely free and in tune with nature—the symbol of all things American.

Jean Baptiste Point DuSable

Jean Baptiste. Point DuSable (du-SAH-bleh), last name variously given as Sable, Point Sable, Point du Sable, Pointe Du Sable, and Point de Saible. Born circa 1750, probably in Saint Domingue (now Haiti). Died August 28, 1818, in St. Charles, Missouri.

Today the city of Chicago proudly calls itself "the Second City of the United States." Back in the late eighteenth century, however, the future site of Chicago could not attract a single settler. The weather was harsh; the land, on the shores of Lake Michigan, was marshy and not well suited for crops. The Indians refused to live there because of the strong-smelling wild garlic and skunk grass that grew in abundance. (*Chegagou*, from which the name Chicago comes, is an Indian word that means something like "big strong onion.") There were no white settlements within a hundred miles.

Only one person saw the possibilities in this site. He was Jean Baptiste Point DuSable, an African-American pioneer who made the first

Jean Baptiste Point DuSable

claim of land in Chicago and built its first homestead. As the Potawatomie Indians liked to say, "The first white man in Chicago was a black man."

Records are scarce as to DuSable's early life, but it is likely that he was born a free man sometime around 1750 on the Caribbean island of Hispaniola, in what is now called Haiti but was then the French colony of Saint Domingue. His father was French and his mother was African-American; both were devout Catholics, and so was DuSable. By the early 1770s DuSable had left Haiti for the mainland. Starting from New Orleans, he worked his way up the Mississippi River to the town of Peoria, in the present-day state of Illinois. There he married an Indian woman named Catherine and started a family on a small farm of thirty acres.

According to the accounts of people who knew him, DuSable was a tall, handsome man who was equally skilled as a trader, trapper, and farmer. Often he would travel alone, scouting out new places to trade. Sometime in the late 1770s he headed north from Peoria to the tip of Lake Michigan. The flat, damp lakeside smelled bad and was not much to look at, but DuSable realized that the site was ideal for a trading post. Indian fur traders and white merchants from all over the region—from Illinois and the Mississippi Valley to the south, Michigan to the east, and Canada to the north—had to pass by the spot. DuSable built a large cabin where the mouth of the Chicago River meets Lake Michigan, and by 1779 had made a name for himself buying furs from Indian trappers and selling them to merchants in the Michigan towns of Detroit, St. Joseph, and Mackinac.

These were dangerous times in Illinois. In the summer of 1779 every group that laid claim to the area was at war. Britain's American colonies had declared their independence, and British soldiers were trying to stop the revolution by force. French settlers mainly sided with the Americans, while most Indians sided with the British. DuSable saw himself as both French and American.

DuSable braved Lake Michigan's harsh weather to establish a trading post that attracted brisk business. This drawing shows Chicago in 1820.

The British were suspicious of his activities and accused him of being an American spy. Fearing capture, he fled from Chicago but was arrested by British soldiers near Michigan City in present-day Indiana. He was taken to the British fort at Mackinac, Michigan, where he so impressed the commander that within a year he was made manager of a British trading post. In 1784 DuSable was released and returned to Chicago with his wife and children.

Now DuSable expanded his trading post to nine buildings. He planted corn and wheat fields, raised livestock, and ran a small mill and bakery. (A model of the DuSable homestead can be seen at the National DuSable Memorial Society in Chicago.) Within a few years he was the wealthiest man in the area, able to afford such rare luxuries as a feather bed, a collection of oil paintings by European artists, and a French-made walnut chest with glass doors. The land he owned along the lakefront is today some of the most valuable in Chicago, worth more than two billion dollars.

DuSable, his wife, their children, and their grandchildren lived in Chicago for sixteen years.

By the Civil War years, Chicago was the center of the nation's railroad system and the hub of the Midwest's water transportation routes.

Then, in May, 1800, he sold his lands and holdings for $1,200 to a Frenchman named Jean Lalime and moved away. The property was later purchased by John Kinzie, a white Canadian still called by many "the father of Chicago." DuSable's cabin was long known only as "the Kinzie House."

Why would DuSable move, in the prime of his life and at the height of his wealth? At this time there was an influx of white slave-trading Southerners to Chicago, and some historians think that DuSable, a free black man, no longer felt safe. Other historians say that DuSable was pushed out by land speculators. In any case, we know little more about him. He moved with his family first to Peoria, then to St. Charles, Missouri. There he died a poor man in 1819.

For nearly 150 years, DuSable's reputation was eclipsed by that of John Kinzie. Kinzie's daughter-in-law even wrote a book suggesting that DuSable was a runaway slave with no real claim to the land. It was not until the 1960s, after DuSable's bill of sale to Lalime was discovered in old records, that he was again recognized as Chicago's founder and first citizen.

Sacagawea

Sacagawea (sak-uh-ga-WAY-uh; also spelled Sacajawea). Born sometime between 1784 and 1788, near present-day Lemhi, Idaho. Died December 12 or December 20, 1812, at Fort Manuel, Dakota Territory (now South Dakota).

Only one American woman has had her name given to four mountains, two lakes, a river, and a museum. The woman is Sacagawea, the nineteenth-century Shoshoni Indian who accompanied the expedition of Meriwether Lewis and William Clark through the heart of America to the Pacific coast. [For more about the expedition, see the article on Lewis and Clark in this book]. Without her help, it is unlikely that the expedition could have passed peacefully among the Indian tribes of the West, or made it back safely to St. Louis with news about the vast western frontier.

It is hard today to know which of the many stories told about her are true. We do know that she was born into a Shoshoni tribe that lived in the Rocky Mountains, where the state of Utah is today. Her birth name, Boinaiv (Boy-NAH-eev), is a Shoshoni word meaning "Grass Maiden." Around the year 1800, when Sacagawea was about fourteen years old, she was kidnapped by Crow or Minataree warriors and sold to the Hidatsa, another tribe living hundreds of miles to the east along the Missouri River in present-day North Dakota. There she was sold and "married" to Toussaint Charbonneau, a French-Canadian fur trader who was living with at least one other Indian woman at the same time.

In 1804 Lewis and Clark were wintering on the upper Missouri, seeking Indian-language interpreters for their great expedition to survey the unknown American West. They hired Charbonneau, who spoke Hidatsa. Sacagawea, who spoke Hidatsa and the Shoshoni tongue as well, came with him, carrying her infant son Baptiste on her back. She was just sixteen or seventeen years old.

Lewis and Clark both mention her often in their diaries of the expedition, but they rarely call her by her Indian name, and when they do, her name is rarely spelled the same way twice. Sacagawea may be Hidatsa for Bird Woman, or may be a version of the Shoshoni word *tsikikawias*, for Boat Pusher, after the river longboats the Indians saw her in. William Clark saw the Indians pointing to her and flapping their arms to show the action of the boat's oars. He thought that meant the flapping wings of birds, so he translated the name as Bird Woman. She seems to have had yet another name: Lewis always called her "Jenny" in his diary. He wrote of her that she was good-natured and easygoing. "If she has enough to eat and a few trinkets to wear, I believe she would be perfectly content anywhere." But he also said that, when dealing with the Indians they met along the way, she was "the inspiration, the genius of the occasion."

Lewis and Clark had planned to live off the land, but the hunting was not always good and the expedition often went hungry. Sacagawea helped them find and cook wild plants. She showed a cooler head than her husband when their canoe almost capsized on the fast-running Missouri River. While Charbonneau panicked and prayed to God, she calmly balanced her baby on one knee and retrieved the valuables that fell from the boat as it spun about. More than once, Sacagawea also saved the expedition from hostile Indians, sometimes by her skill with languages, sometimes simply by being there. The expedition must be peaceful, the Indians believed, if it included a mother with a young child.

But Sacagawea was directly responsible for saving the lives of all when they reached her home village in the Rockies. This was pure luck, for Sacagawea herself was not sure exactly where her home was. There her brother Cameahwait was now chief. Lewis and Clark begged Cameahwait for horses to carry the expedition's gear and to use for hunting. Without horses the explorers would starve. The chief was curious about the white men but did not want to give them the horses they asked for; horses were the only wealth the Shoshoni owned. But he changed his mind upon seeing Sacagawea, whom he embraced, calling her *Wadze-wipe* ("Lost Woman"). Sacagawea, for her part, was overjoyed to see her people again, which would never have happened had she not gone along with the expedition. Clark wrote that when she suddenly recognized her brother, "she instantly jumped up and embraced him, throwing over him her blanket, and weeping profusely." With her help, Lewis convinced Cameahwait to give them twenty-nine horses and valuable information about the lands west.

Sacagawea traveled with Lewis and Clark for the rest of their journey, across the Rockies, down the Snake River to the Columbia River, to the Pacific Ocean in November 1805, and then back to St. Louis in 1806. With the help of William Clark, her family settled on a farm in St. Louis in 1809. In 1811 Charbonneau and Sacagawea returned west with an expedition led by Manuel Lisa.

Sacagawea

While Clark and Charbonneau look on, the long-lost Sacagawea identifies herself to her people. The reunion took place on August 17, 1805.

Little else is known about her life. The records of the Lisa expedition show that Sacagawea died of a fever sometime in December 1812, at the age of about twenty-five, a few months after giving birth to a daughter, Lizette. (Clark later adopted the little girl, and helped her son Baptiste in his career as an army guide and mountain man.) But there are a number of stories that say she left Charbonneau about that time and returned to her Shoshoni village. Supposedly, she lived with her people until 1884, when she would have been close to a hundred years old. Whichever story is true, there is no doubt that she is one of the most honored women in American history.

Meriwether Lewis and William Clark

Meriwether Lewis. Born August 18, 1774, near Charlottesville, Virginia. Died October 11, 1809, near Nashville, Tennessee.

William Clark. Born August 1, 1770, in Caroline County, Virginia. Died September 1, 1838, in St. Louis, Missouri.

"Great joy in camp," wrote American explorer William Clark on November 7, 1805. "We are in view of the ocean . . . this great Pacific Ocean which we have been so long anxious to see, and the roaring of the waves breaking on the rocky shores may be heard distinctly." He had good reason to be glad, for Clark, his fellow explorer Meriwether Lewis, and their small party had finally reached the Pacific after a grueling two-year journey across the unmapped American West. The Lewis and Clark expedition is one of the best-known epics of American exploration.

Both of the expedition's leaders were born in Virginia, not far from the home of Thomas Jefferson, who knew Lewis and his family well. In 1795 Lewis served under Clark in the U.S. Army on the frontier in Ohio, where they formed a close friendship. Lewis was well educated and well spoken, a risk-taker who liked to go off on his own. Clark was gruff and practical, a seasoned soldier who had spied on Spanish forts along the Mississippi. Both were expert hunters and woodsmen, with knowledge of the frontier and experience dealing with Indians.

In 1801 President Thomas Jefferson hired Lewis as his private secretary. Jefferson soon decided that Lewis was the ideal leader for a special mission he had long planned: an expedition of discovery across the American continent to the Pacific Ocean, the first official exploration to be sponsored by the young United States. At that time the U.S. owned only lands east of the Mississippi River, but Jefferson was bargaining to buy from France much of the land between the Mississippi and the Rocky Mountains. This deal, called the Louisiana Purchase, was completed in 1803 and instantly doubled the size of the country. Few Americans had been to the Louisiana Territory, and none knew for sure what lay beyond it.

Jefferson outlined several goals for the expedition. The most important was to discover a water route from the Missouri River to the west-flowing Columbia River, and finally to the Pacific Ocean. Such a route was the key to opening the West to American settlement and commerce. It would tie together the East and West coasts, which at that time could communicate only by the long ocean trip around the southern tip of South America. Lewis was also to map the lands the expedition passed through, gather specimens of local plants and animals, and observe the character and customs of the Indians. Finally, Jefferson asked Lewis to act as envoy to the Indians he would meet and judge the potential for trading with them.

At Jefferson's orders, Lewis studied surveying, navigation, medicine, and natural science with the best experts the government could provide. Jefferson urged him to choose a second-in-command, but Lewis preferred to have an equal partner and asked Clark to be his co-captain. In the fall of 1803 the two leaders met in Clarksville, on the Ohio River in present-day Indiana. They assembled their party on the eastern side of the Missouri River near St. Louis, where they spent the winter. In the spring of 1804 they set out up

Meriwether Lewis and William Clark, portraits by Charles Willson Peale

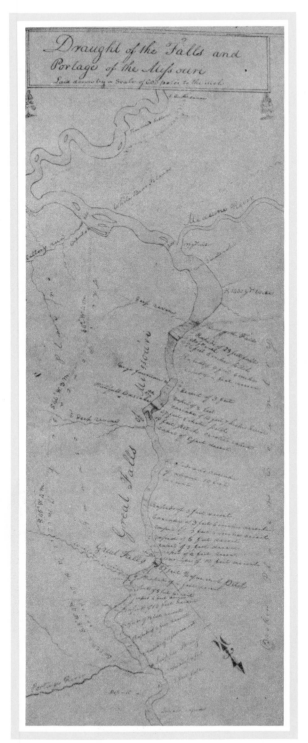

The explorers had to carry their boats past the Great Falls of the Missouri River, which cascade 93 feet. Clark drew this map in his notebook.

the Missouri in a wooden riverboat with twenty-five explorers, more than half of them soldiers, as well as fifteen boatmen, an Indian scout, and Clark's African-American servant.

Throughout the summer they made their way upriver. Rowing against the fast-moving current of the Missouri was back-breaking work; the men often had to pull the boat upstream with a tow rope, or push the boat using poles. Late in the fall of 1804, having traveled some 1,600 miles, they reached the Mandan Indian villages of the upper Missouri River, near the present site of Bismarck, North Dakota. There they made camp in a cottonwood grove. Seeking interpreters who knew the languages of the Indians they would meet farther west, they hired a French trader, Toussaint Charbonneau, and his wife, Sacagawea, a woman of the Rocky Mountain Shoshoni tribe. [For Sacagawea's story, see the article on her in this book.] Sacagawea, who traveled with Lewis and Clark all the way to the Pacific and back, turned out to be one of the most important members of the expedition.

In April of 1805 Lewis and Clark pushed on again, this time in canoes made of cottonwood. These soaked up so much water that they soon had to be abandoned. Beyond the great falls of the Missouri, only a few stretches of the river could be navigated by boat, and from then on the explorers had to go forward mainly on foot. The party saw vast herds of elk and buffalo, so many and so tame that they had to be pushed aside with sticks to make way. They also met several grizzly bears. One huge bear chased six armed men through the woods and leaped after them over a 20-foot cliff. Lewis, who had thought the grizzly's fierce reputation overrated, soon changed his mind. "I had rather fight two Indians than one bear," he wrote.

By midsummer the party had reached the Rocky Mountains, near the villages where Sacagawea had been born. There they came to the stream that was the source of the Missouri River. Crossing the high ridge beyond, Lewis could see "immense ranges of high mountains still to the west of us with their tops partially covered with snow. I now descended the mountain to a handsome bold running stream of cold, clear water. Here I first tasted the water [that flowed into] the great Columbia River." This stream flowed west,

Hungry for food, Clark and some of his men shoot at bears. This woodcut was made from one of the sketches Clark added to his journal.

toward the Pacific Ocean. They had crossed the Continental Divide, the ridge line that separates waters that empty into the Atlantic from waters that empty into the Pacific.

The men were hungry, weary, and footsore. What they needed most was horses, and the only way to get them was from the local Indians, the Mountain Shoshoni. Luckily they made contact with a band of Shoshoni led by a chief named Cameahwait, who turned out to be Sacagawea's brother. With Sacagawea's help, the two captains were able to convince Cameahwait to sell them twenty-nine horses in return for some trade goods and promises of a favorable treaty with the United States.

Now the explorers had to make their way through the roughest country they had yet seen. They led their packhorses up and down ridge after ridge, in each valley cutting their way through dense tangles of dead trees. Autumn was coming on, and snow was already thick on some of the higher ridges. They ran out of food and began eating the horses. Again they were lucky to meet an Indian tribe, the Nez Percé, who fed them and

helped them build canoes for the final leg of their journey to the Pacific. After a swift run down the Snake River they reached the churning rapids of the great Columbia River. Finally, in November 1805, they reached the mouth of the Columbia, in what is now Washington State, and saw their goal—the Pacific Ocean. They had traveled, by Lewis's estimate, more than 5,000 miles.

Though Lewis and Clark had hoped to meet the ships of American or European fur traders at the mouth of the river, there were none so late in the season. They built a camp and miserably waited out the winter. There was not much to eat beyond elk meat, whale blubber, and roots fried in whale oil. Clark, who had written with such joy of finally seeing the Pacific Ocean, ended up hating the cold, wet coastal weather. "I have not seen one Pacific [peaceful] day," he wrote, only endless storms "tempestuous and horrible." They left as early in the spring as possible.

The expedition's return trip was much faster than its trip out. After trudging up the banks of the Columbia for many miles, past thousands of Indians gathering for the annual salmon run, the expedition divided. Lewis took a northern route, and Clark a southern one, seeking the best waterway through the mountains. They charted large sections of the Jefferson, Maria's, and Yellowstone Rivers, in what are now the states of Idaho, Montana, and Wyoming. Here they found countless beaver and otter, rich hunting grounds for fur trappers.

Along the way Lewis had the one violent encounter with Indians of the entire journey. A band of Piegan Blackfeet Indians he met near the source of the Maria's River tried to steal his guns and horses. After a breathless chase down a canyon, one Piegan turned and took aim at Lewis, but Lewis got his shot off first and wounded him. Another Piegan was stabbed in the heart by one of Lewis's men. (This battle was not forgotten by the Blackfeet; when American traders appeared in the area some years later, the Blackfeet attacked them in revenge.) Lewis himself was shot a few days after, but not by vengeful Indians; one of his own men mistook him for a deer. It took him the rest of the journey to recover.

Reunited in August at the junction of the Yellowstone and Missouri Rivers, the two captains spent much of the remainder of their trip trying unsuccessfully to make peace among the Mandan, Hidatsa, Sioux, and other tribes bordering American lands, and to convince their chiefs to visit the president in Washington. As they drifted down the Missouri, the sight of a few ordinary cows standing on the riverbank made them shout with joy. They reached St. Louis in September 1806 and learned that they had long ago been given up for dead.

Now Lewis and Clark were national heroes—the first white Americans to cross the continent. They had found a water route to the Pacific (though it was not as easy to travel as Jefferson had hoped), returned with priceless maps, and opened new areas to the American fur trade. They had been less successful as envoys to the Indians, but Clark went on to make the government's relations with the Indians his life's work.

In 1807 Clark became brigadier-general of militia and superintendent of Indian affairs of the Upper Louisiana Territory, and Lewis was appointed governor of the same region. But Lewis did not serve long. For reasons that are not clear he became depressed and took to drink. During a trip back to Washington, D.C., in 1809 to defend himself against charges that he had misused govern-

To cross the Rocky Mountains, Lewis and Clark followed Indian trails along the natural passes that cut through the mountain range.

The route of Lewis and Clark

ment money, he stayed alone in an inn near the present site of Nashville, Tennessee. There, drunk and despairing, he shot himself to death. Clark succeeded Lewis as governor in 1813. For the rest of his life, Clark showed a passionate concern for the rights of Indians, promoting laws that protected Indian lands and negotiating several treaties. Tribal chiefs were often guests at his home in St. Louis. After Sacagawea died in 1812, he adopted her daughter.

Zebulon Montgomery Pike

Zebulon Montgomery Pike. Born January 5, 1779, in Lamberton (now Lamington), New Jersey. Died April 27, 1813, in York (now Toronto), Ontario, Canada.

"We gave three cheers to Mexican Mountains," wrote American explorer Zebulon Montgomery Pike in his journal. It was the year 1806, and he and his men had been traveling for weeks in the wilderness of the West, coming ever closer to the Spanish territory of New Mexico. They had reached what is now the state of Colorado. On the horizon was a line of purple hills.

Nearer, they could see a tall peak like a blue cloud standing alone on the plain. Pike and three companions set out to climb the 14,000-foot peak. Without water, food, and warm clothes, they could make it only as far as the foothills. The great snowcapped mountain was still fifteen miles away. "I believe that no human being could have ascended to its pinnacle," Pike wrote in disappointment. Pike's Peak, as the mountain is now called, is the chief monument to the exploring career of Zebulon Montgomery Pike. But historians today are more interested in Pike's role in the first great conspiracy against the government of the United States.

Pike was the son of a officer in the new army of

Zebulon Montgomery Pike, portrait by Charles Willson Peale

James Wilkinson

the United States. At the age of fifteen he joined his father's company as a cadet. Five years later, in 1799, he became a lieutenant serving on the western frontier. Pike's energy, ambition, and patriotism brought him to the attention of General James Wilkinson, governor of the Upper Louisiana Territory, then the westernmost part of the United States. [For the story of how this vast territory was claimed by France and sold to the United States, see the articles on La Salle and Lewis and Clark in this book.]

Pike believed that Wilkinson was a great and honorable soldier, but Wilkinson's own actions show that he was a spy and a traitor. Spain, which at that time managed a huge empire that stretched from South America to present-day New Mexico and California, hired Wilkinson in 1787 to spy on the United States. He regularly sold information about American military plans to Spanish officials, who feared the United States as their chief rival in North America. At the same time Wilkinson passed secret Spanish documents to the U.S. Army. Much of what he gave to both sides was completely false, made up by Wilkinson himself to further his real goal. This was to start a war between the United States and Spain, then to use that war as an excuse to conquer parts of the southwestern United States and Mexico for himself. His co-conspirator in this grandiose scheme was Aaron Burr, who had recently served as Thomas Jefferson's vice-president but had not been nominated for a second term. Zebulon Pike was an important part of Burr and Wilkinson's plans.

In 1805 Wilkinson sent Pike on an expedition to seek the source of the Mississippi River and make peace among the Indian tribes of the region. Pike led twenty men on a 2,000-mile round trip from St. Louis, Missouri, to what is now upper Minnesota. It is not clear how this expedition furthered Wilkinson's plans. Perhaps he wanted Pike to help him gain control of the rich fur trade in the area, which was then controlled by Britain. In any case, Pike accomplished little of importance. He even failed to identify the true source of the Mississippi River, though it was well known to local traders.

Only a few days after Pike's return in the spring of 1806, Wilkinson asked him to set out on a new expedition, this time to the Southwest. Wilkinson

Pike's Peak towers over the town of Colorado Springs in this 1906 photograph. At 14,110 feet, the peak was a landmark for travelers.

commissioned him to arrange a peace between the Kansas and Osage Indians in the Louisiana Territory, and then explore as far south and west as the headwaters of the Arkansas and Red Rivers, in present-day Colorado. This would take him close to Spanish-owned New Mexico. [For the story of Spain's conquest of New Mexico, see the articles on Coronado and Estevanico in this book.] But Wilkinson had a secret set of orders for Pike. He asked Pike to spy on the Spanish. The United States and Spain were nearly at war over the location of the border between Spanish and American territory in Texas, and Pike was quite willing to spy on his country's enemies. Did Pike know that Wilkinson and Burr intended to use what he found out for their own ends? There is no proof either way, and the answer may never be known.

The expedition set out for the Southwest in July of 1806. Pike returned some Osage Indian captives to their village on the Osage River, then struck out across the plains of Kansas along what would later be called the Santa Fe Trail. In late November, as the weather was turning bitterly cold, the party made camp at the present-day site of Pueblo, Colorado. That became the base camp for Pike's attempt to climb the mountain now called Pike's Peak.

Some books claim that Pike discovered Pike's Peak and named it for himself. In fact, Pike called it "the Grand Peak" and was by no means the first person, or even the first citizen of the United States, to see it. The Indians had known of the mountain for thousands of years, and the Spanish passed by it often in their trading expeditions to

American troops led by Pike defeated the British at Toronto in 1813. Pike was killed when the British set fire to their own powder supply.

the plains. Probably the first American to see it was James Purcell, a trapper who was in the area in 1804. But a later American explorer, John Charles Frémont, called it Pike's Peak in his journals, and the name stuck. Despite Pike's belief that it could never be climbed, the peak was scaled just fourteen years later by four Americans.

All through the winter of 1807 Pike's party wandered in the Rocky Mountains, looking for the source of the Red River. The men were poorly dressed for a winter expedition in the mountains. Several suffered so badly from frostbite that they had to be left behind in makeshift camps. In February 1807 Pike built a small fort on the banks of the Rio Grande river, well within territory claimed by Spain. Pike always maintained that he thought he was camped on the Red River, within

U.S. territory, but it is more probable that he knew where he was and wanted the Spanish to capture him and take him to Santa Fe, the capital of New Mexico. That way he could talk with Spanish officials and scout out possible invasion routes. Soon enough, Spanish troops arrived to escort Pike and his group to Santa Fe. Unknown to him, someone had leaked his secret mission to Spanish officials, and a Spanish army had been searching for Pike all over the West.

The ragged band of Americans, unshaven and dirty, with rags wrapped around their feet in place of boots, arrived in Santa Fe at the end of February. After reading Pike's orders and journals, the Spanish knew for certain that he was a spy. The usual punishment for spying was death, but the Spanish did not want to risk starting a war with the United States over Pike. Instead, he and his men were escorted back to the border by Spanish troops. On the trip home Pike secretly made detailed notes of everything he had seen, writing on scraps of paper and hiding them in rifle barrels. When Pike arrived back in U.S. territory in June 1807, these notes gave American officials their first clear picture of conditions in Spanish New Mexico.

While Pike was still in the wilderness, Wilkinson's plans were discovered. President Jefferson, hearing rumors of the general's misconduct, relieved him of his command. In desperation, Wilkinson tried to save his career by betraying Burr. Wilkinson revealed Burr's plan to separate the lower part of Louisiana from the United States and to use New Orleans as a base to invade Mexico, but he said nothing about his own role in the plot. In May 1807, Burr was put on trial for treason, with Wilkinson as the star witness against him. The trial was an international sensation. Burr was acquitted, but his political career was ruined. Wilkinson, who had hoped to make himself a hero, was branded a traitor by the press. (Jefferson continued to trust him, however, and Wilkinson later returned to the army.) Even Pike's reputation was damaged. Some of Pike's papers were shown in court as evidence that he knew of the conspiracy. Because of this, Pike was denied the honors and fame he thought he deserved.

Pike continued his career in the Army. In 1813,

Route of Pike's expedition

during the War of 1812 between the United States and Britain, he was made a brigadier general. That April he led American troops to victory in the Battle of York, one of the three important battles of the war. As Pike met with his officers outside the British fort, a nearby store of ammunition exploded, sending debris rocketing in all directions. A flying rock hit him in the back, fatally wounding him. According to witnesses, Pike died smiling as he heard the sounds of the British surrender.

The African Continent

Ibn Battutah

Ibn Battutah (IH-bin bat-TU-tah), full name Abu Abd Allah Muhammad ibn Abd Allah ibn Ibrahim al-Lawati at-Tanji ibn Battutah. Born February 24, 1304, in Tangier, Morocco. Died 1368 or 1369 in Morocco.

In the fourteenth century, most people stayed in their home village all their lives. A sailor might travel, or a merchant, or a soldier in the Crusades, but even these people wouldn't travel far compared to people today. There was one man of the fourteenth century, however, who became the greatest traveler the world had yet seen. He was Ibn Battutah, a Muslim scholar from Morocco who vowed never to take any road twice. It has been estimated that he traveled more than 75,000 miles on foot, camelback, and aboard ship, more miles than any one person traveled before the voyages of Francis Drake in the sixteenth century. [See the article on Drake in this book.] Making his way through mountains, deserts, jungles, and storms at sea, Ibn Battutah visited every corner of the Muslim world, which included parts of Europe, Africa, the Middle East, India, and southern Asia, We know about his journeys because Ibn Battutah wrote a book, one of the most famous books of his age.

When Ibn Battutah was twenty-one years old, he left his native Morocco to make the pilgrimage to Mecca (the Muslim holy city in what is now Saudi Arabia) that is required of every Muslim. For several years he was a student of Islamic law and literature at schools in Syria, Egypt, Mecca, and Medina. At some point he decided that he would visit every Muslim country in the world—a vast undertaking, since the Muslim lands stretched from western Europe through Africa to Central Asia and the Far East. He began by sailing down the east coast of Africa to the rich trading city of Kilwa, in the country we now call Tanzania. Next he decided to visit the court of Muhammad ibn Tuhluq, the sultan of Delhi in India, who was a famous patron of Muslim scholars. To get there, he took a long, winding route through Turkey, Constantinople, and southern Russia, and then followed the ancient silk road through Samarkhand, Khorasan, and Afghanistan.

Ibn Battutah was well received by the sultan, who appointed him grand judge of Delhi. But the sultan was a mistrustful man who might reward a favorite one day and execute him the next. More than once, Ibn Battutah himself narrowly escaped death. In the end, he managed to regain the sultan's confidence, but he was glad to leave India for China in 1342 bearing rich gifts from the sultan to the Chinese emperor.

This was the most dangerous journey of Ibn Battutah's life. His party was attacked by Hindu bandits shortly after he left Delhi. He lost the gifts for the emperor in a shipwreck off the Malabar Coast. He spent two years in the Maldive Islands, where he considered becoming sultan himself, but his political opponents made life there too risky. After another shipwreck and further adventures in Java and Sumatra, he finally reached the coast of China. Ibn Battutah claimed to have traveled as far as Beijing, the

Travelers from many different parts of the Muslim world journey together on a seagoing ship in this drawing from a Persian manuscript.

capital of China, though he gives few details of this trip, and historians today doubt that he made it that far. In China he saw, among other wonders, the immense navies of the emperor, far larger than any assembled in the Muslim or Christian worlds. He returned by ship around India and through the Persian Gulf to Syria, where he encountered many people dying from the Black Death (bubonic plague).

Ibn Battutah returned safely to his home in 1348, but within two years he was off again to visit the kingdom of Granada in Spain, and two years after that to the Sudan. Though he was now tiring

of endless travel, the sultan of Morocco commanded him to make one last journey, a diplomatic mission to the West African kingdom of Mali. There he was to observe the rule of the African sultan Mansa Sulayman.

Ibn Battutah's account of this trip shows his curiosity about the people he met and his sharp eye for the details of their lives. He was used to the generosity of the sultans of the east and thought Mansa Sulayman "a miserly king, not a man from whom one may hope for a rich present." From this tight-fisted sultan he received only "three loaves of bread, a piece of beef fried in oil,

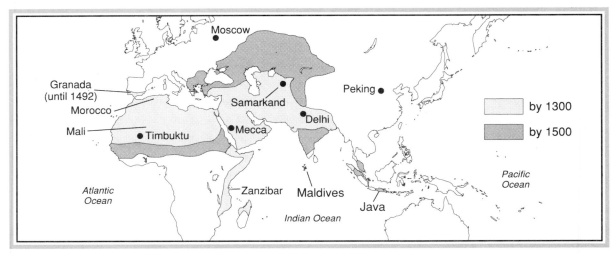

The Muslim world in the 14th century

and a gourd full of sour yogurt." As a strict Muslim, Ibn Battutah did not approve of some of the local customs, such as women walking about without clothes. But he was impressed with the richness of Mansa Sulayman's court. When the sultan left his palace he was accompanied by musicians, dancers, and three hundred slaves with swords and spears. In his outdoor court the sultan sat under a multicolored silk tent crowned by a golden bird. Ibn Battutah also reported back that the sultan's rule was just and orderly, though not very merciful. "The Sultan pardons no one who is guilty of doing wrong," he wrote. "There is complete safety throughout the land. The traveler here has no more reason to fear bandits or robbers than the man who stays at home."

Having achieved his lifelong goal of visiting every Muslim country, Ibn Battutah began the return trip to his home in Morocco, traveling in a caravan of six hundred slaves. The sultan of Morocco asked him to write a book about his adventures. He told his story, called simply *Rihlah* ("Travels"), to a scribe named Ibn Juzayy, who retold it in more formal language. But readers of his book can still hear Ibn Battutah's own sensible voice underneath.

In his last years Ibn Battutah lived a quiet life as a judge in an unknown Moroccan town. He did not die a famous man. But many people read his book. Its tales of the fabulous treasures of Asia were an inspiration to the Portuguese and Spanish explorers who sailed in search of the Indies a century later. Today his stories of fourteenth-century Muslim life are still important. They open a window into the lives of people we would otherwise know little about.

After spending more than a quarter of a century traveling, Ibn Battutah dictates his book to a scribe at the request of the sultan of Morocco.

Leo Africanus

Leo Africanus (af-rih-KAY-nus), birth name al-Hasan ibn Muhammad al-Wezzan al-Fasi (or al-Zaiyati), also called Giovanni Leone. Born circa 1495, probably in Granada, Spain. Died between 1551 and 1554, probably in Tunis.

In the year 1523, an unusual meeting took place in the chambers of Pope Leo X in Rome. Before the pope stood a Moor, a Muslim from North Africa, dressed in the white robes of an Islamic judge. The man was a gift from some Venetian pirates who had captured him on the seas near Constantinople. Usually such captives became slaves and were set to menial work. But even the pirates realized that this Moor was different. Though he was less than thirty years old, he was already a learned man and a great traveler. In addition to Arabic, he spoke excellent Spanish and even some Italian.

The pope listened with interest as the Moor, whose name was al-Hasan ibn Muhammad al-Wezzan al-Fasi, told his story. He explained that he had been born to a wealthy Muslim family of Granada, Spain, some years after the conquest of Granada by the Christian armies of King Fernando and Queen Isabel. [For more on the conflict between Christians and Muslims in Spain, see the article on Christopher Columbus.] In the terms of Granada's surrender, the king and queen had promised not to persecute their Muslim subjects, but they did not honor this promise. When he was still an infant, the captive and his family had moved to the safer city of Fez, in Morocco. As he grew up, the Moor had studied Islamic law and gained a reputation as a scholar. Then he traveled

In the garden of his palace in Rome, Pope Leo X and his entourage listen as Leo Africanus tells the story of his capture by Venetian pirates.

throughout Arabia, Persia, and Africa with his uncle, a diplomat and merchant. It was on his return from a voyage to Constantinople (present-day Istanbul, the capital of Turkey) that he was captured by the pirates and brought to the pope.

Pope Leo took an immediate liking to the man. He ordered him to be set free and given a handsome pension, and arranged for him to be baptized as a Christian. For his Christian name, the pope gave him his own name, Giovanni Leone ("John Leo"). For many years, the Moor lived in Rome, studying and writing books about his adventures. His most famous and only surviving book, *The History and Description of Africa*, earned him the name Leo Africanus ("The Lion of Africa"), which is the name by which he is known to us today.

Some years later, Leo Africanus left Rome, never to return. He took up residence in Tunis, where he renounced Christianity and returned to Islam. Nothing is known of his life after this, except that he died in Tunis sometime around the year 1554.

For three hundred years, Leo's book was the best source of information available to Europeans interested in Central and West Africa. Leo painted a picture of an opulent world supported by slavery, scholarship, and gold. Of all his accounts, the most intriguing to Europeans was the one about Timbuktu, an ancient city located on the southern edge of the Sahara in the present-day Republic of Mali. (Another great Muslim traveler, Ibn Batuttah, had visited the Muslim colony in Timbuktu in the fourteenth century, but he barely mentions the city in his famous travel book. See the article about Ibn Batuttah in this book.) In the fifteenth century Timbuktu was conquered by the Central African empire of the Songhai and developed into a wealthy trade center on the main caravan route across the Sahara.

This map of Africa from Leo's book is oriented with south at the top. The Mediterranean Sea is at the bottom, the Atlantic Ocean at right.

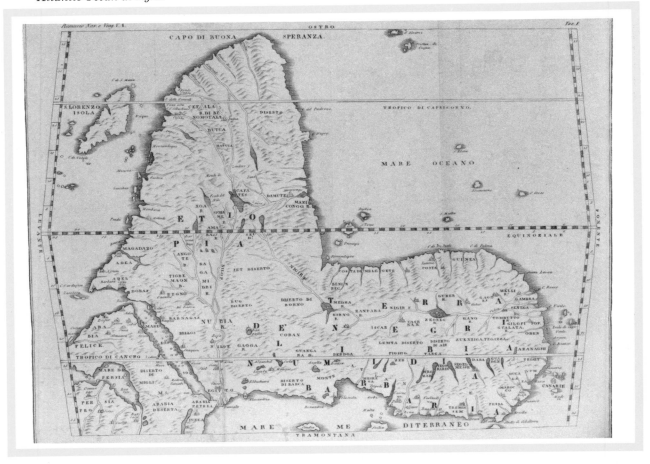

Salt and gold were the most important items of trade, and in that dry region, they were nearly equal in value.

When Leo visited Timbuktu in the year 1514, he saw "many shops of artisans and merchants, especially of such as weave linen and cotton cloth. Corn, cattle, milk, and butter this regions yields in great abundance. The inhabitants, and especially the strangers there residing, are exceedingly rich, insomuch as the king has married both his daughters to two rich merchants. The rich king of Timbuktu has many plates and sceptres of gold, some weighing 1,300 pounds, and he keeps a magnificent and well-furnished court. Whosoever will speak to this king must first fall down before the king's feet, then take up earth and sprinkle it upon his head and shoulders. Even ambassadors and strangers must do this."

Leo was most impressed with Timbuktu's universities and libraries. "Here are a great many doctors, judges, priests, and other learned men, bountifully maintained at the king's cost," he wrote. "And hither are brought diverse books out of Barbary [North Africa], which are sold for more money than any other merchandise." The universities of Timbuktu and other Songhai towns were famous throughout the Muslim world and produced books on Islamic law that are still in use today.

The inhabitants of Timbuktu, noted Leo, were "of a gentle and cheerful disposition, and spend a great part of the night in singing and dancing throughout the streets of the city." But Timbuktu was too rich for its own good. In 1591, not long after Leo's death, the army of the Sultan of Morocco, armed with muskets, overran the Songhai empire and captured Timbuktu. The city was repeatedly plundered of its gold and books, and its scholars were killed or exiled. In short order it was reduced to a dusty desert town.

Europeans, however, knew nothing of Timbuktu's sad fate and were inspired by Leo's book to make long journeys in search of the prosperous, learned city that he described. Many lost their lives in the baking deserts of the Sahara. In the nineteenth century, when European explorers finally reached Timbuktu, they were bitterly disappointed. "The city is nothing but a mass of ill-looking houses built of earth," wrote one visitor, the French explorer René Caillié. "Timbuktu and its environs present the most monotonous and barren scene I ever beheld." Yet the legend of Timbuktu as described by Leo retains some of its power even today. The town is a popular attraction for tourists to the Sahara, though nothing of its former splendor remains. And Timbuktu is still the name we use when we refer to a place that is as far from where we are as it is possible to be.

Nzinga

Nzinga (in-ZING-ga). Born circa 1580 in Ndongo (now Angola). Died December 17, 1663, probably in Matamba (now Angola).

The kingdom of Ndongo lay in ruins. Its people, the Mbundus, had been conquered by a Portuguese army three years before. Their king had taken refuge on an island in the Kwanza River. Their villages were raided by soldiers who enslaved the people and sent them to the New World to toil in Portugal's mines and plantations.

Yet the Portuguese were not entirely happy with the way things were going. Using soldiers to round up slaves was not efficient. The job had been easier in the old days, when they had simply bought slaves from Ndongo's royal family. The Portuguese governor sent a message to the exiled king, Mbandi, inviting him to come to his palace in the city of Luanda to discuss a settlement. The king sent his younger sister, Nzinga, as his ambassador.

Nzinga arrived at the palace escorted by an honor guard of women. The room held only one chair, and it had been set aside for the governor.

A Dutch engraving shows Nzinga sitting on the back of a servant while she negotiates a treaty with the Portuguese governor in Luanda.

At a signal from Nzinga, one of the women in the honor guard knelt down on her hands and knees so that the ambassador could sit on her back. Thus Nzinga met the Portuguese governor as an equal. The result of this discussion was a treaty in which the Portuguese agreed to help restore Ndongo as an independent kingdom in exchange for Mbandi's assistance with the slave trade. Both parties also agreed to cooperate in the fight against their common enemy, a ferocious gang of bandits called the Mbangala.

The scene in the governor's palace has become part of the legend of Nzinga, who is regarded by the people of Angola, in west central Africa, as a national heroine. (The name Angola is derived from the word *ngola*, meaning "ruler.")

The Portuguese had been present in Angola for one hundred years before Nzinga was born. During the fifteenth century, as part of their search for a sea route to India, they had become the first Europeans to sail along the African coast and around the Cape of Good Hope. By the middle of the sixteenth century they were the masters of an empire that stretched from Brazil halfway across the globe to Indonesia. [See the series of articles from Prince Henry the Navigator to Afonso de Albuquerque in this book.] Their interest in the area they called Angola was sparked by rumors of silver mines, and by the plans of the Jesuits, a group of missionary priests, to introduce African peoples to Christianity.

But the need for slave labor pushed all other goals aside. The Portuguese plantations in Brazil and the West Indies used up slave workers at a terrible rate. Soon the Portuguese were shipping tens of thousands of people every year from Angola to the New World. They preferred to buy their slaves from African trading partners rather than venture into the countryside on their own to take captives. First they made a deal with the rulers of the kingdom of Kongo, who raided neighboring Ndongo for prisoners to sell. When Kongo collapsed, they made a deal with the rulers of Ndongo. Nzinga's father, the ngola Kiluanji, received payments of cloth and wine in exchange for criminals and war captives.

Even so, the Portuguese needed more slaves. They began conducting mass raiding campaigns of their own. In 1575, a military expedition led by Paulo Novais de Dias, the grandson of the explorer Bartolomeu Dias [see the article on him in this book], invaded the Kwanza river valley with the intention of establishing a Portuguese settlement there. The Mbundus tried to force them back. So began one hundred years of war.

Nzinga was born five years after the invasion. As the years of fighting went by, she grew up, married, and became the mother of a son. In 1618 there was a crisis in the royal family of Ndongo. Kiluanji was overthrown by his own people as a tyrant, and Mbandi took his place. Some of the Mbundu chiefs tried to prevent him from taking the throne. Mbandi protected himself by killing these chiefs, as well as his own younger brother and his nephew, Nzinga's only child. Soon afterward, he was defeated by the Portuguese, and Ndongo fell.

Nzinga about forty years old when she went on the mission to the governor at Luanda. Before she returned home, she allowed the Jesuit priests to baptize her as a Christian, in the hope that this would result in better treatment for her people from the Portuguese.

The Mbundus began to regard Nzinga as their leader, rather than Mbandi. Though the Portuguese failed to honor the treaty, Mbandi did nothing. In fact, he went to Luanda to ask the Portuguese governor for help against those of his people who opposed him. But it was too late. Nzinga had made a deal with the Mbangala bandit tribe. On her orders, they ambushed Mbandi on his way home from Luanda and killed him. She also ordered the murder of his son.

The Portuguese wanted a more docile person than Nzinga to deal with. They appointed a kinsman of hers as the new ngola. The Mbundu chiefs joined Nzinga in rebelling against him. Rather than risk a battle against the well-armed foreigners, Nzinga's army used guerrilla tactics, staying on the move and attacking wherever they

For political reasons, Nzinga agreed to accept baptism. She was baptized again four decades later after founding the kingdom of Matamba.

had the chance. Eventually they went eastward to the country of Matamba, overthrew its queen, and set up their own state, with Nzinga as its head. From this refuge, they launched one military campaign after another, in the hope of getting back their own territory. To the south of them, the Mbangalas set up their own state, called Kasanje.

Although Nzinga promised to marry their leader, the Mbangalas were dangerous allies. To avoid having to take care of families, they killed their own children at birth and in their place adopted teenagers captured on raids. They were notorious for eating human flesh.

In 1641 the Portuguese suddenly found themselves with two new enemies: the Dutch, who were intent on building a trading empire of their own, and the conquered people of Kongo, who launched a rebellion. Over the next decade, all these groups played a game of shifting alliances and changing rivalries. First the Dutch captured Luanda and blockaded its harbor. The Portuguese found themselves bottled up in the forts they had built along the Kwanza. They beat off a major attack by Nzinga and her soldiers, killing some two thousand of them. At last Nzinga persuaded the Dutch and the Kongo people to join her campaign, but the Mbangalas threw their support to the Portuguese, in the hope of getting the slave trade running smoothly once again.

Then, as quickly as they had come, the Dutch were gone. In 1648 a Portuguese fleet arrived from Brazil and recaptured Luanda. Nzinga's Kongo allies gave up the fight and submitted to the Portuguese. The Mbundus went back to Matamba and carried on their guerrilla attacks. During these years of warfare, Nzinga was the Mbundu army's chief military strategist and commander. Because she had a position of authority that was usually held by a man, she dressed in men's clothing, and since it was the custom for the ngola to have several wives, she had several husbands, who dressed as women.

Without the help of allies, the Mbundus did not have the military power to take Ndongo back from the Portuguese. Eventually they gave up that idea and turned their attention to creating a strong Mbundu state in their new territory of Matamba. They needed to build a secure economy for their country, and supplying the Portuguese

with slaves was still a very profitable business. In 1656, a treaty of friendship was signed by the former enemies. One of Nzinga's sisters, who had spent ten years as a Portuguese prisoner, was sent home in exchange for a ransom of 130 slaves. (Another sister, captured at the same time, had been strangled.)

Matamba and the Mbangala state of Kasanje became centers of the slave trade in west central Africa. Many of the people they captured were from Kongo, which had once been a strong kingdom but was now so weak that it could not defend its villages from Nzinga's raiders. Nzinga herself once again accepted baptism and sent ambassadors to Rome to greet the pope. She died in 1663, more than eighty years old.

A few years after her death, the Portuguese put down one final rebellion in Ndongo, and Nzinga's former kingdom lost its last remnant of independence. Angola thus became the first African state to be ruled as a colony of a European power. It remained under Portugal's control until 1975. [For more about the division of Africa into European colonies in the nineteenth century, see the article about Henry Morton Stanley in this book.] The Angolans who fought for independence in the 1960s used many of the same guerrilla tactics developed by Nzinga three centuries earlier.

The kingdoms and tribes of west central Africa in the 16th century

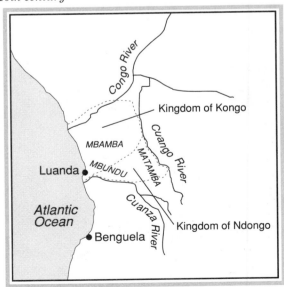

Shaka

Shaka (u-CHA-ka). Born circa 1787 in a
Zulu village in present-day South Africa.
Died September 22, 1828, in Dukuza (in
present-day South Africa).

Shaka, drawn by one of the European traders who visited him in the 1820s

For thirteen days, the small group of European
traders had been traveling northeast through
the African countryside, escorted by an ambassador from the king of the Zulu tribe. Ever since
they had landed at Port Natal, on the southeastern coast of what is now South Africa, they
had heard rumors about this powerful king. The
Africans they met near the coast were clearly terrified of him. One of the traders, Henry Francis
Fynn, had made an excursion some distance inland and had encountered an army of the king's
warriors, twenty thousand strong, marching
through the forest in perfect regimental discipline. Soon afterward, the traders had received a
summons from the king to visit him in his village
of Bulawayo, a hundred miles away.

Now they were entering the king's village,
called in the Bantu language a *kraal*. In the center was a huge circular pen in which the king, as
the leader of a cattle-herding people, kept his
stock of cows and goats. From this hub, lines of
hive-shaped huts extended in all directions over
an area three miles square. An immense crowd of
chanting, dancing people, perhaps eighty thousand in all, were packed into the kraal, including
thousands of warriors armed with shields and
spears. As the traders took their assigned places,
their attention was caught by a tall man with a
regal look, wearing a skirt of monkey tails and a
blue crane feather in his headband, who leaped
forward out of the warrior host. It was Shaka, the
king whose name was feared by everyone for hundreds of miles, the military genius who had
turned the Zulu tribe into an organization of virtually unbeatable fighters.

By the time the European traders arrived at his

doorstep, in the summer of 1824, Shaka had been king of the Zulus for eight years. Before his time, the Nguni people of southeastern Africa, including the Zulus, were divided into about eight hundred clans, each clan ruled over by a chieftain. Their life of cattle-herding had been going on in much the same way for two centuries. Shaka was the son of Senzangakhona, the head of the Zulu clan, and Nandi, a woman of the Langeni clan who became Senzangakhona's third wife. For half of Shaka's childhood, he and his mother lived with the Zulus, and for the other half with the Langenis, but in both places they were treated with contempt and their lives were made miserable.

Finally, young Shaka was sent to live with the Mtetwa clan. He arrived at a crucial time. The chief of the Mtetwas, Dingiswayo, was setting out to construct a political entity much bigger than just his clan. He began by building up an army of warriors grouped into regiments, each with its own leaders and uniforms, and he used this army to gain control of nearby clans, whose warriors then joined with the Mtetwas. The result was a confederacy of clans that were no longer independent, but now owed allegiance to the chief of the dominant clan. Shaka was drafted into the army, along with all the young men his age, when he was in his early twenties. He quickly distinguished himself as a promising soldier who had courage and ingenuity in plenty. Dissatisfied with the long-handled spear that was the traditional weapon of the Ngunis, he invented a short stabbing spear that was more useful in hand-to-hand fighting. He demonstrated the effectiveness of his invention in a fight against a clan called the Butelezi, when he answered a challenge to single combat and killed his opponent so quickly that the Butelezis turned and ran. Dingiswayo rewarded him by promoting him to commander of his regiment and allowing him to experiment with new battle tactics.

When Senzangakhona died in 1816, Shaka, with Dingiswayo's approval, returned to his father's kraal at the head of a Mtetwa escort and made himself chief, after sending an assassin ahead to kill the half-brother who had already inherited the position. That very day, he began to shape the clan that had rejected him into one whose people obeyed his every whim without question. He did this by clubbing to death every person in the village who had once slighted him or

his mother. During the eight years of his reign he ruled his subjects by terror, ordering the immediate execution of anyone, adult or child, who interfered in his plans, whether by intention or by mistake. Zulus were put to death every day for such minor offenses as sneezing while Shaka was speaking, or appearing in one of his dreams. They quickly became a people dedicated to keeping their king happy at any cost.

In return, the Zulus learned what it meant to belong to a first-rate army. Shaka lost no time in putting his military innovations into effect. He divided his warriors, who numbered about 400, into four regiments according to age. These regiments lived together in their own kraals and each had distinctive battle dress and war cries. Unmarried men were sworn to celibacy, for Shaka wanted their loyalty to be to him, rather than to wives and families. All warriors were trained to be absolutely obedient to Shaka's orders. They learned to understand hand signals given by their leaders; to march across country for hours without breaking ranks; to use the stabbing spear that Shaka had invented for the Mtetwas; to go barefoot on any terrain at top speed (to toughen their feet, they were forced to dance on thorns). The smallest breach of discipline resulted in immediate execution.

Before Shaka's time, battles between tribes in this region usually consisted of the two opposing sides coming face-to-face and exchanging volleys of spears, with the bigger army almost always the

The Zulu empire in the early 1820s

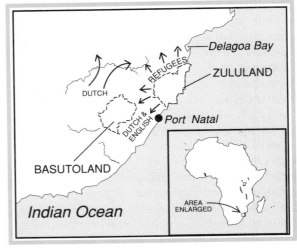

victor. Shaka introduced a battle plan that enabled his army to defeat much larger forces. The strongest regiments were put in the center. As they advanced, two lines of warriors on either side of the main group moved rapidly forward and closed around the enemy in a pincer motion, preventing the enemy warriors from retreating. Behind the main group came a reserve unit, ready to replace wounded soldiers as needed. Boys too young for combat carried equipment The Zulu army on the march could go fifty miles in a day, taking whatever food it needed from nearby kraals. After each battle, Shaka executed anyone who had shown the slightest cowardice.

For a year, as Dingiswayo's vassal, Shaka sent his army to assist the Mtetwas in their wars and confined his own attacks to neighboring clans, including the Langenis, his mother's clan, whom he punished just as he had the Zulus. The survivors of these attacks were absorbed into the Zulu tribe. When Dingiswayo died in 1817, Shaka's army had grown to two thousand, and the Zulu territories, originally about ten miles square, had quadrupled in size. Shaka was now free to move against more distant clans. The Zulus became ever more powerful, and Shaka, assisted by his organization of spies, informers, and executioners, became the ruler of an empire. This is how Henry Francis Fynn and his fellow European traders saw him when they came to the royal kraal at Bulawayo in the summer of 1824.

Like shock waves, the effects of Shaka's power radiated in every direction. Tribes fleeing from the Zulu onslaught pushed their way into the territories of other tribes and created even more refugees. The old, established way of life was broken up from Lake Tanganyika in the north to the Dutch-English settlement called the Cape Colony in the south. An estimated two million people died in this upheaval, which is known as the *Mfecane* ("the crushing"). When the Dutch soldier-farmers called the Boers pushed northward from the Cape Colony in the 1830s, the devastated tribes were in no position to stop them.

But by that time, Shaka was no longer the king of the Zulus. His downfall had its beginnings in 1827, with the death from dysentery of his mother, Nandi. The king was gripped by grief so intense that the his subjects, in a mass demonstration of their devotion to him, began to slaughter one another, until some seven thousand lay dead.

People who tried to escape by staying in their huts were hunted down and killed. Shaka gave orders that for an entire year no one was to drink milk, grow crops, or give birth, so that the whole Zulu kingdom might share in his suffering. He began to push his army even harder than before, sending them on raids into distant territories without giving them rest.

Convinced that Shaka was insane and bent on destroying his people, two of his half-brothers and his own servant assassinated him at his kraal in Dukuza in September 1828. One of the brothers, Dingane, took his place as king. Neither Dingane nor his successor Mpande, another son of Senzangakona, had the military expertise or the unquestioned authority of Shaka. They were unable to prevent the reduction of the Zulus' territory by the Boers and the British, who made Zululand a British protectorate in 1887.

A modern African artist painted this scene of the assassination of Shaka by his half-brother, Dingane, who succeeded him as king.

David Livingstone

*David Livingstone, birth name David
Livingston. Born March 19, 1813, in
Blantyre, Scotland. Died May 1, 1873, in
Ifala (in present-day Zambia).*

The little group of travelers—a Scottish doctor and a handful of helpers—struggled through the forest near Lake Tanganyika, in what is now the nation of Zaire in Africa. They were on their way to Ujiji, an Arab slave-trading post on the eastern shore of the lake. They were all that was left of a much larger expedition that had set out six years before, searching for the sources of the River Nile.

The group's leader was the famous David Livingstone, who had spent most of his life mapping Central Africa, preaching the Christian religion as he went. Unlike most other European explorers of Africa, Livingstone had earned the friendship of the people among whom he traveled. They called him Ngaka, "the Doctor." The slave traders who dealt in African lives disliked him because he had roused public opinion against their work.

Livingstone was in a hurry to reach Ujiji. Medicines and supplies were waiting for him there. His own medical kit had been stolen months before. He had suffered from dysentery, rheumatic fever, pneumonia, cholera, bleeding hemorrhoids, and ulcerated feet. He had lost most of his teeth. But when he reached Ujiji, he found that the medicines had been sold by a slave trader. Without them, he would soon be dead.

A few days later, an enormous caravan came marching into town with the American flag at its head. Its leader was not an explorer, a soldier, or a scientist, but a reporter named Henry Morton Stanley, who had sent by his newspaper to find the missing Livingstone. He had brought food, medicine, supplies, and letters.

To Stanley's surprise, Livingstone refused to go back with him. He insisted on finishing the task he had set himself. Stanley accompanied him on a journey to the northern end of Lake Tanganyika to find out whether it produced a north-flowing river that might be the Nile. (They discovered that the river flows south.) When Stanley left, Livingstone stayed behind.

If it had not been for this kind of stubbornness and independence, Livingstone would never have undertaken his journeys through south-central Africa. Indeed, he might never have left his birthplace in Scotland. He was the son of a poor tea dealer. At the age of ten, he was sent to work in a cotton mill. Like many other children, he had to run machines fourteen hours a day, from six in the morning to eight at night. The young mill workers were beaten if they fell asleep on the job. Still, Livingstone went to school in the evenings and read books until midnight. When he got older, he used his earnings from the mill to pay for classes at a Glasgow college. He received his medical degree when he was twenty-seven and went to Cape Town, at the southern tip of Africa, to work for the London Missionary Society.

Livingstone was intensely curious about his adopted land. He began to explore the countryside north of Cape Town, establishing mission stations as he went. In 1849 he and two friends, led by an African guide, became the first Europeans to succeed in crossing the Kalahari Desert, though they nearly died of thirst on the way. Two years later he brought his wife and children through the desert, at the risk of their lives, so that he could meet Sebetwane, the chief of the Makololo tribe, whom he much admired. Sebetwane's capital was located near the Zambezi River, in what is now the panhandle of Namibia. Livingstone realized that the deep Zambezi, which runs across southwestern Africa to the Indian Ocean, would make a good water route for European traders and missionaries. It was Livingstone's hope that the arrival of such people would put an end to the international slave-exporting trade that was devastating this part of Africa.

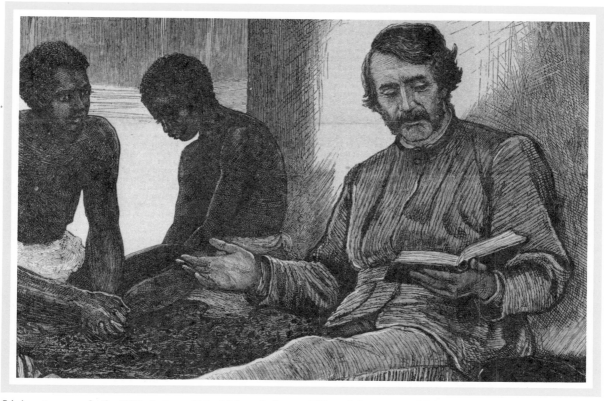

Livingstone reads the Bible to two of his African helpers. Although he went to Africa as a missionary, he made no permanent converts.

Slavery had existed in most parts of the globe for many centuries. It was a common aftermath of wars and territorial conquests. Since the Middle Ages, Arab traders had been selling Africans as slaves throughout the Muslim world. The situation worsened in the fifteenth century, when the Portuguese began to capture African people by the thousands to work in their New World colonies. [See the article on Nzinga of Angola.]

By the nineteenth century, when Livingstone came to Africa, slave trading was a giant business. The slave dealers stayed on the coast. They hired warriors from local tribes to round up captives for them. These raiders would attack a village, kill the defenders, tie up the survivors, and march them in chains to the coastal slave markets. There they were paid in cloth, guns, and other items. If Africans could buy such goods directly from European traders, Livingstone thought, they would have no need to work for the dealers, and the slave trade would collapse.

Livingstone decided to find out for himself whether the Zambezi River would make a good water highway. Before he began his explorations, he studied the techniques used by geographers so that he could make accurate notes of what he found. He also sent his family back to Britain. His four children rarely saw him while they were growing up.

In June of 1852, Livingstone left Cape Town and headed north to visit the capital of the Makololo empire, where Sebetwane's son Sekelutu was now chief. After Livingstone had explored the upper Zambezi River by canoe, he set out westward to the Portuguese capital of Luanda, on the Atlantic coast, accompanied by twenty-seven Makololo warriors. They arrived in May 1854. They had covered hundreds of miles of dense forest, endured exhaustion and malaria, suffered threats from armed tribesfolk who extorted protection money, and received help from compassionate tribesfolk who offered food and shelter.

Then they returned to the Makololo country and set out in the opposite direction, following the Zambezi River eastward to the Indian Ocean. On the way, Livingstone became the first European to see the spectacular Victoria Falls, a mile long and 355 feet high. He made written reports describing in great detail everything he saw in the course of a 4,000-mile journey.

At the Portuguese town of Quelimane, the emaciated Livingstone, sick with malaria and dysentery, boarded a ship that took him to England. He was surprised to find that his travels through Africa had made him a celebrity at home. Queen Victoria invited him to visit her. The Royal Geographical Society gave him an award. Scholars and journalists begged for a chance to speak with him. Livingstone took every opportunity to let the public know how much he respected the peoples of Africa, how devastating the slave trade was to them, and how important he believed it was for the nations of Europe to follow a policy of "commerce, civilization, and Christianity" in order to stop the slavers and "introduce the Negro family into the body of nations, no one member of which can suffer without the others suffering with it." The British, who had outlawed slavery in their own territories only twenty years earlier, received his message with enthusiasm. Livingstone's book *Missionary Travels and Researches in South Africa* sold 12,000 copies as soon as it was published.

The government was so impressed with Livingstone's work that in March 1858 it sent him back at the head of an expedition with orders to establish a trade route through south-central Africa. At Quelimane he was reunited with his Makololo escorts, who had waited for him there, and together they traveled up the Zambezi River in a leaky steamship. But this expedition, which lasted for five years, was beset with troubles. Livingstone found it hard to work with the British members of the team, one of whom was his own brother. He was willing to endure constant suffering, including exhaustion, debilitating fevers, lack of food and water, insect stings, and dangerous animals (he once had his shoulder crushed by a lion). But his colleagues were not. They thought he was arrogant and reckless, and he thought they were weak and quarrelsome.

To his disappointment, Livingstone discovered that his hopes for using the Zambezi as a water highway were in vain. The river was broken by stretches of rough water that trade boats could not cross. He tried other rivers, but none of them were navigable either.

Evidence of the devastation wrought by the slave trade was everywhere. Livingstone was horrified to discover that the geographical knowledge he had gained from his previous journeys had made it possible for the slave traders to extend their terror deeper and deeper into Africa's interior. On voyages up the Shire River to Lake Nyasa, which he was the first European to see, he witnessed the destruction of Makanga villages by slave raiders from the Ajawa and Yao tribes hired by the Arabs and Portuguese. The ruined villages were strewn with dead bodies. In the nearby countryside, he came across a group of prisoners, including children, who were being whipped along the trail by slave raiders. Livingstone and his group chased the raiders off with gunfire and freed the captives, but the raiders would be back.

There were other disappointments as well. Livingstone's Makololo friends were about to lose their empire and their way of life. Their king Sekelutu was near death from leprosy. Livingstone's wife died of fever on a visit to Africa. One of their children who had emigrated to the United States was killed in the Civil War, fighting for the Union side.

Livingstone returned to England in 1863. He was in London the following year, at the height of the dispute between the explorers John Hanning Speke and Richard Burton over the sources of the Nile. [For the story of their travels and an explanation of the Nile mystery, see the article on Burton in this book.] Livingstone, too, became fascinated with the problem of the Nile's source and decided to go back to Africa to solve it. He arrived in Zanzibar in March 1866, determined to meet three goals: to find the source of the Nile, to explore the region around Lakes Nyasa and Tanganyika, and to report on the human costs of the slave trade.

This journey lasted seven years. During the first three years, the expedition reached Lake Nyasa, made its way through steaming forestland toward Lake Tanganyika, and struggled onward to Lake Bangweulu, which no non-African had ever seen. Livingstone's progress was sometimes blocked by tribal warfare and by Arab slave traders who did not like his interference in their work.

Yet he was so weakened by hunger and disease that he finally had no choice but to travel with their caravans. The Arabs had the medical skills he needed, and when he was too sick to walk, they had their slaves carry him.

In spite of his sickness, Livingstone continued to explore the Lualaba River, which he thought might be the beginning of the Nile. In July, while visiting the village of Nyangwe, he was an eyewitness to the massacre of four hundred villagers, including children, who were shot to death by Arab traders or drowned in the river as they tried to escape. He was nearly killed three times in one day by Manyuema warriors, who hurled spears at him and aimed a falling tree in his direction.

It was in November 1871 that Livingstone crawled into Ujiji more dead than alive and was saved by Henry Morton Stanley, the reporter from the *New York Herald*. Livingstone impressed Stanley so much that he decided to become an explorer himself. [Stanley's explorations, and his subsequent role in the European colonization of Africa, are covered in the article on Stanley in this book.]

The source of the Nile still remained to be discovered. But the mystery was destined to be solved by Stanley, not by his mentor. Livingstone spent the next year crisscrossing the lands west and south of Lake Tanganyika. Once again he became desperately ill. The entry in his journal for April 10, 1873, reads: "I am pale and weak from bleeding profusely ever since 31st March. Oh! how I long to be permitted by the Over Power to finish my work." On April 29th, he and two

Some of Livingstone's journeys

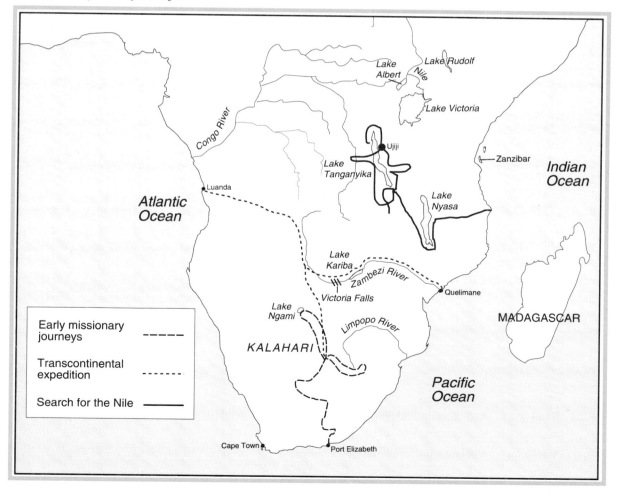

After nine months of searching, Stanley greets the emaciated Livingstone at Ujiji with the now-famous question: "Dr. Livingstone, I presume?"

servants—all that was left of the expedition—reached a village on the banks of the Molilamo River. Two days later, he was dead. His servants carried his embalmed body all the way to the coast and escorted it back to England, where it was buried in Westminster Abbey.

The legend of Livingstone helped shape British and American attitudes toward Africa for a long time to come. Interestingly, although Livingstone always thought of himself as a missionary, in all his years in Africa he made not a single permanent convert.

Richard Francis Burton

Richard Francis Burton. Born March 19, 1921, in Torquay, Devonshire, England. Died October 20, 1890, in Trieste, Italy.

In the fall of 1853, a caravan of Muslim pilgrims set out across the Arabian Desert. Their destination was the city of Mecca, revered by Muslims as the birthplace of Muhammad, the founder of their religion, Islam. Only Muslims are allowed to

enter Mecca, and nonbelievers caught inside used to be put to death.

The caravan traveled at night to escape the burning sun. There was very little water, and along the road lay the rotting carcasses of camels and ponies who had died of the heat. The pilgrims had to fend off an attack by robbers. Just before they reached the city, the pilgrims bathed and put on the cotton robes worn by all visitors to Mecca, and the men had their heads shaved. The following day they joined the crowd of worshippers at the Great Mosque, the shrine that all faithful Muslims are expected to visit at least once. In accordance with Muslim ritual, they walked in procession seven times around the Kaaba, the square stone building that stands in the mosque's courtyard.

Of all the places that are cherished by Muslims, the Kaaba is considered the holiest, and some of the pilgrims entered it to pray. Among them was Mirza Abdullah, an Indian doctor of Afghan descent. This Mirza Abdullah wore a long beard, spoke perfect Arabic, and performed the pilgrim ceremonies with precision. If his fellow pilgrims had not been engrossed in their own prayers, they might have noticed the doctor writing tiny notes on his sleeve with a pencil. It would have meant instant death for him if they had. For underneath his robes, Mirza Abdullah was really Richard Burton, an Englishman in disguise.

It wasn't the first time that Burton had gone undercover to forbidden places, and it would not be the last. He was intensely curious about the way other people live, especially in places that most Englishmen considered exotic. Forbidden things and places fascinated him. Not only was he a master of disguises and a good actor, but he had a talent for languages (by the end of his life he knew forty different languages and dialects). He also had an enormous hunger for learning. He was studying ancient ruins and writing books about the places he visited when the sciences of archeology, anthropology, and sociology were just getting started. He was an expert swordsman and an accomplished poet. He explored three continents, sometimes in disguise, often in danger. He translated Arab and Hindu books on sexual themes, books that shocked the English public in the Victorian era. Some people called him a genius; others called him "Ruffian Dick."

Even in childhood, Burton had had a restless life. His family left England when he was very young and moved from place to place in France and Italy. The three children were educated mainly by tutors rather than in schools. By Burton's

Burton liked to experience for himself the kinds of lives different peoples led. He posed for this photograph in the clothes of a Turkish Muslim.

own account, they grew up wild and uncontrollable. The two boys were sent to Oxford University, but Richard soon got himself expelled. He joined the army and was sent out to India, at that time a part of the British empire, where he learned eight languages in eight years and served as a surveyor and intelligence officer. After he returned to England, he wrote the first of his anthropological studies, on the peoples of the Sind province. (Eventually he published 43 books about his travels and 30 volumes of translations.)

Burton was thirty-two years old when he set out to visit Mecca disguised as Mirza Abdullah. His journey took him through Egypt and down the Red Sea in a crowded pilgrim ship, then on to what is now Saudi Arabia and the city of Medina, another place holy to Muslims and closed to nonbelievers. When he joined the pilgrim caravan, he became the first European to cross the Arabian desert from Medina to Mecca, and the only one ever to do it before the twentieth century. After making a thorough observation of Mecca, he traveled to Harer, a closed Muslim slave-trading center in Somaliland (now in Ethiopia). He was not the first European ever to enter Harer, but he was the first to leave it alive.

By early 1855, Burton was organizing his most ambitious expedition yet: to find the source of Africa's great Nile River. According to ancient legends, the Nile flowed from vast "fountains" somewhere in Central Africa. Portuguese, Scottish, and German explorers had tried in vain to find them. Always ready for a challenge, Burton set out westward into the Somali desert with forty-five men, including three British army officers with experience in India. One of these was John Hanning Speke, a young lieutenant with a passion for hunting.

One night, camped near the city of Berbera, they were attacked by a group of Somalis who suspected them of spying on the slave trade for the British government. Burton was pierced through the jaws by a javelin blade, Speke received eleven spear wounds, and a third officer was killed. Speke and Burton had to go back to England to recuperate, and then went off to fight against Russia in the Crimean War. Two years later, in 1857, they went back to Africa to try again, with money from the Royal Geographical Society and the British government.

They set out from the island of Zanzibar, notorious as an Arab slave market. With a freed slave named Sidi Bombay as their guide, they made their way slowly westward over a course of six hundred miles, through jungles and grasslands and across three mountain ranges. Both of them, as well as their African bearers, suffered from malaria and traveled in feverish misery. Both lost their sight for a time. Speke temporarily lost his hearing. Burton's hands and feet became paralyzed, and his mouth was filled with ulcers. But in February 1858 they climbed a hill and looked down on something no European had ever seen: Lake Tanganyika, 420 miles long, the longest freshwater lake in the world.

In two rickety hired canoes Burton and Speke paddled through its stormy, crocodile-infested waters, trying to find out if the river at the north end of the lake flowed out—in which case it might be the source of the Nile—or in. But the bearers refused to go that far because the northern shores were inhabited by a cannibal tribe, the Wavira. Nonetheless, Burton was convinced that the Nile arose in Lake Tanganyika.

By this time, the two Englishmen, who had started the journey as friends, were barely able to

Lands explored by Burton and Speke

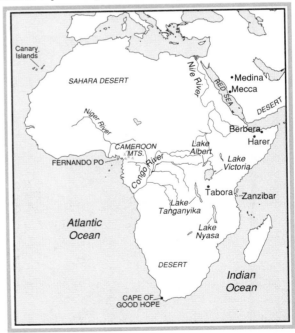

tolerate each other's company. Their personalities were too different. Speke was a prudish man who kept his distance from Africans and Arabs; Burton was fascinated by all the peoples he met and studied their customs and traditions with intense curiosity. Matters of life and death—marriage, sex, birth, slavery, murder, burial—preoccupied him. When he visited an African village, he would join in the villagers' ritual dances and sample their foods and drugs. Because he was so quick to learn languages, he could hold a conversation almost anywhere, but Speke was unable to talk with anyone except Burton and Sidi Bombay. Burton began to think that Speke was useless for anything except hunting, and Speke began to think that Burton intended to steal all the glory of the expedition for himself.

On its way back to the east coast, the expedition stopped at the Arab settlement of Kazeh (now the city of Tabora in Tanzania). While Burton rested and studied the inhabitants, Speke set off northwards to search for a huge lake that the local people called Ukerewe. He came to a body of water more like a sea than a lake (it was afterwards shown to be 250 miles long and 200 miles wide, about as big as the whole country of Scotland). Speke called it Lake Victoria, after the queen of England. Using a thermometer to measure altitude—the higher the land, the lower the temperature at which water boils—he calculated that this lake was higher than Lake Tanganyika, and decided that it must be the true source of the Nile. But when Speke returned to Kazeh to announce that the mystery of the Nile was solved, Burton refused to believe him.

The expedition ended in bitterness, and it had a bitter sequel. When Burton got back to London, he found that the Royal Geographical Society had already acclaimed Speke as the hero of the trip and had given him the command of a new expedition to Lake Victoria. The rivalry between the two men erupted into a public argument. In speeches and articles each accused the other of mismanagement and bad science. They differed not only on the source of the Nile but also on the location of the fabled Mountains of the Moon, mentioned by the ancient geographer Ptolemy. Speke insisted that these were the hills near Lake Tanganyika. Burton said that the mountains were yet to be found.

John Hanning Speke

In the spring of the following year, Speke's expedition left London for Zanzibar. His second-in-command was James Augustus Grant, a young army officer who had once gone hunting with Speke in the Himalayas; his guide, as before, was Sidi Bombay. They were gone for three years. At the head of a caravan of two hundred bearers, they made their way through hostile kingdoms to the northern end of Lake Victoria, made contact with the Nile, and followed it all the way through the Sudan and Egypt to the Mediterranean Sea, despite acute sickness and hunger. On the way, they met a pair of big-game hunters and adventurers, Florence and Samuel Baker, who were inspired to go in search of Luta Nzige, another lake that was rumored to be a source of the Nile. Under constant danger from suspicious slave traders, the Bakers found the lake, which they renamed Lake Albert, and confirmed that a branch of the Nile receives its waters. (Some years later, Baker returned to the area as head of a military expedition to stop the slave trade there.)

While Speke and Grant were making their momentous journey, Burton went to the United States to see the Mormon settlement in Utah, then took a job as British consul on the island of Fernando Po, off the coast of Nigeria. While he was there, he made a series of excursions into western Africa, climbing peaks in the Cameroon Mountains and exploring four rivers, including part of the Congo. On an extended visit to Dahomey, he made an official protest to the king against the local custom of sacrificing humans—some 500 a year, by his estimate—as part of religious celebrations.

The controversy over the Nile heated up again when Speke got back to London. The Royal Geographical Society decided to resolve the matter with a public debate between the two rivals. But the debate came to an abrupt end. While Burton was making his opening statement to the audience, Speke went hunting and was killed by his own gun. It was ruled an accident, but many people thought it was suicide.

The scandal over Speke's death put an end to Burton's career as an explorer. He spent the last thirty years of his life in the service of the Foreign Office, which assigned him to various consulates, first in Santos, Brazil, then in Damascus, Syria, and finally in Trieste (now part of Italy). He was knighted in 1886. Most of his time was spent writing and translating.

Burton's knowledge of the sexual customs of people in other parts of the world made him despise the prudishness of the English. He set out to enlighten them by translating ancient Indian texts on the art of love, including the *Ananga Ranga* and the *Kama Sutra*, and narrowly escaped being haled into court on obscenity

After their arrival at Lake Tanganyika, Burton and Speke visited the town of Ujiji, where Arab slave traders had a thriving business.

charges. His most famous work is his translation from the Arabic of *Alf Layla Wa-Layla* ("A Thousand Nights and a Night," the collection of stories better known in the West as the *Arabian Nights*). He rendered this classic of Muslim literature in a supple, vivid prose that has never been equaled, and added a wealth of scholarly notes and comments. His diaries and journals, together with his last manuscript, were burned by his wife after he died, in a misguided effort to control the reputation of one of Victorian England's most formidable geniuses.

The search for the Nile and the Mountains of the Moon went on. The missionary and explorer David Livingstone, who had spent years roaming through Central Africa, was present in London during the debate. He returned to Africa full of zeal to solve the Nile mystery himself, but he failed too. The reporter Henry Morton Stanley, who led a rescue expedition to Lake Tanganyika to find the missing Livingstone, took up the quest himself. Twenty years later, Stanley confirmed conclusively that Lake Victoria is the source of the Nile, and Lake Tanganyika the source of the Congo River. He also found the Mountains of the Moon south of Samuel and Florence Baker's Lake Albert. [For the full stories of Livingstone and Stanley, see the articles on them in this book.]

Henry Morton Stanley

Henry Morton Stanley, birth name John Rowlands. Born January 28, 1841, in Denbigh, Wales. Died May 10, 1904, in London.

In 1869, James Gordon Bennett, Jr., the publisher of the *New York Herald*, decided to send an enterprising reporter to Africa in search of the missing explorer David Livingstone. He had just the man for the job: Henry Morton Stanley, his special correspondent, who had already filed war stories for the *Herald* from Abyssinia (Ethiopia) and Spain.

Livingstone had been gone for six years. After a lifetime's work in Africa as a missionary, explorer, and antislavery crusader, he had gone back once more to see if he could solve the mystery of the Nile River's source. A decade earlier, the explorers Richard Burton and John Hanning Speke had gone on a harrowing journey through Central Africa to find the answer, but their discovery of two immense lakes, Tanganyika and Victoria, had only deepened the mystery. [For the full stories, see the articles on Livingstone and Burton in this book.]

Stanley was a scrappy young man who had

Henry Morton Stanley

made his way up in the world from rough beginnings. His real name was John Rowlands. He was the first of four illegitimate children born to a housemaid from a rural village in northern Wales. His mother refused to keep him, so for most of his childhood he lived in a workhouse where beatings and abuse were frequent. At the age of seventeen he came to the United States as a cabin boy and went to work as a storekeeper in Arkansas, taking the name of the New Orleans merchant who set him up in business. Over the next ten years, Stanley kept on the move. After fighting on both sides of the Civil War and spending time in a prison camp, he joined the merchant marine and then the U.S. Navy, went west to the American frontier and east to Turkey, and became a journalist. He was known at the *Herald* as a reporter who would go to any lengths to get his stories and who could write them up with plenty of dramatic flair.

For his Livingstone assignment, Stanley went to Zanzibar, the island off the east coast of Africa that was the usual port of entry for Europeans. With money from his publisher, he put together a huge expedition that required more than 150

Stanley's rescue of Livingstone inspired this 1872 caricature. The camel is labeled with the name of the newspaper that paid for the trip.

hired bearers and two dozen pack animals to carry. The head of his armed escort was Sidi Bombay, the guide who had accompanied Burton and Speke on their journeys ten years before. During the nine-month trek, Stanley encountered all the usual hardships that beset explorers in Africa: tropical heat and humidity, rainstorms and flooded rivers, starvation and thirst, tribal kings who demanded payment, rebellious bearers, mutinous colleagues, hostile warriors, and debilitating bouts of fever. His party passed many slave caravans. From one of them, they learned that a thin old man with pale skin and white hair was staying at the slave-trading post of Ujiji, on the shore of Lake Tanganyika. On November 24, 1871, they reached Ujiji and found Livingstone, weak from illness and just barely alive.

With the help of the medicine Stanley had brought, Livingstone recovered enough to set out once again. He was determined to find out whether Lake Tanganyika is the source of the Nile, as Burton had insisted it was. Stanley went with him. They found that the river at the northern end of the lake flows south, not north. It was not the Nile after all.

On his way back to Zanzibar, Stanley passed an official rescue expedition, including one of Livingstone's sons, that was searching for Livingstone. He went to London in 1872 to announce his success. But the British were not pleased that an American journalist had gotten there first. He was denounced as a braggart and a liar.

The following year the news came that Livingstone had died in Africa without finding the source of the Nile. Stanley decided to carry on the work of the man whose life he had saved. With money from the *Herald* and from London's *Daily Telegraph*, he left for Zanzibar in August 1874.

The expedition, loaded with nine tons of baggage and equipment, pushed rapidly through unexplored territory towards Lake Victoria. Stanley used different methods from the peaceable Livingstone. He forced his men forward with threats of flogging and hanging. When the caravan was attacked by local tribespeople, he fought back, earning himself a reputation back home as a man of violence rather than a scientist. By the time the caravan reached the lake, more than half its members had been lost to sickness, desertion, and combat.

Hired bearers carry a disassembled boat from Zanzibar to Lake Victoria. Stanley used the boat to prove that the lake is the source of the Nile.

Putting together a boat that the bearers had carried in pieces from Zanzibar, Stanley spent the next several months circumnavigating Lake Victoria, fending off attacks by the local inhabitants as he went. He confirmed that Speke had been right about the lake. It is a single enormous unit, not a collection of smaller lakes, and its waters flow out through a waterfall at the northern end. Here at last was proof that Lake Victoria is indeed the main source of the Nile.

In the course of exploring the lake, Stanley paid a visit to Mutesa, the king of Buganda (part of the modern nation of Uganda). Speke had visited him fifteen years before and had described him as a despot who enjoyed watching his executioners kill several of his own people, mostly women, every day. Stanley thought Mutesa could be converted to Christianity. His appeal for missionaries, printed in the newspapers that had financed his trip, resulted in the arrival of missions

from England and France. (The competition between these missions contributed to civil war in Uganda and eventually resulted in the establishment of a British protectorate there that lasted until 1962.)

By the fall of 1876, Stanley, still pursuing Livingstone's unfinished plans, had circumnavigated and mapped Lake Tanganyika and was preparing to make a trip down one of its rivers, the Lualaba. Livingstone had believed that the Lualaba fed into the Nile. Stanley intended to find out. Although he had written disgusted reports of the suffering inflicted on Africans by the slave traders, he found it convenient to hire additional bearers from a man called Tippu Tib (Hamed bin Muhammad), the best-known and most ruthless of the Arab slavers operating out of Zanzibar.

Stanley found that the Lualaba feeds into the Congo River, which winds through some of the densest jungle in Central Africa before emptying into the Atlantic Ocean. The trip down the river, in a boat and a fleet of canoes, was one long nightmare of bloody clashes with unfriendly tribes, losses to smallpox and dysentery, torture from swarms of red ants, and struggles to get past the many rapids and waterfalls. Not one of the four friends who had accompanied Stanley from England survived the journey, nor did many of the African helpers and guides. The starving remnants of the expedition were finally forced to leave their boats and hike across country. They reached the Atlantic in August 1877, having followed the Congo River almost its entire length of 2,700 miles.

Stanley had at last put to rest some of the vital questions that had been troubling London's Royal Geographical Society for decades. He had also found what Livingstone had so desperately wanted to find: a river highway that could bring legitimate traders into Central Africa, thus wiping out the slave traders. He did his best to persuade the British to appropriate the land around the Congo as a colony. But the British, already the administrators of a vast empire that included the Sudan and India, were not interested.

However, someone else was. King Leopold of Belgium, a tiny country with no colonies, was eager to take control of the Congo basin, an area eighty times the size of his own nation. In February 1879 Stanley headed back to Africa with a five-year contract and funds for another expedition. His job was to make travel possible along the Congo River by building a highway to bypass its many waterfalls and by setting up a chain of river stations.

This was an enormous feat of engineering that involved cutting through hardwood forests and filling in ravines in the tropical heat. The hard work nearly killed Stanley. Sickness and exhaustion reduced him to 100 pounds. His tenacity in pushing the road through earned him the nickname Bula Matari, "the Rock Smasher," from the Africans who worked on it with him. By the time his contract expired, in 1884, he had outfitted twenty-two stations, built a small railway, and set up a steamboat operation on the Congo. He had also purchased for his sponsors—by fraud, his critics said—huge tracts of land in the river basin.

That winter, Stanley attended a meeting, the Berlin Conference, in which seven European nations signed an agreement dividing most of Africa into colonies. The chief result was the establishment of the Congo Free State, an area of 900,000 square miles. This colony did not belong to the country of Belgium but to King Leopold personally. Over the next twenty-four years, his agents and soldiers built ivory and rubber plantations and forced the Africans to work on them, while Leopold received the profits. An estimated one and a half million Africans died under his harsh administration.

But though the division of Africa into European colonies was a direct result of Stanley's expeditions along the Congo, Stanley himself had nothing more to do with the political developments that arose from his work. His last trip through Africa was a relief mission, just as his first had been. This time, his goal was to save Mehmed Emin Pasha, the governor of Equatoria, the southernmost province of Sudan.

Emin Pasha was in reality Eduard Schnitzer, a Prussian physician who had served the British administrators of the Sudan as a doctor and a diplomat. As the British-appointed governor of Equatoria, he had explored the entire province and had put a stop to the practice of slavery there. In 1884 an Islamic revolutionary known as the Mahdi led a rebellion against Egyptian and British rule in the Sudan, and Emin Pasha was left stranded in Equatoria.

The British-financed rescue expedition, with Stanley in charge, reached the mouth of the Congo River in March 1887 and headed east under the protection of Tippu Tib, who was still the leading slave dealer in Central Africa. Leaving a detachment of men behind to follow later, Stanley and the main body of the expedition set out to cross the Great Forest, a dense jungle that no European had ever passed through. For five months they pressed on, losing men daily to starvation, insect bites, tropical diseases, and the poisoned weapons of Pygmy tribesmen who thought they were slave raiders. Yet when the survivors reached Emin Pasha's headquarters in April 1888, after a boat trip to Lake Albert, they found that the man for whom they had suffered so much was not sure he wanted to leave. While the governor dithered, Stanley had to make two more trips through the Great Forest to find out what had happened to the men of the detachment. Death and desertion had taken most of them.

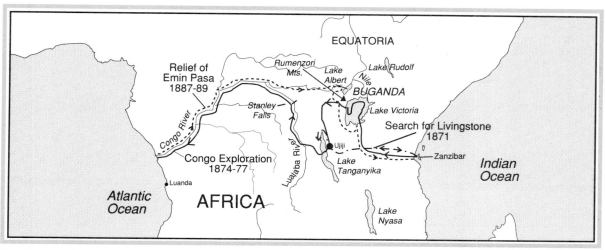

Stanley's explorations

Finally, in April 1889, the rescue expedition started its homeward journey, with the governor and his entourage. They reached the coast of the Indian Ocean that December. Only a quarter of the 800 people who had set out with Stanley at the beginning of the journey lived to see the end. Emin Pasha, who survived, was murdered by Arab slave raiders two years later.

But during the trek Stanley managed to find the answer to yet another question that had been plaguing geographers for a long time: the identity of the snow-capped Mountains of the Moon, which the ancient geographer Ptolemy had claimed to exist in the heart of Africa. Speke had been sure these mountains were near Lake Tanganyika, but Burton had disagreed.

When Stanley was going back to find the missing detachment, the mist on the horizon lifted for a moment, and he suddenly caught sight of a mountain range, the Ruwenzori. British explorers had passed close to the mountains before—Samuel Baker in 1864 and Stanley himself in 1876—but the mountains had always been hidden by the mist.

This was the last major expedition Stanley led. Returning to Britain, he married, adopted a child, was knighted, and won a seat in Parliament. Stanley had fulfilled Livingstone's dream of making Africa accessible to European traders and missionaries. He had also made possible the European domination of Africa that was to persist into the last half of the twentieth century.

China and Japan

Marco Polo

Marco Polo. Born circa 1254 in Venice. Died 1324 in Venice.

"**E**mperors and kings, dukes and marquises, counts, knights, and townsfolk, and all people who wish to know the many races of men and the strange customs of the many regions of the world, take this book and have it read to you." So begins the greatest travel book of all time, *The Travels of Marco Polo.* Marco Polo was a thirteenth-century Venetian trader who journeyed far into Asia at a time when few Europeans had ever been east of the Mediterranean. His famous book, filled with vivid stories of China and other exotic lands, spurred the European desire to explore the world as had no other work before. For three centuries after, Europeans went voyaging in search of the wonders that Marco Polo had described. Indeed, it has been said that without Marco Polo, there could have been no Christopher Columbus.

Marco Polo's book was so widely read because Europeans knew almost nothing about Asia and were hungry to know more. For centuries all routes from Europe to Asia had been blocked by the Muslim empire, which stretched from the shores of the Black Sea to the northern coast of Africa. No European could travel by land further east than the ports of the eastern Mediterranean, which were controlled by the Turks. No European was allowed to take a ship to India or Asia from the Egyptian ports on the Red Sea or from the city of Basra on the Persian Gulf. The sea route around Africa to Asia had not yet been discovered. So European merchants who wanted to trade in desirable goods from the Orient—pepper and spices from the Indies, or silk and lacquered boxes from China—had to purchase them at inflated prices from Muslim dealers or from a few merchant families from the Italian seafaring states of Venice and Genoa.

Then suddenly the routes were opened. In the year 1214, hordes of horsemen and archers swept out of Mongolia in Central Asia to conquer China. These skilled and ruthless soldiers were the Tatars (sometimes spelled Tartars). Led by Genghis Khan and his descendants, the Tatars conquered

Marco Polo

Three travelers of Marco Polo's era set off on a journey. Medieval merchants often traveled, but few went as far as Marco Polo did, to Beijing.

an empire from the Yellow River in China west to the shores of the Danube River in Hungary, and from Central Russia south to Persia and the Middle East. Only the death of one of Genghis Khan's sons kept the Tatar armies from invading Western Europe as well. By the year 1250, the Tatars had conquered Turkey, Persia, and Syria and therefore controlled all the main roads between East and West.

Though fierce in battle, the Tatars made surprisingly tolerant rulers. Unlike the Muslims, they believed in free trade and open roads, and did not care if many religions existed side by side in their empire. Soon a trickle of Europeans, mostly Christian missionaries and a few daring merchants, began to make their way into Asia. Among these were two Venetian traders, the brothers Niccolò and Maffeo Polo.

The Polos belonged to a wealthy family that had long done business with traders in Constantinople (the present-day Turkish capital of Istanbul) and the cities of the Crimea, a peninsula on the Black Sea. About the year 1260 the Polos sold

their holdings in Constantinople and sailed with a cargo of jewels up the Volga River to the court of Berke Khan, a son of Genghis Khan and the ruler of the western part of the Tatar empire. (The word *khan* means "king" or "emperor.") The Polos sold all their jewels to Berke Khan at double their value and prepared to return to Venice. But a war between the khan and another Tatar lord made it impossible for them to return the way they had come. Instead, they decided to accompany a party of Tatar envoys who were traveling east to the court of Kublai Khan, overlord of all the Tatars. The Great Khan, these envoys said, was intensely curious about Europeans and the West and would welcome them with honor.

After a four-year journey, the Polos reached Kublai's Khan's summer palace in Shang-tu (also called Xanadu) in Mongolia. The khan welcomed them warmly and questioned them closely about events in Europe. According to Marco's account, Kublai Khan desired to become a Christian but wanted the Christians to prove themselves first. He sent Maffeo and Niccolò back to Italy to be his envoys to the pope, the leader of the Catholic Church. "Go to the pope," said the khan, "and plead with him to send me one hundred Christians acquainted with the seven arts of wisdom." To safeguard the brothers on their return trip, Kublai Khan gave them a golden tablet. They had merely to show this tablet to anyone within the Tatar empire and they would receive whatever help they required. The Polos arrived back in Venice in 1269.

At this point Marco himself enters the story. He was now a boy of about fifteen, and had never seen his father Niccolò. When, after two years, his father and uncle set off to Shang-tu with letters of greeting from the pope, Marco went with them. The pope, unwilling to spare a hundred priests, sent along two Dominican friars who lost their nerve and left the expedition before it got anywhere near the Tatar lands.

The Polos' journey took them through some of the most rugged and hostile terrain on earth. They traveled through the deserts of Persia (present-day Iraq and Iran); over the mountains of Afghanistan, where Marco spent a year recovering from an illness (possibly malaria); and across the Pamir Knot at the meeting of China, Afghanistan, and Kashmir, a barrier of 20,000-foot peaks called "the roof of the world." Descending from the Pamir, they followed the Silk Road, the main trading route between China and the West. It passed through one of the driest places in the world, the Gobi Desert. According to Marco, the Gobi was a menacing place, where strange things could happen. "Someone lagging behind his fellows will suddenly hear spirits, calling him by name as if they were his companions. Tricked by the voices, he may stray from the path and be hopelessly lost. . . . The desert spirits can do amazing and unbelievable things. Even in the daytime one can hear their voices, and sometimes there is a clashing of swords and armor, a roll of war drums, or the sound of musical instruments."

About the year 1275 the Polos arrived at Shang-tu and presented themselves and their gifts to Kublai Khan. The khan took an immediate liking to Marco, who was now about twenty and could

The Polos approach the throne of Emperor Kublai Khan, grandson of the famed Mongol leader Genghis Khan and conqueror of China.

The Tatars (also known as Mongols) had well-organized armies of horsemen who were known for their quick and devastating attacks.

speak Turkish, a Persian dialect of Mongol, and some other languages quite well. Kublai Khan seemed to be most pleased with Marco's ability to tell vivid tales about the places he had seen. Soon after Marco arrived, Kublai asked him to go on a six-month diplomatic mission and report back in detail on what he saw along the way. This was the first of many such trips for Marco, who was to serve the khan for the next sixteen years. It was not unusual for Kublai to employ a foreigner such as Marco as an agent. The Tatars preferred to trust foreigners in high positions rather than the Chinese or other peoples under their rule.

The young Polo was mightily impressed with the splendor of the khan and his court, and willingly entered his service. Kublai Khan, wrote Marco, "has every right to be called the Great Khan because no man since Adam has ever ruled over so many people or such a vast empire, nor possessed such treasures or so much power." The emperor was a man "of medium height, sturdily built but not fat. . . . with pink and white skin like a rose, fine black eyes, and a handsome nose." As a direct descendant of Genghis Khan, he was entitled to the throne by birth, but Marco also thought he deserved it by virtue of "his spirit, his courage, and his superior wisdom."

According to Marco, Kublai Khan's court was the most magnificent in the world. The khan spent part of every year at his vast palace in Beijing, the capital of China. The palace's hundreds of rooms were decorated with silver and gold leaf, and painted with scenes of horsemen, dragons, and other creatures. The domed roof was painted deep colors so that it shone like a jewel. Surrounding the palace were gardens of unsurpassed beauty, and beyond them, fields where the khan would hunt and fly his hawks. At his summer palace at Shang-tu, the khan maintained sixteen miles of enclosed parks and hunting grounds, in the midst of which was a palace made of varnished wicker. This wicker palace was held to the ground by silk cords, and could be picked up and moved whenever the khan desired.

What was the key to the Tatars' success as conquerors? Marco believed it was the Tatar soldiers, who, he claimed, were "excellent fighters and bold in battle. They value their lives so little that they are willing to face any danger. They are certainly the toughest fighting men in the world. Often they spend a whole month living on nothing but mare's milk and what game they can catch. . . . No army is tougher, cheaper to feed, or better adapted to conquest." Polo also described the tactics that enabled the Tatars to defeat armies much larger than their own. "In battle they never confront the enemy army directly; they try instead to surround it. They do not care if they are thought to be in retreat; they move with great quickness, dashing from one part of the battle to another. . . . Just when the enemy thinks it is near victory, the retreating Tatars turn about and shoot them with arrows, leaving the battlefield strewn with dead men and horses. Then they violently attack and overrun their enemy." Yet, Polo noted, the Tatar armies were becoming soft from living in China and other civilized places.

Other aspects of Chinese culture fascinated Marco. For the first time, he saw paper money and was astounded that people would accept paper in place of of gold or silver. (Paper money was a Chinese invention, as was the printing press used to print it; neither invention was used in the West until much later.) Bathing was not a popular custom in Europe in those days, and Marco noted with interest that the Chinese bathed often and had the most elaborate baths he had ever seen. He also wrote the first Western accounts of some great historical events, such as Kublai's failed invasion of Japan, the island nation that Marco called "Cipango." As Marco heard it (he was not there himself), the Tatar armies sailed to Japan, disembarked, and began to move inland. Before they had made much progress, however, they saw that a powerful storm was coming. The armies piled back into the ships and took to sea, but nearly all the ships were wrecked in the storm, and tens of thousands of men were lost. This great disaster was as important in Japanese history as was the defeat of the Spanish Armada in English history. [See the article on Francis Drake for more on the Battle of the Armada.]

It is not clear from Marco's book exactly what the Polos did for Kublai Khan during their long stay at his court. In fact, Marco tells little about his own activities, preferring instead to write about the places he saw. Much of what he says agrees with the findings of historians, but some of his tales are plainly gossip and legend. We do know that he traveled on the khan's business to southern China, Malaysia, and Indonesia, as well as to India, perhaps as far as Kashmir. He describes some places that no European saw again until the twentieth century. Occasionally Marco tells us something about himself. From around 1283 to 1286 he may have been the governor of Yang-chou, in the Chinese province of Kansu. At another time the Polos may have helped in the siege of the Chinese city of Hsiang-yang by overseeing the construction and use of great siege engines called *mangonels*, but historians are somewhat skeptical of Marco's account. Possibly Marco was involved in managing the trade in salt, for he mentions it often in his book.

At length the Polos began to feel homesick for Venice and begged Kublai Khan to let them return. The elderly khan was reluctant to let them go, but in the year 1292 he finally consented when they offered to escort a seventeen-year-old Mongol princess named Kokachin to her future husband, the king of Persia. Laden with the wealth they had gathered during their years in the East, the Polos set sail for the Indian Ocean in a fleet of fourteen ships bearing some six hundred courtiers, sailors, and soldiers. The voyage was a stormy one, and by the time the Polos reached Persia, only eighteen of the travelers were left alive, including the princess. When Kokachin was delivered to her destination, according to Marco, she bade farewell to her Venetian friends with many tears. Finally, in 1295, the Polos arrived in Venice. Marco's book ends here, but there are other accounts that tell of their return. According to one story, at first no one recognized the long-lost travelers, who looked more like hard-bitten Tatar horsemen than wealthy Venetians. But when Marco opened his robe to show the dazzling collection of jewels he had been given by Kublai Khan, his family suddenly welcomed him with open arms.

Not long after Marco's return, Venice and its rival, Genoa, went to war. Marco was captured in a sea battle and thrown into a Genoese prison. He shared his cell with a prisoner named Rustichello, a writer of romantic stories and tales of chivalry. With nothing else to do, Marco began to dictate the events of his life to Rustichello, who fashioned them into a book and added a few flourishes of his own. The result was *The Travels of Marco Polo*, published about the year 1300. It was enjoyed both as a source of information about the geography and customs of the East and as a diverting entertainment. (In those days, most Europeans could not read, which is why the author recomended that the owner "should take this book and have it read to you.") The book took on even greater importance when the Tatar Empire collapsed around the year 1350 and land travel between Europe and Asia again became impossi-ble. For many years, Marco's book was the only one about Asia based on first-hand reporting. Even as late as the early 1600s, European map-makers still drew upon his rather vague descriptions of Asian geography.

More than one hundred handwritten editions of *The Travels of Marco Polo* still exist from the years before the European invention of the printing press, but the manuscript written out by Rustichello has been lost. The meaning of the book's original title, *Il millione* ("The Million"), is a mystery. It may refer to a Polo family nickname.

Little is known of Marco's life after he was freed from prison. He returned to Venice, where he lived quietly on his fortune until he died at the age of seventy. On his deathbed, as one story goes, he was asked to confess that his book was all lies and fables. But Marco replied that he had not told the half of it.

Zheng He

Zheng He (zheng-hay, also spelled Cheng Ho), birth name Ma Sanpao. Born circa 1371 in Kunming, Yunnan, China. Died sometime after 1433 in China.

The mightiest navies of the early Age of Exploration were not possessed by the adventurous Portuguese or the far-flung Arabs. It was China, a country not usually noted for its interest in exploration, that mounted the greatest voyages of discovery of the fifteenth century. China's grand fleets, with scores of ships much larger than any floated by Europeans, explored as far west as the east coast of Africa. The admiral of these voyages was a Chinese official named Zheng He.

Not much is known of Zheng He's early life. He was born Ma Sanpao in Yunnan Province in southwestern China, the son of a Muslim who had made the religious pilgrimage to Mecca in the Arabian desert. At that time, Yunnan was ruled by the Mongols, the people who had conquered China two centuries earlier under Genghis Khan, but when Ma He (as he was by then known) was about ten years old, the province was recaptured by armies of the Ming dynasty of China. Along with hundreds of other boys, Ma He was taken from his family, castrated, and made an orderly in the Chinese army. It was common Chinese practice to castrate boys who were chosen for Imperial service, so that they could not marry or have children when they grew up. This, the Chinese thought, would ensure their undivided loyalty to the emperor. These eunuchs, as they were called, could rise to the highest levels of civil service and attain great power at court.

Ma He soon proved to be one of the most talented. Within a few years he was a ambitious junior officer in the service of the Prince of Yen and had made many useful friends at the imperial court. When the Prince of Yen became Emperor Yongle in 1402, Ma He, now called Zheng He, became chief eunuch at the court, where he attained considerable influence.

Yongle, whose imperial name means "eternal contentment," was not at all content with his reputation. He desired above all to impress the world with the unmatched splendor of his imperial rule. So he ordered that a great fleet be assembled to collect tribute from coastal states and as-yet unknown new lands along the "Western Oceans." Zheng He was put in charge of the vast undertaking. The fleet set sail in 1405 with 300 ships and 27,000 men. The largest ship was the nine-masted Treasure Ship, 444 feet long and 180 feet wide; it could carry nearly a thousand people. All three of Columbus's ships could have fit easily within this great vessel. Other huge ships carried horses,

Yongle was the greatest of the Ming emperors of China. He ordered Zheng He to lead naval expeditions to distant Arabia and East Africa.

supplies, and trade goods. The smallest ship was the Fighting Ship, for this was not an expedition of war or conquest but of diplomacy.

The Chinese ships were larger than anything Europeans would build for hundreds of years and were more advanced in their construction. For example, the Chinese divided their ships into separate compartments with watertight walls called bulkheads. The bulkheads prevented a leak in one compartment from flooding the whole ship, and made the hull much stronger, too. Passengers lived on the many decks, which with their windows and decorations gave the larger ships the look of floating castles. The majestic square sails and great rudders, forty or more feet high, made these ships truly impressive. With their superior compasses and well-drawn seacharts, the Chinese were truly the premier mariners of the age.

For the first part of its journey, the fleet sailed to a number of places in Southeast Asia, including what are now the countries of Vietnam, Thailand, and Java. Then it crossed the Indian Ocean to visit the Malabar Coast of India and the island of Sri Lanka. Chinese junks had been trading in these ports for hundreds of years, but no fleet like Zheng He's had ever been seen. The admiral collected much treasure and received assurances of the greatness of China from every group of people he met. He returned to Sri Lanka in 1409 and after a brief battle captured its king and took him back to the emperor as a prisoner.

Two years later, the enormous ships of Zheng He's fleet made their first appearance in the part of the world that we now call the Middle East, arriving at the straits of Hormuz at the mouth of the Persian Gulf. The next time the ships appeared at Hormuz, in 1414, they carried a delegation of Chinese diplomats bound for Egypt by way of the Red Sea. Zheng He sailed his fleet southward along the east coast of Africa almost to Mozambique on this fourth journey. On his way back, he took aboard some three hundred foreign diplomats who wished to pay their respects to Emperor Yongle. The envoy from Malindi in East Africa brought an unusual gift to the emperor: a giraffe, an animal never seen before by the Chinese. The long-necked creature caused a sensation at court —Chinese naturalists decided it must be a unicorn, an animal thought to bring good luck—and it was given a prominent place in the imperial zoo.

A junk similar to those used by Zheng He. Junks have exceptionally strong hulls and bamboo-ribbed sails that are easy to raise and lower.

Zheng He's fifth and sixth voyages retraced the route of the fourth. During his sixth voyage, Yongle died (in 1424) and was succeeded by Emperor Hungzhi, who did not support the voyages and canceled the trip planned for that year. Zheng He was sent to Nanking, the southern capital of China, where he was ordered to disband his men.

But Hung Hsi's reign was short, and in 1431, with the backing of a new emperor, Zheng He was able to launch one more voyage, the grandest of all. With 27,550 men and more than 300 ships, he visited nearly every major port in Southeast Asia, India, the Persian Gulf, the Red Sea, and East Africa. Diplomatic relations were established and tribute collected from more than twenty foreign kingdoms.

For all the tribute collected by Zheng He, these voyages did not make a profit for China, nor were they meant to—their main purpose was to impress the rest of the world with the wealth and grandeur of the Chinese empire. Zheng He was instructed to give lavish gifts to each leader he met, and he himself was given the title "Admiral of the Triple Treasure." (A more popular nickname for him was the "Three-Jeweled Eunuch.") One marker stone left by the Chinese in Sri Lanka lists the treasures Zheng He presented to the Buddhist temple there: 1,000 pieces of gold, 5,000 pieces of silver, 100 rolls of silk cloth, 2,500 jars of perfumed oil, and many bronze ornaments. In the end, gifts like these cost far more than the tribute Zheng He collected. There was no attempt to set up colonies or trading posts, for the Chinese—

unlike the Europeans and the Arabs—were not interested in expanding into other lands and did not feel that they needed what others had to sell.

This seventh voyage proved to be Zheng He's last, as well as China's last official voyage of discovery. The new emperor, seeing no practical benefit from the expeditions, put an end to them, and perhaps to Zheng He as well. Upon his return from the seventh voyage in 1433, the admiral's name disappears from the court records, and no more is known of him. Zheng He's own accounts of his voyages were destroyed. With the passing of Zheng He, China gave up its role as the premiere exploring power of the fifteenth century, and instead became an object of discovery for adventurous Europeans.

Matteo Ricci

Matteo Ricci (REET-chee). Born October 6, 1552, in Macerata, Marches, Italy. Died May 11, 1610, in Beijing, China.

The conquest of China in the early thirteenth century by the Tatar armies of Genghis Khan opened the way for a century of contacts between the Chinese and the Europeans. But in the middle of the fourteenth century, China again closed its doors to Europeans. No European diplomats, traders, or missionaries were allowed to enter the country. Even when contacts between Europe and China became more common, in the sixteenth century, the Chinese were still suspicious of foreigners, and with some reason. In 1557, the Chinese allowed Portugal to establish the first Western trading colony on the Chinese mainland in the city of Macao. While they accepted the European presence as useful for trade, Chinese officials constantly worried that the newcomers were planning to occupy more territory. They were particularly alarmed by the fighting between the Portuguese and the Dutch, who were competing for Asian business. Dutch privateers sought to break Portugal's control of the Asian spice trade by raiding Portuguese ships and ports in Southeast Asia. Chinese people were often killed in these skirmishes. In 1603, the Spanish, who had absorbed the Portuguese empire, massacred more than 20,000 Chinese living in the Philippines, for reasons that are still not clear today. Then there were the Japanese pirates, who made damaging attacks on Chinese ports every year, so that finally the Chinese feared to conduct any sea trade at all. Instead they moved their goods along inland waterways, even though that took twice as long.

Just as troubling to the Chinese were the rivalries between Western religions. Most Chinese held to the beliefs of more than one religion at once; they might be Confucian, Buddhist, and Taoist all at the same time, without worrying that these systems of belief sometimes conflicted. Yet the Muslims and Christians were always at odds with one another. Muslims had lived in China for centuries, and their leaders argued that Christian missionaries should never be allowed to enter. The Roman Catholic missionaries of Macao, who hoped someday to turn China into a Christian country, dreamed of driving the Muslims out of China altogether. (One of the few things that Muslims and Christians agreed upon was that it was proper to persecute the small communities of Chinese Jews.) The two main groups of Christians, the Roman Catholics and the Protestants, hated one another, and even the different groups of Catholic missionaries—the Augustinians, Dominicans, Franciscans, and Jesuits—quarreled among themselves and had different approaches to teaching religion. Some Chinese argued that all these worrisome *huihui* (god-worshipping foreigners) wanted entry to China only to lay the groundwork for a future invasion.

Few Europeans were willing to learn about the Chinese and earn their trust. Among those who tried to do this was Matteo Ricci, the first and most brilliant of the Jesuit missionaries allowed into China. Ricci was born in the Italian town of Macerata, the eldest son of a well-to-do family. In 1561 he entered a school run by the Jesuits. (Jesuits are members of the Society of Jesus, a missionary order of Catholic priests and brothers.) At the age of sixteen he traveled to Rome to study law, then, in 1571, joined the Jesuits as a novice, a student training to become a priest. The Jesuits were eager to establish missions in the new lands opening to Europeans in the sixteenth century. China, with its millions of potential converts, was one of the main areas of Jesuit interest. Their hope was to convert the Chinese emperor, who might then order that all his subjects to become Christians as well. The Jesuit leader Francis Xavier had died in 1552, the year Ricci was born, while waiting to gain entrance to China for just this purpose.

For the task of founding the first Jesuit mission in China, the Jesuits sought priests and novices of the highest intelligence and dedication. Ricci, one of the most talented of their students in Rome, was granted permission in 1577 to travel to the Portuguese colony of Goa, on the central west coast of India. [For the story of the Portuguese capture of Goa, see the article on Afonso de Albuquerque in this book.] In 1582, two years after he was ordained a priest, he settled in Macao and began his study of the Chinese language, which he was probably the first European to master. Within a few months he had learned to speak Chinese fluently, but it took him ten years to read and write well enough to begin translating European books into Chinese.

In 1583 Ricci and another priest, Michele Ruggieri, won permission from the emperor to found a small mission in the Chinese town of Zhaoqing. When they were expelled by hostile officials in 1589, they moved to the town of Shaozhou. Later, after Ruggieri left China, Ricci moved to the city of Nancheng. Finally, in 1601, the emperor allowed him to settle in the imperial capital of Beijing, where he lived for the rest of his life. Ricci's letters to his Jesuit superiors, which describe everything he learned about Chinese life, were the first detailed reports on China to reach the West since the thirteenth-century book written by Marco Polo. [For more on Marco Polo's travels in Asia, see the article about him in this book.]

Matteo Ricci, in Chinese dress

For all Ricci's cleverness, it was many years before he was accepted by the Chinese. They would stare at him as he walked in the streets, call him "foreign devil" and "barbarian" to his face, and throw stones on his roof at night. Once a gang of young men broke into Ricci's house, beat some of his followers, and attacked him with an axe. Chinese officials deliberately made it difficult for him to travel. The Emperor Wanli himself denied Ricci permission to live in Beijing. When, after many years, Ricci finally received an audience with Wanli, the emperor chose not to appear in person. Ricci had to pay his compliments to an empty throne.

Ricci never made many converts to Catholicism

Ricci needed to win the respect of the learned scholars, like those shown here, who held important positions in China's government.

during his years in China—perhaps a dozen or so every year—but he did open the way for other missionaries. One of Ricci's goals was to dispel Chinese suspicion of Europeans. It had been decided by Ricci's Jesuit superior that Ricci would be more likely to succeed in his mission if he adopted Chinese customs and dress. This approach was far different than that taken by most Europeans of the era. At first Ricci wore the robes of a Buddhist monk, but he made little progress. After some years, a Chinese friend told him that monks were held in less esteem than were Confucian scholars (followers of the philosopher Confucius, who had lived in the fifth century B.C.). As soon as Ricci began dressing and acting like a Confucian, he was able to move in a higher level of Chinese society and attracted the attention of Chinese scholars curious about the West.

In Ricci's time, China had enjoyed many unbroken centuries of scholarship and scientific innovation. The Chinese were using paper money, the printing press, gunpowder, and maps laid out on a grid of lines long before Europeans had ever heard of such things. Chinese art, philosophy, and literature were perhaps the most sophisticated in the world, and scholars there were respected and influential members of society. Ricci found that the best way to reach the Chinese scholars was to share his knowledge with them, in the hope that they would move from curiosity about Western art and science to curiosity about Christianity. From 1584 to 1602, Ricci worked on the first Western map of the world designed for a Chinese audience. The place names were labeled in Chinese, and small descriptions gave the Jesuit view of Western religion, politics, and culture. This map was much copied, studied, and discussed by the Chinese, who rarely saw a picture of their country that showed it as part of the larger world. "When they saw on the map what an almost unlimited stretch of land and sea lay between Europe and the Kingdom of China," wrote Ricci, "they seemed to be less fearful of us." Emperor Wanli had a copy made that covered one whole wall of his inner palace.

Western technology, mathematics, history, and literature were new and of great interest to the Chinese, and Ricci spent much time teaching these subjects. But the Chinese were most impressed with Ricci's skill in the arts of memory. At that time, when printed books were not yet common in the West, most people still had to memorize everything they needed to know. Over many centuries, techniques were developed that used visual images, puns, and relations between ideas to help boost a person's power of remembering. Among these techniques was the "memory palace," first used by the ancient Greeks. Ricci kept in his mind an imaginary palace of many rooms; in each room he placed an image that helped him remember something of importance. Using this system, he was able to memorize long lists of names and thousands of Chinese words.

After a few public demonstrations of his memory skills, famous Chinese scholars came to Ricci for training. Ever watchful for a chance to teach some aspect of Christianity to his hosts, he suggested that the Chinese break up long lists of things to remember into groups of ten—the Chinese symbol for the number ten resembles the Christian symbol of a cross. However, the Chinese did not accept Christian ideas easily. When the powerful court official Ma Tang discovered in Ricci's luggage a crucifix (a small statue showing the execution of Jesus), he became angry, saying that it was bad luck for Ricci to carry such an image of suffering and death. Ricci, surrounded by a threatening crowd, was unable to explain the crucifix's religious meaning and barely got away with his life. After that, he kept his crucifixes hidden and instead displayed pictures of the Madonna and Child (the baby Jesus and his mother).

By the time Ricci was finally allowed to settle in Beijing, he had become famous as "the Wise Man from the West," the only European the Chinese had ever known who had taken the trouble to learn their language and study their philosophy. Several of his books, such as a treatise on memory and a Chinese translation of the works of the Greek mathematician Euclid, were widely printed. With the support of important Chinese scholars and two princes of the royal family, he was able to publish Christian works in Chinese translation and lay the foundations for a permanent Catholic community in China. When Ricci died in Beijing at the age of fifty-seven, he was granted the right to be buried in the Imperial City by special order of the emperor—the first of the very few Europeans ever given that honor.

William Adams

William Adams. Born 1564 in
Gillingham, Kent, England. Died May 16,
1620, in Japan, probably in Hirado.

The Dutch sailors and their English pilot had never seen a house like this one. It was built of wood, but it looked nothing like the wooden houses of Europe. The rooms were big, wide spaces with hardly any furniture in them. The floors were covered by reed mats. Everything was clean and spare, not at all like the houses they were used to. The people who lived here spoke not a word of any language the mariners knew. Their clothes, their food, their behavior were utterly strange.

The mariners had come all the way to the other side of the world, to the islands of Japan. They were all that was left of a five-ship expedition that had started out from Holland many months before. They were weak from starvation, and some of them were close to death. As soon as they had anchored their battered ship off the coast, they had been taken prisoner and put under guard. Their only visitors were a few Portuguese priests who were living in Japan as missionaries. The English pilot, Will Adams, who knew how to speak Portuguese, tried to find out from the priests what would happen next. But Portugal was at war with England and Holland, and the priests were not inclined to help them. All they would say was that the sailors were now in the hands of a man named Ieyasu, the Mighty Lord of Edo, head of the Tokugawa clan and the greatest warlord in the land. Ieyasu would decide what to do with them in his own good time.

Will Adams lived in the same era as Francis Drake, Martin Frobisher, and the other "sea-dogs" of Elizabethan England. Born in a coastal town, he was apprenticed as a boy to a well-known shipwright and must often have gone to sea. When the Spanish Armada attacked England in the year 1588, Adams, who was only twenty-four years old, captained his own vessel, running supplies to Drake's ship and the rest of the defending English fleet. [See the article on Drake in this book for more about the Armada.] After that, he hired himself out as a ship's pilot to any employer who could meet his price. Most often, he worked for Dutch merchants who traded overseas.

Holland had recently broken free from Spain, but this rebellion had cost the Dutch their profitable trade in Asian goods. The Portuguese and the Spanish, who had built huge empires in the East and together controlled the sea routes that linked Asia and Europe, refused to continue their former practice of shipping Indian spices and Chinese cloth to the merchants of Holland for resale in northern Europe. So the Dutch decided to start their own trade with Asian countries. In 1598 they sent out a fleet of ships with instructions to head southwest across the Atlantic Ocean, round Cape Horn, plunder whatever Spanish ships and ports they found on the South American coast, and continue west across the Pacific to China, Japan, or the Indies, whichever place seemed best to the captain. (This was basically the same route that Francis Drake had used in his circumnavigation of the world in 1577.) Because this was as much a military expedition as a commercial one, one of the ships, the Liefde ("Charity"), carried a great store of weapons.

Adams was hired as chief pilot for the voyage. As he said goodbye to his wife and his newborn daughter, he told them not to be worried, for he expected to come back in two or three years' time as a rich man. But the voyage was a disaster. Of the five ships that set out from Holland, one turned back, one was captured by the Portuguese, another was seized by the Spanish, and the fourth was lost in a storm in the Pacific. Adams urged the crew of the remaining ship, the Liefde, to sail on toward Japan, which none of them had ever seen but which was thought to be a land of great wealth. On the way they ran out of food and water and suffered terribly from scurvy.

Only 24 of the original 110-man crew were still alive when the *Liefde* anchored off the Japanese island of Kyushu in April 1600. The guns and ammunition in the *Liefde*'s hold were taken directly to Tokugawa Ieyasu, who was happy to get them. He planned to put them to good use in his war against his rivals. Japan was ruled by an emperor, but the real power was held by the *shogun*, the Great General of the empire. Hideyoshi, the old shogun, had just died, and the emperor had not yet appointed the next shogun. Ieyasu had waited many years, patiently serving other shoguns, and now he believed that his moment was at hand. He expected that the Dutch weapons that had fallen into his hands would prove very useful.

Among the visitors at Ieyasu's court were a group of Roman Catholic priests known as Jesuits (members of the Society of Jesus, a missionary order) who had been coming to Japan over the last sixty years. They were working hard to establish the Catholic Church in Japan. Fearing competition from the Dutch, who were Protestants, they urged Ieyasu to have the sailors killed. Only renegades or pirates, they argued, would carry such an immense cargo of arms.

Ieyasu decided to talk to one of these dangerous foreigners himself. The only Europeans he had yet encountered were the Portuguese and the Spanish. No Dutch or English mariners had ever reached Japan. He ordered their leader to be brought before him. As the captain-general of the expedition was too ill to move, Adams was sent in his place.

When Adams entered Ieyasu's court, the warlord was sitting cross-legged, alone on a low platform, dressed in the stiff, boxy clothes of a *daimyo*, or Japanese baron. Around Ieyasu were his courtiers, attendants, and guards, who kept a respectful distance and bowed very low to him. Adams did the same. He could see that everyone respected and feared this man. Plainly, if he said the wrong thing to Ieyasu, he and his sailors would be executed. But he could not communicate with Ieyasu directly. He had to rely on one of the Portuguese priests to serve as his interpreter, and he was not at all sure that his words would be translated accurately.

First, Ieyasu asked Adams where he came from and what was his business in Japan. With

Tokugawa Ieyasu, shogun of Japan

the help of some charts he had saved from his ship, Adams showed Ieyasu how he had sailed from Europe around the tip of South America and all the way across the Pacific Ocean to the east coast of Japan. Ieyasu pressed him with many more questions. Then he asked, "Is your country at war just now?" Adams, glancing at the Jesuit interpreter, described how England and Holland were peaceful countries seeking only profitable trade with all other nations, including Japan. Their only war, he said, was a war of defense against Portugal and Spain. "Do you worship any gods?" asked Ieyasu. Adams replied, "I believe in the one God that made heaven and earth."

But, though this answer seemed to satisfy Ieyasu, Adams was led away to a prison. He was left there for nearly seven weeks. During that time, he heard no news of his fellow crewmen. Had the Portuguese convinced Ieyasu to let him rot forever in his cell?

In fact, the interpreter had translated Adams's words faithfully, and Ieyasu had taken an immediate liking to the Englishman. Here was a brave man who could give him a different view of the outside world than he would get from the Portuguese or the Spanish. And Adams did not appear to be interested in converting the Japanese to Christianity, as were the Jesuits and the Spanish Franciscan missionaries. That, in Ieyasu's opinion, was a mark in his favor. But Ieyasu decided to test Adams once more. He had Adams released and reunited with the crew. Then he ordered Adams to build a ship similar to the *Liefde*. The warlord was delighted when, a few months later, Adams presented him with a European-style sailing ship.

As a reward, Ieyasu made Adams one of his personal retainers, an unheard-of honor for a foreigner. It may be that Ieyasu felt he could trust Adams precisely because he was a foreigner, someone who was not involved in the intrigues and schemes of the Japanese nobles. Ieyasu also granted Adams an estate outside the town of Edo, where Ieyasu had his headquarters, and allowed him to marry the daughter of a local official. (Edo is now Tokyo, the capital of Japan.) Adams had little choice but to make a new life for himself in

Japan because Ieyasu told him that he would never be allowed to leave. As a retainer, he had to serve his lord, and Ieyasu found him too valuable a man to lose. From time to time, Adams sent money to his wife and child in England through the Dutch sailors who now came frequently to Japan to trade.

In 1603, Ieyasu was made shogun by the emperor and began to establish a powerful dynasty. Adams became his most important advisor on European affairs. Adams spoke his mind freely to Ieyasu and gave the shogun useful though not entirely impartial information concerning the Spanish and Portuguese. He described the religious wars between Catholics and Protestants that were then raging in Europe, and told Ieyasu about the vast Spanish conquests in the New World. When the Spanish asked Ieyasu's permission to go on a surveying expedition around Japan, Adams warned him that this might be the first step toward an invasion. (In fact, all the Spanish wanted to do was find the mythical "Islands of Gold and Silver" that were rumored to lie off the coast of Japan.) Adams's stories of

Ieyasu established his court at Edo (now called Tokyo) in 1603. This engraving shows the court as it looked when Will Adams lived there.

the battle of the Spanish Armada—a battle in which England, an island nation like Japan, had fended off a naval invasion by a much larger rival—must have been especially interesting to Ieyasu. Three centuries before, Japan had been threatened with a sea invasion from China, and had been saved by a storm that destroyed most of the attacking ships. [See the article on Marco Polo in this book for more on the first Western account of this invasion.] And Ieyasu's predecessor, Hideyoshi, had mounted two disastrous overseas invasions of Korea.

Ieyasu wanted to increase trade between Japan and all the Western nations that sent ships to Asia. He well understood the great usefulness of their guns, warships, and other inventions. On the other hand, he was alarmed by the number of Japanese converts to Christianity. He saw Christianity as a threat to the traditional social order that kept him in power. In 1614, he ordered all Western missionaries out of the country. Western traders were allowed to remain, and for a while they prospered. Adams obtained a favorable trading patent for the Dutch, and even the Portuguese and Spanish merchants were quite willing to use his services as a translator and go-between because the shogun held him in such high esteem. When an English trading expedition reached Japan in 1613, its captain was dismayed to find that Adams was so busy working for the Japanese, the Dutch, the Portuguese, and the Spanish that he had little time for the English!

In 1616, Ieyasu died. The new shogun, Ieyasu's son Hidetada, cared little for Europeans and even less for Adams. Apparently Hidetada was jealous of the affection that his father had shown for Adams, and he was now of a mind to humiliate the Englishman. When Adams came to the palace to ask Hidetada for assistance against the Dutch, who had captured an English trading ship, the shogun kept him waiting for two months while he went out hunting and hawking. Finally Hidetada gave his answer: the whole affair was none of his concern.

Adams knew that his influence at the court of the shoguns was over. It was possible now for him to return to England, but he decided not to leave his Japanese family and his estates. In Japan he was a rich man, but in England he would be no more than an aging ship's pilot.

A drawing by a Japanese artist of a 17th-century Dutch ship. With Adams's help, Ieyasu negotiated treaties with European traders.

Not long after his rebuff from Hidetada, Adams died from a disease he contracted on a trading voyage to China. The English trading post, unable to prosper against fierce competition from the Dutch, was closed soon after. Once the English left, the Tokugawa shoguns saw that the European presence in Japan was not permanent, and decided that the only way to preserve the stability and harmony of the country was rid themselves of all Westerners and of any Japanese who had adopted their ways. The Portuguese and Spaniards were driven out—only a few Dutch were allowed to keep a trading post on a nearby island—and thousands of Japanese Christians were killed by crucifixion. In 1638 Japan closed itself off completely from the West and entered a period of isolation under Tokugawa rule that lasted for more than two hundred years.

Science and Medicine

Nicolaus Copernicus

Nicolaus Copernicus (ko-PER-ni-kus), birth name Mikolaj Kopernik. Born February 19, 1473, in Torun, Poland. Died May 24, 1543, in Frauenberg (now Frombork), Poland.

For some two thousand years, most Europeans looked at the sky and felt they understood what they saw. The earth stood at the center of the universe, and everything else—sun, moon, planets, and stars—circled around it, embedded

Nicholas Copernicus

in great crystal spheres. Ptolemy, a Greek philosopher of the second century, had described such a system (we call his idea the *Ptolemaic theory* today), and nearly all European astronomers accepted it. Besides, this is just how the heavens really look from Earth, so believing in an earth-centered universe seemed to be only common sense. It was so obvious that most people gave it no more thought.

A sixteenth-century Polish astronomer was not satisfied with the obvious explanations. His name was Mikolaj Kopernik, or in Latin Nicolaus Copernicus. He was born in Torun, a prosperous town on the banks of the Vistula River in northern Poland. His father, a well-to-do merchant, died when he was ten years old, and his uncle, a bishop in the Catholic Church, became his guardian. Copernicus's uncle helped him become a canon at the church in Frauenberg at the age of twenty-four. That is how Copernicus earned his living for the rest of his life. But Copernicus also attended the universities at Bologna and Cracow, where he studied mathematics, church law, medicine, and astronomy. Astronomy was his true love, though he did not have as much time for it as he wished, being busy with church matters and medical care of the people in his diocese. His first recorded observation was of the star Aldebaran being occulted (covered over) by the moon. He also undertook regular observations of the paths of the sun, moon, and planets and tried to calculate their orbits.

Many astronomers, including Copernicus, were troubled by problems with the Ptolemaic system. They saw that the planets changed in brightness and sometimes even appeared to move backward in the sky. No simple system of circular orbits could explain that. Ptolemy himself had recognized the problems, but he had believed that the planets made smaller circles as they traveled along their main circles, which would account for some of their odd motions. Eventually, as observations of the planets and stars became more accurate, astronomers had to imagine more and more complex circles within circles to explain the motion of planets. Even so, the Ptolemaic system didn't work very well. Copernicus wasn't the only astronomer of his day who thought the Ptolemaic system was too complicated and inaccurate to be true, but he was the first to put forward an idea to replace it.

Copernicus reread the works of the old Greek astronomers, and there he found the germ of a new idea. It was breathtakingly simple. Suppose the earth was *not* at the center of the universe at all—suppose it circled around the sun instead, just one of many celestial bodies in the sun's family? Right away this idea solved several of the problems of the Ptolemaic system, such as why planets appear to change in brightness and move backwards. Even more important to Copernicus, a sun-centered view of the universe seemed more beautiful, and thus, he believed, more likely to be true.

It isn't enough in science just to think up a new idea; the idea has to be tested for its truth. So Copernicus spent many years making astronomical observations to find support for his theory. His observations showed him the true order of the planets in relation to the earth. The ancients believed that the earth was circled by the moon, Mercury, Venus, the sun, Mars, Jupiter, and Saturn, in that order. (These were all the planets that astronomers knew about then; they considered the moon and sun to be planets too.) Copernicus saw that the correct arrangement put the sun at the center, circled by Mercury, Venus, Earth, Mars, Jupiter, and Saturn. The moon is the only celestial body that actually does revolve around the earth.

Still Copernicus hesitated to publish his work. In 1510, he began showing a handwritten paper about his theory to his friends. They were excited about it and urged him to make his views more widely known. But it wasn't until 1543, the year of

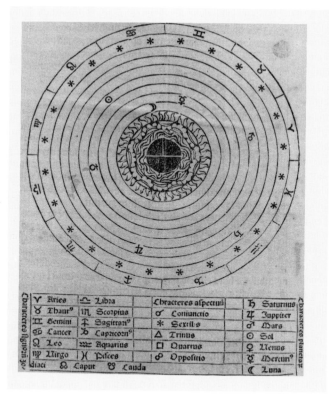

Ptolemy put Earth at the center of the universe, surrounded by the elements of water, air, and fire and the orbits of the moon, sun, and planets.

Copernicus placed the sun at the center, orbited by Earth and the other planets within an outer sphere of fixed stars. The moon orbits Earth.

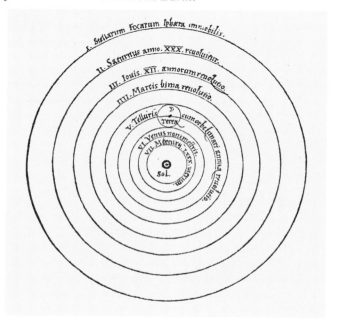

his death, that his work was published as a book, called *De revolutionibus orbium coelestium* ("On the Revolutions of the Celestial Spheres"). It is said that Copernicus was given the first copy of the book on the very day he died.

The book's introduction, supposedly written by Copernicus himself, said that his new theory was offered more as an approach to astronomical calculations than as scientific truth, and was not to be taken too seriously. But the astronomer Johannes Kepler discovered that the book's editor, Andreas Osiander, had secretly removed Copernicus's original introduction and put in his own instead. "Copernicus thought his hypotheses were true," wrote Kepler in his journals, "no less than did the ancient philosophers. He did not merely think so, but he proves that they are true." (In fact, nowhere in his writings did Copernicus offer what scientists today would consider convincing proof of his ideas. That was left to later astronomers, notably Kepler himself.)

Osiander believed that leaders of the Church would be hostile to Copernicus's theories because his ideas contradicted the Church's view of the universe, which had for centuries been based on the ideas of Ptolemy. If the life of Jesus was the most important event in history, as Christians believed, then the earth, where Jesus lived, had to be the center of the universe, as Ptolemy claimed.

To put the sun at the center, as Copernicus did, turned everything upside down and opened the way for all kinds of other questions about Church teachings. As it turned out, Osiander was right. Decades later, other astronomers, notably Giordano Bruno and Galileo Galilei, did suffer at the hands of the Church for speaking out in favor of the Copernican theory. [See the articles on Kepler, Bruno, and Galileo in this book.]

The impact of Copernicus's theory was profound. In less than one hundred years no serious astronomer believed in the Ptolemaic system. Yet predictions of astronomical events based on the new system alone were not much more accurate than those based on the old, because Copernicus still believed that celestial bodies moved in perfectly circular orbits. It was left to Copernicus's follower Kepler to show that planets and all other objects in space follow elliptical orbits, not circular ones. Once this was discovered, predictions based the Copernican theory could be made with great accuracy. This was the best test of its truth.

As time went on Copernicus's simple idea would lead to the questioning of many other old beliefs, not just in astronomy but also in physics, medicine, mathematics, and religion. Today we call this the Copernican Revolution, in honor of the astronomer who first understood our real place in the universe.

Giordano Bruno

Giordano Bruno (BREW-no), birth name Filippo Bruno. Born 1548 in Nola, Campania, Italy. Died February 17, 1600, in Rome.

In the sixteenth century, when the Catholic Church was the most powerful institution in Europe, anyone whose ideas went against its teachings could be tried by the Inquisition, a special court set up by the Church. The Inquisition had convicted many such people over the years, including *heretics* (Christians with unorthodox beliefs), women accused of witchcraft, and Jews. Persons brought before the Inquisition faced the possibility of being tortured to force a confession, or, if they refused to cooperate, of being burned at the stake. Most people quickly confessed to whatever error they were charged with in order to save their lives. One who would not back down before the Inquisition was Giordano Bruno, the first person to be executed for advancing scientific theories in conflict with Church teachings.

Bruno, named Filippo Bruno at birth, was the son of a soldier. He studied literature, logic, and

Giordano Bruno

debating before entering a Dominican convent in the Italian kingdom of Naples to train as a Catholic priest. Early on he began to have trouble with the Church authorities. He read several books forbidden by the Church and, even worse in the view of the Church, he discussed them with others. He was seen studying controversial subjects, like astronomy and astrology. A charge of heresy was brought against him in 1576 and he had to leave Naples, which was controlled at that time by Spain, for the relative safety of Rome. (The Spanish Inquisition was the most severe and the most likely to lead to death for the accused; the Inquisition in Rome was considered more lenient.) But he got in trouble for speaking his mind there as well, so he fled to northern Italy, then to Switzerland, and in 1781 to Paris, France. Along the way Bruno briefly joined the Protestant Reformed Church, but the Protestants also decided that he was a heretic. By the time he reached Paris, Bruno had been excommunicated (exiled from the congregation) by both the Catholic and Protestant churches. He now settled into the life of a wandering scholar, earning his living by teaching his skills and his ideas to whoever would listen.

Bruno found safety for a while in Paris under the tolerant rule of King Henry III. In 1583 he moved to England, where he was befriended by the French ambassador to England, Michel de Castelnau. During his time in England, Bruno mixed with the highest levels of English society and wrote some of his best-known books. (Some historians think that he may have spied on Castelnau and passed French secrets to the English statesman and spymaster Sir Francis Walsingham. But the evidence for this is not conclusive.)

About this time, Bruno began to teach Copernicus's sun-centered theory of the universe at Oxford University. [See the article on Copernicus in this book.] Bruno's own astronomical ideas were quite modern, more modern than those of Copernicus. He thought that the universe was endless, that it might be filled with solar systems and worlds like our own, that the form and matter of the universe were one and the same, and that the universe was made up of atoms. Bruno also questioned the Bible's scientific accuracy.

Upon returning to Paris, Bruno made the mistake of writing four short books that made fun of a prominent politician whose philosophical ideas he disliked. For this and other critical writings he was forced to leave Paris in 1586. He wandered for several years in Germany, writing and lecturing on his philosophy and on the need for all religions to live together in peace. He could stay nowhere for long, because once it was known who he was, the local clergy would try to make him leave.

A diagram from Bruno's book, On the Composition of Images, Signs, and Ideas, *in which he sought to unify Christian, classical, and occult lore.*

Bruno made a special study of the arts of memory. In the sixteenth century, when printed books were not yet common, most people had to memorize everything they might need to know. The Dominican friars were famous for having created a "science" of improving and expanding memory. This "science" was really no more than a few simple mental tricks and games, but since the Dominicans kept it a secret, most people thought it was a great mystery. Bruno wrote that he had developed this science of memory to the point where it helped "not only the memory but also all the powers of the soul in a wonderful manner." A Venetian nobleman, Giovanni Mocenigo, wanted to learn Bruno's methods and invited him to come to Venice in 1591. Bruno judged that enough time had passed that it was now safe for him to return to Italy. He also hoped to get a post teaching mathematics at the University of Padua. [The post instead went to Galileo Galilei; see the article on him in this book.]

But Mocenigo got little benefit from Bruno's teachings. He felt that Bruno had tricked him, and he knew how to take his revenge. Mocenigo denounced Bruno to the Church authorities as a heretic. Bruno was arrested and put on trial in Venice by the Inquisition. In 1593 he was sent to Rome, where he spent seven years in prison while his case was debated. Bruno's accusers wanted

him to make a full confession of error and deny his ideas, but he would not. He claimed that his ideas were philosophic, not religious, and thus no threat to the Church.

In the end, Bruno's stubbornness cost him his life. The Church did not accept his defense, and in February of 1600 he was sentenced to death. "Perhaps your fear in passing judgment on me is greater than mine in receiving it," he told his judges. A week later he was taken from his cell, bound, gagged, tied to a stake, and burned alive.

Bruno's fate shocked many people. More than thirty years later, the Church tried Galileo for a similar crime, and Galileo, thinking of what had happened to Bruno, quickly confessed. After that, Bruno's role as an early champion of scientific ideas was gradually forgotten. One eighteenth-century historian even questioned whether he had been burned at all. But in the nineteenth century, the revolutionaries and statesmen who united the small states of Italy into one nation took Bruno as one of their heroes because of his courage and his dedication to free thought. Streets and plazas were named after him, and a statue of him was raised at the place where he was burned. Bruno himself, however, remains an elusive figure. We still know little of the details of his life, or of why he chose to make the ultimate sacrifice for his ideas.

Tycho Brahe

Tycho Brahe (BRA-heh), known as Tycho (TEE-ko). Born December 14, 1546, in Knudstrup, Skåne, Denmark. Died October 24, 1601, in Prague, Holy Roman Empire (in present-day Czechoslovakia).

The most important center for astronomical research in the sixteenth century was not to be found at a great university, or at the court of a mighty emperor, but on a small island in the sound between Sweden and Denmark. Here

Tycho Brahe, astronomer to King Frederick II of Denmark, built an observatory that was the envy of scientists everywhere. Tycho, who had a taste for grand ideas and projects and always thought of grand names for them, called his observatory Uraniborg, which means "Castle of the Heavens."

Uraniborg was more like a palace of science than a laboratory as we think of one today. There were large libraries and studies; elegant rooms to house visiting astronomers and their assistants; well-tended fish ponds, gardens, and forests; and busy workshops to make everything from paper to printed books. The furnishings at Uraniborg were the most beautiful and finely crafted of their kind. Tycho even invented new kinds of plumbing and installed running water and toilets for his heavenly castle, rare things indeed in the sixteenth century. And of course there were the best astronomical instruments of the time: crystal globes with the celestial bodies marked on them, and giant rulers and circles to measure the angles between the planets and stars. All Tycho's observations were made with the naked eye, for no one had thought of using lenses to study the heavens. [See the article on Galileo in this book for the story of his discoveries with the telescope.] But Tycho and his followers did achieve their goal: the most accurate measurements of the stars and planets that had yet been made.

Tycho (who is almost always referred to by his first name) is one of the most colorful figures in the history of science. Born to a noble family, he was stolen by a rich, childless uncle when very young and raised in the uncle's castle. Entering the University of Copenhagen in 1559, Tycho began to study law at his uncle's request. However, when he observed the solar eclipse of August 21, 1560, his life was set on a course that led far away from laws and courts. Tycho thought it was miraculous that astronomers could predict an event in the heavens and decided on that day to become an astronomer himself. He studied law during the day as his uncle wished, but at night he secretly pursued his passion for the stars, working with a simple draftsman's compass, a small star globe, and a measuring cross-staff. Tycho found to his surprise that the best astronomical tables he could obtain were days and even months off in their predictions of where celestial bodies would be in the sky on any particular night. So he set himself the huge task of redoing all those calculations to make them as correct as he could. Ingenious as well as curious, Tycho designed and made his own instruments, and he invented many other things as well. When he had part of his nose cut off in a duel with another student over who was the better mathematician, he made a new nose for himself out of silver and gold.

Returning from years of schooling and travel, Tycho inherited the estates of his father and uncle and built a small observatory. There he made his single most important observation. On

Tycho Brahe

Tycho Brahe, sitting at his desk, imagines himself directing astronomical research in the observatory of his palace at Uraniborg.

November 11, 1572, he saw a bright new star in the constellation of Cassiopeia, where no star like it had ever been seen before. The publication of his discovery, in his 1573 book *De nova stella* ("The New Star"), shook the world of science. (We call bright exploding stars "novas" today because of Tycho's book.) Astronomers had always assumed that the stars were fixed and unchanging, but Tycho's discovery proved this idea was wrong.

Tycho was now considered one of the best astronomers in Europe, and he used his fame to convince King Frederick II in 1576 to give him the island of Ven, where he built Uraniborg. Among the discoveries made at Uraniborg was proof that a comet seen in 1577 was farther away than the moon. He also made a catalogue of the exact posi-

tions of 777 stars, and later added 223 more. His catalogue of celestial bodies became the standard work of astronomy, replacing that of Ptolemy.

One reason that Tycho's observations were so accurate was that he always tried to make allowances for the defects of his instruments. He even drew up tables of errors for each instrument, so observations could be adjusted for the greatest accuracy. Tycho also kept careful records, and repeated his observations many times to check his results. All these things are now considered part of the standard method of scientific research. Tycho was an observer rather than a maker of theories, but he did put forth his own version of the sun-centered universe pictured by Copernicus. [See the article on Copernicus.] In

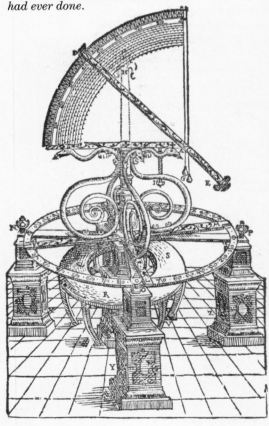

The giant quadrant at Uraniborg allowed Tycho to measure the altitudes of celestial bodies more accurately than anyone else had ever done.

The library of Tycho's observatory was equipped with a five-foot celestial globe that showed the location of the stars and planets.

Tycho's view, the earth was still at the center of the universe, with the sun orbiting the earth, but the planets and stars orbited around the sun.

When King Frederick died, his son Christian IV decided that Uraniborg was too expensive to maintain and stopped sending Tycho money. Tycho would accept nothing less than what he had received from King Frederick, so in disgust he left Denmark in 1597 and settled in Prague. Under the patronage of Emperor Rudolph II, he continued his work, using instruments he brought with him from Uraniborg, but made no more important discoveries before his death in 1601. It was left to his brilliant pupil Johannes Kepler to carry on and expand his work. [See the article on Kepler that follows.]

Johannes Kepler

Johannes Kepler. Born December 27, 1571, in Weir der Stadt, Württemberg, Germany. Died November 15, 1630, in Regensburg, Germany.

In the sixteenth and seventeenth centuries there was no clear distinction between astronomy, the study of the universe according to the principles of science, and theology, the study of the ways of God. The German astronomer Johannes Kepler was both a religious mystic and a brilliant scientist, and the two parts of him worked together. His mystical belief that the perfection of God could be seen in the geometry of the stars and planets led him to discover the astronomical laws of celestial motion that have made him famous.

Born in 1571, Kepler was the son of a roving soldier and an innkeeper's daughter. Recognizing Kepler's talent at an early age, the dukes of his region gave him a scholarship to attend the University of Tübingen, where he decided to study for the Lutheran ministry. At Tübingen he also studied mathematics and learned of the new Copernican picture of the universe, which he intuitively felt was the truth. [See the article about Copernicus in this book.] Kepler never became a minister, which he sometimes regretted. Instead, in 1594, he took a job as a mathematics teacher in Graz, Austria. He earned extra money by selling astrological calendars that predicted the weather, the course of wars, and other future events.

Johannes Kepler

One day, while drawing shapes to teach his students about the orbits of the planets, Kepler had a flash of inspiration. He knew of five planets (not including the earth, which was not considered a planet at that time), and also of five Platonic solids, solid objects made of sides that are all the same shape. (A cube is a good example of a Platonic solid—all the sides of a cube are identical squares.) The Platonic solids were thought to be the most harmonious and beautiful of all forms. Kepler made a sudden connection between the perfection of the Platonic solids and the imagined perfection of the orbits of the planets. He reasoned that perhaps it was no coincidence that there were the same number of planets and perfect solids. Perhaps the invisible spheres that define the orbits of the five planets each fit on the outside of a Platonic solid.

The idea fired his imagination. "Day and night I was consumed by the computing," he wrote, "to see if this idea would agree with the Copernican orbits, or if my joy would be carried away by the wind." Much to his satisfaction, Kepler was able to make this scheme work, with only a small margin of error. Today we know that there is no real connection between the orbits of the planets and the Platonic solids, but it was all very convincing to Kepler, and drove him on to make more investigations into planetary orbits. He published his findings as a book, the *Mysterium cosmographicum* ("Cosmographic Mysteries"), in 1596, when he was only twenty-five years old. To his old teacher at the University of Tübingen he wrote: "Behold how through my effort God is being celebrated in astronomy."

Tycho Brahe, the greatest observational astronomer of the day, admired Kepler's book and invited him to join the staff of Tycho's new observatory outside the city of Prague in Bohemia, which was then part of the Holy Roman Empire (it is now in Czechoslovakia). When Tycho died in 1601, Kepler was appointed imperial mathematician to the Holy Roman Empire by Emperor Rudolf II. Kepler's main job was to carry on Tycho's work in astronomy. [See the article about Tycho in this book.]

Tycho had set Kepler the task of making a new survey of the planet Mars. Kepler began at the very beginning. He felt he had to understand how light moved through the atmosphere before he could understand how to look at Mars. Other thinkers about vision had believed that the eye itself somehow creates the images of the things we see. But Kepler was the first to understand that light rays come from objects in the world and are focused by a lens within the eye, just as the lenses of eyeglasses and telescopes focus light. He also gave a description of how the lenses in eyeglasses change the focal point of the rays to focus the image more clearly on the retina, the part of the eye that senses light. And he realized that the earth's air bends light from the stars as a glass

lens does, which is why stars and planets seem to twinkle. This was an important advance in *optics*, the science of light and lenses. When telescopes came into general use a few years later, Kepler had the best explanation of how they worked.

He also tried to explain what they showed. Astronomers had long believed that the planets and even the stars moved in perfect circles around the earth, which was at the center of the universe. Since the heavens were close to God, the orbits of the celestial bodies would naturally take the most perfect possible shape—the circle. However, this beautiful and harmonious picture of the universe did not agree very well with the way planets were seen to move in reality. They slowed down, speeded up, and sometimes even appeared to move backwards. To account for these odd motions, the astronomers figured that the orbits of the planets must consist of circles upon circles. After a while, this system, called the Ptolemaic system after the second-century astronomer Ptolemy, became so complicated that it lost much of its simple beauty. It was challenged by the Copernican system, which put the sun at the center with the planets traveling around it, in perfect circles. Even Copernicus was not willing to consider that orbits might take some other shape, for if the celestial bodies did not move in perfect circles, then perhaps the heavens themselves were not perfect—and that was too disturbing a thought to contemplate.

Kepler's mind was not closed to other possibilities, however, and he sought for a new explanation that might be even more beautiful. After trying and failing to make Tycho's observations of Mars fit a circular orbit, Kepler searched for a shape that would fit the facts. He discovered that Mars, and all the other planets, orbit the sun not in a circle but in an ellipse (an oval), with the sun toward one end of the ellipse. This is known as Kepler's first law of planetary motion. At the same time he saw that the planets, as they move, must speed up as they come near the sun and slow down as they swing around the far end of their orbit. The change in speed was not random, Kepler found, but beautifully exact. Kepler worked out his ideas for all the known planets, but we will take Mars as an example. He imagined the elliptical orbit of Mars as a flat, oval-shaped plane, with the planet traveling around the oval's edge. He

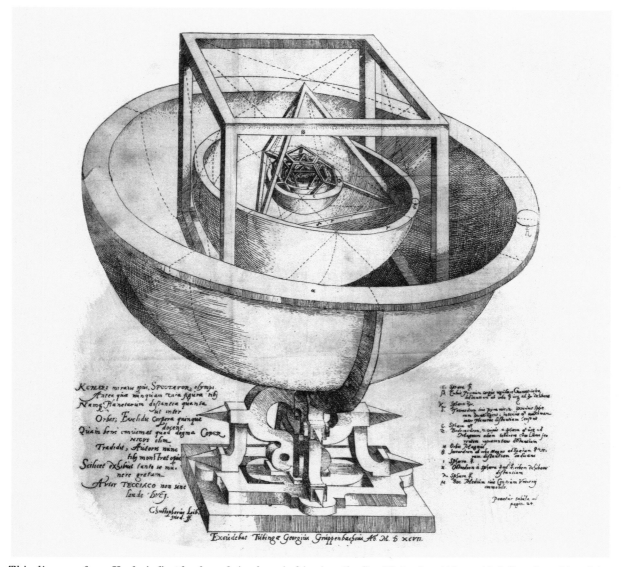

This diagram from Kepler's first book explains how, in his view, the five Platonic solids could define the orbits of the five known planets.

then divided the amount of time Mars took to orbit the sun—the Martian year—into equal parts. He then measured and marked the distance Mars traveled along the edge of the oval during a part of the Martian year when it was near the sun, and the distance Mars traveled during a part of the year when it was far from the sun. Then he drew lines from the starting and ending points of each marked section of the oval to the center of the sun. These made two-pie shaped wedges: the one near the sun was wide and short, and the one far from

the sun was narrow and long. But each wedge was the same area in square units. In other words, each planet sweeps out an equal area of its orbital plane in equal lengths of time. This law, called Kepler's second law, accounts for the observation that planets speed up and slow down when they are in different parts of the sky. These two discoveries were made public in his book *Astronomia nova* ("New Astronomy") in 1609.

Another problem Kepler tried to understand is why Mars takes longer to orbit the sun than

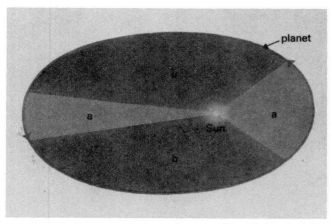

A planet sweeps out equal areas of its elliptical orbit in equal periods of time, as described by Kepler's second law of planetary motion.

does the earth. The farther planets, Jupiter and Saturn, move more slowly still; Mercury and Venus, the planets closer to the sun than Earth, move fastest. Perhaps, Kepler thought, there was some invisible force coming from the sun that makes the planets move in their orbits at a speed in proportion to their distance from the sun. Kepler guessed that this force might be magnetism, which had just been discovered. (It was Isaac Newton who realized that a different force was involved—the force of gravity. See the article on Newton in this book.) Kepler was able to show mathematically that a planet's distance

from the sun is directly related to the time that planet takes to orbit the sun—his third law of planetary motion, which he published in 1619 in a book called *Harmonices mundi* ("Harmonies of the World").

When Emperor Rudolf II was forced out of power in 1608, Kepler thought it best to leave Prague. He spent several years in Linz, Austria, still holding the job of imperial mathematician. During this time his mother was accused of being a witch. She would have been tortured and burned at the stake, like many other unfortunate women in those years, if Kepler had not managed to convince her accusers that she was innocent. Kepler himself left Linz when he was unable to publish his final work, a book of tables of celestial objects, because of a peasant revolt there; the book was later published in Germany. In 1630, traveling through Germany to collect some money in Austria, he fell ill suddenly and died.

Kepler's laws of planetary motion made sense of the solar system that Copernicus had described. They also suggested the existence of the force that Isaac Newton later called gravity, and enabled astronomers to predict the positions of the planets with great accuracy, which had been hard to do before. In fact, Kepler's ideas mark the beginning of modern ways of thinking not only about astronomy, but about physics as well. To Kepler himself, however, his work was most importantly an insight into God's creation.

Galileo Galilei

Galileo Galilei (gah-lee-LEH-ee), known as Galileo (gah-lee-LAY-oh). Born February 15, 1564, in Pisa, Italy. Died January 8, 1642, in Arcetri, Italy.

The old, ill man was on trial for a crime no one had ever been accused of before—showing proof that the earth revolved around the sun. It was the year 1633; he was in the Vatican in Rome.

Around him was a solemn assembly of priests, and before him was the pope, Urban VIII. The old man kneeled and confessed his crime. "I have been judged to be vehemently suspected of heresy, that is, of having held and believed that the sun is the center of the world and immobile and that the earth is not the center and moves. With sincere heart and unpretended faith I abjure, curse, and detest the aforesaid errors and heresies." Pope Urban then pronounced the sentence: life imprisonment and the banning of the prisoner's most important book. The old man was led away, to spend the rest of his life in a small house, cut off from the rest of the world.

The man was Galileo Galilei, the great Italian astronomer, the first person to turn a telescope toward the sky. Why was he on trial for a belief that had been held by many astronomers for close to a century, without challenge from the Church? The Church had been able to ignore the idea of a sun-centered universe as described by Copernicus and Kepler because their arguments were based on mathematics, and few people could understand them. Even Giordano Bruno, who had been burned at the stake years earlier for teaching Copernicus's views, had been condemned mainly for his religious heresies. But Galileo's astronomical discoveries were such a hard blow against the old view of an unchanging universe under God that the Church could not ignore them. Anyone with a telescope could see what Galileo had seen. [See the articles on Copernicus, Bruno, and Kepler in this book.] The pope feared that the scientific truth would shake people's faith and weaken the great power of the Church.

As a young man, Galileo, the son of a musician, had studied religion and medicine but showed no early interest in mathematics. One day he saw a lamp swinging on a chain in the cathedral of Pisa and realized that all the swings took the same length of time, even though the distance of each swing grew shorter as the lamp slowed to a stop. (Later he suggested that a swinging weight, called a pendulum, might be used in clock mechanisms.) This was the first time Galileo understood that common events in the world can be described with mathematical ideas. At the University of Pisa he turned to the study of mathematics but had to leave before he graduated because he had no money. For a while he made his living as a lecturer, instrument-maker, and lens-grinder.

In 1592 Galileo became a professor of mathematics at the University of Padua. There he studied the nature of motion and gravity. He showed that objects of different weights fall at the same speed; that rising and falling objects slow down and speed up smoothly; and that objects thrown into the air will always fall back to earth along a certain curve called a *parabola*. (The story that Galileo dropped two weights from the Leaning Tower of Pisa is probably not true, but he must

have performed experiments like that.) Galileo followed a very modern way of doing science: he did many experiments and then found a mathematical way to describe his results. It was his belief that "the Book of Nature is written in mathematical characters."

The telescope was not invented by Galileo, as has sometimes been claimed, but by an unknown lens-grinder sometime in the sixteenth century. A Dutch eyeglass maker, Hans Lippershey, tried to sell a telescope to his government around 1600. Soon many people were making them throughout Europe. Galileo heard of the telescope in 1609, and within a month had built a better one himself. He gave it to the Venetian senate and was promised a generous reward.

Most people of the time saw the telescope as a tool of war, to help aim cannons better and to see ships far off at sea. Galileo had the novel idea of using a telescope to look at the heavens. Late in 1609 he looked at the moon with his telescope, and was astonished to find that it was not smooth but had sharp mountains and pitted craters. He also saw, as he wrote, "stars in myriads which have

Galileo Galilei

never been seen before," as well as the rings of Saturn and four moons orbiting Jupiter. (These four large moons we now call the "Galilean satellites" in his honor.) This last discovery gave new weight to Copernicus's idea of a sun-centered universe. It seemed much more likely that the sun could have planets orbiting around it if the planets themselves had smaller bodies orbiting around them. When Galileo published his findings, his book, *Siderius nuncius* ("The Starry Messenger"), caused a sensation and made him famous. In other writings Galileo strongly defended the theory of Copernicus.

Galileo soon discovered that he had made many enemies. Other professors were jealous of his fame, and some in the Church were preaching that his work went against the teachings of the Bible. He defended himself to Church leaders, writing that it would be "a terrible harm for the souls if people found themselves convinced by proof of something that it was made a sin for them to believe." At first Galileo had the support of the Vatican, but when he began to insist that scripture had to be revised to conform to Copernican ideas, many felt he had gone too far. Stubbornly, he even made a trip to Rome in 1616 to argue his case. Cardinal Bellarmine in Rome, though sympathetic, did not agree with Galileo. The cardinal decreed that the theory of Copernicus had not yet

been proved—which, at the time, was so—and that Galileo should not write about it except as one among several intellectual notions.

For several years, Galileo lived in a small house near Florence, writing little and staying out of the public eye. However, he did not change his mind about the meaning of his discoveries. He even grew vain about his accomplishments, claiming once that he was the only man to discover anything new in the skies. In 1624 he made another trip to Rome and received permission to write a book simply explaining the two main ideas about the universe—Ptolemaic (earth-centered) and Copernican (sun-centered)—so long as he did not claim that either one them was the truth. When the book, titled "Dialogue Concerning the Two Chief World Systems," was published in 1632, it was hailed as a masterpiece. Though the Church censors had approved the book, careful readers could tell that Galileo favored the Copernican theory. His arguments were so persuasive that the "Dialogue," more than any other work, convinced open-minded people that Copernicus must have been right. Soon Galileo's enemies began to argue that he had tried to fool the censors, that he really was claiming that the Copernican ideas were the truth after all.

The pope, Urban VIII, was an old friend of Galileo's, and had once called him a "great man,

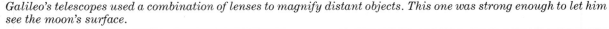

Galileo's telescopes used a combination of lenses to magnify distant objects. This one was strong enough to let him see the moon's surface.

On the title page of Galileo's Dialogue, *Galileo converses with Ptolemy (wearing a turban) and Copernicus (wearing a three-cornered fur hat).*

whose fame shines in the heavens." But Urban felt that Galileo's persistence was a threat to the Catholic Church and its traditional Christian ideas. He summoned Galileo to Rome in 1633 to stand trial for breaking his agreement with Cardinal Bellarmine. Galileo, who was too ill to walk or ride, was carried all the way to Rome in the dead of winter.

Galileo's accusers claimed that he had been ordered by Cardinal Bellarmine never to defend the theory of Copernicus in speech or writing, and they produced papers to prove it. Historians now believe these papers were forged. But the pope was convinced, and Galileo knew that he had to admit to the crime or face torture. At his age and with his bad health, that would mean death. He may also have had in mind the fate of Giordano Bruno. So Galileo confessed. Legend has it that he murmured, "The earth moves, just the same," as he was led away. Galileo was ordered to spend the rest of his life under house arrest at his small house in Arcetri, near Florence. The death of his beloved daughter a short time later seemed to complete his misery.

But he could not stay idle for long. He resumed his work, though it was not published in Italy, and used his telescopes to make more discoveries, including the monthly wobble of the moon. He went blind in 1638 but dictated his ideas to his helpers until he died of a fever four years later.

Galileo's discoveries with the telescope are what we most often remember him for today. But he was also the person who first understood that events in the world can be described by mathematics, which is one of the basic principles of modern physics.

Isaac Newton

Isaac Newton. Born January 4, 1643, in Woolsthorpe, Lincolnshire, England. Died March 31, 1727, in London.

What makes things fall? How do objects move? Where do colors come from? One great figure of science was able to provide answers to these basic questions about our world. He was the English physicist and mathematician Isaac Newton, who did more to widen our understanding of the universe than anyone before or since.

Newton was a sickly baby and a frail child. His

Isaac Newton

father, a village landowner, died before Isaac was born. When his mother remarried, she went to live with her new husband in another village, leaving young Newton in the care of his grandmother. He hated his stepfather and never forgave his mother for abandoning him, even after she returned when he was about twelve years old. Newton's mother wanted him to run the farm, but he would go off to read and think instead of minding the cows, so she sent him to school instead.

In 1661, Newton entered Cambridge University. After less than two years of study, he had mastered the math and physics of the day and begun to work on his own. His most important achievement in these early years was his invention of differential calculus, a new kind of math for analyzing curved shapes. This was quite an achievement for a college undergraduate. When the plague struck Cambridge in 1665, Newton moved back home to his farm in Woolsthorpe. There he continued his work in mathematics and embarked on new lines of thought about light and the movement of celestial bodies.

In 1669, Newton was elected professor of mathematics at Cambridge. His first lectures were on the nature of light and color. Earlier scientists, beginning with the Greek philosopher Aristotle, had thought that white light somehow changed to make colors. Newton did a series of experiments in 1665 and 1666 that corrected this notion. His equipment was simple: a darkened room, a set of glass prisms, and some paper pierced with slits and holes. A sunbeam entering the room through a small hole in the window hit the prism and cast a rainbow—or *spectrum*, as scientists call it—on the opposite wall. Newton found that individual colors of the spectrum could not be changed back to white light, or divided into yet other colors, but that all the colors together could be combined by another prism to make white light again. So white light was not one thing, as the earlier scientists had thought, but a combination of many colors of light. An account of this work was published in 1704—nearly forty years later—as part of his major book on light, *Opticks*.

Newton made another important discovery in optics: he invented a new kind of telescope that used a curved mirror to gather light and enlarge the image. This design works so much better than the type of telescope used by Galileo, which has a large lens in front to gather light, that today nearly all astronomical telescopes use mirrors. [See the article on Galileo in this book.] The Royal Society of London, the top scientific body in England, asked to see Newton's invention in 1671 and elected him a member of the Society a short time later.

During the years 1679 to 1685, Newton worked on what would be his most important contributions to science. These were his three laws of motion and his theory of universal gravitation. The laws of motion came to him as he puzzled over the motions of the planets. Why did they move in ellipses around the sun? Why did they keep moving? It came to him that all objects must have inertia, that is, they stay at rest until a force is applied to move them, and then they stay in motion until another force is applied to stop them (his first law). He also found that when a force is applied to an object, the change in motion of the object is proportional to the amount of force and the mass of the object (the second law). Finally, he could see that on earth every action has an equal and opposite reaction, which must be true in the rest of the universe as well (the third law). Newton stated his laws in mathematical terms, so anyone could experiment with different objects and forces and see whether the laws held true.

The experience of weight and gravity is so common that everyone takes it for granted. It was a great leap of imagination when Newton realized that gravity is a force that belongs to every object, not just the earth, and that gravity can act over great distances. The sun must attract the planets just as the earth attracts an apple falling from a tree. (The story that Newton came to his theory of gravity by watching the fall of an apple is probably true; he mentions the apple in his writings. It did not hit him on the head, as is sometimes pictured, but fell outside the window of his mother's farmhouse.) Moreover, he proved mathematically that this force decreases by the square of the distance between objects. It was Newton who first applied the word "gravity" (from the Latin *gravitas*, meaning weight or heaviness) to this universal phenomenon.

Beginning in 1686, Newton published his findings on motion and gravity in what many people consider the single greatest book of science ever written, the *Philosophiae naturalis principia mathematica* ("Mathematical Principles of Natural Philosophy"), usually called the *Principia mathematica*. Newton himself was rather indifferent about publishing the work; it was produced

The title page of Newton's book Principia Mathematica. *In those days, all scientific books published in Europe were written in Latin.*

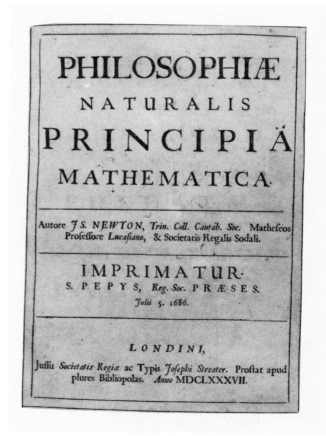

at the expense of his friend, the astronomer Edmund Halley, who was the first to see its genius. In this book Newton tied together the different observations made by the natural scientists who lived before him and created a single, unifying explanation for these events using simple mathematical statements. On its publication Newton was hailed as the chief scientist of England, and younger scientists began to gather around him. Within a generation all the important scientific positions in England were held by his followers.

Now famous, Newton found that he enjoyed the city life in London, so he sought a position that would allow him to live there. In 1696 he left Cambridge to become master of the Royal Mint, a job he took seriously. Not only did he oversee the minting of a new set of coins, but he also made it his business to hunt down and punish counterfeiters. With strict justice and little mercy, he sent many to the gallows.

Newton was not an easy person to get along with. He was very careful to protect his rights and could not stand any criticism. The scientist

Newton's reflecting telecope used a concave mirror to gather light. All earlier designs, including Galileo's, used a lens for this purpose.

Robert Hooke had claimed that Newton stole from him some of the ideas in the *Principia*. Instead of giving Hooke credit for important early thinking on gravity, Newton in a fury deleted from the *Principia* every reference to Hooke and his work. When Newton was elected president of the Royal Society in 1703, he used his power to help his own followers and to bully any scientist who challenged him or displeased him. Any argument might make him boil over with anger that could last for years. A few times he gave way to fits of rage that seemed close to madness. Other times he would retreat into himself and refuse to see or write to anyone. He took no interest in the usual pleasures of life—he never married and had a family, or listened to music, or even seemed to enjoy his food—and was rarely heard to laugh. The twentieth-century English writer Aldous Huxley said of him, "As a man, he was a failure; as a monster, he was superb."

Newton's most famous scientific battle was with the German mathematician and philosopher Baron Gottfried Wilhelm von Leibniz over who first invented calculus. Newton had thought of calculus years before Leibniz did, but Leibniz came to an understanding of it on his own, without seeing Newton's work, and then published his results twenty years before Newton finally published his own version. The argument between the two reached such a pitch that it became the talk of London. But Newton was in a better position than Leibniz to win the battle. A committee of the Royal Society was formed to settle once and for all the question of who was first, and the committee chose Newton. Much later, it came out that Newton had written the committee's report himself! Leibniz had the last laugh, however, for it is his methods of calculus that are used today, not Newton's.

Newton did little new scientific work in his later years, except to bring out new editions of his books. He died at the age of eighty-four. People were already calling him the greatest scientist of all time. For his part, Newton was proud of his own discoveries, but he also knew that there was much more to find. "I do not know what I may appear to the world," he wrote, "but to myself I seem to have been only like a boy playing on the seashore . . . whilst the great ocean of truth lay all undiscovered before me."

William, Caroline, and John Herschel

Frederick William Herschel (HER-shel), birth name Friedrich Wilhelm Herschel. Born November 15, 1738, in Hanover, Germany. Died August 25, 1822, in Slough, Buckinghamshire, England.

Caroline Lucretia Herschel. Born March 16, 1750 in Hanover, Germany. Died January 9, 1848, in Hanover.

John Frederick William Herschel. Born March 7, 1792, in Slough, Buckingham-shire, England. Died May 11, 1871, in Collingwood, Kent, England.

One day in August 1789, King George III of England brought his friend the Archbishop of Canterbury out to the countryside to see a new marvel. Rising up before them was a construction like nothing they had ever seen before. To the archbishop, it looked like a combination of cannon, house, and sailing ship. No, explained the king, it was the largest telescope in the world. Suspended from a confusion of scaffolding and spars, pulleys and ropes, was the telescope itself, a mighty tube forty feet long and as beautifully fashioned as a musical instrument. Its dark wood was polished and its brass fittings gleamed. Within was a huge mirror to catch the light from distant suns and reflect it into a tiny eyepiece that could be used only by climbing to a platform many feet above the ground. "Come, my lord archbishop," said the king, "I will show you the way to heaven."

The maker of this grand instrument for seeing the cosmos was a man named Frederick William Herschel, the most famous telescope-maker and astronomer of his time. William, his younger sister Caroline, and his son John extended human vision beyond our solar system and the stars of our galaxy to reveal the vast sea of galaxies that fills the universe.

William Herschel was born Friedrich Wilhelm Herschel in Hanover, a city in what is now northwest Germany. He inherited his love of music and of the stars from his father, an army musician who often took William out to look at the night sky. As a young man, William played the oboe and violin in his father's band, which was attached to the Hanoverian Guards. He fled Europe during the Seven Years' War (1756–1763) and came to England, which was then ruled by King George II, a member of the Hanoverian royal family. William was a skillful musician and teacher and was soon able to make a comfortable living for himself as organist of the chapel in the resort city of Bath. His sister Caroline joined him in 1772, hoping to find work as a singer.

This comfortable life did not satisfy William. Music did not keep him busy enough, and he knew he did not have the genius of a Handel or a Mozart. Instead, after reading several books on

William Herschel

astronomy, he developed a passion for stargazing. At first he used a small refracting telescope (the type that collects light through a lens in the front of a long tube), but he was unhappy with the poor images it provided. Also, such telescopes needed very long tubes to focus properly, making them awkward to handle. Then he tried a reflecting telescope (the type that collects light with a mirror at the back of a tube) and was so pleased with it that he decided to build one for himself. [Isaac Newton was the inventor of the reflecting telescope. For more on telescopes, see the articles on Newton and Galileo in this book.] Through several years of patient effort Herschel taught himself how to grind glass into lenses and cast shining metal into concave mirrors. His telescopes were

William and Caroline Herschel spend one of many long nights surveying the sky through a telescope, looking for unknown objects.

works of art. They were as finely crafted as violins or oboes, and they were also the most powerful optical instruments of their day. The more powerful the telescope, William knew, the farther it could see into space, and the more celestial objects it would uncover.

Together with Caroline, William set out to build a telescope that required a giant mirror three feet wide, bigger than any that had yet been tried. Unable to find a foundry that would handle such a large and exacting job, they set up their own foundry in the basement of their house. The mold for the mirror was made of a great pile of horse dung that William, Caroline, and some helpers had carefully collected and pounded into shape. When the molten metal was poured in, however, the mold cracked, spilling the metal onto the floor of the basement. The floorstones exploded with the heat, sending William and his crew running out to the garden to escape the flying rocks and jetting streams of hot metal.

It is unlikely that there have ever been stargazers more dedicated than the Herschels. Beginning in 1775, William used telescopes of increasing power to make four complete surveys of the night sky. The method he adopted was to "sweep" the sky in a back-and-forth pattern so that no area of the heavens was left unobserved. Each time he came to an interesting object he would pause to note it in his "Book of Sweeps." In this way he came to memorize the entire night sky as it could be seen through his telescopes. He could not have managed this work without the help of Caroline, who had long since given up her dreams of becoming a singer to devote her life to astronomy. She took her own turns at the eyepiece and discovered eight comets. When William was using the telescope, she read aloud from *The Arabian Nights*, *Don Quixote*, and other books to keep him awake while he stared into space, a black velvet hood over his head to block out the light from her lamp. She wrote down his observations in the "sweep books." Their studies went on night after night, summer and winter; every spare moment was devoted to astronomy. They would even steal away during intermission at plays and concerts to grab a few minutes with the telescope. "If it had not been for the intervention of a cloudy or moonlit night," wrote Caroline, "I know not when he or I either would have got any sleep."

Because William and Caroline had better telescopes than anyone else, they saw things that no one else could see. On the night of March 13, 1781, William did something that had not been done since prehistoric times: he discovered a new planet. During one of his sweeps of the heavens, William saw a large green star in the constellation of Gemini. Familiar as he was with every star in Gemini, he knew that this one did not belong there. He thought the mysterious star might be a comet, but within a few months of his announcement other astronomers proved that it was a new planet traveling in an orbit far beyond Saturn.

Before the Herschels, astronomers knew of only five planets beyond the earth: Mercury, Venus, Mars, Jupiter, and Saturn. They did not think that there could be any others. With this discovery, the solar system was suddenly understood to be a much bigger place than anyone had thought—in fact, nearly twice as big.

As the planet's discoverer, William wanted to call it "Georgium Sidus" (George's Star) after King George III, but the name never caught on. Nor did an attempt by French astronomers to name the planet "Herschel," after William himself. Astronomers finally decided to follow the usual practice of giving celestial objects names from Greek and Roman mythology and settled on Uranus, the name of the husband of Gaea (Earth) and the father of the giant Titans.

The discovery of Uranus made William famous. By the end of the year he had been named a Fellow of the Royal Society, the chief scientific organization in England. A few months later he was summoned to display his telescopes to King George, who appointed him to the post of Astronomer Royal. This enabled William to give up his job at the chapel and spend all his time on astronomy. With money given him by the king, he built the great forty-foot telescope that was shown to the archbishop in 1789. It was considered a modern wonder of the world. On the very first night it was used, William found two moons of Saturn no one had seen before. But the big telescope was so clumsy that he did not use it often. He used smaller scopes to do what he now considered his most important work, investigating the strange milk-white patches visible in the night sky.

William believed that these milky patches, which astronomers call *nebulae* (from the Latin

Caroline Herschel at the age of ninety-two

word for cloud), were clusters of stars so far away that even viewed through the best telescopes they looked like clouds. He described these nebulae as "island universes" and claimed that they glowed with "the united luster of millions of stars." Today we know that some of Herschel's nebulae are indeed vast star clusters, and we call them *galaxies*; we still use the word "nebulae" to describe glowing clouds of gas or clusters of stars within our own galaxy, the Milky Way. William was the first to guess at the true nature of galaxies. Realizing that the sun is also part of an "island universe," he tried to discover the size and shape of the "island" by counting the stars in all directions. This did not work, for at that time he had no way of knowing how far away a star really is, but it marked the beginning of that branch of astronomy that deals with the Milky Way galaxy. Not until the twentieth century did astronomers finally discover the its size and shape.

At the age of forty-nine, William married a widow named Mary Pitt. In 1792 they had a son, John Herschel. John attended Cambridge University, where he showed a talent for mathematics and chemistry. When William died in 1822, Caroline and John undertook to complete different parts of William's studies. Caroline returned to Hanover to work on William's catalog of nebulae and star clusters. In 1828, when she was seventy-eight years old, she was awarded a gold medal by the Royal Astronomical Society for her work.

John Herschel

through. The change in a star's position can be seen most clearly in double-star systems, in which one star revolves around a close neighbor. Working from his father's catalog of double stars, John carefully observed the changes in position of the stars in each pair and, using simple geometry, made the most accurate measurements to date of star distances.

In 1833 John undertook another major task, to survey the skies of the southern hemisphere, which his father had never seen. He set up an observatory outside the city of Cape Town in South Africa. Over the course of four years, he cataloged more than 68,000 stars and thousands of nebulae, double stars, and star clusters. When this work was made public after his return, John became nearly as famous as his father. But unlike his father, John had other interests in addition to astronomy. In 1850 he was made master of the mint, a job Isaac Newton had performed a century before. The next year he agreed to do all the planning for the scientific parts of the Great Exhibition of 1851, a nineteenth-century version of the modern World's Fair. This intense effort led to a nervous breakdown and eventually to his death, in 1871, after years of failing health.

Taken together, the work of these three people did more to bring astronomy into the modern age than any effort before or since. No wonder the Herschels have been called "the first family of astronomy."

John set himself the task of finding a way to measure accurately the distance to a star, a problem that had stumped his father. It was already known that some stars appear in slightly different places in the sky when the earth is at the extremes of its orbit around the sun. This is called *stellar parallax*. You can see a similar effect yourself by holding an upright finger in front of your nose and looking at it with each eye in turn. The finger covers a different part of the background, depending on which eye you are looking

Antonie van Leeuwenhoek

Antonie van Leeuwenhoek (LAY-ven-huke). Born October 24, 1632, in Delft, Holland. Died August 26, 1723, in Delft.

While the great astronomers of the seventeenth century were pointing their telescopes to the sky to find new wonders beyond the earth, an ordinary Dutch merchant named Antonie van Leeuwenhoek turned his gaze down to a drop of water and found equally miraculous wonders there. Using a simple microscope, he found living creatures smaller than any that had ever been imagined—and found them everywhere.

As a young man, Leeuwenhoek was apprenticed to a draper (a cloth seller) in Amsterdam. In 1653 he started his own business in his home town of Delft, selling fine silk, linen, ribbons, buttons, and other wares to the well-to-do merchants of the town. The business was a success, and he was able to live comfortably. Eventually he became

Antonie van Leeuwenhoek

head of the Delft city council and chamberlain to the city sheriffs.

Drapers and others who worked with fabric had long used low-power lenses as magnifying glasses to inspect the weave of cloth. Leeuwenhoek learned how to grind his own lenses, and soon lens-grinding became his hobby. Over the years he made more than five hundred lenses; some could magnify objects up to 300 times their real size. His microscopes were the simplest kind possible, with just a single lens held between two brass plates, but they were powerful enough to reveal an unimagined world of invisible life.

Leeuwenhoek had never studied science or mathematics, but he was very curious about the world around him. All kinds of objects passed under his lenses, and his eye was the first to gaze on many things that had been in the world, unseen,

for ages. He soon gained a reputation as an skilled lens-maker and amateur scientist. In 1673 the Dutch doctor Regnier de Graaf sent a letter to the Royal Society of London, then the top scientific body in the world, describing some of Leeuwenhoek's early work. De Graaf asked the Society to encourage Leeuwenhoek and set him new and more difficult problems. Most of what we know of his microscope research comes from the one hundred and ninety letters about his findings that he sent to the Society beginning in 1673. Leeuwenhoek rarely left Delft, but he was able to carry on an entire scientific career mainly by these letters.

In September 1674 he used his lenses to examine a drop of pond water. There he saw to his surprise a host of protozoa, tiny animals that he called "small animalcules." In another drop of water he observed bacteria, the first time anyone had seen them. "I saw very plainly that these were little eels, or worms," he wrote in a letter to the Royal Society, "lying all huddled up together and wriggling . . . and the whole water seemed to be alive with these multifarious animalcules. This was, for me, among all the marvels that I have discovered in nature, the most marvelous of all." Through careful measurements Leeuwenhoek was able to show that a single drop of water could hold millions of these creatures. No one had suspected the existence of such tiny beings. And Leeuwenhoek found them everywhere he looked,

Leeuwenhoek's microscopes were made of two small metal plates enclosing a tiny lens, with an adjustable pin to hold the specimen in place.

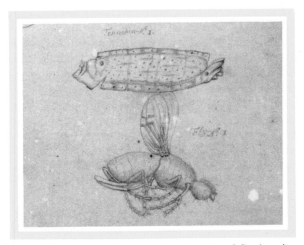

One of Leeuwenhoek's reports to the Royal Society included these detailed drawings of maggots and flies, drawn by a hired artist.

"for these animalcules can be carried by the wind, along with the bits of dust floating in the air."

Leeuwenhoek delighted in finding life everywhere and discovering the hidden ways small creatures led their lives. He looked at fleas, ants, weevils, and other insects, and found that each was "endowed with as great perfection in its kind as any large animal." Before Leeuwenhoek, most people believed that fleas and other "pests" were born out of dust, filth, or mud. He showed that the fleas and other creatures he observed were born from eggs laid by animals of the same kind. This helped to prove the unity of all living things, from the largest creature to the smallest. Leeuwenhoek also looked at the fibers of muscles, at the lens of the eye, and at blood—he was the first person to see red blood cells. He was also the first to see human sperm and realize that they must fertilize the human egg.

Some scientists did not believe him, but Leeuwenhoek always made sure to have witnesses, even if he had to invite people in off the street. He asked these witnesses to observe through his lens and sign a statement about what they had seen. Soon the famous began to hear of his discoveries, and he was visited by Peter the Great, Tsar of Russia, and Queen Anne of England. But what pleased him most was to be elected a fellow of the Royal Society in 1680.

Visitors to the Royal Society of London today can still see some of Leeuwenhoek's microscopes. None of these are strong enough to resolve bacteria, so we know that Leeuwenhoek must have made even more powerful instruments that he kept secret, or perhaps he discovered ways of lighting his specimens that brought out more detail. In fact, Leeuwenhoek always claimed that he had more powerful tools that he could not show to visitors. He felt that if all his secrets were known, no one would think that his discoveries were so miraculous after all.

Gerardus Mercator

Gerardus Mercator (mer-KAYT-er), birth name Gerhard Kremer. Born March 5, 1512, in Rupelmonde, Flanders (now Belgium). Died December 2, 1594, in Duisburg, Kleve (in present-day Germany).

The great voyages of discovery of the sixteenth and seventeenth centuries all depended on mapmakers for their success. If you were a ship's captain, having a good map made reaching your goal easier; having a bad map meant going astray and maybe perishing on the wide seas. Of the many sixteenth-century mapmakers, the greatest was Gerardus Mercator, who invented a new way to map the world that is still used more than any other, to this day.

Mercator was born into a poor family that had moved to Flanders (now Belgium) from Germany. He was a good scholar and was able to attend the best schools. He studied humanities, religion, and philosophy at the University of Louvain, and on his own became an expert calligrapher, engraver, surveyor, and instrument-maker. Then, around 1533, he turned to the study of mathematics, geography, and astronomy. Along the way he became fascinated by maps, and decided that making maps would be his life work.

With his two partners, the mathematician Gemma Frisius and the master engraver Gaspar a Myrica, Mercator began work on a series of globes and maps that soon made him famous. He produced a globe of the earth in 1536 and a celestial globe in 1537. That same year he also made his first map (a small map of the Holy Land), and the next year, a map of the world shaped something like two rounded hearts set back to back. This map was the first to name both North and South America. Mercator's precise map of Flanders, for which he did all the surveying and engraving himself, won him a commission from Holy Roman Emperor Charles V to make a much bigger world globe.

The year 1544 was nearly Mercator's last. The regent of Flanders ordered the execution of all heretics, people whose ideas contradicted the teachings of the Catholic Church. Mercator was arrested along with more than forty other citizens of Louvain who were suspected of being Protestants. Most of the prisoners were killed—some burned at the stake, others beheaded or

Gerardus Mercator

buried alive—but Mercator was saved by the intervention of his parish priest and officials at the University of Louvain. He was released from prison after a few months and allowed to continue his work. A few years later he moved to a safer home in Duisburg, in the duchy of Kleve (now

Mercator's world map of 1538 was projected on double heart shapes. He did not develop his revolutionary "Mercator projection" until 1569.

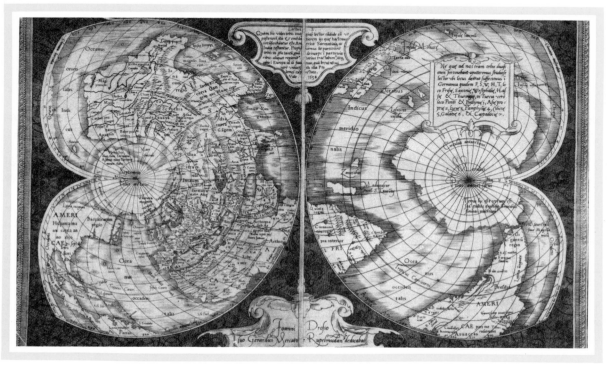

part of Germany). The Duke of Kleve hired him as court cosmographer (someone who maps the earth and heavens) in 1564. Mercator set up his own mapmaking workshop and engraving studio, and here he did his most important work.

Mercator made maps that were clear in design and a pleasure to use. One of his trademarks was his beautifully formed italic lettering, which was soon copied by other mapmakers. But what set Mercator's maps apart from most others of the time was their accuracy. Many mapmakers added their own imaginary details to the known outlines of the lands they drew; Mercator did not. He traveled often to see new charts, talk to explorers, and get the latest geographic information. His passion for accuracy lead him to develop his most important innovation, the Mercator projection.

The most accurate way to map the earth is make an image of it on a globe, since the earth is itself a globe. If you take this spherical map and put it on a piece of flat paper, you get a distorted image, since the flat plane of the paper is very different from the globe's curved surface. Earlier mapmakers often ignored this distortion, which made for wrong, useless maps.

Mercator went at this problem in a new and practical way. He wanted to make a map in which the lines of longitude (the vertical lines on a map) and latitude (the horizontal lines on a map) were always at right angles to each other. The lines of latitude and longitude are imaginary lines of measurement that allow navigators to plot their positions on the earth's surface, and they are easier to use when they are arranged in a neat grid. But there is no neat grid on a globe, because the lines of longitude come together at the poles. Mercator saw that if he stretched out the surface of the globe into a rectangle and made the longitude lines parallel, he would have to adjust the scale of his drawing as well. There would be more area to fill at the top and bottom of the map than there is on the globe, so the lands and oceans in those parts of the map would have to be drawn bigger to keep the coastlines looking as much as possible as they really do.

Mercator worked on his idea for several years. His first "Mercator projection" of the world, published in 1569, was an immediate success. It marked a revolution in mapmaking, being simple, accurate, and useful. So popular was his invention that if you look at any world map today, chances are it is a Mercator projection.

One of his final projects was a collection of maps. Mercator gave this collection the title *Atlas*, the name we still use today for books of maps. He intended his atlas to include maps and histories covering every age and area of the world, an immense task that he did not live to complete. But his fame was secure as the man who had invented a better way to map the earth.

Carolus Linnaeus

Carolus Linnaeus (lih-NAY-us), birth name Carl von Linné. Born May 23, 1707, in South Råshult, Sweden. Died January 10, 1778, in Uppsala, Sweden.

The great voyages of exploration brought with them an unexpected bonus—the discovery of tens of thousands of new kinds of plants and animals never before seen by Europeans. For naturalists, this was both a delight and a prob-lem, for they could not agree on what to call all these unknown species. An eighteenth-century Swedish botanist (plant scientist) named Carl Linné—better known by the Latin form of his name, Carolus Linnaeus—invented a standard way of naming living things that is now used all over the world. As the leading naturalist in Europe, he encouraged the practice of sending scientists along on expeditions of discovery, a practice we continue today on every manned mission into space.

As a child, Linnaeus took an interest in flowers

while playing in his father's garden and in the woods and meadows around his home in southeastern Sweden. By the time he was eight years old, the story goes, he had already learned so much about plants that he earned the nickname "the little botanist." His father, who was a Lutheran pastor, wanted him to study for the ministry, but Linnaeus turned to medicine and botany instead. At the University of Uppsala in Sweden he lectured in botany, and in 1732 he accompanied an expedition to Lapland organized by the Uppsala Society of Science. The discovery of several new plants on this trip filled him with a lifelong eagerness to find more. Years later, he sponsored expeditions of younger naturalists and carefully studied the specimens they brought back to him.

One of the most important jobs of a naturalist is to identify, describe, and name new types of living things. But before Linnaeus there was no accepted system for identifying the group to which a plant or animal belonged, for picking out the important features that set one group apart from another, or even for giving the plant or animal a name that everyone could agree on. Common names for plants varied from country to country and even from village to village. Scientists used Latin names, but there was still much confusion because different scientists would give the same plant a different name. After his return from Lapland Linnaeus developed a practical system for classifying and naming plants that cleared up much of the confusion.

In Linnaeus's scheme, each kind of plant is a unique *species*. Species that are similar belong to the same *genus*. Similar genuses, in turn, are grouped together into *families*, and so on into broader and broader categories until the most general grouping (plant or animal) is reached. The features that set each plant most reliably apart from all others, Linnaeus decided, are the number, shape, and function of its reproductive organs—the parts of the plant that create new plants. So all his classifications are based on reproductive organs. This was a new idea, and for some people a troubling one. While naturalists found Linnaeus's system to be simple and useful, some other people thought the whole subject of reproduction embarrassing, too shocking even to discuss. In his books Linnaeus was forced to write poetically of the "brides" and "bridegrooms" of the plant world. Reproductive strategies are still

Linnaeus in Lapland dress, holding a sprig of Linnaea, *a wildflower named in his honor.*

"Frumentum Indicum" was the name given to corn by a 16th-century herbalist. Students of Linnaeus gave it the scientific name Zea mays.

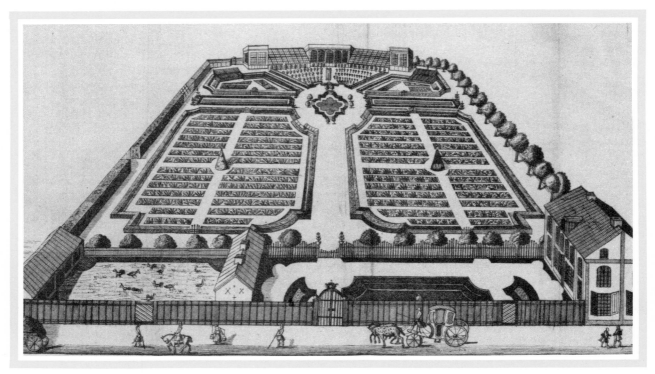

Linnaeus's botanical garden at Uppsala had flower beds, greenhouses, trees, and fishponds. Linnaeus lived in the house at bottom right.

important in classification, although naturalists now consider other traits as well.

Finally, Linnaeus found a simple way to name every plant and animal. He gave each species a two-part name in Latin: first the genus name, and then the species name. An example is *Homo sapiens*, the scientific name Linnaeus invented for human beings. *Homo*, which means "man," is the genus name; *sapiens*, which means "wise," is the species name. In the same way, the purple foxglove, a poisonous plant that is the source of an important heart medicine, was called *Digitalis purpurea* ("purple glove-fingers") from the appearance of its flowers, and its near relatives were named *Digitalis lanata* and *lutea* ("woolly" and "yellow" glove-fingers, respectively).

This system of classification, which Linnaeus published in his book *Systema naturae* ("The System of Nature"), was seen immediately as the answer to many problems of natural science. Naturalists could learn it quickly and apply it to all living things in a consistent way. New species could be named easily, which was very important

in the age of discovery. This simple system is still used today by scientists everywhere, no matter what language they speak, although many of Linnaeus's original classifications have been changed to reflect modern ideas about how living creatures have evolved.

Linnaeus, who became the professor of botany at Uppsala in 1740, was now famous. He gathered around him a group of admiring younger naturalists whom he trained in his method. Then Linnaeus sent his students, whom he called "the true discoverers," around the world to seek out new species. They booked passage on the ships of explorers and merchants and brought back thousands of specimens from everywhere on earth, from the mountains of China and Japan to the jungles of Africa and South America. Even such relatively well-known places as the American colonies had rarely been visited by trained naturalists, and yielded a treasure trove of new plants and animals.

But such journeys were filled with danger. Several of Linnaeus's favorite students died in accidents or of rare diseases before they reached the age of thirty. Linnaeus sometimes wondered if this great scientific effort was worth the cost. "The deaths of many whom I have made to travel have made my hair gray," he wrote, "and what have I gained? A few dried plants, with great anxiety, unrest, and care." The names of his lost students live on in the names of the species they discovered—for example, *Ternstroemia*, a group of tropical plants that Linnaeus named after Christopher Tärnström, who died of a fever in the East Indies.

But the voyages continued. The English naturalists Joseph Banks and David Solander, who went with Captain James Cook on his trip to Australia from 1768 to 1771, were both devoted Linnaeans. [See the article about Captain Cook in this book]. Linnaeus never named any of the fantastic species Solander and Banks collected, for they did not send samples to him and by that time he was too ill to travel to England. He died in 1778, leaving his system of classification and his great catalog of nature to be expanded by the next generation of naturalists.

Alexander von Humboldt

Alexander von Humboldt (HUM-bawlt), birth name Friedrich Wilhelm Karl Heinrich Alexander von Humboldt. Born September 14, 1769, in Berlin, Prussia (now Germany). Died May 6, 1859, in Berlin.

On the brown waters of the Orinoco River in South America drifted a single small canoe. In it were Alexander von Humboldt, perhaps the most enthusiastic scientist-explorer of the nineteenth century, and a few of his companions. Though he was hundreds of miles from any civilized place, Humboldt was just where he wanted to be. Crocodiles hiding in the muddy waters and hungry jaguars watching from the trees along the shore did not worry him. Nor was he deterred by poor food and dirty water to drink. He was even willing to endure the steamy jungle heat that made him sweat with every movement, the daily rains that soaked him to the skin, and the clouds of hungry mosquitoes that were eating him alive. The Indians and missionaries he met thought he was crazy, but Humboldt was a happy man. "I am in my element in this tropical paradise," he wrote in his journal. He had found "a homeland for my soul."

Little in Humboldt's background would seem to have prepared him for the life of an explorer. He was born into a wealthy Prussian family connected with the nobility. Like many another scientist, Humboldt was a sickly child who early on showed a love for nature. Humboldt's mother was determined that her son should make his mark in the civil service, as his father had before him, and Humboldt bowed to her wishes. At the University of Göttingen, where he spent the year of 1789–1790 studying law, he also attended lectures on mineralogy and engineering, and developed a passionate interest in botany. He formed the ambition to travel to far-off countries, though it would be years before he could do so.

Humboldt saw a way to join the civil service while at the same time forwarding his interest in earth sciences. Two years of study at the School of Mines in Freiburg, Saxony (now part of Germany), prepared him for the post of inspector of mines. By 1795 he had made so many improvements in mining practices that he was appointed supervisor-in-chief, with authority over all mining operations. But he gave up this promising career immediately upon the death of his mother in 1797. Now, with the wealth from her estate, he could indulge his interest in science and travel.

With Aimé Bonpland, a young French botanist who would accompany him on most of his travels, Humboldt obtained permission to explore the Spanish empire in South America, an area rarely

Alexander von Humboldt

As he traveled, Humboldt gathered specimens of thousands of new plants and animals. Eventually his canoe was piled so high with specimens that it was in danger of tipping over. But this research helped Humboldt become the first European to understand that each creature of the rain forest, from the highest tree to the smallest ant, has its necessary place in the cycle of jungle life. "Nowhere else are death and life so closely linked as in the tropical jungle," he wrote. Humboldt also measured the air temperature at regular times throughout the day, used his thermometer to estimate the altitude (the higher the land, the lower the temperature at which water boils), and took compass readings of his position. The charts he later made of his findings were the first weather maps.

The trip up the Orinoco was hard and long. The travelers dared not swim, because schools of piranha fish waited just beneath the surface to strip the flesh from any animal that entered the water. Rain and insects spoiled their food, so that they finally were reduced to eating pounded cacao beans and ants and to drinking muddy river water—unboiled, since no cooking fire could be kept going in the humid jungle. Just as they were about to reach their goal, they were arrested by soldiers at a tiny Spanish outpost who believed that they were spies. What other reason could foreigners have for coming to this godforsaken spot?, the soldiers asked. But Humboldt persuaded the soldiers to release his friends from jail and let them continue on their way. Finally they

visited by foreigners. The two explorers landed in Caracas, Venezuela, in 1799 and soon set out for the interior, guided by a Guayaquil Indian river pilot named Carlos de Pinero. Humboldt's goal was to travel by canoe up the Orinoco River, through some of the densest jungles in the world, and find out whether there was a waterway linking the Orinoco and the Amazon River. Along the way they met a Spanish missionary, Father Zea, who acted as their guide along the Orinoco.

Humboldt's journey through the rainforest

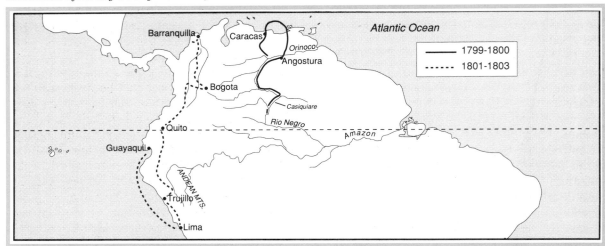

found what they were looking for: the Casiquiare River, a natural canal that connects the upper reaches of the Orinoco with the Rio Negro, the largest tributary of the great Amazon River.

When Humboldt and his party arrived in Angostura (now Ciudad Bolivar, in Venezuela) they had traveled 1,500 miles and were weak with fever and hunger. People in Angostura were amazed to hear that Europeans had traveled all that way to find the canal between the Orinoco and the Amazon, when the inhabitants had known about it all the time. But Humboldt's enthusiasm was undimmed; he wrote in his journal that he felt "a very deep sense of satisfaction" at their accomplishment, and viewed with pride the 12,000 specimens he had collected and the hundreds of scientific measurements he had made.

A few months later Humboldt and Bonpland set off on an exploration of the northwestern spine of South America, traveling down the Andes mountains from Bogotá, Colombia, to Trujillo, Peru. The way was steep, rocky, and dangerous. Humboldt, who loved to climb mountains, made it nearly to the top of Chimborazo, a volcano in Ecuador that is one of the highest peaks in the Andes. At 19,280 feet, just 1,300 feet from the summit, he and Bonpland, both suffering from mountain sickness, had to turn back. (Humboldt was the first to understand that mountain sickness is caused by the lack of oxygen at high altitudes.) Nonetheless, their climb stood as a mountaineering record for thirty years. On the coast, Humboldt discovered the great ocean current which was long called the Humboldt Current (now called the Peru Current).

After further travels in Mexico and the United States, where Humboldt was the guest of President Thomas Jefferson, the companions sailed back to France in 1804. Much of Humboldt's fortune had been spent, and he went on no more great expeditions. Instead he settled down, first in Paris and later in Berlin, to write out his findings and theories. His most influential book, *Kosmos* ("The Cosmos"), attempted to explain the entirety of nature as it was then understood. In this book Humboldt offered quite modern explanations for such mysteries as the earth's magnetic field, the actions of volcanos, and the complex living systems of the rain forest and the oceans. He was working on the fifth volume of *Kosmos* when he died in 1859.

Humboldt and his fellow explorers, reduced to eating insects and mashed beans, camp under huge trees on the banks of the Orinoco River.

René Descartes

René Descartes (day-caht). Born March 31, 1596, in La Haye (now La Haye–Descartes), Touraine, France. Died February 11, 1650, in Stockholm, Sweden.

How do we know what is true? All great philosophers have wrestled with this question, but none more single-mindedly than the seventeenth-century French mathematician and thinker René Descartes, who set himself the goal "never to accept anything as true which I did not clearly and distinctly see to be so."

Descartes had a sad childhood. His mother died when he was only a year old, and his father, a judge and lawyer, was gone half of every year, trying cases in another province. Nor was he close to his brother or sister—later in life, he did not even attend their weddings. The men in the family had been lawyers and judges for generations, and he was expected to become one too. But Descartes soon went his own way. Even as a boy his father called him his "little philosopher" because Descartes constantly asked about the why and how of things. Attending the new school at La Flèche, Descartes came under the influence of an excellent teacher, Father Charlet, who introduced him to literature, philosophy, and mathematics. By the end of his schooling, however, Descartes was complaining that all he had learned was useless, except mathematics. So, as he later wrote, he decided to abandon "the study of letters" and study "the book of the world" instead, traveling wherever he pleased and recording his observations, all the while searching for truths within himself. He was able to live comfortably in this way on the income from an estate his mother had left him.

This was the time of the Thirty Years' War, a conflict that involved most of the states of Europe, both Catholic and Protestant. From 1618 to 1628 Descartes traveled constantly, joining the armies first of Maurice, Prince of Orange, then of Maximilian, Duke of Bavaria, and finally of the Holy Roman Emperor in Hungary. Descartes didn't see much fighting, and the boredom of camp life gave him plenty of time to think. On November 10, 1619, he had a dream that revealed to him his future course. In the dream he glimpsed a new universal science that would draw together all branches of knowledge into one system of true wisdom. It was his job, he believed, to discover the nature of this universal science and explain it to others. After further travels in Hungary, Germany, Italy, and France, he settled in Holland, where he began to write down his ideas.

The searcher for truth, wrote Descartes in his most famous book, the *Discourse on Method*

René Descartes, from a painting by Frans Hals

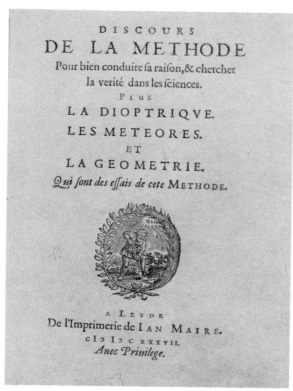

The title page of Descartes's Discourse on Method *shows a man digging in the garden of truth, under a sun bearing the Name of God in Hebrew.*

(published in 1637), must begin by letting go of all opinions and prejudices. Only a scientific, logical approach will result in the discovery of truth. Then the searcher must find a starting point, one absolutely true thing to reason from. To Descartes, there was only one true thing that could not be questioned, and that was the existence of thought itself. This led him to make his famous statement, *"Cogito, ergo sum,"* which is Latin for "I think, therefore I am." From that foothold, all other truths would follow. When tackling a large philosophical problem, the proper approach is to divide it into smaller and smaller problems, until each small problem can be solved on its own. The answers to all the smaller problems yield the answer to the main problem.

Descartes held that the physical world is made up of atoms moving according to purely mechanical principles. Plants, animals, and even human bodies, in his view, are no more than machines made of living tissue which can be understood totally by looking at the type and motion of their atoms, just as philosophical problems can be understood by looking at their smallest parts. The one thing that does not obey mechanical principles, he wrote, is the human mind, which is separate from and above nature. Other than that, there are no unknowable aspects of nature. This idea was most influential on the sciences. Even today, the great majority of scientists hold to a mechanistic view of the universe derived from that of Descartes. Some thinkers go so far as to say that all modern scientists and philosophers are Cartesians, in the sense that they either agree with his ideas or must react against them.

Descartes made several contributions to mathematics as well. The most important was the idea of a *Cartesian plane,* an imaginary flat plane divided horizontally and vertically by two axes (directions of measurement). Each axis can be shown as a line made up of points, with each point assigned a number. Any shape drawn on the Cartesian plane can be described as a set of points on the plane located by the numbers on the horizontal and vertical axes. Descartes showed that many classes of shapes could be defined on the

Among the subjects Descartes pondered was optics, the study of light and vision. Here he demostrates the refraction of light rays.

Cartesian plane entirely by mathematical statements; conversely, many mathematical problems could be solved by geometric means. This formed the basis for the field of mathematics called analytic geometry.

The publication of the *Discourse on Method* and of a later work, *Meditations* (1640), brought Descartes fame as one of the leading philosophers of Europe. While younger thinkers were eager to spread Descartes's ideas, Protestant and Catholic authorities alike saw his books as an attack on religion, and banned them. Descartes himself tried to stay out of the fray. He needed solitude for his work and moved his home often, seeing visitors only when he couldn't avoid it.

In the late 1640s Queen Christina of Sweden wrote him a series of letters asking him to visit her court in Stockholm. After putting her off many times, even after she sent a ship of the Swedish navy to pick him up, he finally agreed. Descartes went to Sweden in 1649 and began to tutor the young queen in philosophy. But the cold climate was bad for his health, and he died there of pneumonia after five months. Already he was seen as one of the great thinkers of his age, and that is still his reputation today.

Ambroise Paré

Ambroise Paré (pah-RAY). Born 1510 in Laval, Mayenne, France. Died December 20, 1590, in Paris.

Death or mutilation on the battlefield was a common fate for European men in the sixteenth century. Wars were fought for economic gain, for the supremacy of one religion over another, for the acquisition of more land or more power. War itself was nothing new, in this part of the world or any other, but the European wars of the sixteenth century were fought with a new kind of weapon, the gun, that inflicted new and horrible kinds of wounds. Surgeons who accompanied armies into battle did not know how to treat gunshot wounds except by burning them with bandages soaked in boiling oil. The heat was supposed to take the poison out of the wound, for in those days surgeons believed that gunpowder was a poison.

Ambroise Paré was the first surgeon to challenge this way of doing things. He was born in northern France, the son of a cabinetmaker, and learned his craft from a barber-surgeon. In France in those days there were two kinds of doctors: the physicians, who taught at the University of Paris and studied Greek and Latin books by ancient writers, and the barber-surgeons, who went from town to town doing such work as setting broken bones and pulling teeth. Paré knew the writings of Galen and Hippocrates and the other ancients, but he was not afraid to contradict what they said when experience taught him otherwise.

After spending four years as a resident surgeon at a hospital in Paris, Paré was recruited to join the French army and went with it in 1537 to the Italian city of Turin, which the French were besieging. During the siege, many soldiers were shot, and Paré took care of them in the way he had been taught—by scalding their wounds with boiling oil. There were so many wounded men that the oil ran short, and Paré had to make do with an ointment made of egg yolks, attar of roses, and turpentine. To his great surprise, the soldiers who had been treated with the egg mixture healed rapidly, while those who had been burned suffered from pain, fever, and inflammations. "And then," Paré wrote, "I resolved with myself never more to burn thus cruelly poor men wounded with gunshot."

From then on, Paré no longer considered book-learning the right way to study medicine. His method was to observe, to think problems through, and to learn from experience. He also felt a sense of compassion for hurt and sick people that was uncommon in his day. Whenever possible, he substituted a gentle form of treatment for a violent one. This is why his work is regarded as the beginning of modern surgery.

The soldiers of France quickly realized that Paré's methods worked. So did the kings and nobles who led them. He was much in demand to accompany military campaigns. Although he had left the army, married, and begun practicing surgery in Paris, he was persuaded to return in 1542 as surgeon to the grand lord of Brittany. During this campaign he developed a useful technique that no one appears to have thought of before. An officer was wounded in the shoulder, but none of the army surgeons could find the bullet. Paré found it by having the officer put himself in the same position he was in when he was shot.

Gunpowder had brought another important change to the battlefields of Europe: it had greatly increased the number of amputations. A gunshot wound in an arm or leg was likely to become

Ambroise Paré at the age of seventy-five

Catholics and Protestants fight in a village near Paris in 1587, producing the cannon, gunshot, and bayonet wounds that Paré learned to treat.

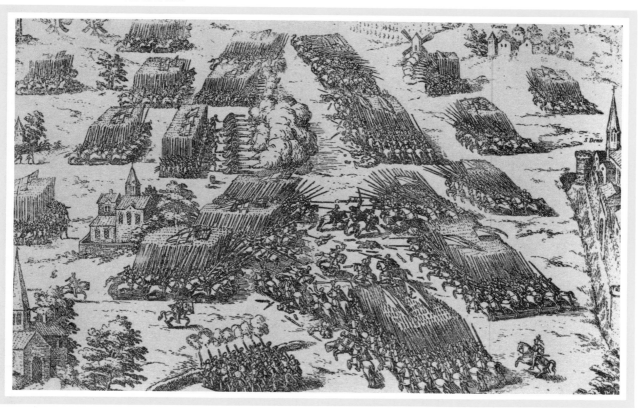

infected, and the surgeons had no way to stop the infection from spreading to the rest of the body other than by cutting off the wounded limb. Once the amputation was done, they would stop the bleeding by cauterizing the stump—that is, searing it with a red-hot iron. In 1552, during the invasion of Lorraine, Paré decided to try a method that had been used in antiquity and then forgotten: instead of burning the wound, he tied off the bleeding arteries with thin threads called ligatures. The survival rate of soldiers undergoing amputations rose dramatically. The following year Paré hit on a way of packing a chest wound with a sponge to stop the flow of air, stabilize the chest, and soak up the blood. This method, too, was a simplified version of the one that modern doctors now use.

In between campaigns, Paré returned to Paris to write up his findings and to practice surgery on civilians. He invented a number of prostheses (artificial body parts) for his patients, including limbs, teeth, and eyes made of silver and gold. He rejected the conventional wisdom that held that

Paré insisted on sharing his medical knowledge. This illustration from one of his books shows how to use leverage to fix a dislocated elbow.

hernia patients had to be castrated before their hernias could be surgically repaired. He also invented new medical instruments and techniques, such as soothing a distressed patient to sleep with the noise of gently pouring water.

But it was never long before he was called again to risk his life on the battlefield. When the French, fighting the Holy Roman Emperor Charles V, found themselves under siege in the town of Metz and facing heavy losses, they had Paré smuggled in to help them. Not long afterward, he was present during a bloody battle in Picardy. The defeated French garrison surrendered, and Paré was captured by the Spanish. They agreed to let him go after he cured a Spanish officer of a leg ulcer.

The wars between France and Spain, fought to decide who would control Italy, came to an end when Princess Elizabeth of France married the new Holy Roman Emperor, Felipe II of Spain. But there was a new war to take the place of the old: the civil war between the Catholics and the Protestants (known in France as the Huguenots). Paré himself, though of Huguenot birth, continued to serve France's Catholic kings; he was appointed to the high offices of premier surgeon by King Charles IX and of valet de chambre by King Henry III. Yet he narrowly escaped being killed alongside thousands of other Huguenots during the St. Bartholomew's Day Massacre of 1572. A mob burst into the house of the Protestant adral Gaspard de Coligny, whom Paré was treating for wounds received in an assassination attempt, and stabbed the admiral to death before Paré's eyes.

In his books, as well as in his practice, Paré did the unusual: he wrote in French, so that any literate person could understand him, rather than in Latin, which only a handful of scholars could read. He did not agree with the physicians of the University of Paris that medical knowledge should be the secret possession of a special group. Any surgeon who wanted to learn his methods was welcome to do so. All Paré's books were translated into many languages, and his methods were widely copied all over Europe. His *Complete Works*, first published in 1575, remained in print for a century and ran to thirteen editions. Paré had thus become the most influential surgeon of his day by the time he died at the age of eighty.

Andreas Vesalius

Andreas Vesalius (veh-SAY-lee-us). Born December 1514 in Brussels, Brabant (now Belgium). Died circa June 1564 on Zacynthus Island (now Zante Island), Greece.

In a classroom at the University of Paris, a learned professor was teaching young medical students about the human body. It was a typical anatomy lesson for the year 1533. The corpse of an executed criminal was laid out on a table in the middle of the room. Over the corpse bent a barber-surgeon with a knife in his hand. As the medical students clustered around him, the barber-surgeon cut the body open and exposed its parts. High above them all sat the professor, reading aloud in Latin from a book written by the Greco-Roman physician Galen. The professor never looked down at the body, so he never saw for himself that most of what Galen had written was wrong. The barber-surgeon did not know Latin, so he could not correct the professor, and he often botched his work so that the students could not see how the body really looks inside. This was the way that anatomy had been taught for centuries, and as a result, the doctors of the sixteenth century knew little more about how human bodies function than had the doctors of the ancient world.

But on this day, something unusual happened. One of the students in the professor's audience pushed the barber-surgeon aside and took up the knife. With great skill he sliced open the body on the table and delicately laid bare the network of muscles, nerves, and blood vessels. For once, the surprised medical students were able to look into a human body and learn something about how it is made. Within a few years, their bold young friend would discredit Galen, shock the professors, and found the modern science of anatomy.

The student was named Andreas Vesalius, and he was nineteen years old. He was a Belgian, born to a family that had long been active in medicine and scholarship. His father had served as apothecary to the Holy Roman Emperor Charles V, who was also the king of Spain, and it was the son's ambition to do even better and become the emperor's royal physician. As a child, Vesalius lived near the city gallows, where he saw the bodies of executed criminals torn open by birds and beasts. In this way he became familiar with the sight and smell of corpses. By the time he was fifteen—the year he went off to the University of Louvain to

Andreas Vesalius

study Greek, Latin, and Hebrew—he had had a good deal of experience in cutting open small animals to see how they were put together. By eighteen, he was ready to enter the medical school at the University of Paris, where he surprised his professors with his self-taught skill at dissection. He was not at all satisfied with the way anatomy was taught there, and he and his fellow students made midnight raids to gallows and graveyards to collect bodies that they could dissect in private.

To finish his training, Vesalius went to the famous medical school at the University of Padua, in Italy. He so impressed his teachers that on the

In a medieval anatomy class, a professor seated on a throne reads from Galen's Latin works while, below, barber-surgeons dissect a corpse.

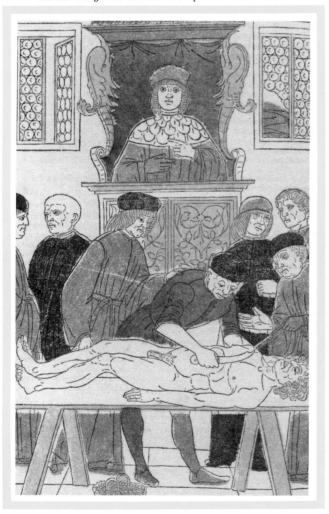

day after his graduation he was appointed professor of surgery and anatomy at the university. Over the next few years, Vesalius developed a teaching method that was intended to help students learn as much as possible. He always did his own dissections, explaining his findings as he went along; he made charts of the body and kept them near the dissection table, together with a human skeleton, to make his explanations even clearer; and he dissected animals, both living and dead, to help the students understand how the organs work. He taught with intensity and enthusiasm, and his classes were crowded with fascinated onlookers.

But although Vesalius had broken with tradition by doing his own dissections, he had not yet broken with Galen. He did his best to make his findings fit in with Galen's writings. In his charts and diagrams, he included organs that Galen insisted were there, even though he knew they did not exist. For example, Galen said that there was a network of nerves and vessels, which he called the *rete mirabile*, at the base of the brain. Vesalius found such a network in animals, but not in humans. Still, in his book *Tabulae Anatomicae Sex* ("Six Anatomical Diagrams"), he included an illustration of the *rete mirabile* and other elements of Galen's teachings.

It gradually dawned on Vesalius that Galen himself had never done any dissections of human bodies. All Galen's information had been gleaned from dissections of apes, dogs, pigs, and other animals, and it was worthless for studying human beings. Vesalius announced his discovery in January 1540, at the University of Bologna, where he had been invited to give classes as a guest lecturer. There was a dramatic confrontation between the professors, who insisted that Galen could not be questioned, and the brash young visitor from Padua, who declared in public that Galen's knowledge of human anatomy was completely untrustworthy.

Vesalius decided to make a textbook that would set forth his findings. He set out to create the first book on human anatomy that was based entirely on dissection, without regard to Galen. To illustrate it, he hired Jan Stephan van Calcar, a young Belgian artist who had studied with the great painter Titian in Venice and who had done some of the drawings for Vesalius's earlier book. For months the two worked together, with Vesalius dissecting a series of executed criminals supplied by the city authorities and Calcar drawing what Vesalius laid bare. When the drawings were done, they were taken to Venice to be engraved on wood blocks; then the blocks were sent to Basel, in Switzerland, where the book was printed on the new printing presses. It was published under the title *De humani corporis fabrica* ("On the Human's Bodily Works") in 1543, the same year in which Nicholas Copernicus published his book *De revolutionibus orbium coelestium*. [See the article on Copernicus in this book.]

The *Fabrica*, as we call it now, is one of the most beautiful books ever published, one of the great masterpieces of the art of printing. Every part of it was designed to be of service to the reader. Vesalius's text, written in Latin, was organized into seven sections that explained the subject matter in precise detail. The illustrations, some three hundred in all, were the most accurate anatomical drawings that had ever been made, and the Swiss printers had brought them to the reader with perfect clarity. There had never been a book like it. It was one of the great achievements of the Renaissance, because it used a new invention—the printing press—to give form to the new scientific way of thinking about the world. Its author was only twenty-eight years old.

The book was famous from the moment it was published. The medical professors loyal to Galen attacked it furiously in their writings, calling Vesalius a monster and a liar. Vesalius soon left the university to fulfill his childhood ambition of becoming court physician to the Holy Roman Emperor, Charles V. He married, had a daughter, built a house in Brussels, took on many important people as his patients, and did so well at the emperor's court that he was given the title of count, even though the other court physicians were Galenists who disliked their freethinking colleague. When Charles abdicated his throne in 1556, his son, Felipe (King Philip II of Spain), appointed Vesalius to the post of court physician in Madrid.

But Vesalius missed his life of research, and in 1564, over the king's objections, he left Madrid to go on a pilgrimage to Jerusalem, with the intention of going back to teach at the University of Padua afterwards. On his way home, his ship was

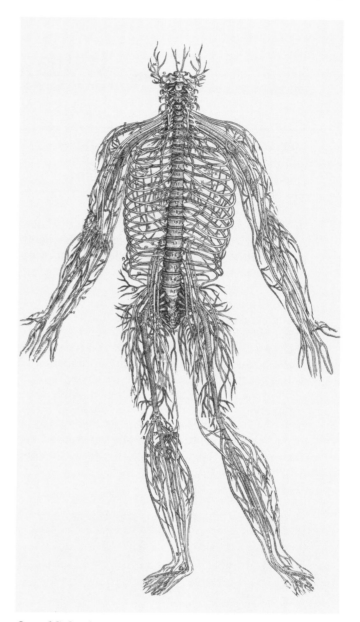

One of Calcar's engravings for Vesalius's book on anatomy, showing the network of nerves that connects the brain with the rest of the body.

nearly wrecked in a storm and he fell ill. He went ashore on a small island off the coast of Greece, and there he died and was buried in an unmarked grave. The woodcuts that were made to illustrate his book outlasted him by four hundred years; they were destroyed by an Allied air attack on Munich during World War II.

William Harvey

William Harvey. Born April 1, 1578 in Folkestone, Kent, England. Died June 3, 1657, in Roehampton, Kent, England.

Most schoolchildren know something of how the circulatory system works. The heart pumps blood into the lungs, where it picks up oxygen, and then through the arteries, which carry the oxygen-rich blood to tiny blood vessels called capillaries in every part of the body. Then the blood passes through the capillaries into the veins, which carry it back to the heart again. In this way, all the cells of the body receive oxygen and food and get rid of their waste products.

Back in the sixteenth century, when William Harvey was in medical school, nobody knew anything about the circulation of the blood, or about how the heart works. Galen, the Greek doctor from the first century who was revered as the final authority on all medical matters, thought

William Harvey

that the right and left sides of the heart were connected, that blood from one side passed through and collected air and "spirit" from the other side, and that the blood then washed down to the rest of the body and ebbed back, like the tides. He also thought that fresh blood was made in the liver from food and that the pulse was caused by the "spirit" carried in the blood. None of this was true, but for fourteen centuries no one realized that Galen was wrong. Even though Galen himself believed that doctors should do experiments to find out how the body really works, all through the Middle Ages doctors had been content to read his books without trying to find out anything for themselves.

Harvey was the first person to find out the truth about how the blood circulates. He was born in a town on the southern coast of England, the eldest of nine children of a well-to-do businessman. Most of his brothers became well-to-do businessmen too, but young Harvey was a boy who loved books. He was sent to the King's School in Canterbury, where the students had to speak Greek and Latin instead of English. Then he went to one of the colleges at Cambridge University and to the famous medical school at the University of Padua, in Italy. One of his professors there was Giralomo Fabrizio (or Fabricius), who had made a special study of the veins and found that they contain little valves, the purpose of which neither he nor anyone else understood.

On his return to England, Harvey married, was admitted as a Fellow to the College of Physicians in London, and joined the staff of St. Bartholomew's Hospital. Over the next several years, he became the physician to many important people, including King James and his Lord Chancellor, the philosopher Francis Bacon. [This was the same king whom Pocahontas visited in London and who ordered the execution of Sir Walter Raleigh. See the articles on them in this book.] The College of Physicians showed its respect for his abilities by giving him a lifelong appointment as a lecturer in anatomy and surgery.

At the same time, he decided to find out for himself how the circulatory system works. Other doctors had already provided him with certain clues to the mystery. Andreas Vesalius, the great anatomist who taught at the University of Padua just before Harvey's time, had proven from dissections that, despite what Galen said, the two sides of the heart are not connected and the inferior *vena cava*, one of two large veins that feed into the heart, does not come from the liver. [See the article on Vesalius in this book.] Vesalius's assistant, Realdus Columbus, had observed that blood travels from the heart to the lungs, where it picks up oxygen. (Another anatomist who made the same observation, Miguel Servetus, was burned at the stake as a religious heretic.) And Harvey's own teacher Fabricius had observed the tiny valves in the veins.

Harvey had an idea that the purpose of these valves was to keep the blood from flowing backward in the vein—to keep it moving forward only. But if it couldn't go backward, then where did the blood end up? There was obviously no place in the body where the used blood collected, and no place for the blood to leave the body. The answer, Harvey reasoned, must be that the blood travels in a circle, moving continuously from the veins to the arteries and back to the veins again. Was the heart, then, a kind of pump that kept the blood in motion, and if so, how did it work? Harvey dissected hundreds of living dogs, pigs, and snakes to find out, and after years of watching, thinking, and trying again, he unraveled the mystery.

Harvey wrote out an explanation of his discoveries in a little book, only seventy-two pages long, known as *De Motu Cordis* ("On the Motion of the Heart"), which was published in 1628. In this book he described the circulation of the blood, the pumping action of the heart, and the way that this pumping action produces the pulse in the arteries. He also did something else that was new: he used measurements to demonstrate the truth of his arguments. Scientists call this "quantitative evidence." They use it all the time in our own day. Harvey calculated the amount of blood the heart pumps in the course of one hour and found that the result was far more than the amount of blood in the body, and more than could be produced by the liver. This was an important element in Harvey's demonstration that the same blood is circulated through the body over and over again.

The only thing Harvey could not explain was how the blood gets from the arteries into the veins. He assumed that there must be pores, or little holes, in the flesh that allow the blood to cross over. Since the microscope had not yet been invented, there was no way for Harvey to see the tiny capillaries where the actual movement from the arteries to the veins takes place. The man who finally discovered the capillaries, Marcello Malpighi, was born the same year that Harvey's book was published.

Some of Harvey's fellow physicians realized immediately that he was right. But there were many others who resisted Harvey's ideas, including a number of his own patients, who no longer wanted him to treat them. Harvey replied to them: "Let my thoughts perish if they are worthless, my experiments if they are erroneous, or if I have not properly understood them. . . . If I am

Harvey was the first person to understand the pumping action of the heart and to describe how blood circulates through the veins and arteries.

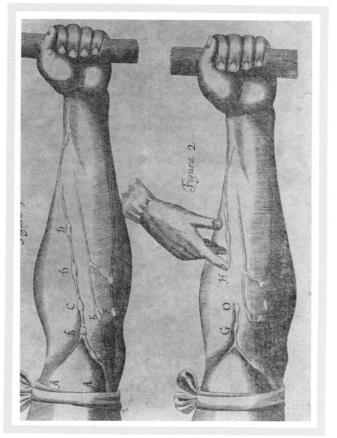

wrong (for after all I am but a man), let what I have written turn sour with neglect, but if I am right sometime at least the human race will not disdain the truth."

A few years before the publication of *De Motu Cordis*, King James died, and Harvey was called to testify for the defense at the trial of the Duke of Buckingham, who had been accused of poisoning the king. The new king, Charles I, befriended Harvey and took a lively interest in his work, reappointing him to the post of physician extraordinary in his court and allowing him to experiment on the royal herd of deer. When the king went on state visits, Harvey accompanied him. But this friendship, in the end, cost Harvey his career and very nearly cost him his life. In 1642 civil war broke out between the king's supporters and his enemies in Parliament, who called for the execution of Harvey and the rest of Charles's friends. [See the articles on Roger Williams and William Bradford in this book for more about the religious and political controversies that produced the civil war.] The following year, Harvey, though he had escaped execution, was fired from the hospital where he had practiced for more than three decades. A troop of Roundheads, as the Parliamentary soldiers were called, ransacked his house and destroyed most of his scientific papers and research notes.

King Charles was beheaded by the Roundheads in 1649. For the next nine years the country was ruled by their leader, Oliver Cromwell. Harvey, though discredited as a political "delinquent," continued his experiments for a time, and in 1651 published a book on the development of the chick within the egg. The College of Physicians, which he had served actively for many years, received from Harvey a donation of books and manuscripts together with money to build a library for them, but the building was destroyed in the Great Fire of London a few years later. Nonetheless, despite his troubles with the new authorities, Harvey lived long enough to see his ideas about the workings of the circulatory system widely accepted and to hear himself acclaimed as a great man. He died of a stroke at the age of eighty.

The importance of Harvey's work lies not only in his discovery of the circulation of the blood, but in his grasp of what we now call the scientific method. His way of getting at the truth by making observations, weighing the evidence, and testing new theories helped make a revolution in the way people think about the world. As Harvey wrote in the preface to *De Motu Cordis*, "I profess both to learn and to teach . . . not from the positions of philosophers but from the fabric of nature. . . . I avow myself the partisan of truth alone."

Jean-François Champollion

Jean-François Champollion (shonh-pohl-yonh). Born December 23, 1790, in Figeac, Auvergne, France. Died March 4, 1832, in Paris.

In 1798 the French Army, led by Napoleon Bonaparte, marched through the North African desert into Cairo, Egypt. In the shadow of the Great Pyramids, the French cut to pieces the armies of the Egyptian sultans, while Napoleon cried to his men, "Soldiers, forty centuries are looking down upon you!" Napoleon soon retreated from Egypt, but in his wake came hundreds of French historians, scientists, and treasure-hunters seeking to unravel the mystery of the pharaohs, the kings of ancient Egypt. But none of them could understand the pharaohs' strange form of writing, called *hieroglyphs* (from the Greek words for "sacred carvings"). These stylized pictures of hawks, boats, reeds, and other symbols were written everywhere on the crumbling temples and yellowing scrolls. Plainly the hieroglyphs told the whole history of the ancient Egyptians, but no one alive knew how to read them. That knowledge had been lost for 1,400 years.

A year after Napoleon's victory, a remarkable discovery was made by a French soldier digging in the ruins of an Egyptian fort near the town of Rashid (called Rosetta in English). It was a broken slab of hard black basalt stone, about three and a half feet long, two feet wide, and a few inches thick. On the Rosetta Stone were carved three inscriptions. One was in classical Greek, written in the familiar Greek letters. The second was in Egyptian, written in an old script called demotic. The third was in hieroglyphs. No one knew how to read either the demotic or the hieroglyphic writings. But the Greek inscription, which Greek scholars could easily read, claimed that the three inscriptions all said the same thing. It would now be possible to compare the texts and figure out the meaning of the hieroglyphs. The task was not as easy as it looked, however. Many scholars tried to solve the mystery, but none succeeded. The years passed until a brilliant young Frenchman named Jean-François Champollion finally deciphered the hieroglyphs and revealed to modern eyes the written history of the ancient Egyptians.

Champollion possessed a genius for languages. At the age of five he taught himself to read French; by age thirteen he had mastered Latin, Greek, Arabic, Syrian, and Chaldean. Later he learned Hebrew, Persian, Chinese, and Coptic, an old Egyptian language written in Greek letters. While he was still in grammar school he saw his first Egyptian antiquities, including samples of hieroglyphs on stone tablets, and declared that he would be the first to read them. From that time onward, Egypt and its hieroglyphic writing were his obsessions.

Applying in 1807 as a student to the *lycée* (high school) at Grenoble, Champollion read for the faculty a proposal for a book called "Egypt Under the Pharaohs." His audience was stunned by the book's ambitious scope. No such history had ever been attempted. Instead of being admitted as a student, Champollion was made a professor.

When he was not teaching in Grenoble, Champollion spent much of his time in Paris, studying copies of the Rosetta Stone and other Egyptian documents in the Louvre Museum. He slept in a damp, dismal little room not far away. Probably it

Jean-François Champollion, by Leon Cogniet

was at this time that he contracted the chronic lung infection that killed him twenty years later. With almost no money, Champollion would have starved if he had not been helped by his brother Jacques-Joseph, a talented archaeologist. In 1814 Champollion was charged with treason for supporting the exiled Napoleon, and narrowly escaped trial. In 1821 he was charged again and had to leave Grenoble for good. But that was also the year that he finally began publishing his translations of the hieroglyphs on the Rosetta Stone.

For centuries, scholars had been making guesses about what the hieroglyphs meant. A Greek named Horapollon of the fourth century B.C. claimed that the hieroglyphs were a form of picture writing, in which each picture stood for a whole word or an idea. Most scholars up to Champollion's time agreed with Horapollon, even though Horapollon himself could not read hieroglyphs and no progress translating them was ever made using his ideas. Even the discovery of the Rosetta Stone did not help scholars much until an important clue was uncovered by the English physicist Thomas Young. Young translated the demotic text of the Rosetta Stone by assigning a sound to each character. But even then Young still could not see how the demotic characters related to the hieroglyphic pictures.

Champollion, studying the Rosetta Stone, abandoned the idea that the hieroglyphs were picture-writing. It was more likely, he reasoned,

The ancient Egyptians used hieroglyphic writing to record religious texts, like prayers, as well as secular texts, like songs and legal documents.

that each symbol stood for a sound, as in demotic script and all other Western languages. He looked at certain hieroglyphs that were enclosed by a ring, called a cartouche. Young and others had already shown that hieroglyphs in cartouches always represented the names of rulers. Comparing the Greek text and the hieroglyphs side by side, he saw that one hieroglyph in a cartouche was the name of Ptolemy, a Greek ruler of Egypt. In other inscriptions he saw the names of Cleopatra, an Egyptian queen, and Rameses, pharaoh at the time of Moses. By looking at the arrangement of the hieroglyphs in each name, which had some symbols in common, Champollion suddenly realized that the hieroglyphs spelled out the names phonetically, that is, by sound. Champollion now knew that certain hieroglyphs stood for certain sounds. He was able to link other hieroglyphs to particular sounds using his knowledge of Coptic, which, he showed, was a more recent version of the ancient Egyptian language. From this small beginning, he eventually compiled a long list of hieroglyphs and their Greek equivalents.

There were many factors that made translation difficult. Champollion discovered that some hieroglyphs stood for whole syllables, some for single letters, and a few were indeed picture-words. Certain hieroglyphs had no sound, but were used as signals to the reader to emphasize a word, to change the order in which the symbols were to be read, or to distinguish one hieroglyph from another that looked the same. Another problem was that hieroglyphic writing had been used for more than three thousand years, and over that time it had changed greatly. Later hieroglyphic writing contained hundreds of new symbols and new rules for using them. To make things even more challenging, the Egyptians enjoyed scrambling the hieroglyphs to make a code. It was a game for them, the way crossword puzzles are for many people today.

Champollion's Egyptian dictionary was quickly denounced by jealous and skeptical historians. Still, by 1826 he had earned enough renown to become curator of the Egyptian collection at the Louvre. Two years later he led an archaeological expedition to Egypt, visiting the great ruins at Dendera. The Egyptians were astounded that a Frenchman could understand the mysterious carvings they themselves could not read. Champollion made no important archeological discoveries on this trip (scientific excavations had not yet begun in Egypt), but after his return he was rewarded with the first chair of Egyptian antiquities, created especially for him at the College of France. He died the next year, in 1832. Despite his achievements, it was not until the late nineteenth century that Champollion was finally recognized as the founder of the modern study of ancient Egypt.

The text of the Rosetta Stone, repeated three times in three languages, concerns Ptolemy V Epiphanes, who ruled Egypt from 205 to 180 B.C.

Heinrich Schliemann

Heinrich Schliemann (SHLEE-mahn). Born January 6, 1822, in Neubukow, Mecklenburg-Schwerin (now Germany). Died December 26, 1890, in Naples, Italy.

The story of the Trojan War had fascinated young Heinrich Schliemann ever since he was a little boy. He loved to hear his father tell about the war between the ancient Greeks and the Trojans three thousand years ago; how after ten years of battle the Greeks, led by the heroes Agamemnon, Achilles, and Odysseus, had defeated the Trojans and destroyed the city of Troy. The great poet Homer had described the Trojan War in his epic poem the *Iliad*. Schliemann always felt sorry for the Trojans, especially their king, Priam, and his brave son, Hector, who were both killed by the Greeks. His father said these were just exciting stories, but to Schliemann they seemed real.

In 1829, when Schliemann was seven years old, his father gave him a book with an engraving that showed Troy with its huge walls and gate engulfed by flames. When he asked his father if Troy were still there, his father answered that it had been so completely destroyed that there was nothing left. "Father," replied Schliemann, "if Troy had such huge walls, they must still be standing, buried under the ground. When I am older, I will go to Greece and find Troy and Priam's treasure."

It took many years for Schliemann to realize his dream. At the age of fourteen he was apprenticed to a grocer. Grinding potatoes, wrapping fish, and sweeping out the shop was such hard, boring work that Schliemann almost forgot about Troy. One day a drunken miller wandered into the shop reciting verses from Homer in classical Greek. Schliemann had never heard Greek before. When he learned that the verses told about the Trojan War, he paid the man out of his meager shopboy's wages to say them over again.

With that event, Schliemann's remarkable luck began to show itself. He left the grocer in 1841 and signed on as a cabin boy on a ship sailing from Hamburg, Germany, to Venezuela. The ship was wrecked off the coast of Holland, and Schliemann made it to shore near the city of Amsterdam, penniless and clothed in rags. A family friend helped him get a job as a clerk with a trading company. He did so well that he became an agent for the company in St. Petersburg, Russia. There he started his own import-export business selling military goods. This was such a success that by the age of thirty-six Schliemann was able to retire with a large fortune.

While Schliemann was making his fortune, he also taught himself many languages, including English, Portuguese, Italian, Latin, Arabic, Russian, Swedish, and Polish. The system for learning languages that he invented worked so well he was able to master a new language in just six weeks. He left the study of Greek for last, fearing he would become obsessed with it and neglect his business. Schliemann would read from Homer in a loud voice to an old man he had hired to listen. This so disturbed his neighbors that he was twice forced to move to new rooms.

Now Schliemann was ready to spend all his wealth to find Troy. His approach was different from that of most scholars of the day. Ancient Greek historians had treated the Trojan War as an actual event, but few nineteenth-century historians thought that there was much truth to Homer's stories. Schliemann, however, was convinced that Homer had described real people whose graves could be found, and real places that could be uncovered with pick and shovel. He was sure that all the clues to the location of Troy could be found in the *Iliad*.

The first problem was to identify the the precise location of ancient Troy. The *Iliad* said that the city lay east of Greece across the Aegean Sea, on the coast of what is now Turkey. (In Schliemann's day it was called Asia Minor, and was the seat of the Ottoman Empire.) The few scholars who believed in the existence of Troy thought it was buried under a hill near the village of Bunarbashi in northwestern Turkey. Schliemann disagreed. According to Homer, the invading Greeks could run back and forth from the walls of Troy to their beached ships several times in a day. Bunarbashi was miles from the sea. Homer described Troy as having four springs. Bunarbashi had forty. Searching for a better site, Schliemann came upon the village of Hisarlik. It was much closer to the sea and seemed a more likely spot to build a great city. And it had a huge mound that might well be hiding ancient ruins.

Schliemann and his young Greek wife, Sophia, began digging at Hisarlik in 1870, aided by one hundred local workmen. Immediately they began uncovering the remains of an ancient city. Below it were the ruins of six older cities, stacked like layers in a cake. (Later, an eighth and ninth layer were discovered.) At twenty-three feet down, Schliemann uncovered the seventh layer, a city with immense stone walls and a gigantic gate just like the engraving he remembered from his childhood. Schliemann was overjoyed—this had to be Troy!

On the last day of excavation, Schliemann was walking alongside a tottering wall of stone when his eye caught the gleam of gold in the dirt. According to Schliemann's own account, he knew right away that this had to be Priam's treasure, buried for three thousand years. Fearing that his workmen would steal any gold they saw, he immediately called a rest break. While the workers ate and relaxed, suspecting nothing, Schliemann frantically dug out the treasure with a penknife and his fingers. All the while the heavy wall swayed overhead, threatening to crash down at any moment. When he examined the treasure later, in private, he found that it included an embossed shield of copper, goblets of solid gold, and nine thousand pieces of gold jewelry. Seeking to preserve the gold for archaeologists to study, Schliemann smuggled it out of the country. Turkish officials were very angry when they found out.

Had Schliemann really discovered Troy? We now know he was digging in the right place but at

Heinrich Schliemann

the wrong depth. According to later scholars, the city of massive walls that Schliemann found was actually built a thousand years before Homer's Troy, which was in the second layer from the top. (Ironically, much of Homer's Troy was destroyed by Schliemann as he dug through it to reach the lower layers.) The gold did not belong to Priam, but to an unknown, even more ancient king.

Still, Schliemann had discovered a civilization that was completely new to scholars and had unearthed a great treasure. Dramatic newspaper accounts of his excavations, some written by Schliemann himself, made him world-famous. He was not above exaggerating his adventures to make them sound even more exciting than they were. For example, he wrote that Sophia was present when he dug up the treasure and that she carried it away hidden in her shawl. But historians have found that she was really hundreds of miles away in the Greek capital of Athens.

Sophia was on the scene at Schliemann's next excavation, however. This was at ruins near Mycenae, in Greece. There, ancient stone walls and a great gate crowned with stone lions had been visible for thousands of years. Acting on another

Sophia Schliemann wearing ancient Trojan jewelry

hunch based on his reading of Greek texts, Schliemann concluded this was the site of the city of Agamemnon, the king from Mycenae who led the Greeks to victory at Troy. Moreover, Schliemann was sure he knew where to find Agamemnon's grave. Earlier researchers had dug about in the ruins but had found no evidence that this was in fact Agamemnon's palace.

Schliemann was just as lucky this time as he had been at Troy. In August 1876 he and Sophia began digging in the middle of the ruins, where no other archaeologists had tried. They soon found a circle of stone slabs. Within the circle, in a dense layer of clay and small stones, they found five graves containing well-preserved bodies. Schliemann identified them as Agamemnon and his followers, who were all murdered upon their return from Troy by Agamemnon's queen Clytemnestra and her lover Aegisthus. The bodies, which were covered with jewels and golden ornaments of high workmanship, had to be uncovered with great care. "It was exceedingly difficult," wrote Sophia, "because, on our knees in the mud, my

Near the Lion Gate at Mycenae, the Schliemanns found the grave of a man they believed to be Agamemnon, brother-in-law of Helen of Troy.

husband and I had to cut out the pebbles, to cut away the layer of clay, and to take out one by one the precious jewels."

The treasure was the most valuable ever found up to that time. (It can be seen today in the national museum at Athens.) Schliemann was hailed throughout the world as an uncoverer of wonders. "It is an entirely new and unsuspected world that I am discovering for archaeology," he boasted. But, just as at Troy, Schliemann did not understand the true nature of his find. Later archaeologists proved that he had not found the grave of Agamemnon, but that of a king belonging to an older culture, the Minoan-Mycenaean, that dominated the Mediterranean world long before the Trojan War.

Schliemann suspected the existence of the Minoan-Mycenaean culture, though he never connected the ruins of Mycenae with it. In 1884 he began digging at the Greek city of Tiryns, another site connected with Mycenae, and uncovered a great palace. The ruins at Tiryns resembled similar ruins he had seen on the island of Crete in the Mediterranean. Schliemann always meant to dig at Crete, but could not agree on a price to pay the owner of the land he was interested in. A few years later the English archaeologist Sir Arthur Evans showed that Crete was the center of the Minoan-Mycenaean civilization, just as Schliemann had predicted.

Schliemann suffered from a painful ear infection much of his life. He was in Italy when, on Christmas Day 1890, the infection suddenly grew worse. He collapsed in the street and died the next morning. Schliemann was buried in Greece, and over his grave was placed a bust of Homer.

Picture Credits

Most of the pictures in this book are used by kind permission of the New York Public Library and come from the Library's Rare Books Division (NYPL/RBD), General Research Division (NYPL/GRD), or Portrait File (NYPL/PF). Picture credits follow page numbers.

THE EMPIRES OF PORTUGAL AND SPAIN. p 2: Henry the Navigator, portrait from the Arquivo Nacional de Fotografia, Instituo Português de Museus, Lisbon. p 3: Star shooter, from *Arte de Navigador*, Medina, Italy 1554. NYPL/RBD. p 3: Sagres: photo by Thomas Nebbia, © National Geographic Society. p 5: King Joao II, engraving from Denis, *Portugal*, Paris 1846. NYPL/GRD. p 6: Prester John, from an atlas by Diego Homem, 1558; reprinted in Cortesao, *Cartas das novas*, Lisbon, 1938. NYPL/RBD. p.8: Padroe, from Cortesao, *Expedicao de Cabral*, Lisbon 1912. NYPL/GRD. p 8: Dias's ships in a storm, from *Newnes' Pictorial Knowledge*, H. A. Pollock, ed., London nd. p 9: Dias and his men, painting by Domingos Rebelo, reproduced in Saraiva, *Temas de Historia de Portugal*, 1968. p 10: Portuguese portrait of Da Gama, © The British Museum. p 11: Da Gama's ships, from a manuscript in Lisbon. The Mansell Collection, London. p 12: Arab potentate. The Mansell Collection, London. p 13: Battle of Surat, © The British Library. p 14: Portrait of Cabral from Cortesao, *A Expedicao de Pedro Alvares Cabral*, Lisbon 1912. NYPL/GRD. p 15: The Cantino Chart of 1502 (watercolor copy 1883). NYPL, Stokes Collection. p 16: View of Malindi by Linschotten. NYPL/RBD. p 18: Portrait of Albuquerque, anonymous engraving (1792?). NYPL/PF. p 19: Albuquerque receiving tribute, from Manuel de Macedo, *Historia de Portugal*, Lisbon 189-. NYPL/GRD. p 21: Portrait of Magellan, Servicio de Reprografia de la Biblioteca Nacional, Madrid. p 22: "Magellan & the Straits," by J.P. Gabler, 1801. NYPL, Print Collection. p 23: "The Death of Magellan," from Mary Evans Picture Library, London. p 27: Zacuto, from the mural painted by J. M. Amshewitz in the William Cullen Library of the University of Witwatersrand, Johannesburg, SA. p 28: Zacuto's almanac. NYPL/RBD. p 28: Interior of synagogue in Cochin, India, © 1993 by George Mott. p 30: The de Orchi portrait of Columbus, undated gravure. NYPL/PF. p 31: Columbus's signature: woodcut by Frank Du Mond, 1891, after the original in the Naval Museum of Madrid. NYPL/PF. p 32: Compass in an ivory box, late 15th c. © National Maritime Museum, London. p 33: Portraits of Fernando and Isabel. The Royal Collection, c1993 Her Majesty Queen Elizabeth II. p 35: Columbus's ships. Anonymous wood engraving from Eggleston's *United States History*. NYPL/PF. p 36: Columbus's map of Hispaniola, NYPL/PF. p 36: Columbus's landing, from Theodor de Bry, [*America*], Frankfurt 1590. NYPL/RBD. p 37: Horse, from The Bancroft Collection, University of California at Berkeley. p 38: Columbus in chains, anonymous woodcut after pastel by Marechal, nd. NYPL/PF. p 42: "Balboa Discovering the Pacific," engraving by Lesestre 1811. NYPL/PF. p 44: Balboa setting dogs on people, from Theodor de Bry, *India Orientalis.*, 1598. NYPL/RBD. p 45: Malintzin with Cortes, from *Lienza de Tlaxcala*, 15th c. neg # 326507, showing the Great Temple of Tenochtitlan as reconstructed by Ignacio Marquina, reproduced courtesy Department of Library Services, American Museum of Natural History, New York. p 48: Moctezuma's house, from the *Codex Mendoza*, neg. 315767, courtesy Department of Library Services, American Museum of Natural History, New York. p 48: feather headdress © Museum fur Volkerkunde, Vienna. p 49: Quetzlcoatl, transparency 4702(2) by J. Beckett, from *Codex Florentino*, courtesy Department of Library Services, American Museum of Natural History, New York. p 50: Portrait of Cortes from Germanisches National Museum, Nurnberg. p 53: Cortes & Malintzin, from *Lienza de Tlaxcala*. neg. 314372, courtesy Department of Library Services, American Museum of Natural History, New York. p 54: Map of Tenochtitlan from *Proeclara Ferdinandi* by Hernan Cortes, 1534. NYPL/RBD. p 55: "Capture of Mexico City by Cortez." Anonymous wood engraving, 1870. NYPL/PF. p 56: Portrait of Pizarro from Thevet, *Les Vrais Pourtraits et vies des hommes illustres*, 1584. NYPL/RBD. p 58: The capture of Atahualpa, from Theodor de Bry, [*America*], 1590. NYPL/RBD. p 59: The mine at Potosi from Theodor de Bry, [*America*], 1590. NYPL/RBD. p 61: European portrait of Atahualpa. Unknown artist, 4056.313 "Atahvallpa Inga XIIII" Hispanic document 186. From the Collection of the Gilcrease Museum, Tulsa. p 62: Llama of silver and cinnabar/resin. neg #330026, Photographer Boltin. Courtesy Department Library Services, American Museum of Natural History, New York. p 63: Portrait of Las Casas, lithograph after painting by Felix Parra, 1899. NYPL/PF. p 64: Burning at stake, from Johannes Gysius, *Le Miroir de la cruelle . . .* , 1620. NYPL/RBD. p 66: Zuni dancer. Lithograph by Ackerman from *Report of an expedition down the Zuni River*, Washington 1853. NYPL, General Research Division. p 67: Indian Pueblo at Acoma, albumen print. NYPL, Dennis Collection. p 68: "The Expedition of Fran-

cisco Coronado" courtesy of the Frederic Remington Art Museum, Ogdensburg, NY. p 70: Grand Canyon: albumen print by Underwood and Underwood, 1908. NYPL, Dennis Collection. p 70: Battle of Hawikuh, lithograph from Twitchell, *Leading Facts of New Mexican History*, Cedar Rapids, 1911. NYPL/GRD. p 71: Portrait of Serra, anonymous 19th c. chromolithograph. NYPL/PF. p 72: San Antonio Mission, albumen print, 19th c. NYPL, Dennis Collection.

MARINERS AND PIRATES. p 74: Portrait of Verrazano, engraving by F. Allegrini after painting by Zocchi. NYPL/GRD. p 75: Robertus de Bailly gilded copper globe, view 5, photography courtesy of The Pierpont Morgan Library, New York. p 76: Portrait of Cartier, engraving by S. Freeman, nd. NYPL/PF. p 77: "Jacques Cartier on the St. Lawrence", engraving by Chavane, nd. NYPL/PF. p 78: Cartier's ship courtesy of Environment Canada, Canadian Parks Service, Quebec Region, Louis Lavoie, illustrator. p 80: Portrait of Drake from a miniature attd. to Hilliard, National Portrait Gallery, London. p 81: *The Golden Hind* from *Expedio Francesi Draki*, Leyden 1588. NYPL/RBD. p 82: Map of Drake's journey from Walter Bigges's *Relation . . .* 1589. NYPL/RBD. p 84: "Drake Playing Bowls." Engraved from the painting by Seymour Lucas, Mansell Collection, London. p 85: "Battle of the Armada." neg. A6717, National Maritime Museum, Greenwich, England. p 86: Portrait of Frobisher. Gravure after the painting by Cornelius Ketel in the Bodliean Library. NYPL/PF. p 87: Kayaker from Dionyse Settle's *De Martini Frobisseri Angli*, Nuremburg, 1580. NYPL/RBD. p 88: Eskimos, drawings by John White. NYPL, Picture Collection. p 89: Relics of Barents' expedition. Anonymous wood engraving, 1873; NYPL/PF. p 91: Barents & men leave their ship, from De Bry, *India Orientalis*, 1598. NYPL/RBD. p 92: Portrait of Hudson, photo of painting by Count Pulaski. NYPL/PF. p 93: *The Half Moon*, gravure by H. A. Marten, 1909 after Hendricks Hallak. NYPL/PF. p 94: "The Last Voyage of Henry Hudson," gravure of John Collier's painting. *Newnes' Pictorial Knowledge*, H. A. Pollock, ed., London nd. p 96: Russian koch, drawing by N. D. Travin from Raymond Fisher's *Voyage of Semen Dezhnev in 1648*, London 1981. NYPL/GRD. p 96: Tunguses, anonymous engraving from Joseph Billings's *Travels in Russia*. NYPL/GRD. p 99: Walruses, from Gerritsz, *Descriptio . . .* , Amsterdam 1613. NYPL/RBD. p 100: Dogsled, from *Cook's Voyages*, London 1784. NYPL/RBD. p 102: Portrait of Morgan, anonymous 18th c. woodcut. NYPL/PF. p 102: Pirates abusing citizens, woodcut from Exquemelin, *Americaensche . . .* (1678). NYPL/RBD. p 103: Maracaibo, woodcut from Esquemeling [Exquemelin], Spanish edition. p 107: Murderers Bay: from Heeres's *Abel Tasman's Journal*, Amsterdam 1898. NYPL/GRD. p 108: World map, from Ortelius, *Theatrum . . . Typus Orbis Terrarum*. [Antwerp] 1579. NYPL/RBD. p 109: Portrait of Cook engraved by W. Holl after the painting "Captain James Cook" by N. Dance. NYPL/PF. p 111: "View of Ice Islands" from Anderson's *Captain Cook's Travels*, London 1784. NYPL/RBD. p 112: "Man of the Sandwich Islands" engraved by Noble from James Cook's *A Voyage to the Pacific Ocean*, London 1784. NYPL/RBD. p 113: "The Death of Captain Cook," drawn by J. Webber, the figures engraved by F. Bartolozzi, RA, the landscape by W. Byrne. published 1785. Special Collections, University of British Columbia Library, Vancouver.

THE SETTLEMENT OF NORTH AMERICA. p 116: Leif Eriksson: Gravure after painting by Edward Moran, 1898. NYPL/PF. p 117: Vinland map, courtesy of the Beinecke Rare Book and Manuscript Library, Yale University. p 118: Sod house at l'Anse aux Meadows, New York Times Pictures, photo by B. Schonback. p 120: Painting of Raleigh attributed to Hilliard, 1588. Courtesy of the National Portrait Gallery, London. p 121: "Arrival of the Englishemen in Virginia," from Thomas Harriot's *A Briefe and true report of the new found land of Virginia*, Frankfort 1590. NYPL/RBD. p 122: Indian village, from Harriot, *op cit*. NYPL/RBD. p 123: The raid on Cadiz, anonymous engraving, nd. NYPL, Picture Collection. p 124: Powhatan in council. Detail from map of Virginia in John Smith's *General History of Virginia*, London 1624. NYPL/RBD. p 125: "Pocahontas pleading for the life of John Smith . . . " Albumen print, 19th c. NYPL, Dennis Collection. p 128: Portrait of Pocahontas in Elizabethan dress, from an anonymous 16th c. miniature. NYPL/PF. p 128: Pocahontas and her son, gravure from anonymous painting owned by Rolfe family. NYPL/PF. p 129: Portrait of John Smith from map of New England, by John Smith and Simon Van der Passe, engraving 1614. NYPL, Stokes Collection. p 132: Map of Virginia from John Smith's *General History of Virginia*, London 1624. NYPL/RBD. p 133: Map of New England by John Smith and Sinon Van der Passe, engraving 1614. NYPL, Stokes Collection. p 135: Statue of Massasoit at Plymouth. Historical Pictures/Stock Montage Inc. Chicago. p 136: Tisquantum planting corn. Historical Pictures/Stock Montage Inc., Chicago. p 138: Statue of

Bradford at Plymouth. Historical Pictures/Stock Montage Inc., Chicago. p 139: *The Mayflower*, wood engraving from John Goodwin's *The Pilgrim Republic*, Boston 1888. NYPL/GRD. p 140: Pilgrims building houses, Historical Pictures/Stock Montage Inc., Chicago. p 141: Woods' map of New England, from John Goodwin, *The Pilgrim Republic*, Boston 1888. NYPL/GRD. p 143: Portrait of Champlain, 19th c. painting, gravure 1924. NYPL/PF. p 144: Map from Champlain's *Voyages et decouvertes*, Paris 1620. NYPL/RBD. p 145: Iroquois club, © 1993 The Denver Art Museum. p 147: Niagara Falls, from Louis Hennepin's *A New Discovery . . .*, London 1698. NYPL/RBD. p 148: "La Salle Taking Possession of Louisiana," reproduction of a painting by J. Marchand, 1903. NYPL/PF. p 149: La Salle Assassinated, from Hennepin, *op. cit.*, London 1698. NYPL/RBD. p 151: Statue of Hutchinson by Cyrus Dallin, anonymous photo, nd. NYPL/PF. p 152: Engraving of Winthrop by J. Kellogg, after a painting by Van Dyke. NYPL/PF. p 153: The trial of Anne Hutchinson. The Granger Collection, New York. p 155: Anonymous 19th c. painting of Metacom. Courtesy of the Haffenreffer Museum of Anthropology, Brown University. p 156: Soapstone pipe found by Daniel Seamans in 1912, photo by Carmelo Guadagno, 1976. Photograph courtesy of National Museum of the American Indian, Smithsonian Institution. p 158: Great Swamp fight, anonymous 19th c. illustration. NYPL/GRD. p 160: Statue of Roger Williams by Franklin Simmons, gravure, nd. NYPL/PF. p 162: "Roger Williams Sheltered by the Narragansetts," wood engraving by J. C. Armytage and A. H. Wray, NYPL/PF. p 165: Portrait engraving of Penn by J. Sartain from a painting done in 1666. NYPL/PF. p 167: "William Penn's Treaty with the Indians," engraving by J. Bannister after Benjamin West's painting. NYPL/PF. p 168: Plan of Philadelphia. Engraved by Thomas Holme after William Penn's plan, 1682. NYPL, Stokes Collection. p 170: Portrait of Boone, courtesy of the John James Audobon Memorial Museum, Henderson, Kentucky. p 171: "Daniel Boone Escorting Settlers Through the Cumberland Gap" by George Caleb Bingham. Washington University Gallery of Art, St. Louis, Gift of Nathaniel Phillips, Boston, 1890. p 172: Portrait of Du Sable from Andreas's *History of Chicago*, 1884. Courtesy of the Photographs and Prints Division, Schomburg Center for Research in Black Culture, NYPL. p 173: "Chicago in 1820": Color Lithograph by John Gemmel, 1820. NYPL, Stokes Collection. p 173: "Mouth of the Chicago River from the Rush Street Bridge ca. 1860s." Albumen print, NYPL, Dennis Collection. p 175: Drawing of Sacagawea by E. S. Paxson from Olin Wheeler's *Trail of Lewis and Clark*, NY 1904. NYPL/GRD. P 176: "Reunion on of Sacajawea and Her People," from Grace Hebard's *Sacajawea*, Glendale 1933. NYPL/GRD. p 177: Portraits of Lewis and Clark by Charles Willson Peale. Courtesy of the Independence National Historical Park Collection. p 178: Falls and Portage of the Missouri, from *Journals of Lewis and Clark*, NY 1904. NYPL/GRD. p 179: "Captain Clark and His Men Shooting Bears" from Gass's *Journal of Lewis and Clark*, Philadelphia 1812. NYPL/RBD. p 180: "View of the Rocky Mountains," lithograph by Hinely after painting by Karl Bodmer. NYPL, Stokes Collection. p 182: Portrait of Pike by Charles Willson Peale. Courtesy of the Independence National Historical Park Collection. p 182: Wilkinson: 1871 engraving by H. B. Hall after a painting in the Philadelphia State House. NYPL/PF. p 183: "Pike's Peak and Colorado Springs," gravure nd. NYPL/PF. p 184: "Victory of York U.C.—Death of General Pike." Anonymous wood engraving, nd. NYPL/PF.

AFRICA. p 187: boat: Firdausi, Shah Nameh. Persia, 19th c. NYPL Spencer Collection, Persian ms #62. p 188: Ibn Battutah telling his story to a scribe, from *Newnes' Pictorial Knowledge*, H. A. Pollock, ed., London nd. p 189: "The Court of Pope Leo X" wood engraving after painting by F. L. Ruben NYPL/PF. p 190: Map by Leo Africanus from *Ramusio il viaggio di Giovan Leone*, Venice 1837. NYPL/GRD. p 192: "Audiance du Vice Roy d'Angole a la Reine Anne Zingha," from J. B. Labat's *Relation Historique de L'Ethiopie Occidentale*. By permission of The Boston Atheneum. p 193: "La Reine Anne Zingha Baptisee en 1622," from Labat, *op cit*. The Boston Atheneum. p 195: Portrait of Shaka courtesy of the South African Library, Cape Town, SA. p 197: Death of Shaka, watercolor by T. Livingstone Sango, courtesy of the Campbell Collections of the University of Natal, SA. p 199: "Dr. Livingstone Reading the Bible to His Men', anonymous wood engraving 1874. NYPL/PF. p 202: "The Meeting of Livingstone and Stanley in Central Africa, 1872," wood engraving by S. Durand. NYPL/PF. p 203: Photo of Burton by Ernest Edwards, from *Portaits of Men of Eminence*, 1865. NYPL, Photography Collection. p 205: Portrait of Speke from his *Journal of the Discovery of the Source of the Nile*, New York, 1861. NYPL/GRD. p 206: View of Ujiji, uncredited, possibly a sketch by Speke. NYPL/PF. p 207: Portrait of Stanley: photogravure after J. Thomson, 1890. NYPL/PF. p 208: Caricature of Stanley, wood engraving by Eaton, 1872. NYPL/PF. p 209: "Mr. Stanley's Boat." Anonymous wood engraving, 1872. NYPL/PF.

ASIA. p 212: Portrait of Marco Polo by Marco Bonatti, line engraving, Italian, 1820. The Granger Collection, New York. p 213: Medieval travelers, from *Livre des Merveilles*, 1375. Bibliotheque Nationale, Paris. p 214: The Polos meet the Khan, from *Livre des Merveilles*, 1375. Bibliotheque Nationale, Paris. p 215: Tatar horseman, courtesy of the Freer Gallery of Art, Smithsonian Institution, Washington, DC, #18.52: Detail from a Chinese painting. "Scenes Among the Mongol Tartars: The Captivity of Ts'ai Wen Chi." Ming, 15th-16th c. Ink outline on paper makimono: 468.3 x 30.5 cm. p 218: Emperor Yong Lo, gravure from a Chinese painting. NYPL/PF. p 219: Junk: anonymous woodcut from *Penny Magazine*, 1835. NYPL, Picture Collection. p 221: A Jesuit missionary in China, believed to be Matteo Ricci. p 222: Chinese scholars, from *Imperial Edicts*, vol 8. 1681. NYPL, Spencer Collection. p 225: Woodcut of Ieyasu. NYPL/PF. p 226: View of Edo from Mortanus's *Atlas Japanensis*, London 1670. NYPL/RBD. p 227: Japanese rendering of a Dutch ship, anonymous woodcut, 17th c. NYPL, Print Collection.

SCIENCE AND MEDICINE. p 228: Portrait engraving of Copernicus by R. Cooper. NYPL/PF. p 229: Ptolemaic system, engraving from Sacrobosto's *Sphaera Mundi*. NYPL/RBD. p 229: Copernican system, from Copernicus's *De Revolutionibus Orbium Coelestium*, Nuremberg 1543. NYPL/RBD. p 231: Portrait of Bruno, engraving by C. Mayer, nd. NYPL/PF. p 230: Diagram from Bruno's *De Compositione . . .*, 1591. By permission of the Houghton Library, Harvard University. p 233: Engraving of Tycho by H. Larmessin. NYPL/PF. p 233: Tycho in his observatory; Quadrans Muralis, from Brahe's *Astronomia*, 1598. NYPL/RBD. p 234: Quadrans Mediocris, from Brahe, *op. cit.* NYPL/RBD. p 234: Globus Magnus, from Brahe, *op. cit.* NYPL/RBD. p 235: Portrait of Kepler from Seidlitz's *Allemaine Historisch Port*, vol 2. NYPL/GRD. p 237: Platonic solids from Kepler's *Mysterium Cosmographium*, Tubingen 1596. NYPL/RBD. p 238: Diagram of Kepler's second law, from NYPL, Picture Collection. p 239: Anonymous engraving of Galileo, nd. NYPL/PF. p 240: Galileo's telescope, courtesy of the Instituto e Museo di Storia della Scienza di Firenze, photograph by Franca Principe. p 241: Frontispiece: engraving by Stefan Della Bella from Galileo's *Dialogo di Galileo Galilei*, Toscana 1562. NYPL/RBD. p 242: Painting of Newton by an unknown artist © 1726, courtesy of the National Portrait Gallery, London. p 243: Title page from Newton's *Philosophiae Naturalis Principia Mathematica*, London 1687. NYPL/RBD. p 244: Newton's telescope, NYPL, Picture Collection. p 245: Painting of William Herschel by L. F. Abbott, courtesy of the National Portrait Gallery, London. p 246: "Herschel and his sister at the telescope," anonymous 19th c. engraving. NYPL/PF. p 247: Anonymous wood engraving of Caroline Herschel, 19th c. NYPL/PF. p 248: Portrait of John Herschel by Schiaboff after painting by H. W. Pickersgill. NYPL/PF. p 249: Engraving of Leeuwenhoek by J. Chapman, nd. NYPL/PF. p 249: Microscope from the Museum Boerhaave, Leiden. p 250: Drawings of flies from a letter of Leeuwenhoek's, courtesy of The Royal Society Library, London. p 251: Anonymous engraving of Mercator, 17th c. NYPL/PF. p 251: Double heart map from Mercator's *Orbis Imago*, 1538. NYPL/RBD. p 253: "Linnaeus in His Lapland Dress," engraving by Dunkarton after a painting by Hoffmann from Thornton's *New Illustration of the Sexual system of Carolus von Linnaeus*, London 1799. NYPL, Print collection. p 253: Corn plant from Matthioli's *Commentarii in Sex Libros . . .*, 1565. NYPL, Arents Collection. p 254: Uppsala botanical garden: engraving from *Amoenitates Academicae Lugduni Batavorum*, 1749. NYPL/GRD. p 256: Anonymous engraving of Humboldt, 19th c. NYPL/PF. p 257: Jungle scene, engraving by A. Cross after a painting by Killie. NYPL/PF. p 258: Engraving of Descartes by Edelinck after the painting by Frans Hals. NYPL/PF. p 259: Title page from Descartes's *Discours de la Methode . . .*, Leyden 1637. NYPL/RBD. p 259: Instrument from Descartes, *op. cit.* NYPL/RBD. p 261: Woodcut of Pare by Horbeck in Stephen Paget's *Pare and his Times*, NY 1897. NYPL/GRD. p 261: Battle of St Denis: old engraving, reproduced from Paget, *op. cit.* NYPL/GRD. p 262: Physcians setting a dislocated elbow: reproduced from Pare's *Works* in Paget, *op cit.* NYPL/GRD. p 263: Wood engraving of Vesalius after Morin, nd. NYPL/PF. p 264: Barber surgeon: Italy 1496. NYPL, Spencer Collection. p 265: Anatomical drawing: woodcut by Calcar from Vesalius's *De Humani Corporis*, facsimile of 1568 ed. NYPL, Print Collection. p 262: Engraving of Harvey by E. Scriven, nd. NYPL/PF. p 267: Arms, from Harvey's *Exercitatio anatomica . . .*, Frankfurt 1628. NYPL/RBD. p 269: Painting of Champollion by Leon Cogniet, courtesy of Musee du Louvre, Paris. p 270: Hieroglyphics, detail of the Stela of Tjetji, Egypt, now in the British Museum. NYPL, Picture Collection. p 271: Rosetta stone. The British Museum, London. © British Museum. p 273: Wood engraving of Schliemann by M. S. Brown, 1889. NYPL/PF. p 274: "Mrs. Schliemann in the parure of Helen of Troy," anonymous wood engraving. NYPL/PF. p 275: Lion Gate, Mycenae. NYPL/GRD.

Index

References to full articles are given in **boldface**